GODS
with
THUNDERBOLTS

RELIGION
IN
ROMAN BRITAIN

Should I have answer'd Caius Cassius so?
When Marcus Brutus grows so covetous,
To lock such rascal counters from his friends,
Be ready, Gods, with all your Thunderbolts;
Dash him to pieces!

William Shakespeare, *Julius Caesar* IV.iii.78

GODS
with
THUNDERBOLTS

RELIGION
IN
ROMAN BRITAIN

GUY DE LA BÉDOYÈRE

TEMPUS

First published 2002
This edition 2007

Tempus Publishing Ltd
The Mill, Brimscombe Port
Stroud, Gloucestershire GL5 2QG
www.tempus-publishing.com

British Library Cataloguing in Publication Data.
A catalogue record for this book is available from the British Library.

ISBN 978 0 7524 4291 4

Typesetting and origination by Tempus Publishing.
Printed in Great Britain.

Contents

List of illustrations

Text figures

Colour plates

Map 1

RELIGION IN THE
SOUTH-EAST

LINCOLN ●✚

■ CHESTER

ANCASTER ●

◈? Walsingham

WALL ●　　● LEICESTER　　　CAISTER ●

WATER NEWTON ●★✚

■ Legionary fortress
■ Fort
▣ Fort of the Saxon Shore
● Colony, Municipium etc
● Civitas capital ● Town
✱ Villa　◈ Temple
★ Treasure ✚ Christian site

GODMANCHESTER ●　Mildenhall ★
　　　　　　　　　　✚ ● ICKLINGHAM

★ Thetford

COLCHESTER ●

GLOUCESTER ●
　　　✱ Chedworth ◈ Wood Eaton
LYDNEY ◈ ◈ ULEY　● CIRENCESTER　　● VERULAMIUM
● CAERWENT　　　　　　　　　　◈ Harlow
　　　　　　　　　　　　　　　　　　▣ ✚ BRADWELL
◈ Nettleton　✱ Littlecote　LONDON ●
● BATH　　SILCHESTER ●✚　　　● SPRINGHEAD　✚ RECULVER
✕◈ Brean Down　　　　　Lullingstone ✱✚　CANTERBURY ●　▣
◈ Lamyatt　　　　　　　　　　　　　　　　✚ R'BOROUGH

● WINCHESTER　　　　　　　▣ LYMPNE

Fishbourne ✱　● CHICHESTER

Maiden ● DORCHESTER
Castle ◈
　　　　✱ Brading

0　　　　　　30 miles

50 kilometres

9

Map 2

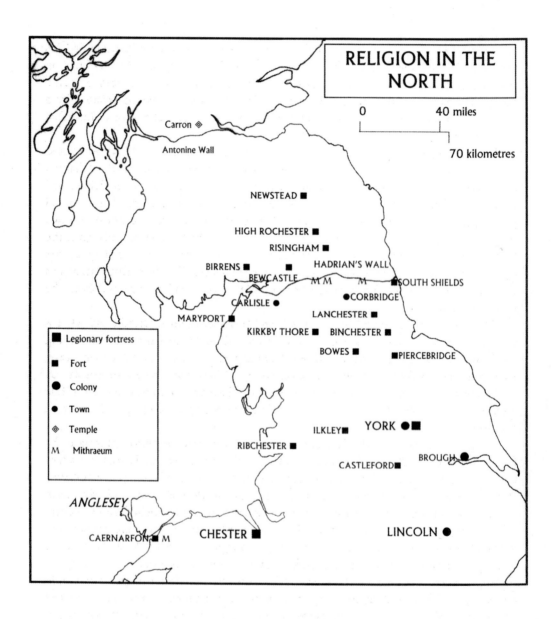

RELIGION IN THE NORTH

0   40 miles

70 kilometres

Carron ◈

Antonine Wall

NEWSTEAD ■

HIGH ROCHESTER ■

RISINGHAM ■

BIRRENS ■   HADRIAN'S WALL

BEWCASTLE ■   M M   M ■SOUTH SHIELDS

CARLISLE ●   ●CORBRIDGE

MARYPORT ■   LANCHESTER ■

KIRKBY THORE ■   BINCHESTER ■

BOWES ■   ■PIERCEBRIDGE

■ Legionary fortress

■ Fort

● Colony

• Town

◈ Temple

M Mithraeum

ILKLEY■   YORK ●■

RIBCHESTER ■   BROUGH ●

CASTLEFORD■

ANGLESEY

CAERNARFON■ M   CHESTER ■   LINCOLN ●

10

Foreword and introduction

In the year 60 Gaius Suetonius Paullinus, the Roman governor of Britain, led his army across the Menai Straits from north-west Wales to Anglesey. He was bent on destroying the centre of Druid power, believing it to be where resistance to the conquest was being masterminded. The bewildered soldiers were confronted by a frenzy and noise that was the very definition of barbarity and chaos, or at least that was how the army saw it.

Less than a generation before, the troops who came to Britain in 43 demonstrated their natural sense of spiritual superstition in their reluctance to cross the Channel and invade. The truth was that Roman religion and the Celtic spirits of Britain had much in common. Omens, superstition, natural phenomena, and the landscape all played parts in the theatricality of pagan beliefs. Over the next few centuries the two worlds combined to create a remarkable mixture in which classical gods from the Greek and Roman worlds were integrated into a new pantheon where they sat side by side with deities whose names had never been recorded before. But within less than four centuries the Romano-British and Celtic gods had disappeared from the record we have.

This book is a narrative history of cult and belief in Roman Britain and what it tells us about the minds of men and women in that time. There is no great underlying thesis or series of unexpected revelations. The purpose is simply to tell the story, using examples from as far and wide as possible, though I have tried wherever possible to challenge some accepted views which seem more based on opinions than facts. The record is unavoidably limited but I have tried assiduously to keep speculation to a minimum.

Religion is a subject that attracts some of the more intense philosophising to be found in books on Roman Britain, or indeed antiquity in general. Ritual, in particular, is one of those words used as an explanation but which often explains nothing. Perhaps in an age when the spiritual side to human life seems increasingly under threat there is some solace and satisfaction in speculating on the beliefs and priorities of a different time. It's also true that religion above all is one of those areas where the archaeologist and historian can fly unchecked through footless halls of air in their quest to reach out and touch the hands of those elusive gods. For example, is questioning the very existence of the martyr Alban a sensible academic enquiry, or simply an example of futile indulgence, made safe by the impossibility of proving it one way or the other? One of the consequent problems is expressing an interpretation of, say, the Celtic and Roman belief in an afterlife as if this was a universally-held creed. Yet it is clear from the sources that not everyone in antiquity did subscribe to some sort of generic cultural religious identity or indeed any religious identity at all.

11

At the very least this can leave the modern reader wondering on the basis for intellectual flights of fancy, and worst leave him or her drowning in a sea of florid pronouncements and dense, crypto-theological debates. The average Romano-British passer-by purchasing a knick-knack horse-and-rider brooch from a wayside shrine vendor might have been astonished by what his souvenir would lead to one day. The same could be true for a Roman soldier tipping refuse into a handy pit in the fort of Newstead, who now has the chance from the safety of Elysium to watch an entertaining debate over whether he was binning routine military debris or instead engaging in creating a structured deposit in a 'ritual continuity' from prehistoric times.

Religion, while appearing to be a well-defined topic, is anything but. Ritual has a habit in archaeological minds of expanding to fill the space available, while conveniently overlooking common sense or the absence of much critical evidence. The difference between religious imagery as an artistic convention, and religious imagery as a sacred symbol, is not always taken into account. Both of course occurred, and in differing degrees of overlap, but differentiating them in the archaeological record is often impossible. Pagan imagery, for example, provided the Christian world with an enduring source of visual and literary decoration, as well as metaphor − and it still does. Equally there seems to be a strange reluctance to allow the ancient world the right to have engaged in activities for straightforward practical reasons. At the time of writing the celebrated Bronze Age 'Iceman' of the Ötzal Alps is in the news once more following the discovery that he probably died from an arrow wound, and not the cold as once thought. Inevitably the debate has now moved to whether this was straightforward murder, or 'ritual sacrifice'. With their usual reckless subjectivity the proponents of the 'ritual' interpretation cite 'mountain worship' and the fact that the man retained his possessions as supporting evidence. That he had been wounded after theft or during a fight over food or other resources, and died while making his escape, is barely considered a possibility. Likewise, it was originally thought that there was some significance in how his possessions had been laid out, but it has since been shown that periods of ice-melting caused the artefacts to float about and settle in new places.

I hope I have kept a sober and clear head. Instead, I have tried to let the Romans, the Romano-British, and all the others who lived here tell us about the gods and spirits they believed controlled their lives, and how they sought to influence them when, or if, they did. Primary sources are much better evidence for explaining behaviour than an archaeological imagination, in spite of problems with interpretation. It would be absurd to accept literary sources at face value but works like Ovid's *Fasti*, a poem recording religious festivals, contain detail that it would be impossible to imagine from archaeological evidence. Rejecting primary sources just because they are 'biased' or 'selective' overlooks the fact that 'bias' is the basis of individuality. One could equally well reject many archaeological interpretations for exactly the same reason. The difference is that the latter belong to our own time, but the literary sources have the advantage of belonging to the time we are trying to study.

In other words, observing bias is the path to understanding what people wanted to say about themselves, and how they saw themselves and other people. Without it, we would all be the same and there would be nothing to say. Caesar's perspective on the Druids, for example, tells us not just about his need to depict his enemies in a certain way, but also how the Romans liked to differentiate themselves from 'barbarians'. Modern historians study Nazi propaganda because its perverse interpretation of German destiny tells us about the ideology, cynicism and bigotry that drove the Third Reich. Excavating a Messerschmitt Bf109 fighter of 1940 tells us no more about Nazi ideology than excavating bones and pottery from a pit in a Roman temple precinct tells us about the beliefs and superstitions involved. Both circumstances give us information about *how* the ideologies or beliefs were expressed, but not *why*. Archaeological interpretations sometimes fail to make this subtle distinction, and assume that the *why* can be reliably inferred from the *how*. The perfect example is the coin hoard. We can excavate the coins, analyse the contents and draw up a list. But the coins, which are all we have, cannot tell us *why* they were collected, buried and remained unrecovered. Conversely, Samuel Pepys' description of his own coin hoard does give us that critical information and illustrates what archaeology does not, and cannot, tell us (*Diary* 19 June, 10 October 1667).

However, the literary evidence, whether extracted from a source like Ovid, or from an inscription on a ragged altar found near Housesteads fort, presents the archaeologist and historian with a frustrating, and unresolvable, paradox. At a stroke the written record reveals the abundantly unpredictable panorama of human religious perspective, experience and expression. It shows at the same instant that without it we cannot hope to reconstruct that experience and expression reliably. The Druids, for example, have absolutely no recognisable manifestation in archaeology. Nothing: not a potsherd and not a single sprig of petrified mistletoe. Likewise, a host of gods appear in the written record of the Roman period and vanish when Roman Britain ended.

Primary sources also lead us to Roman scepticism, and humour, facets of human perceptions entirely beyond an archaeologist to extract from potsherds, megaliths and ditches. Martial's scathing attack on a pompous soothsayer and his accidental castration is one of the delights of Roman literature. Wherever possible I have tried to trace contemporary evidence for what was symbolic of what, rather than state a connection as given. There are some revelations. The archaeological evidence ranges from personal talismans to monumental classical temple complexes. I have also let the Roman cynics enter the fray. Religious debate and scepticism was as much a part of the Roman world as it is of our own, though they scarcely seem to find a mention in many modern books. Left to their own devices the ancients all tell just as remarkable a story, and being in their own words it is all the better for it.

So that this book remains as useful as possible, I have appended a complete list of all gods and goddesses mentioned by name in inscriptions found in Britain, or in literary texts referring to Roman Britain, and a brief description of the dedication or reference. This is an adapted, improved and updated version of the list published in my *Companion to Roman Britain* (Tempus 1999). It is, to my knowledge, the only such list ever compiled and published. Readers might also care to consult my *Buildings of Roman Britain* (Tempus 2001), which contains a very large number of reconstruction drawings of Romano-British structures including temples and shrines. It is one of the ironies of contemporary Romano-British studies that the best sources of an illustrated series of artefacts and coins are those produced by and for collectors, rather than by scholars and museums. Nigel Mills' *Celtic and Roman Artefacts* (Witham 2000) is, for example, an unparalleled collection of colour photographs of statuettes, busts, brooches and other votive items.

As ever I am very grateful to Catherine Johns of the British Museum and Peter Kemmis Betty for their observations on, and corrections to, the text and Tim Clarke at Tempus for seeing it through the press. Any errors that remain are my own. I would also like to thank Philip Clarke, Tim Taylor and Michael Douglas of Channel 4's *Time Team* for taking up my suggestion to excavate at the small Roman town of Ancaster, where the work provided much of the stimulation for this book. Thanks are also due to the people of Ancaster, especially at Ancaster Primary School, who allowed the digs to happen and made previous finds available for study, and Anna Brearley and her staff at Grantham Museum. As in previous works, all drawings, paintings and photographs are by the author unless otherwise stated. The finished book was submitted to Tempus entirely in electronic form on CD-ROM.

Guy de la Bédoyère, Welby by Ermine Street, 2002

1 Fulgur Divorum

In 1848, a mile west of Haltonchesters fort on Hadrian's Wall, a slab was found with the letters *Fulgur Div(or)um* inscribed on it. Meaning 'thunderbolt of the gods' it commemorates the place where a thunderbolt fell to earth and an awe-struck local, probably a soldier, recorded the moment when he witnessed divine force at its most terrifying (*RIB* 1426). Religion dominates much of our evidence for Roman Britain. Most surviving inscriptions record dedications to gods of gifts, or even of buildings (**1**). Temples and shrines are mentioned on inscribed slabs more frequently than any other class of structure. Some of the most outstanding and exceptional finds from Roman Britain bear visual or written references to gods. Even where a primary religious purpose is not evident, the imagery of gods and spirits monopolises the art of Roman Britain. Cults, great and small, proliferated across Britain and range from the windswept obscurity of a hunter god carved on a Northumberland rock to the architectural maze of temples, arcades, vaults and altars which surrounded the sacred spring at Bath (**39, 57**). We call some of them 'Roman', some 'Celtic', some 'Romano-Celtic', and the rest exotic imports. There is an inherent bias in the record, which is important to remember. The greater majority of the known inscriptions come from military sites in northern England and the Hadrian's Wall zone.

The word 'Celtic' needs defining because it recurs throughout this book. In antiquity, the term was applied to the peoples beyond the Roman frontiers in northern Europe. It was a catch-all label that has become almost as convenient for us as it was for the Romans, though we use it more liberally than they did. In both cases it papers over a multitude of different tribes and traditions. Being illiterate, the peoples concerned never call themselves Celts in a form we can recognise. In other words, there is no instance of a Celt creating a piece of primary evidence, other than via the media of the Roman world in the form of Latin, however garbled. The Romans never applied the term 'Celtic' to Britain or its inhabitants. Nevertheless, the word is now commonly used to describe the non-Roman traditions, art, style and peoples of the provinces of the north-west.

The religious sculpture, the inscribed religious texts, and the religious artefacts provide us with almost all we know about the ordinary people of Roman Britain. Take Priscus for example. He made a dedication to Sulis at Bath and on his altar recorded that he was a *lapidarius*, 'stonemason', and came from the Chartres region in Gaul (*RIB* 149). Two coppersmiths, Celatus and Cintusmus, are exceptionally recorded on dedications to Mars and Silvanus Callirius respectively (*RIB* 274, 194).

So, the body of evidence is of unparalleled importance to anyone trying to people Roman Britain with individuals and to understand it as an historical and social epoch.

1 *(left) Lincoln. Face-pot (heavily restored) with a painted inscription 'to the God Mercury'. RIB 2499.1. Height 270mm*

2 *(right) Epona. Bronze statuette of the 'Celtic' fertility goddess, accompanied by a pair of miniature horses or foals. Epona holds ears of corn and a yoke, to make her identity clear. Epona is known in Britain by name on altars from Auchendavy and Carvoran. Said to be from Wiltshire. Height 75mm*

Religion also experienced an extraordinary amount of change in the 360 or so years that Britain was a province. What began with tension evolved into a new pantheon of gods and beliefs. The process was not continuous. Gods favoured by individual emperors were liable to enjoy episodes of greater popularity, like Minerva under Domitian, or Serapis under Caracalla (**colour plate 5**). The arrival of exotic cults blended in to create an unprecedented and unrepeated mix. Egyptian Isis could be worshipped a few minutes walk from a temple housing Persian Mithras, itself a stone's throw from another dedicated to Jupiter, while altars and shrines dedicated to local and regional deities like the Celtic horse and fertility goddess Epona were dotted around (**2**). A soldier at Housesteads fort on Hadrian's Wall would have struggled not to trip over the shrines, altars and dedications cluttering the slope below the stronghold.

It is almost impossible to measure the quality and nature of symbolism, ritual and belief. One man's religious symbol is another man's decorative motif, and yet another's nightmare (**8**). In the Roman world there were many grades of the amount of trust placed in the gods, or even the use of their symbols. That even extended to the outright cynicism felt by others for the self-imposed tyranny of ritual. Silvanus

3 *Silvanus. Altar dedicated by Marcus Aurelius Quirinus, prefect of* cohors I Lingonum *at Lanchester (Durham) during the reign of Gordian III (238-44). From Eastgate near Stanhope (Durham).* RIB *1042*

4 *Bronze bust from Great Walsingham (Norfolk). This curious figure has been described as a 'three-horned deity', and was perhaps a furniture or bucket fitting. Horns are a familiar attribute of regional cult figures in the north-western provinces (see for example 5), but it is impossible to know who or what this represents. It may be pre-Roman in date, which might make it evidence of an Iron Age origin for the cult centre thought to have existed here. But the piece is so unusual, even a medieval date is possible. Height 49mm*

was a woodland god (**3**), for example, but the name was also a well-known family name (*cognomen*). Does an altar to, or symbol of, Silvanus, for example on a gemstone, mean the owner was a member of a *collegium* (guild) of Silvanus worshippers unless it specifically says so as one ring from Wendens Ambo does? Or was it simply that the owner shared the name and made his choice on that basis? It is easy to assume that ancient religion was a deadly, straight-faced affair, but some Romans like Pliny the Elder, Martial and Lucian found pompous priests, self-important soothsayers, and credulous crowds to be ridiculous and amusing.

The other miracle of the Roman period is the light it sheds on what had come before. The record may not be perfect, and the record within a Roman idiom, but it is better than nothing, and it is certainly better than what we might invent for ourselves without their help. The coming of literacy and realistic sculpture meant 'the gods are come down to us in the likeness of men' (*Acts* xiv.11), propelling the silent cults and spirits of the prehistoric past into our own gaze. That raises the question of whether the perception of those gods had changed, now that they had found a tangible human form. As we have little idea how they were perceived before, the question is unanswerable. Thus we are left none the wiser, which only serves to emphasise our dependence on Roman records and chance finds (**4**). From this material deities like Antenociticus or Viridios emerge from the primeval fog that cloaks so much (**5, 70, colour plate 32**).

5 *Antenociticus. Stone head of the cult statue from the small temple outside Benwell fort (see* **98***) on Hadrian's Wall. Note the horns amongst the hair. Life-size*

This record comes to us through the writings of Roman authors, the inscriptions from towns, forts and official bodies and the innumerable altars, dedications, offerings and possessions of the population of Britain. Its disappearance by the early fifth century is as abrupt as the opened window of four centuries before. When religious life in Britain comes back into focus in the sixth century the warrior cults of Mars Cocidius have vanished along with a phalanx of spirits whose identities subsist for us only in the evidence of the veneration shown in the Roman years.

The prehistoric mists

In ancient Britain, influencing and communicating with the spirits behind natural forces was essential if disasters were to be averted, and omens heeded. Gods with all their thunderbolts were interpreted literally as just that. Even the physical evidence was there to prove it. As late as the early nineteenth century the Jurassic belemnite fossils that lie scattered across the beach at Lyme Regis in Dorset were still believed to be the petrified remains of thunderbolts. The ammonites of the same beaches were traditionally considered to be charms that offered protection from serpents, and cures for various ailments including blindness (**6**). Impossible not to notice, Britain's fossil remains added to what was already an astonishingly diverse landscape

6 *Ammonite, Lyme Regis (Dorset). Fossil remains of these sea creatures abound on the beach at Lyme Regis, though they are commonly found in other places in Britain. They were once thought to be petrified snakes, or even people turned into snakes and petrified as a punishment. Ammonites were widely attributed with powers over serpents and disease. Such a tradition almost certainly stretched back into antiquity. In the Middle Ages, ammonites were even occasionally embellished with a carved 'serpent's head'. This example is around 200 million years old. Diameter approx. 0.5m*

(**146**), a perfect stage on which to set an array of divine forces. Gentle lowlands with abundant rivers and streams provided spots for river and water deities, while woodlands provided another fertile setting for spirits. The highlands, always close enough to have their presence felt, supplied wildernesses for hunting, havens for wild game, and dramatic settings for battles (**30**). Unfortunately, we can only imagine what meant what to whom.

Within and through all this terrain, Britain's characteristically unpredictable weather compromised the capacity of human settlement to cope but was rarely bad enough to prevent survival. This is crucial: Britain is relatively benign. Living off the land is hard, but this is not an island of tidal waves, tornadoes, catastrophic earthquakes, or desperate frosts. Yet elements of all these do take place in Britain. There are severe storms, damaging floods, and even occasional earth tremors (**7**). A dramatic change in the sky was a portentous event, and was interpreted the same way by the Romans (**colour plate 1**).

Dedications and offerings were a way of trying to exercise control over powerful natural forces, or to commemorate great and significant events. We can see the

7 *Thunderstorms. Natural forces determined ancient man's prosperity and security. Violent natural phenomena were terrifying not just because of their destructive power, but also because of what they might portend for the future*

importance placed on such megalithic monuments as Stonehenge, and the many other stone circles and henge monuments scattered across the landscape though we have no idea how they were used. A modern example illustrates the point perfectly. The symbolic erection of a cross above the ruins of the World Trade Center in New York is a potent gesture lost on almost no one today. But without the documentation in the form of written history or an inscription, in thousands of years' time there would be no possibility of understanding its original significance and the world-changing events it symbolises (**8**). It is exactly this that plagues the prehistorian, and no amount of speculation makes good the gap in his or her knowledge. We can estimate the investment in time alone needed to produce and transport megalithic stones, and then assemble them into the finished design, but not *why* it was done. It is a conceit to believe otherwise.

Conversely, we know why the World Trade Center cross was selected from the debris, and we know what it took to build medieval cathedrals because some of the records survive. We also know the spiritual and intellectual background to these projects, why they were designed in the way they were and the purpose they served in ritual. And we know the god whose glory they commemorated. But we know nothing in detail about prehistoric religion. We do not even know the names of the gods. Only in records of the Roman period do representations of deities emerge that we can understand (**9**). We can do no more than guess the fears and hopes these people had, and the way in which they expressed these relationships. Even if we

8 *No. 3, World Financial Center, New York, overlooks the steel-girder cross on the site of the Twin Towers. The spiritual symbolism the cross stands for of 11 September 2001, the deaths and the hope, are clear to us. But without the documentation, buried and dispersed across millennia the cross's significance would be lost. So it is for us, when we try to understand prehistoric religious monuments*

are correct in assuming that stone circles and the like had a powerful role to play in religion, rather than, say, acting purely as measuring instruments, it is no less true that we are impossibly distanced from the details of how these facilities and centres functioned in spiritual activities. We cannot come close to the truth, and even if we did we could not know that we had. The barriers of illiteracy and anonymity prevent transmission across lost generations.

The natural world

Until recently, anticipating natural events depended entirely upon observation and experience. This could be very effective when it came to cycles, like the phases of the moon, or the seasons. It was much less easy to expect the unexpected. Today, our knowledge of worldwide weather systems and other scientific data makes it possible to predict violent storms, droughts and heatwaves. We can also track the movement of diseases, and link their impact according to human or animal genetics. Although we still struggle to predict disasters like earthquakes, we at least know what causes them. Lucretius provided a clear explanation of the physical forces behind lightning and thunderbolts and asked what god could possibly be strong enough to control these

9 *Bath, pediment depicting Luna. This carving seems to have formed part of a façade looking over the altar in the temple precinct. The crescent moon behind the goddess's head makes it easy to recognise her, and is typical of classical anthropomorphic religious sculpture in presenting the viewer with the features necessary to identify the deity. Appropriately enough the entrance to the sacred spring opposite seems to have displayed a matching bust of Sol, the Sun*

forces and even allow them to destroy his own temples (*DRN* vi.160ff, ii.1093ff). Pliny the Elder knew that most of his contemporaries attributed thunderbolts to gods, but was able to cite the geographical circumstances and times of years that favoured them (*NH* ii.136ff). However, Lucretius and Pliny were highly-educated, literate and able to draw on a wide range of sources. More often people depended on the belief that chance could be controlled in advance through the formulae of rites.

In the natural world opportunities lie side by side with the confounding frustrations of epidemics, eruptions and ecological disasters. In modern times there is no better example of the battle than the North American settlers of the nineteenth century. These people were driven in part by their search for religious freedom and of them, the Mormons are the most conspicuous to this day. Far from losing their faith in the face of unspeakable hardships, it became deeper, more entrenched, and cemented the community together. The magnificence of the landscape and its breathtaking weather only confirmed them in their respect for the spiritual power that lay behind its creation. Native Americans were already even more in tune with

10 *Sacred landscapes are a worldwide phenomenon. Monument Valley, on the Arizona-Utah border, is now the protected sacred home of the Navajo people. In ancient religion a deity could be synonymous with the landscape he or she was associated with*

the natural world. Sundance, in Wyoming, takes its name from the self-explanatory ritual carried out there. Further south, in Arizona, the sanctity and symbolism of Monument Valley to the Navajo have been recognised and ownership restored to the tribe (**10**). To this day, the United States remains one of the most religious of all the developed nations.

But Salt Lake City, the capital of the Mormon state of Utah, is paradoxically a measure of how in little over a century human beings have taken increasing control of their day-to-day concerns. Despite the state's arid conditions, water usage per capita is amongst the very highest in the entire United States, and the rate of population growth is also amongst the nation's highest. This power has distanced some of us from the sense of divine action and it makes it harder to understand what ancient man thought and felt. During the year 2001 Great Britain was struck by an epidemic of foot-and-mouth disease. The condition hits cattle, sheep and pigs (amongst others) and has a drastic effect on the farming communities it affects. Yet, few shoppers in Britain experienced much inconvenience – if any at all. The consequences of this disastrous natural phenomenon (notwithstanding the involvement of modern farming methods in its spread) had next to no impact on modern British society apart from ruining farmers. Vast international modern markets, high-speed transportation, food surpluses, and the spending power of a developed country, simply erased the disease's effects from high streets. At any other time the temple precincts, or churches, would have been filled to bursting.

Throughout all recorded history, and in many parts of the world today, disease, weather and earthquakes have played dramatic roles in destroying cities and communities. A remote volcanic eruption, triggering dust clouds and thus diminished sunlight, could have a desperate effect on societies thousands of miles away for decades to come. Bad harvests lead to starvation, starvation to political and social dissent, perhaps even the collapse of regimes. In other words a single disaster can act as a catalyst for change stretching across generations. In the year 283 the emperor Carus was killed by a bolt of lightning. This prevented him from following up military successes against the Persians. Within two years both his sons and heirs were murdered and the Roman Empire fell into the hands of Diocletian who reconstructed it on a different model. Human history turns on unpredictable moments like these.

Ritual and social order

Speaking of the gods, the politician Gracchus in the motion picture *Spartacus*, announces to the young Julius Caesar that 'privately I believe in none of them, neither do you — publicly I believe in them all'. A Hollywood script it might be, but many real Roman politicians might have shared the character's sentiment. At Bath, one of the curse tablets lists six members of the same family who had been seen lying while swearing oaths by the spring on the Ides (12th) of April. Evidently, someone watching thought they were committing perjury and cursed them for it, asking that whoever was responsible paid 'for it to the goddess Sulis in his own blood' (Cunliffe 1988, 226). Insulting the gods could threaten the very foundations of society.

Polybius, a Roman historian of the second century BC, attributed Rome's astonishing rise to the phenomenon of superstition and called it 'the element which binds the Roman state together' (*Histories* vi.56). Polybius was blunt about what he saw as the credulity of the masses, and saw Roman religion as a political necessity operated by the upper classes in order to contain the 'fickle' and capricious rabble so inclined to 'lawless desires'. By exposing them to 'mysterious terrors', religion not only kept ordinary people in check but also provided social bedrock in a system where men made undertakings on oath, and kept their word. The result, he said, was a vast bias to honourable behaviour. That would change as the Roman Republic went the way of all systems of government, but Polybius had an acute grasp of *realpolitick*.

In our own time, there is no doubt that a decline in religious observation has been matched by an increase in social dislocation, conflict and moral crises. But we can still see how religious belief and the practice of ritual act as cultural and social ties, over and above spiritual sensibilities. Attending church, the mosque or the synagogue is an important way of publicising one's identity as the member of a group. This is particularly evident in Britain's minority religions, like Roman Catholicism or Islam. Such behaviour confirms a sense of belonging and provides opportunities to develop social, and commercial, relationships. Ritual also provides a continuity that transcends life and allows individuals, families and communities to mark and absorb the endless cycle of birth and death. In this way religion infiltrates and holds society together with a mixture of compliance and control.

Ritual, superstition and charismatics

Pliny the Elder was a man transfixed by the world and he set down in writing everything he could find out about it. His *Natural History* is the greatest work of general knowledge, anecdotes, facts and fallacies, insight and credulity, to survive from antiquity. Pliny discussed the nature of God in an early part of his work and concluded that if God existed at all, he must be 'the complete embodiment' of all senses, the mind and the soul (ii.14). But Pliny recognised that a divinity had limitations: he could not commit suicide, or change the fact that two times 10 made 20. Therefore what men really meant by God was Nature, because in the end Nature was all-powerful, with the facts of nature and natural laws being beyond anyone or any deity to alter. This was reflected in the identities of gods across the ancient world. In Germany, the tribes placed their trust in 'Nerhus – Mother Earth – and believe that she intervenes in human affairs' (Tacitus, *Germania* 38.2). Back in the second century BC Cato the Elder advised on appropriate rituals for propitiating the spirits of woodland groves when the trees were thinned for agriculture (*DA*, 139-40). In the late first century AD Martial fondly remembered the gods of the farm he had sold, which included Mars, Jupiter, Silvanus, Flora and Priapus (*E* x.92).

It is very easy for modern commentators to produce interpretations of sites and artefacts and present these as if they were universal and all-encompassing in antiquity. The spoked-wheel motif, for example, is almost invariably described as a symbol of a 'Celtic solar god', with the implication that this was a constant and conscious motive behind its display and use (**11**, and see chapter 5 where its symbolism is discussed in much greater detail). Likewise, the potency of ritual and its regimented observation is often seen as something observed with stone-faced seriousness by all and sundry. In fact the ancient world was also inclined to debate the point. Sadly though, we can only know about this from literary sources, and these are scarce compared to the votive gifts from those who had fewer doubts or at least were less inclined to take a chance.

Rome's intelligentsia, like Cicero, pondered on whether the superstitious observation of ritual, the attention paid to omens and their interpretation, amounted to self-induced imprisonment. Particularly popular was the examination of entrails of sacrificial victims for appropriate indicators of impending doom or great prospects. Conversely, Epicurean philosophy, which motivated the work of Lucretius, celebrated the natural world and expounded the idea that superstition simply created terror, and was an unwarranted artificial imposition (Cicero, *DND*, i.55-6). Lucretius asked how it was that 'fear of gods crept into the heart, which in our earth keeps holy their shrines and pools and groves, their altars and images'. He promised to explain that rather it was natural forces which controlled the sun and moon, and the produce of the soil – such an explanation was essential to avoid reverting to the gods, those 'cruel taskmasters' (*DRN* v.73-90). The Epicurean aspired to what Cicero called *cum dignitate otium*, 'dignified withdrawal' (*pro Sestio*, xlv.98), retiring from the rigours of public life and seeking a spiritual and inner peace. Perhaps this was whom the 'philosopher' at Brading represents (**colour plate 28**).

11 *Stone figure of a god, perhaps a Genius, with a cornucopia. The spoked wheel, a solar symbol, has been incorporated into the scene, here propped on an altar. From Netherby, an outpost fort to the north-west of Hadrian's Wall*

Such alternative thinking seems to have had little effect on entrenched tradition. Writing in the early third century AD, Herodian said of omens and entrails that 'the Italians place particular faith in this kind of divination' (viii.3.7). Almost all of us succumb to superstitious behaviour under the right circumstances. Surviving air crew of the Second World War, especially those who flew in bombers, can almost all recount the mascots they carried and rituals they underwent on a daily basis, and the pathological dread which followed the discovery that a mascot had been left behind, or an important ritual overlooked. Making one's bed before a mission, for instance, was considered a disastrous omen. Others left games of chess perpetually unfinished.

Writing in his *Alexander* in the second century, the satirist Lucian was amused at how the highly-successful religious charlatan, Alexander of Abonuteichos in Bithynia and Pontus, fiddled prophecies that had not been fulfilled so that it looked as if he had been right all along. All that is except the prophecy that he would die at the age of 150, since he expired before he was 70. Alexander is, incidentally, a reminder of the potent role charismatic individuals can play in religion, regardless of their integrity or lack of. So often in archaeology we find that explanations are sought in generalities when the truth is that ancient lives, just as our own, were impacted on by the idiosyncratic and random experiences of real life. These include people whose personalities and circumstance act as social and historical catalysts, and whom in retrospect we regard as defining parts of their time. The establishment of the late-Roman shrine at Lydney with its dream interpreter could just as easily have been generated by an influential individual who had captured the spiritual imagination of a group of wealthy admirers, as it could have been by a more general pagan revival. That we cannot distinguish either possibility from the record is a function of its inadequacy, not that such people did not exist.

Ritual and power

Pliny the Elder was disparaging about human vanities and concerns, but he was devastatingly acute in his analysis of what provokes much religious behaviour. We only need look at the curse tablets from the sacred spring at Bath to see what he meant (**43**). Men and women went through life confronted by Nature and exercised themselves to minimise the bad and increase the good. The means was 'chance divination': the control of chance events by spiritual force and insight. This way their prosperity and security could be enhanced, and their posthumous prospects improved. This helps explain the importance of healing cults, of which Bath is the prime Romano-British example. Celsus, a Roman author of the early first century AD, mentioned in his *de Medicina* that before medical science advanced disease was traditionally attributed to *iram deorum*, 'anger of the gods' and 'from them help used to be sought' (*Prooemium* 4). But the reality was that in spite of improvements in medical knowledge, belief in healing cults thrived while quackery and miraculous cures were rife and notorious. This reflected popular susceptibility to the promise of power over unknown and unknowable forces.

The essence of the relationship was seeking control, though as Cicero, Lucretius and Pliny pointed out the question was, who really *was* in control? Control is sought according to the means and knowledge available. In general, the less sophisticated a community, the more an explanation will be sought in confidence in ritual rather than hard facts or analysis. This restores a measure of control – or at least the illusion of it, especially if mechanisms of influence and power are introduced into the relationship.

Ritual inspires trust and a sense of influence over the moral neutrality of natural forces. By following ritual to the letter, the process of obtaining divine favour was enacted and it was an integral part of being a member of the Roman community. In Roman Britain this sense of ritual and civic duty turns up in occasional inscriptions like that of Lucius Viducius Placidus from Rouen at York in 221 (**55**). Pliny the Elder was also disparaging about the complicated manpower needed not only to utter the right words, but also to check the text, and make sure that silence was observed throughout. A wrong word, or unsolicited interjection, could destroy the chances of the ritual working (*NH* xxviii.10-11). There was some central direction of these public events. Under Elagabalus (218-22), the time when Viducius Placidus was in office, 'instructions were also sent out to all Roman magistrates or people conducting public sacrifices that the new god Elagabalus' name should precede all the others being invoked by the officiating priests' (Herodian iv.5.7). Here we see how the exercise of ritual, ostensibly to assert power over natural forces, functioned also as a means of exercising power over other people.

12 *Vitalis, probably a soldier at Carrawburgh (Hadrian's Wall), places his trust in the Goddess Fortuna on a simple altar he made himself. Pliny the Elder was fascinated by how much store men and women set by her power.* RIB 1537

Gods for all seasons

Pliny the Elder found the division of human virtues and vices into divine personifications such as Concord ridiculous and self-serving. He was especially interested how people fixated on Fortuna ('chance') believing her to be the source of all their advantages, and her caprices the cause of their disasters (**12**). Fortuna was particularly popular in Britain amongst military units, and usually benefited from dedications made by commanding officers rather than ordinary soldiers, an interesting instance of the hierarchy apparent amongst some of the deities. Here, amongst others, she appeared as Fortuna Conservatrix ('the Preserver'), Redux ('the Home-Bringer'), and even as Fortuna Balneari ('Fortuna of the Baths') where the frequent destruction by fire and subsequent rebuilding was recorded on other inscriptions. More often she was just known as Fortuna.

Other men, Pliny said, took fate a stage further and decided that God cast a die for each man before birth (**colour plate 11**). Pliny concluded that the only certainty was that nothing was certain. He envied animals whose sole concern was food, while human beings worried themselves sick over money, injustice, status, glory and, more than anything else, death. A popular theme on imperial coinage was the figure of

13 Aequitas, *the spirit of equity and justice, on a silver* denarius *of Trajan (struck 103-12), promoting the idea that the Roman state could promise relief from the unfairness and injustice of life. She holds a pair of scales to represent her control over fair dealing, and a cornucopia, symbol of abundance*

14 *(opposite) Altar to Jupiter and the Matres Ollototae, 'Mothers of Other Peoples', by Pomponius Dubitatus,* beneficiarius consularis, *'detached to the governor's staff', from Binchester fort (Durham).* RIB 1030

Aequitas, 'equity' or 'fair dealing', suggesting that the Roman state could promise some relief from the unfairness of life (**13**). Much later, St Augustine in the *City of God* looked back from a Christian perspective on what he regarded as the extraordinary Roman habit of having a different god for almost everything. In particular he found it amazing that three gods had separate protective duties over a door: Forculus for the actual doors, Cardea for the hinges, and Limentinus for the threshold (*op. cit.* 4.8). Augustine was intrigued by the idea that no one god could be 'entrusted' with the guardianship of a broad portfolio by 'men who loved a multitude of gods'. There are few better descriptions of a Roman cult centre than Pliny the Younger's account of the source of the Clitumnus in Italy. Not only did Clitumnus himself benefit from his own temple but 'all round is a number of little shrines. Each has its own god, name and cult, and some also their own springs . . .' (*Letters* viii.8).

The Roman capacity to entrust their world to an infinite range of spirits meant that they were equally sensitive to the needs and interests of new gods whether they were found in conquered territories, or imported by private individuals. Minucius Felix, writing in the third century AD, commented on how one could see nations and empires worshipping their own gods, but that the Romans accepted them all. Felix concluded that this was the secret to Rome's success, 'even at the first moment of victory, they worship the conquered gods in captured citadels' (*Octavius* 6). As late as the beginning of the fifth century, Macrobius recorded a traditional veneration even for the gods of Rome's ancient enemy, Carthage (*SC* iii.9.7-8). Even so, a Christian writer like Lactantius had already expressed the view that Roman civilisation debased itself by welcoming barbaric gods (see chapter 7). This was not a simple expression of unconditional tolerance. The Roman world hoped it presented a more attractive prospect to the new gods, and could appropriate the protective powers instead.

In Britain, several undated altars from the fort at Binchester (Durham) are dedicated to the marvellously catch-all Matres Ollototae, 'the Mother Goddesses from other peoples' (*RIB* 1030-2) (**14**). Several other altars from elsewhere in the military north record the Matres Tramarinae, 'the Mother Goddesses from overseas' (for example, *RIB* 1989 from Castlesteads). Places and regional identities now start to appear in divine anthropomorphic form, drawing on a well-established tradition from Mediterranean civilisation (**colour plates 5 & 6**), and particularly conspicuous amongst the Greek cities of the Roman East. Brigantia, a female goddess modelled on Minerva, represented the tribal and geographical identity of northern Britain. At Brough-on-Noe (Derbys), a goddess called Arnomecta appears on a dedication by Aelius Motio (*RIB* 281). Unknown elsewhere she has been plausibly linked to the Roman name for Buxton, *Aquae Arnemetiae*, 'waters of Arnemetia', itself a name linked to the word for a sacred grove (see chapter 2).

There was an implicit, and sometimes explicit, hierarchy in this great ecumenical society. Institutions and official bodies were more likely to make offerings to gods from the top of the pantheon like Jupiter Optimus Maximus, taking care to add the Spirits of the Emperors, often using heavily abbreviated verbal formulae. Conversely, the Veteres are best-known from a series of poorly-fashioned and inscribed altars in northern Britain dedicated by individuals of modest status (**106**). Epona, a strange deity linked to horses and the countryside, is most familiar from a variety of inscriptions and representations in the north-west provinces (**2**). She was also known well enough in Rome to be sneered at by Juvenal as *solam Eponam*, 'earthy Epona', in a context that associates her with the stink of stables (*Satires* viii.157), and later with pack-horses by Tertullian (*Apologeticum* xvi). She may have been represented in some of the sculpture groups we usually label 'Mother Goddesses' (**14**). Juvenal seems to have spent time in Britain as the tribune commanding an auxiliary cohort, and perhaps this was where he picked up his first-hand knowledge (*op. cit.* ii.161). It is precisely this kind of *literary* reference that provides us with direct testimony for how some of these more obscure spirits were regarded and what their powers were, and often even their names. The less 'Roman' a deity was, the greater the need to portray him or her with their associates or paraphernalia to make their identities clear in a non-verbal way.

The invasion of Britain might have involved suppressing certain religious activities, primarily those of the Druids, but this was more of a political necessity rather than a specifically religious persecution. On the whole, the domestic pagan gods of Britain enjoyed an Indian summer under Roman rule. Venerated and conflated with classical deities by the imported culture of the Roman world, hunter gods like Cocidius and the spectral figures of Britain's forests were brought out into the everyday world of the Roman province and found themselves commemorated in ways which have preserved them for us.

Identifying 'ritual' in archaeology

Common themes throughout much Roman religion were the cycle of festivals, and the devices of the offering and the vow. Priests like Lucius Viducius Placidus (above), helped fulfil the requisite ceremonies in the annual calendar of festivals, available to us from inscriptions and literary sources like Ovid's *Fasti*, 'days of the year and all their festivals' (though only January to June is extant). Thanks to these we know a little about how Roman communities participated in rites, some of the sacrifices or rituals followed, and the integral part festivals played in drawing people together in ways that reinforced their ties through entertainment and shared interests in fertility, harvests, and security.

The offering was a gift, usually in the form of a sacrifice. It served as an advance payment for a service that, it was hoped, the god would provide (**colour plate 8**). Conversely, the vow was a deal with a god. A man or woman decided to seek a favour from a deity. It could be anything from the survival of a child from illness, to the punishment of a cloak or mule thief. This might involve a visit to the temple or shrine of the selected deity. At Bath, Basilia seems to have promised her missing silver ring to the temple of Mars, before recording this and the requested punishment for the evil-doer on a curse tablet she deposited in the sacred spring of Sulis (Cunliffe 1988, no. 97). The curse tablets are rare instances of where we know how the transaction began. In these cases, the lost or stolen item was 'given' to the deity and that represented the human being's side of the bargain. But the other way was to make a request, and promise a gift in return. Such requests and promised gifts may have been recorded on scrolls deposited at temples. The numerous seal-boxes found at Great Walsingham (Norfolk), where a cult site may have existed (see chapter 4), are thought to be possible, albeit rather tenuous, evidence for archiving of such vows.

All we normally find is the end-product: the gift that fulfilled the vow. Such gifts range from money to statues but by far and away the majority that survive are coins, followed by brooches, jewellery, and miniature tools or weapons, as well as an array of personal and domestic flotsam and jetsam like buckles, bells and furniture fittings. Others include altars (**10, 94, 96**), but we have no means of measuring the gifts that have rotted away like wooden vessels, or food and drink. The miniature tools and weapons at any rate were good examples of 'it's the thought that counts' which prevailed in ancient votive practice. Describing them as 'symbolic' fabricates a kind spiritual significance to a handy device that also simply helped avoid throwing away useful equipment, just as generally using worn and outdated coinage for the same purpose avoided chucking good money down a literal drain. This was not always true.

15 *Carlisle (Cumbria). Fragmentary altar dedicated to Aesculapius, found reused in the foundation of a late fourth-century timber building. This is a good example of how much chance plays in the preservation and discovery of the evidence. Diameter 332mm*

Gifts like the Fossdike Mars (which cost its maker and givers 28 *denarii*, see *RIB* 274), or the two gold *aurei* of Allectus and a catapult washer in the Bath spring represent heftier investment but they are exceptional finds compared to most offerings. For every piece of expensive metalwork or jewellery thrown into a sacred well there were hundreds of coins in execrable condition.

Stone altars have a good chance of surviving (**15**). They usually bear an inscribed text recording the god and dedicant names, and variants on the formula *V S L M*, an abbreviation for *votum soluit libens merito*, 'fulfilled the vow willingly and deservedly'. Equally, by definition, we only have access to gifts by people sufficiently 'Latinized' to use words and abbreviations, or with access to someone to do it for them (**43**). So we may have a rather distorted idea of what a vow-fulfilling gift amounted to. Altars did not have to be made of stone. A turf one sufficed for the reconstruction dedication of the Capitol in Rome in 70 (*H* iv.53), so we can take it that many other dedications in Britain took place on earth or timber altars, which have rotted away. Far from being the work of professional masons, many altars were ad-hoc pieces produced when required. This much is obvious from the great range of competence exhibited by those found in Britain. This was normal. Martial's farm bailiff made several 'with his own hands' (*Epigrams* x.92) (**113**).

When artefacts are found in a context like a grave, the Bath spring or a temple precinct, it is fairly obvious that some sort of ritual has probably been involved. It is less obvious whether the artefacts were made or used for that purpose in the first instance. Coins as votive gifts are a particularly good example. A sacred pool or spring, or at a river crossing, provides us with the archaeological context for their use in this way, while references like Sozomen (see below) or Lucretius' account of the Cybele parade (see chapter 6) give us the written historical verification for their use as religious offerings.

But the argument does not work backwards. Most of the time we have no written evidence that particular classes of artefacts were used as votive gifts. Coins, like brooches, had day-to-day functions as well. Found in the absence of any other corroborative evidence they cannot be taken to be been deposited as votive gifts, and the same applies to brooches, miniatures and so on. It is an endless archaeological 'joke' that coins or artefacts found in a context where a practical reason is difficult to discern, are frequently described as being 'ritual' or 'votive'. At Great Walsingham in Norfolk there is no evidence yet for a temple, shrine, or sacred well, yet it has been assumed this was a religious site for a variety of reasons, some good and some bad (see chapter 4). This simply illustrates our separation from the consciousness of the man or woman who deposited an artefact, when there is no written evidence to specify its purpose.

The shrine of Coventina's Well on Hadrian's Wall produced, amongst many other things, a 47mm-wide flat bronze plaque in the shape of a horse. The publication of the finds cites two opinions: 'a mass-produced trinket, doubtless for fixing to the wall of the well-goddess's shrine'; and, 'from a box or piece of furniture'. Although in this case we can infer it was thrown into the well for votive reasons, it is clear that experts cannot decide whether it was manufactured *for that purpose*, and this will materially affect the interpretation of similar items found in more neutral contexts.

In any case, what does 'ritual' really mean? Ritual is a word covering behaviour that follows some sort of prescribed routine. In its most elementary sense, making the beds every morning is a 'ritual'. In fact, our lives are almost completely defined by 'rituals' because we follow set patterns about when and how we go to sleep, when and what we eat, and so on. Ritual, in the form of day-to-day repetition provides us with a sense of security. Much of this daily pattern is unconscious; few of us give much thought to what we do as we do it, which is why we remember so little about these mundane tasks. The patterns are observed as much out of habit than anything else. Generally, only disruption to the routine excites any attention.

In archaeology use of the term 'ritual' tends to mean routines associated with cult activity. This is where the trouble starts because whenever the word is used, the implication is that ritual is not only a primarily *religious* activity but that it is performed with conscious, concentrated, attention. Some primary sources, like Ovid's *Fasti*, describe such events and provide us with information like dates, the gods concerned, the context and the offering. But tying archaeological finds like goods or buried animals interpreted as 'votive' to the rituals testified in the sources we have is quite another thing. It is almost impossible to be certain what some artefacts are or how they were used, and whether something apparently used in religious activity had been made for that purpose. Occasionally, an artefact bears an inscription that makes its religious function beyond doubt. But more often, too much of the story is missing from the archaeological record to make sense of it. On 26 April 1662, the celebrated diarist Samuel Pepys visited the grounds of the earl of Southampton at Titchfield (Hants). He 'observed a little churchyard, where the graves are accustomed to be all Sowed with Sage'. The practice seems to have been based on the myth that white spots on longwort sage had been caused by the Virgin Mary's tears. The myth probably had much more ancient origins, and the custom survived into more modern times in Wales. Pepys's anecdote, or other records of the sage-sowed graves, is all the evidence we could have for this. It will not survive in an archaeologically-identifiable form, and thus we must be hopelessly divorced from other ancient practices we do not know about this way.

In the fifth century AD, the church historian Sozomen included a description of a shrine near Hebron in Palestine as it had functioned in the early fourth century before the Christian authorities dealt with it. Centred on a sacred tree, 'the oak of Mature', the shrine attracted an annual festival. Its holiness was based on the belief that this was where the God and two angels had appeared to the aged Abraham and foretold the birth of a son to him and his elderly wife Sarah (*Genesis* xviii), but it attracted a broader clientele. The Jews were attracted by the connection with their patriarch Abraham, the Christians by the story of a virgin birth, and the pagans by the appearance of the angels. Sozomen described the activities there:

> Here some prayed to the God of all. Some called upon the angels, poured out wine, burnt incense, or offered an ox, or he-goat, a sheep, or a cock. Each man created some beautiful product of his labour. After tending it carefully for a whole year, he offered it according to his vow, as provision for that feast, both for himself and his dependents. And either out of honour to the place, or fear of Divine wrath, they all abstained from coming near their wives, although during the feast they attended more to their beauty and adornment than usual. Nor, if they chanced to appear and to take part in the public processions, did they act at all licentiously. Nor did they behave imprudently in any other respect, although the tents were contiguous to each other, and they all lay promiscuously together. The place is open country, and arable, and without houses, with the exception of the buildings around Abraham's old oak and the well he prepared. No one during the time of the feast drew water from that well. According to pagan custom, some placed burning lamps near it, some poured out wine or cast in cakes. Others offered coins, myrrh, or incense. In this way I suppose the water was rendered undrinkable by contamination with the things thrown into it.
>
> Sozomen, *Ecclesiastical History* ii.4

Firstly, it is plain that a shrine attracted a variety of pilgrims, sometimes from quite different traditions. Secondly, many of the offerings would not survive in the archaeological record. We have little or no idea what the bulk offerings were at any given religious site in Britain. There are many other instances. The festival of Pales (goddess of shepherds and cattle) included fumigation with horse blood, calves' ashes, and beanstalks (Ovid, *Fasti* iv.731ff). Ovid's account of this festival incorporates the tale of Rome's foundation when fruit and crops were thrown into a trench that was backfilled and an altar set on top (*ibid* iv.821-5), a reminder that almost any house or place was liable to involve a similar foundation deposit that would be wholly undetectable by an archaeologist. The *paterae* found in the sacred spring at Bath, many of which were worn, had probably been used for pouring libations and other liquid offerings long before they ended up in the spring. The Hebron shrine's downfall came with a visit by Constantine's mother-in-law, Eutropia. Shocked by the pagan rites at a place celebrated in the Bible, she informed Constantine who arranged for the destruction of pagan monuments and the installation of a church.

If we take isolated 'religious artefacts', such as the bronze statuette of Venus from Verulamium (**132**), the complications even of tangible artefacts become obvious. That it represents a deity at all is something of a subjective assertion – it *could* be Venus but it comes with no label to that effect and the figure is accompanied by no accessory or associate that would confirm the fact by implication. Even if we accept that it is Venus then we have no means of knowing where that Venus was 'used' when she was first made or acquired. The figure may have stood in a household shrine, or remained as unsold stock in a temple shop. Either way she ended up in a deposit otherwise made up of what looks like metalworking debris. Was she buried by accident, awaiting melting-down? Or was she buried as some sort of propitiatory offering to the 'gods of the workshop'? Picking any sort of 'ritual' out of this is impossible, but we can at least see that the Venus, like a brooch or buckle in a sacred spring, might have existed in a number of contexts throughout its life. The same applies to sporadic finds, like bronze figures of animals such as rams.

Another example is the artefact, which seems to have been deliberately mutilated. Perhaps the best instance is the so-called 'ritually-killed' weapon, for example the bent swords found in some of the controversial pits at Newstead (see below). In modern warfare it is routine – even ritual! – practice to disable an enemy's guns by bending the rifle barrel, or exploding a grenade in the barrel of a bigger gun. Both render the arms beyond reuse. The intention is entirely a practical one and it is most unlikely that, say, any soldier in the Second World War gave any spiritual consideration to what he was doing apart from perhaps 'thanking God' he was still alive as he picked up his gear and carried on. Nevertheless, and this is critical, the archaeological manifestation of 'ritually-broken' artefact and one disabled for a practical reason are the same: weapons destroyed in a fashion which leaves the same results time after time but which preserves the basic form and appearance. How we can possibly distinguish routine disabling as standard practice on the battlefield from ritual as spiritual and symbolic death of an inert object? The answer of course is that we cannot, at least not from the archaeological evidence.

Disabling a weapon at least has a clear, practical, purpose. More innocuous objects, like brooches, found in a broken state are more of an enigma and well-known from sites interpreted as being religious. At Harlow (Essex), for example, a number of damaged brooches were recovered from levels preceding the construction of a temple. We lack any information to help us understand the reason – for example, whether it was customary to replace brooches at an annual ceremony, or to dispose of brooches belonging to someone who had died. But damaged goods are not exclusively recovered from religious sites and nor are religious sites exclusively associated with damaged goods (**colour plate 7**). Metal was a much more expensive commodity than it is now. Breaking up discarded or damaged items makes it easier to melt them down for reuse. On the other hand, we also have certain types of brooch that are specifically associated with temples, like the 'horse-and-rider' type (**79, colour plate 13**). These seem to be souvenirs of shrines, a tradition vastly better-known to us from the pilgrim badges of the Middle Ages.

Likewise, it is not unusual for pottery vessels to have been pierced with drilled holes. This was sometimes to repair them with metal staples, but not always. Could this be some process of ritually rendering a vessel unusable? Inevitably, the idea has proved attractive to experts whose knowledge of practical everyday life is limited. A recent sober paper points out that there were many day-to-day reasons for piercing pottery vessels including extant ancient recipes directing the user to do this (Fulford and Timby 2001). The same explanation has been offered for vessels used in burials, drilled or pierced in some way. The entirely practical possibility that it might have been to help drainage, or suspension, is usually ignored. The idea that it might only have been for a ritual purpose is exposed for the intellectually lazy solution it is.

One assumption sometimes made is that votive gifts represented high value to their owners. This was sometimes the case but in fact, as we have already seen, the reverse is more usually true. The finds from the spring at Bath include thousands of coins, most of which were extremely worn, and a handful of brooches where the missing pins and other damage are probably attributable to corrosion and wear. None is convincingly the victim of deliberate mutilation and like the coins, low-value bronze brooches were selected for this purpose far more commonly than expensive gold or silver ones. The possibility must subsist that, once damaged, some brooches were retained as votive gifts, perhaps even being sold for the purpose. Interestingly, broken brooches rarely turn up with all their parts in the same context, which rather suggests they were broken somewhere else at some other time. But such prosaic explanations rarely satisfy most commentators on this sort of subject, so the archaeologist resorts to 'ritual killing' as an explanation, although this doesn't really explain anything at all.

Hoards, rubbish, graves and ritual

The idea that an 'unusual' deposit is likely to have a religious connection is an increasingly popular one in some Romano-British studies. One of the justifications is apparently that there is a 'growing acceptance' of this, according to one recent paper. It's an intriguing statement that seems to substitute acceptance for facts. The basis of the theory is what is perceived to be a diversion from 'normal' deposits (whatever those are), itself a subjective judgement. This same paper discusses the significance of snake jewellery in hoards. It makes much of the large number of Minerva types on coins in the Snettisham jeweller's hoard, and the link of the goddess to conquering death in association with snake jewellery as a symbol of rebirth. It's an attractive way of connecting the evidence, but is it justified?

In fact, 74 of the 83 Snettisham hoard silver coins are of Domitian (81-96), a reign known for producing good-quality silver and in considerable quantity (particularly between 88-96). Domitian favoured Minerva above all other deities (**colour plate 5**), and she appears much more often on his coins than any other subject. So it is inevitable that selection of his coinage *for whatever purpose* would favour coins featuring Minerva. Indeed, it is something of a challenge to find a silver coin of Domitian *without* a reference to Minerva on it, whether one is excavating the piece, or buying one from a modern dealer. It is also much easier to buy a silver coin of Domitian today than any other first-century emperor apart from his father, Vespasian, for the simple reason that almost all his predecessors struck silver erratically and in far smaller amounts.

The latest Snettisham coin was *c*.155, so the hoard must post-date that year. The wear on all the coins shows that they were withdrawn from currency that had been circulating for some time. It has long been known that the gradual debasement of Roman silver issues led each generation to prefer the coins of previous reigns. This is manifested in hoards across the Roman world, though Snettisham shows an exceptional degree of bias to Domitian's series. Even so, the hoarder only accumulated Domitian's silver from the period 85-96, when the silver was produced to a standard of 93.5 per cent fine. There are two possible explanations. By the 150s the 98 per cent fine issues of the period 82-5 are likely to have been already withdrawn by the state or earlier hoarders and were no longer available. This pattern is extremely well-established and is found in every time and place where bullion coinage suffers debasement. But of course 98 per cent fine silver is softer, and therefore less desirable for durable jewellery. Modern sterling, at 92.5 per cent fine, is much closer to the silver the Snettisham hoarder selected and provides the optimum combination of hardness and purity. Either way, the standard of all of Domitian's silver was very accurately maintained, making it a thoroughly reliable means of storing wealth.

The obvious explanation for the hoard, given the context, is that the Snettisham silver coin was accumulated as a stock of reliable bullion for savings or for making new jewellery. Indeed, much of the rest of the hoard was jewellery in various stages of completion (**colour plate 14**). The alternative, that it was a votive deposit of carefully-selected symbolic coin types, flies in the face of normal practice observed on votive sites. Almost all coins selected for votive gifts at religious sites were low value, worn or even counterfeit. The coins at Bath show absolutely no bias to issues depicting Minerva, the principal classical goddess of that shrine (**colour plate 18**). Religious activity might be inherently irrational, but the average Roman who threw three coins in the fountain made a very rational decision about which ones he spent on his wish. Here then, we have a good example of a well-intentioned scholarly interpretation of the Snettisham hoard that is based on an elementary misunderstanding of basic numismatic evidence, and overlooks the overall content of the hoard. The point is not that Snettisham *cannot* be a votive deposit, but that the coins are emphatically *not* reliable evidence for it. Taken together the evidence supports a more practical explanation.

The so-called 'ritual shafts' represent a more complex problem of analysis as the pits at Newstead highlight. When does a rubbish pit become a ritual deposit? The answer is when an archaeologist calls it one, or when its contents are not just rubbish, but that still leaves us often fumbling in the dark for a more expansive explanation. A group of nine third- or fourth-century shafts in Cambridge each contained a dog and a baby, or babies. Was the place and the act of burial primarily a ritual intended to propitiate or appease some third-party force? Or were the babies and dogs first and foremost deceased, and needing burial that was duly performed according to the appropriate rites? There is a critical difference in priority, but distinguishing one from the other in the archaeological record is generally impossible. There is a little help from Columella who tells us that unweaned puppies were sacrificed to provide blood and guts for propitiating the goddess Robigo, 'mildew' (Columella *DRR* x.342-4). This was supposed to protect crops and took place on 25 April, although the entrails of dogs or sheep could also be used (Ovid, *Fasti* iv.901-10). Obviously, that can't explain every buried dog or puppy, but it provides a possible context without involving archaeological conjecture. One recent archaeology television programme made a great deal of fifth-century puppy burials at a site in Italy without once mentioning the relevant primary sources.

The roughly 3m-deep first- or second-century pit at Deal (Kent) which contained a crude chalk figure consisting of little more than a block with a head is rather more likely to have been a subterranean shrine of sorts than just a fortuitous combination of features. Needless to say we cannot know who or what was being worshipped or how. A pit containing the complete skeleton of a young horse, bar its two front feet, is precisely the sort of deposit that excites attention. Is it, for example, an offering to Epona or just the burial of a favourite animal whose feet were retained, much as a lock of hair might be kept as a memento? Of course we cannot answer this.

A number of late-Roman pits were cut into the ruins of an earlier house in Insula IX at Silchester. Some of these had finds, mostly pottery, but one had included a beef joint and another the skeleton of a dog. These were interpreted by excavators as evidence for a 'ritual closing' of the site prior to later reuse. The essence of the problem is not having any contemporary statement of intent to help us. The Silchester pits are no less likely to be rubbish and, as for the dog – what else do you do with a dead dog apart from bury it? On this basis, every modern dead cat or dog buried in its own suburban back garden could be interpreted as a ritual deposit. No doubt many are indeed buried with a tear and a prayer but the primary purpose is burial for entirely practical reasons. Just because we have literary evidence for dog sacrifice does not mean every dead dog was the result of one.

Such problems complicate interpretation of human burial practices. This is a ritual we can all identify with because every society has its own method of disposing of dead bodies and commemorating the deceased person, even in our thoroughly secularised modern community. In general, burials in Roman Britain are cremation in the first and second centuries, with a gradual transition to inhumation thereafter. Grave goods are a common feature until the fourth century when Christian customs began to take over. Christian burials are thought to be defined by an east-west orientation of the body (to greet the Second Coming) and an absence of grave goods, though a few continued to combine the two. Some graves are different. At the Winchester (Hants) Lankhills cemetery seven late fourth-century graves contained decapitated bodies (it is not clear if they were necessarily *killed* this way, or whether it occurred after death). Most of these have been identified as elderly women. Their skulls had been placed beside their legs. One woman was buried with the remains of two dogs. One of the dogs had been cut to pieces and its backbone wrapped round and tied together.

The dogs are an unusual addition, but the action of decapitating bodies, again often of elderly women, is known from a number of other places such as Kimmeridge (Dorset) and Orton Longueville (Cambs). The practice of beheading has been interpreted as an 'essentially Celtic religious' practice (Green 1997). There is some evidence for this. The interest in the head and its potency is apparent not only from examples of sculpture, but also in their treatment of foes. The Gauls 'were accustomed to embalming the heads of notorious enemies in cedar-oil, and showing them off to their guests' (Strabo iv.4.5). Although the Lankhills-type burials are known from several places they are by definition unusual. However, this judgement must in part be qualified by the general shortage of extensive cemetery excavations and even fewer which have been properly published.

Ideally, what we need is to know whether punishment played a part in the women's burials, and whether their behaviour in life had singled them out for a special form of execution. Of course we never will, but historical instances show how ritual and retribution become blurred. In 1660, Charles II was restored to the throne in England. The Restoration was an occasion of great celebration but the regime moved immediately to punish those responsible for executing Charles I in 1649. The living miscreants were sentenced to death by the particularly grisly process of being hanged, drawn and quartered, and even the corpse of Oliver Cromwell was exhumed and treated the same way. In every sense this was far more complex a statement than the word 'ritual' could convey. It was an act of political consolidation, a practical means of disposing of enemies in an instant. It satisfied a popular need for the age to turn its back on the past, and Charles II made a statement about the power he could wield over his opponents. None of this would be recoverable from the archaeological record. History alone provides the story. Nevertheless, it is easy to see that hanging, drawing and quartering – by going beyond what was necessary to kill someone – had features that resemble what was found at Lankhills. The answer must be that the way the elderly women had been buried had something to do with what they had done in life being made to echo through eternity. The obvious parallel is the ruthless medieval treatment of women accused of witchcraft: a viciousness borne out of fear and a determination to contain the women through death.

It ought usually to be possible to rule out everyday rubbish from possible 'ritual' deposits. Dumps of pottery and bone in ditches and pits must surely represent everyday refuse. On the other hand, where pottery vessels have been carefully inserted into holes in the floor in a cellar near a niche depicting nymphs and accompanied by a well as they were in the house at Lullingstone (Kent), we are clearly dealing with something different. In general, complete pottery vessels – even if broken in situ – normally belong to coin hoards, graves or turn up in and around temples. Now, of course, having said that we can't go very much further with what the ritual involved, if ritual it was – the sage graves recorded by Pepys and mentioned above illustrate this perfectly. The miniature pots buried in the precinct of the Triangular Temple at Verulamium might have been revisited for refilling with gifts of food and drink but since we do not even know what god was worshipped there we have no idea at all of what was being sought, or even any sense of frequency, date or indeed anything else at all.

One of the latest novelty archaeology concepts for separating the ritual from the everyday is the so-called 'structured deposit'. The definition of a 'structured deposit' seems to be where artefacts and organic remains like bones are organised into patterns, and where the assemblage seems to be dominated by particular classes at the expense of others, thus differing from those found in 'occupation horizons'. It ought to be fairly obvious to anyone with common sense that most households even today go through a certain amount of rubbish organisation prior to its disposal, so it becomes instantly plain that subjectivity is going to play a large part in how pits filled with debris might be interpreted. And, not surprisingly, that is precisely what turns out to be the case. Newstead is a fort site in southern Scotland where a large number of pits were excavated in the fort and its vicinity. They contained weapons, human remains, quern stones and pottery amongst other things. These have been variously interpreted as:

- normal rubbish and debris from a fort
- burial of rubbish and valuables to prevent their use to an enemy
- votive offerings to Celtic gods of the underworld
- continuity by the Roman occupants of local prehistoric ritual

The options speak for themselves, and tell us a lot about archaeological mindsets. That the last depends on how one interprets 'vertical patterning of finds' shows how tenuous they are. The truth is that it is impossible to know. Archaeologists have never been ashamed to obfuscate where clarity would do, and nor have they been ashamed to ascribe profound and complex motives to rubbish pits, forgetting that rubbish pits come before anything else in human settlement except eating and sex. The problem is that although the literary and epigraphic record bears witness to ritual and cult activity, bits of pot, bone and metalwork cannot be automatically joined up other than in one's own imagination. Archaeology only offers answers manufactured in our own consciousness.

One anecdote told by a professional archaeologist in London is worth mentioning. Owing to costs, a training excavation was carried out on the remains of a Second World War Anderson shelter – a kind of semi-buried hut made of corrugated sheets of steel. According to the archaeologist who had directed the dig, no archaeologists working on the site were able to identify the shelter *unless they were old enough to know already what it was*. Given how much we do not know of what went on at

Newstead or anywhere else, it ought to be obvious that some of this speculation is intellectually bankrupt, in spite of the defence that such practices only seem illogical to us because of our different mind-set.

Even if the speculation borders on the futile that does leave us with tantalisingly unanswered questions. Prehistoric monuments, such as Neolithic chambered tombs, are highly conspicuous now and would have been even more so in the Roman period. There is no doubt that they attracted attention, but the problem is to what end? At Crickley Hill (Glos), the long mound seems to belong at least to the Bronze Age, though Neolithic pottery dating back to 3000 BC was found in association with it. But it had proved a source of interest to someone in the Roman period, someone sufficiently motivated to dig a narrow hole into the mound and drop a Roman brooch into it. Not only that but a miniature of the mound seems also to have been built beside the original. Holes had been dug elsewhere on the mound and Roman coins dropped in. Carsington Pasture cave (Derbys) contained a very large number of human remains from the Neolithic right through to the Iron Age. But the surface of the cave also yielded Roman coins dating up to the middle of the second century, a plate brooch and some pottery. That two of the coins were silver suggests they were not casual losses. More recently the Neolithic group of megaliths at Beckhampton Cove (Wilts), connected to the Avebury henge by Beckhampton Avenue, was visited in the Roman period. As well as samian pottery, the finds included a Roman spearhead and sections of armour.

These are very far from being the only examples. In one sense it seems reasonable to see the phenomenon as a respectful votive gesture to ancient, and barely under-stood, monuments. It has also been suggested that the coins might represent gifts following a bout of Roman grave-robbing in search of valuables. Neolithic hand-axes were used as Romano-British votive goods, for example at Hayling Island. Certainly, some of the Derbyshire chambered tombs like Minninglow seem to have been cleared in the Roman period, but it is also possible that the reason was just to create usable shelters – or just pure curiosity. In the absence of anything conclusive, more extreme explanations have been offered, like the idea that the Roman artefacts were gifts from the local political élite in an effort to legitimise their power by connecting with spirits residing in the monuments.

Taken to its logical extremes, this means everything is possible, however ludicrous, leaving us with such vast open plains of inconclusive scenarios that we are no better off than when we started. Even if the Newstead pits do represent ritual continuity from prehistory we have absolutely no way of identifying anything useful about that ritual, such as what it was for, to whom it was directed and when it happened. The conceptual gulf between a curse, or an inscription, which identifies a moment of ritual or cult, and pits with layers of bones in them, is only bridgeable when we have definitive contexts, for example when they appear in temple precincts. So, on the whole, this book will focus on places and deposits where we are in a good deal less doubt about what was going on.

2 Jove's dread clamours

Cult and power in late prehistory

For a century or more before the Roman invasion of 43, the Iron Age tribes of southern Britain were constantly aware of the classical world emerging intermittently through the fog across the sea. We know from classical accounts, and the distribution of coinage, that Britain's landscape was divided up amongst tribes. Those in the south-east were more 'developed' in the sense that they interacted with the Roman world. Social structures, lineage, kingship, and farming communities had all grown in a direction that was coherent to commentators like Caesar. He described the inhabitants of Kent as *humanissimi*, 'the most civilised' (*BG* v.14), and by implication dismissed those who were not. In Roman perception the less civilised were less visible, to the point of oblivion.

It is correspondingly easy to see why the archaeological evidence for Iron Age cult centres of a form which links to later, Roman, traditions is more dominant in the south and east. Late Iron Age temple-like structures are not infrequently found under Roman temples in this region, for example at Hayling Island (Hants), Wanborough (Surrey) (**16**) and Harlow (Essex). Generally such structures are circular, though the Heathrow temple was square. But buildings were not an essential component of the Iron Age sacred site and further afield they are even more rare. Being in the areas where coinage was produced is reflected in the relatively prolific finds of Iron Age coin finds in temple zones. Such coinage is rare at other contemporary occupation sites. But the connections can be traced further afield. Iron Age features, pottery and coins imported from other tribal areas, have been found near the church at Ancaster (Lincs), itself the focal point of various cult items of Roman date connected with the Mother Goddesses, and the spectral deity of Viridios (**colour plates 32 & 33**). In this instance it is impossible to say whether the pre-Roman features all pre-date the conquest or whether Ancaster was a pre-Roman cult centre, but it seems likely that it was.

Unfortunately, it is scarcely ever the case that finds from Iron Age levels on such sites are unequivocally 'sacred', simply because there was no meaningful sculptural or epigraphic tradition which survives. Caesar said that in Gaul there were *plurima simulacra*, 'numerous likenesses', of Mercury (*BG* vi.17), but such pre-Roman Celtic sculpture is now almost unknown. When it does survive, it never carries an inscription, making it impossible to be certain of function or symbolism. Even structures of a type we can choose to interpret as temples or shrines are far from common. Natural features like trees, springs or waterfalls could all serve as the focus of a cult.

16 *Wanborough (Surrey). A reconstruction drawing of what the first-century circular temple might have looked like. It may well have been built before the Roman invasion, but it was later replaced by a Romano-Celtic temple (see for example* **136***)*

The veneration of the naturalness of any of these left them intact and, to us, virtually unrecognisable as cult focal points unless the Romans developed them into more identifiable forms.

Tacitus gives one simple clue in his statement that Britain featured the same beliefs and religious practices to be found in Gaul (*Agr* 11). He of course was writing in the late first century AD, but his comment reflects Caesar's claim over a century earlier that the tribes in the south-east were made up by immigrants from the continent (*BG* v.12). Inevitably then we need to look closer at Caesar and see what he has to say about Gaulish cults (*ibid*, vi. 13-19). Caesar concentrated on the Druids. Crucially, Caesar was told that the Druid tradition had begun in Britain, and his account includes a number of important points, several of which do not appear in other descriptions of the Druids. He describes a caste of priests led by an elective leader, enjoying elevated social status including exemption from taxes and warfare, total control of all religious activity and belief, including teaching it and excluding people from it, and a major controlling interest in settling disputes and crimes. They taught that the soul was immortal. Cicero added the observation that some Druids were believed to be able to prophesy the future (*DD* i.90), some of whom employed the grisly device of stabbing a man in the back and 'interpreting' his death groans (Strabo iv.4). Another version of this anecdote is recounted by Diodorus Siculus (v.31), making it slightly more likely that it is based on truth. One of the reasons this was perceived as acceptable was the promulgation of the belief that each man's soul was immortal.

The ultimate sanction Druids could impose was exclusion of a miscreant from participating in sacrifices, and thus effectively exclusion from all society. The implications for an individual were deadly serious, because religious rites involving human sacrifice were considered the only means of appeasing the gods and ensuring survival in war or from disease. The poet Lucan called their activities 'strange rites and hateful practices' (*Pharsalia* i.507). The actual gods appeased are misleadingly familiar because Caesar gave them classical names, listing Mercury as the most popular (*BG* vi.17), along with Jupiter, Juno, Minerva, Apollo and Mars (**17**). To what extent he was describing conflated cults, where local gods had been identified with classical equivalents, is not known. A problem for us is that the Celtic deities had relatively ill-defined attributes and identities. This means that although they were often identified with classical gods, that identification could vary from place to place. The Celtic deity Cocidius, for example, was conflated in Britain with both Mars and Silvanus at different locations, perhaps really representing a multitude of now-indistinguishable local hero deities. It is, incidentally, worth establishing that 'conflation' should not be taken to mean that there was a deliberate policy of identifying native and Roman deities. Rather it was probably a handy device, which was simply a consequence of a literate society seeking to label what it found, when and as convenient.

Druids regarded the spoils of war as gifts to be deposited at sacred spots. Removal or retention was punishable by torture and death. One item seems to have been exempt – the human head, an item of the highest totemic importance in this world of tribal military might (Strabo iv.4). Swaggering warriors left the battlefield brandishing the decapitated heads of their enemies, which they then proudly displayed outside their homes. Alien though this might sound to us, and it certainly sounded alien to the Romans, there was in fact much in common between the Druid priesthood and the medieval church in Europe, or even with extremist religious fundamentalist groups today. Medieval Christian bishops exercised unparalleled control and influence over their societies, as well as monopolising education and law. Elevated amongst their flocks, like their popes they were able to manipulate people, restrain dissent, provide spiritual justification for wars, and exert violent retribution on anyone who dared to question their pronouncements.

17 *Mercury and his consort Rosmerta on a relief from Gloucester. Mercury has his* caduceus *(staff) and cockerel – items sometimes found as individual bronze miniatures, or detached from bronze statue groups. Mercury was an extremely popular god in the north-western provinces, even before the Romans arrived. Height 500mm*

The Druids' self-contained religious status challenged the Roman concept of authority where religious identities reflected and enhanced political executive power exercised through the offices of the Roman Republic, and later the person of the emperor. The post of priest was subsumed into the standard portfolio of the élite. It was as if the prime minister was the archbishop of Canterbury. In this way Augustus and his successors served as *pontifex maximus*, 'chief priest'. City councillors and other worthies around the Empire included priestly roles amongst their duties (**55-6**), and estate owners took care of the temples and shrines on their land. In medieval England the friction between the separate authorities of state and church was eventually resolved by identifying one with the other during the Reformation. In Roman Britain the existence of the Druid caste, so long as it functioned in a self-determining way, was wholly intolerable to any external source of authority. Had the Druids integrated emperor worship into their activities there would have been no serious problem: Druid power would have been redirected to serve imperial interests. But it was not, and this left the Roman state no choice.

Matching this sort of information to the archaeological evidence is altogether another matter. For a start, Caesar, Cicero and Strabo had their own agendas or obtained their information from third parties. Caesar, more than any other, wrote for a Roman public in order to publicise his own achievements and promote his own interests. The more exotic and barbarous his opponents could be seen to be, so much the better for Caesar. The *Bellum Gallicum* (Gallic War) was as much a self-serving propaganda tool as it was an armchair travelogue. Unfortunately, whatever the Druids wrote down, it has not survived. Caesar says that in fact they considered it irreligious to write their beliefs and teachings down at all, and used Greek letters when they had to record something (*BG* vi.14). We are left with remarks like Strabo's that Druid human sacrifices extended to 'impaling victims in temples', and hurling cattle and human beings into a huge wooden figure which was then set on fire (iv.4.5, and repeated by Caesar, *BG* vi.16). Doubtless leaving his readers (including us) agog with fascinated horror, Strabo leaves us none the wiser about his sources and whether there was a semblance of truth in his account. What matters is the popular belief such accounts engendered. Even today, similar tensions exist. A controversy broke out in early 2002 when it was revealed that, following police investigations, the body of young boy found in the Thames had been linked to a human sacrifice carried out by a voodoo group sheltering under the cloak of 'cultural diversity'. The result was instantaneous expressions of revulsion, suspicion and confusion.

Coinage and sculpture gives us some sense of the totemic imagery current in late Iron Age Britain. Coinage was issued in small quantities, and by only a few of the tribes proliferating across the prehistoric landscape. Its designs are characterised by the multitude of abstract shapes and fantastical animals depicted which reflect the lack of concern with representational art (**18**). Some of the tribes had begun to flirt with a Latinized literacy, and their issues feature the names of kings, lineages and strongholds. Likewise, their coins feature an increased consciousness of classical design. Tasciovanus of the Catuvellauni was one of the more prominently featured monarchs (**19**). His name appears alongside depictions of winged horses, griffins,

18 *(left) Silver stater (reverse) struck by the Durotriges (roughly Dorset, Somerset and Wiltshire). The abstract figure is in fact a stylised horse, and the type can be traced back to the anatomically realistic designs on Macedonian gold coins of the fourth century BC. Late first century BC to early first century AD*

19 *(right) Gold stater struck during the reign of Tasciovanus of the Catuvellauni or just afterwards. A hunting horseman is featured on the reverse with the letters SEGO, perhaps for a would-be successor trying to associate himself with the dynasty or for an otherwise-unknown stronghold. Note the recurrence of the spoked wheel motif. Diameter 17mm. Early first century AD*

bulls, boars and lions. Some of the figures were modelled on Roman coin designs and images though they often exaggerate key features of the animals, in particular the antlers of stags – antlers recur again and again on representations of deities with a local tradition (**5**).

Epaticcus, Tasciovanus' son, issued one coin type with the head of Hercules and on the other side, a thoroughly Roman-looking eagle. Even the wild boar on another of his issues is barely distinguishable from a silver coin of Augustus, itself modelled on a Roman Republican silver coin struck in 86 BC by Caius Hosidius Geta. These are not the only instances. One theory is that the Romans trained amenable tribal rulers, and that part of the consequence was an increasing perception by those rulers of themselves in a Roman idiom through Roman symbols. In this respect it is very hard to know whether a boar on a tribal coin denotes traditional tribal values of strength and vigour in an animal that might have spiritual symbolism; or, was simply a device that reflected, and appropriated, Roman and Greek metaphors of power. Classical models were widely available anyway, familiar from the silver coinage of the Roman world that circulated far beyond its boundaries, as the US dollar does today. There is no doubt that in the period between Caesar's exploits in Britain in 55 and 54 BC, and the invasion of 43, the coinage of the south and south-east becomes increasingly representational. Even so, the choice tells us something. Most Roman coin types were not copied. The emphasis is on prestigious beasts evoking a clear sense of power, vigour and strength. The same sort of association is as endemic today in the names of military aircraft, expensive and prestigious cars, or even in the ludicrous names of some accessories available for computers.

These priorities are mirrored in some of the rare surviving Celtic sculpture of the period. Bronze figurines of boars, bulls and stags are known – often from grave goods. Stone is even rarer, but wood was more widely used than we will ever know. That the figure mentioned by Strabo above was (a) wooden and (b) burned, should act as a reminder to us above all that what we lack in the archaeological record leaves us hopelessly handicapped from the outset. Lucan, describing what he regarded as the barbaric rites conducted at a sacred Gaulish place, refers to 'effigies of gods, rude, scarce fashioned from some fallen trunk' (*Pharsalia* iii.468-9), and occasional finds of examples preserved in waterlogged conditions reflect this. Metal-detecting finds have altered the picture a little. Small bronze figurines show that anthropomorphic representations did exist but they seem to have been much scarcer than in the Roman period. One example, said to be from Cambridgeshire, depicts a human bust on a body in the form of a tree trunk (**20**, left). This seems to represent a Gaulish woodland god called Erriapus or Eriappus (*AE* 1982, 700-1). Altars to him from Gaul depict the god within tree foliage. A characteristic that these representations share with the regional sculpture

20 *Left: The Gaulish tree god Erriapus, apparently depicted on a small bronze figurine from Cambridgeshire as a human head with the body of a tree trunk. Height 78mm*

*Right: Bronze plaque from South Cadbury (Somerset). Found in the guard-chamber of the hillfort's south-west gate in levels associated with fighting between the Roman army and the tribal defenders in the mid- to late 40s AD. It perhaps depicts a god or ruler. The style is a mix of the cruder so-called 'Celtic' (most noticeable in the eyes), and classical realism. During the Roman period in Britain deities were often depicted in a stylistically similar manner (**68**). Height 134mm*

21 *Building stone from Corbridge depicting a boar, the emblem of* XX Valeria Victrix. *Does this denote simply strength and aggression, or is the association more subtle (see text)? Second or third century. Diameter 308mm*

of Roman Britain is the so-called 'Celtic' style, typically a disproportionately large head, protuberant eyes and mouth and a lack of emphasis on proportion or realism. This varies a good deal, but in Britain figures approximating true classical proportions are rare at any time. Some authorities see the 'Celtic' forms as a distinct, even provocatively idiosyncratic, art. Others recognise it as sharing features found on work by less proficient sculptors or artists. It is interesting that in the Renaissance, once the skills and techniques were revived to produce realistic sculptures and paintings, this became the norm across Europe and was aped to differing levels by lesser artists. The question of whether incompetence, imitation or symbolism is enshrined in Celtic styles will forever remain a potent intellectual battleground.

The choice of animals as symbols is scarcely surprising; or is it? This was an age of warrior cults. Tribes rose and fell according to their skills in warfare and the prestige of their leaders. Later on, Tacitus would note that it was this perpetual preoccupation with squabbling and fighting that made the tribes of Britain so easy to deal with (*Agr* 12). The landscape was a battleground in which tribes constantly fabricated territorial disputes, doubtless provoked by imagined or genuine sleights, but ultimately motivated by no more than greed and the desire to instil in life a sense of purpose, even if it was based on the desire for tribal aggrandisement. Warriors boasted, and berated their opponents, recalled their mighty heroic deeds around roaring fires, and sang songs to relive their dead and glorious comrades. Boars and stags, triumphantly hunted and killed, surely helped reflect and evoke this imagery and it is no surprise that the Roman army also used similar motifs – the boar, for example, was the emblem of the XX legion (**21**), while the bull represented Jupiter.

In fact the imagery was subtler, much subtler than we would normally imagine. Tacitus describes the German tribe of the Aestii as venerating the Mother of the Gods and 'as a symbol of that superstition they wear representations of the wild boar. The boar supplants protection by arms or other human beings, and guarantees to the believer complete peace of mind even while being in the middle of the enemy' (*Germania* 44). The anecdote is an important one – it is most unlikely that modern speculation would come up with a similar connection as mother goddesses and boars seem inherently unrelated. We could speculate on whether Tacitus is wrong, or confused two different stories. Of course, he was not in a position to make a direct assessment – he worked on hearsay. As an objection this isn't a great deal of use as we are in exactly the same position, apart from being also separated by much more time. To refute him needs something better than modern scepticism – perhaps an alternative source of equal stature. We have no such thing, and the result is that we have to recognise he is more likely to be right, and certainly more likely to be right than us, for the time being. The implications are obvious. All the other sorts of association we read into boars, stags, lions and so on, could be nonsense.

Into this confusing world, the Roman army arrived, bringing its own mesmerising array of gods, cults and religious traditions. In spite of the shared traditions of ritual and the veneration of the landscape, fertility and martial themes, a violent clash lay ahead.

Omens and armies

The army that came to Britain in 43 could be confident that Rome firmly associated her destiny with the gods, a relationship evoked by Virgil in his epic poem, the *Aeneid*. Virgil matched myth and verse to create a literary propaganda foundation to imperial military expansion and power. Jupiter announces in the poem that 'I set no boundaries in space or time for the deeds of the Roman people. I have given them unlimited power.' Composed in the years leading up to his death in 19 BC, its purpose was poetically to 'legitimise' Roman expansion. Roman conquest was thus sanctioned by the ultimate divine power – one of man's great religious traditions.

We can take it as read that the military participants in the Claudian conquest, led by the commander Aulus Plautius, took time to make sacrifices and other spiritual preparations before they embarked on their ships and made for Britain (**22**). Omens and signs will have been eagerly looked for in the run-up to a campaign that was feared with an almost pathological dread. Vespasian, then commander of the *II Augusta* legion, perhaps gave thanks for the fact that Claudius' freedman Narcissus had given him the legionary command in the first place. It would be 26 years before he became emperor himself, but Suetonius recounted the omens of his future greatness, which had already occurred (*Vespasian* v). Omens counted for a lot. In the year 16, during the war in Germany, Germanicus took the Roman forces into battle against the barbarian leader, Arminius. The night before, he had a dream in which he was sacrificing. During the ceremony, his clothes were spattered with blood and he dreamed that his grandmother, Livia, gave him a fresh, and better, costume to put on (*Annals* ii.14). During the Civil War of 68-9, the short-lived emperor Vitellius prepared his troops to hold Italy against the approaching army of Vespasian. Vitellius made a speech to his forces but was distressed by an unexpected turn of events. A cloud of vultures flew over and blanked out the sun. An ox being readied for sacrifice escaped, scattering all the ritual and sacrificial equipment and had to be chased and killed in a thoroughly inappropriate way (*Histories* iii.56).

22 *Modern re-enactors perform a sacrifice and dedication of an altar at South Shields (Arbeia) Roman fort (Tyne and Wear). Occasions like these took place to prevent disasters or propitiate the divine forces responsible, or fulfilled obligations set out in the military religious calendar*

Neither of these incidents had anything directly to do with Britain but they illustrate the Roman frame of mind. This sophisticated military machine could be completely upset by the wrong 'signs', and so used sacrifices to propitiate the gods in advance of and after the event. Of course, there was a literary device at play here too. Bad omens made a good story better and men like Tacitus used them wherever possible to drive home the symmetrical inevitability of a bad lot failing while being surrounded with signals that he was doomed all the way along. Good omens were similarly useful because they helped confirm a hero's destiny.

The lead-up to the invasion of Britain was plagued by bad omens, which makes it all the more remarkable that it happened at all. Caligula (37-41) had played with the idea of invading Britain when Adminius, son of Cunobelinus of the Catuvellauni, was banished by his father and fled to the Romans for sanctuary. Caligula prepared his forces to invade, and then proceeded to order them to gather up seashells on the shore. For this 'triumph' he rewarded the soldiers with a cash donative, and displayed the seashells in Rome as booty.

Perhaps Caligula was bent on making fools of his troops, especially if they had expressed fear of crossing to Britain. Or, more likely, it was simply an expression of his caprices. Either way it hardly boded well, but the real victim was Caligula. Tacitus and Suetonius relished the evidence of his dementia and megalomania. But it was true that Britain held a fearful prospect for continentals. Writing to his brother a century before, then participating in Caesar's campaigns, Cicero said he was 'terrified' by the sea and the thought of Britain's coastline, though he could scarcely wait to hear

23 *A stretch of the south coast of Britain, perhaps one of the places first seen by part of the Roman army as it crossed the Channel. It presented a daunting prospect to the invaders – it was literally 'the end of the world'*

about Britain's features and peculiarities (*Letters to his friends* ii.16.4) (**23**). Britain was literally on the edge of the known world, and dangerously close to mythical hinterlands occupied by spectres and demons.

Within a few years, Claudius revived Caligula's plans. The purpose and policy of the invasion are of no concern here, beyond the fact that the expedition sustained the Augustan vision of divinely-inspired destiny through military conquest. Claudius, however, found himself with an army viewing the thought of invading Britain with a mixture of fear and rage at being asked to campaign in the ends of the earth. Their minds were changed with the humiliation of being sent the ex-slave Narcissus to talk them into it. They chanted *Io Saturnalia*, referring to the mid-winter festival of Saturn when slaves took the place of their masters (and vice-versa) for a day, then went to their ships and set sail.

Oppression and quislings

Once underway, there were problems for the reluctant heroes. Contrary winds sent the fleet sailing backwards, but a bolt of lightning was seen to dash across the sky in the direction they were supposed to be sailing. This restored a positive sense of purpose, which on the whole characterised the process of the conquest in the immediate future. Capitulation of the south was not guaranteed but a decisive river battle led to the area being secured and a triumphant entry by Claudius to the principal native stronghold at Colchester (**24**).

24 *The River Thames as it might have appeared in the first century when the Roman army fought a battle to cross here. In fact this is the Potomac at Mount Vernon, Virginia, near Washington DC but it gives an extremely good impression of how much of southern Britain looked in antiquity, helping to explain the popularity of rural gods like Epona and Silvanus*

The forcefulness of the exercise was amply expressed in the form of the new colony of troops at Colchester. Founded about four years after the invasion in about the year 47, it seems to have been instigated as effectively the Roman capital of Britain. This made sense as it was close to the tribal centre of *Camulodunum*. Formerly a Trinovantian stronghold, it became the Catuvellaunian capital during that tribe's vast expansion in the years prior to the Roman invasion. Part of the Camulodunum complex was nearby at Gosbecks, later developed as a Roman religious site with a theatre. Appropriation of all this into a Roman colony with attendant facilities both suppressed and converted the native symbolism into something the Roman government could exploit for its own ends.

Utterly new though was the Temple of Claudius, dedicated to the deified Claudius after his death in 54 (**25**). The town itself was given the formal name *Colonia Claudia Victriciensis*, 'Colony of the Claudian Victories', though in practice it remained known usually as *Camulodunum*. We have half an idea of what might have happened when the temple site was consecrated and the building begun. In the year 70, following the Civil War, Vespasian restored the Capitol in Rome. The area was purified with the sacrifice of a pig, sheep and an ox. Their entrails were offered on an earthen altar to Jupiter, Juno and Minerva to protect the building. On the instructions of the soothsayers unrefined lumps of raw gold and silver were hurled into the foundations (Tacitus, *H* iv.53).

The imperial cult was a knotty issue in the early Empire. In the East the identity of a ruler as a divine being was an integral part of kingship and supreme power. But in Rome the idea was an anathema; it was far too close to the idea of a monarchy.

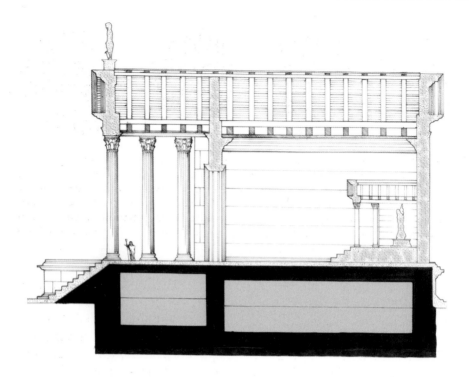

25 *The mid-first-century temple of Claudius at Colchester in cross-section. The solid area at the bottom is the extant vault complex. Its dimensions provide the basis for reconstructing the classical temple that stood on top*

We use the word 'emperor' and see it as meaning an absolute monarch. Now, this is precisely what a Roman emperor was, the only difference being that it was politically and socially impossible to admit the fact. The Roman Republic was initially founded after the expulsion of the kings. Throughout its existence the Republic's political systems constantly struggled to balance ambition against the requirement that monarchies remain dead.

Julius Caesar himself was murdered precisely because of the fears that his dictatorial powers and self-aggrandisement were turning him into a king. But Caesar was eventually deified after his death, providing a neat compromise. Augustus, as the first 'emperor', functioned within the Republican system by simply holding an exceptional number of positions. He was 'emperor', all but in name. Instead he was normally referred to as *princeps*, or literally 'the first man', a handy euphemism. Over succeeding decades the fiction would gradually fade, but at the time of the invasion of Britain the deification of the ruling house could have destroyed the new system by providing grist for the reactionary mill. Tiberius had, for example, rejected any notion of his own divinity, and outlawed any religious building or office in his honour. Caligula, on the other hand, veered recklessly towards self-deification and paid the price.

26 *Left to right: reverse of a* denarius *struck by Vespasian between 73-9 showing him as* pontifex maximus, *'chief priest';* denarius *of Vespasian struck during the reign of his son Titus in 80 showing the deceased emperor as* divus Vespasianus, *'the divine Vespasian'; reverse of a* denarius *struck the same year for Titus' brother and heir, Domitian, showing Minerva's characteristic helmet on a draped table — he 'worshipped her with superstitious veneration' (Suetonius,* Domitian *xv.3);* antoninianus *struck by Elagabalus (218-22) here using the titles of Antoninus Pius — his pose as a sun-god, and his fanaticism and cruelty, guaranteed his early demise*

Claudius came to power as a buffoon, and a tool in the hands of the Republicans. Declaring himself a god would have caused riots, probably of hilarity. But the conquest of Britain and other evidence of his competence defied his critics. Claudius took the creation of priesthoods very seriously, reviving old posts and creating new ones. We can assume therefore that the new temple at Colchester was something he involved himself in if it was begun before his death, though at this stage it would have been dedicated to the Imperial House, or his Victory rather than Claudius the God. Eventually Claudius, too, would be posthumously deified but during his lifetime he showed a marked interest in religious practices and titles 'at home and abroad' (Suetonius, *Claudius* xxii). Vespasian mused with irony on his deathbed that 'I am already becoming a god' (Dio lxvi.17.3). Later Domitian, who was entranced with Minerva (**26**), was to instruct his procurators to address him as *Dominus et Deus noster*, 'Our Lord and God' (Suetonius, *Domitian* xiii), but his infamous reign guaranteed not only that he was denied deification but also suffered the official damnation of his memory. Even Trajan came within an inch of being denied posthumous deification for killing too many opponents (Dio lxix.2.5).

This process of imperial posthumous deification, selectively awarded and (as Suetonius enthusiastically pointed out) selectively taken away, created a means of emperor worship which avoided actually worshipping the current incumbent (for the meantime), regardless of how he was regarded in the Eastern provinces (**26**). The other way to do this was to make a dedication to the *numen*, 'spirit', of the emperor — a sort of guiding force or spirit behind the person of the emperor, or to make it to the welfare of the emperor's family (**67**). The Temple of Claudius was probably initially dedicated to his Victories because he spurned 'excessive honorifics' (*ibid* 12), and became a temple to him, and by extension Augustus, after his death in 54. However the temple was planned, it unavoidably represented a blatant imposition of the imperial power structure on Britain, and acted as a symbol of defeat and oppression. For the Trinovantes, the compulsory contributions to the cult were far more unpleasant. These were interpreted, probably accurately, as nothing more than a blatant way of confiscating native fortunes.

Part of the problem was that as a colony, Colchester was filled with ex-soldiers. Granted land and property as retirement rewards, their very presence provoked hostility only made worse by gratuitous high-handedness.

Quislings within the British tribal system gave the imperial cult more momentum. Cogidubnus/Togidubnus is a figure about who we know a good deal less than is often implied – even the spelling of his name is uncertain. Tacitus called him 'King Cogidumnus', a British king during the governorship of Ostorius Scapula (47–51), and says that 'certain states' were handed over to him as part of the Roman policy to 'employ even kings to enslave others' (*Agr* 14). Today the form Togidubnus is considered to be more reliable though this is surmise rather than fact. From this we can conclude that he was of British aristocratic origin, selected for client-king status either for his malleability or allegiance to Rome (or both), and his territories suitably enlarged by grants of tribal areas acquired by force. But with one literary reference and one inscription spelled differently it is even possible the names are of different men, perhaps father and son. The sole evidence we have for where the territory was, is the inscription from Chichester that records the dedication of a temple to Neptune and Minerva and includes the name of a man normally assumed to be the same individual mentioned by Tacitus. Here it appears as Tiberius Claudius [Co- *or* To]gidubnus. The Roman name for Chichester was *Noviomagus Reg(i)norum*, 'new place of the people of the Kingdom'. The 'tribal name' *Regni* is simply derived from the Latin for King, *rex*, and suggests a fabricated identity connected with the client kingdom phase.

The significance of the Chichester temple text is considerable, though unlike the Temple of Claudius at Colchester, we have no idea of the temple's structural form. The dedication includes a reference to the *Domus Divina*, 'Divine House', which means the imperial family. The *Domus Divina* also recurs with a dedication to Jupiter Optimus Maximus on a possible Jupiter column base from the town (*RIB* 89). This slab is too incomplete to be dated, but continental parallels are mostly of late second- or early third-century date so it is unlikely to be more evidence of client-king obsequiousness. The combination of Neptune and Minerva is not common, in spite of the association of their Greek equivalents, Poseidon and Athena, who competed for Attica and later made their peace. The tone here is explicitly loyal to the rule of Rome. Togidubnus is not the dedicant – he is only cited as the approving authority. As a client king he is effectively proxy for the emperor or his delegate, the governor. The text records that a man, whose name is lost, but was a son of Pudentinus, donated the site to the *collegium fabrorum*, 'guild of smiths', who paid for the temple out of their pockets.

Neptune's appeal is not hard to understand (**27**). Chichester is a coastal town, and its proximity to the harbour at Fishbourne must have made it an entry point to the burgeoning province. The elaborate house or palace at Fishbourne was substantially constructed, in both its Neronian and Flavian forms, by highly-skilled masons, using imported materials. They themselves had perhaps been brought over the Channel – not necessarily permanently. Seasonal commuting may have been the norm. Seeking protection from Neptune was therefore self-protection, recalling Pliny's

27 *Neptune, as depicted on a second-century mosaic from a townhouse at Verulamium*

cynical assessment of how self-interest dictated 'beliefs'. Early timber buildings on the later palace site almost certainly preserve a Claudian military base beforehand. Most of Neptune's other dedications in Britain are of later date and military, for example an altar at Castlecary on the Antonine Wall (*RIB* 2149), perhaps in thanks for a successful voyage up the coast to the Wall. A possible one from York is by a Gaulish trader (see chapter 3), though in this case the name is entirely restored. The connection between Fishbourne and the Chichester smiths is entirely speculative though it fits the context. Equally, the smiths might have been locals, well-established artisans whose careers had been built in and around working for philo-Roman tribal aristocrats. It is perhaps no coincidence that one of Silchester's early temples seems to have been funded by another guild (*RIB* 69-71).

All of Minerva's other dedications in verbal form are from the military zone, apart from in her conflated identity with the god of the sacred spring at Bath, Sulis,

28 *Gilt-bronze bust of Minerva from Bath. Probably once the cult statue's head, the bust has a recess at the back for the goddess's helmet. Probably late first century. Height 248mm*

as Sulis-Minerva (**28, colour plate 18**). At Chichester, her appeal to smiths as the goddess of the arts and crafts seems logical but there is no direct parallel. Unlike Neptune though, Minerva enjoyed wide popularity in the north-west provinces. Although her portrayal varied in crudity depending on the sculptor's ability, she is usually explicitly presented in Roman form as a robed martial female equipped with helmet and spear (**29**). In this sense, despite being one of the principal classical deities, it is probably better to see her on the Chichester dedication in connection with a more regional appeal. Combining Minerva with Neptune and the Divine House was an early example of cult conflation in Britain based on the practical combination of interests amongst artisans who imported their own favourite deities.

Exactly when the Chichester inscription was dedicated will remain uncertain. Togidubnus is said by Tacitus to have remained loyal until 'our own times', which can only mean the late first century. This places it somewhere between *c*.50-90 but the likelihood is that it belongs to the reign of Nero. Another inscription from Chichester is a dedication to Nero (**89, colour plate 6**) for about the year 59 (*RIB* 92). The Boudican Revolt the next year discredited the use of client kings in Britain, but Togidubnus may have lasted in position until his death at an advanced age.

By the year 60 St Paul had reached Rome. By then he had been spreading Christianity for the best part of 20 years. There is no datable evidence for it in Roman Britain until the late third and fourth centuries (**colour plates 20 & 26**). However, a curious aside in Tacitus raises the exceedingly slim possibility that some

[handwritten margin note: ? Pomponius Graecina wife of Aulus Plautius and "foreign superstition"]

29 *Carved relief of Minerva from Lower Slaughter (Glos), but not from the cache of sculptures hidden in a well. The goddess appears in her typical pose with spear, shield, and helmet. Height 370mm*

of the Roman ruling élite in Britain were not only familiar with it, but might even have practised it. In the year 58 Pomponia Graecina was accused in Rome of participating in *superstitionis externae*, 'foreign superstition' (*A* xiii.32). The point is that Pomponia was the wife of Aulus Plautius, governor of Britain from 43-7. Identifying the 'foreign superstition' is a problem. The name Pomponius Graecinus, surely a relation, appears in the Christian catacombs. Pomponia herself can scarcely have become a Christian as early as the time of her husband's British governorship, but the social circles she moved in will have included those who later filled the post. Another possibility is that she had become entranced by the superstition Britain was so notorious for, and which emperors had tried repeatedly to outlaw: Druids and their 'magic'. At this time, the Druids of Britain attracted much more violent sanctions than Christianity.

Druids and Furies

If Jupiter and his classical colleagues were finding new homes in Britain to share with the imperial cult, it was at a price. Resistance to Roman advances found spiritual sustenance from the Druids. Arbiters of war and justice, they provided the ideological basis, and focus, for challenging the invasion. That was hardly surprising: if any group stood to lose from the Roman invasion, it was the Druids. Caesar's description of

30 *The hills of Wales. Barren and forbidding, they provided an easy bolthole for some of the British tribes to retreat into, led by the Druids towards Anglesey. The Roman army was fully prepared to cross this territory to suppress the Druids*

them makes perfect sense in this context. The Druid stronghold was the Isle of Anglesey, though not the slightest trace of any base survives today. Whether Anglesey had always been the Druid heartland is unknown. It is quite possible that by the year 60 this was to where the Druids had withdrawn, gathering refugees as they went as Roman domination spread across the south and east. The ancient name for the island, *Mona*, provides no clues because it means no more than 'mountain'. Perhaps they had wind that Nero, who acceded in 54, had considered withdrawing from Britain altogether – though we do not know exactly when he thought of this (Suetonius, *Nero* xviii).

The further the Druids retreated into Britain the more distanced they became from the part-classicised south-east. The world of prehistoric north Wales was in a different sphere of existence. Remote and barren, it challenged invaders with its hills and impenetrable valleys (**30**). It was devoid of coinage, and most manufactured goods of any kind. Here the Roman world became more easily perceived as the embodiment of evil. It is an intriguing state of affairs. If the Romans were despised for their obsessions with power and control it is every bit as clear that the Druids were obsessed with their own version of the same.

There is a very important aspect to this. The Roman world is something we know a lot about and can visualise as a reflection of our own international west-ernised society. From a Druid perspective, it was easier – if not even more natural – to perceive the Romans as a literal personification of evil demons. Rome herself, her cities, roads, career lawyers and so on, were not only invisible through distance, but were perhaps also almost entirely incomprehensible. Today, the United States is sometimes regarded in a similar fashion and we can see that when screaming mobs burn the American flag and effigies of the president. The coming of the Roman army just equated with destruction of liberty (that is, the Druids' liberty), appropriation of sacred places, and also the threat to vested interests. Druid leaders had enjoyed unparalleled levels of power and influence over their people, and also acted as the only significant unifying influence, though we do not know how much compliance they enjoyed, and how much oppression they had to use to keep their power. Ruling through ignorance and fear they were unchallenged, until the governor Gaius Suetonius Paullinus arrived in north Wales in about the year 59. If this all seems a little extreme an interpretation we need only consider the international turmoil of 2001 when the terrorist attacks in New York and Washington polarised the forces of western governments against the Islamic fundamentalists known as the Taliban. The parallels of mutual suspicion, misunderstanding, ignorance and abuses of power are remarkable.

Anglesey had become a refugee stronghold and helped sustain resistance to Roman control elsewhere in Britain. The retreat into Wales had begun earlier, when Caratacus of the Catuvellauni, another son of Cunobelinus, fled there to lead the resistance against Rome in the mid-40s. He was captured in 51, but Wales had proved durably intractable. Tacitus' image of Anglesey is colourfully fearful. He called it a *novitate aspectus*, 'strange sight', and described the Roman army being presented with a rabble on the beach (*A* xiv.30). Although he did not go there himself, he wrote at a time when it was just still possible to talk to eye-witnesses. There is no real reason why we should query him any more than we query the authority of contemporary authors writing about the Second World War. The tribesmen were gathered in arms, but amongst them women dressed in black and with their hair in a tousled mess wandered, waving their torches. In the background Druids stood in a circle and held their hands skyward while muttering prayers. This picture of barbaric frenzy left the soldiers struck dumb with amazement, to the extent that they entirely forgot to cover themselves against attack. Their feelings were probably ambivalent. On one hand, the image will have been something they despised. On the other, their natural superstition will have been stirred into apprehension and downright terror at the prospect of alien magic being worked against them.

But Paullinus galvanised the soldiers by encouraging them to march forwards and destroy a crowd of 'females and fanatics'. The moment of paralysis passed and the battle was quick and decisive. The image of raving Druids was an attractive device for Tacitus. It allowed him to present his readers with a graphic representation of barbarity. The dishevelled women, for example, were likened to Furies. The Druids represented the spiritual opposition and he used them again in the *Histories* for the Civil War in 69, nine years later. The death of Vitellius in that conflict had followed fighting in Rome herself, and the destruction of the Temple of Capitoline Jupiter. Tacitus described how the Gaulish Druids put it about that this was a portent for the end of the Roman Empire, which of course it turned out not to be (*H* iv.54).

Back in Anglesey, Paullinus took care not only to garrison the island of Anglesey but also to destroy the *sacri luci*, 'sacred groves' (**31**). Pliny the Elder provides some insight on the importance of the groves to Druids:

> There is nothing the Druids regard as holier than mistletoe, and the tree it grows on – so long as that is a very hard oak. Groves of such trees are chosen for this reason alone and without the leaves and branches of those trees they will not perform their rites. We can suppose that this custom is the reason they are called Druids from the Greek word for an oak ['drys']. In addition, they believe anything growing on an oak tree is a gift from heaven, and indicates that the tree has been chosen by God himself.
>
> But mistletoe is only found on these oaks very rarely. When it is found, a great ritual surrounds its collection, especially on the sixth day of the lunar cycle – this is from when these tribes count the first days of the months and the year – and after every thirty years of a new generation because at that point it is still gaining strength and is not even half its full size.
>
> They welcome the moon with a local word which translates as 'all things healed', and prepare a ritual sacrifice and feast beneath a tree. Two bulls are brought up, with horns bound for the first time for the event. A priest, wearing white vestments, climbs up the tree and cuts off the mistletoe with a gold sickle. It is caught in a white cloak. Finally, the victims are killed and pray that God will make his gift propitious on the people he has given it to. The Druids believe that mistletoe in drink while make a sterile animal fertile, and can act as a poison antidote.
>
> Such is the power of superstition connected with such trifles, and it is extremely common amongst the peoples of the world.
> Pliny the Elder, *NH* xvi.249

Groves remained thereafter in lore and memory, even if they were later replaced or obscured by larger settlements. The Latin for a grove is *nemus*, derived from a similar Greek word. Both were derived from an ancient common source that also provides the Celtic *nemeton*. This turns up in place-names like *Vernemetum* (a settlement in Nottinghamshire, near Willoughby-on-the-Wolds) and *Aquae Arnemetiae* (Buxton, Derbys), here integrated into the name of the local goddess. Mars Rigonemetos, 'Mars, King of the Grove', also turns up in Nettleham (Lincs). At Bath an altar was dedicated to Mars and what seems to have been a personification of the grove, Nemetona (*RIB* 140). Such gods also appear in Germany, and indeed the Bath dedicant, Peregrinus, says he came from Trier. The groves were a relatively innocuous part of Druid life. There was another side to their activities the Romans drew the line at. The Romans managed to organise a civilisation, which indulged in fights-to-the-death entertainment, but which abhorred human sacrifice. The Druid love of soothsaying through entrails taken from executed human victims symbolised a stark point of tension with Roman religious attitudes or just plain sensibilities. Pliny the Elder commented on what he called British 'magic' and the essential problem:

31 *Trees played an important symbolic role in pre-Roman religion in Britain. Groves of trees were venerated by Druids, especially those where mistletoe grew*

Right up until living memory, magic has been practised in the two Gaulish provinces. The Druids were suppressed under Tiberius [14–37], along with all their soothsayers and doctors. But such an observation is of little matter, because magic crossed the sea and pervaded even the remotest parts of Nature. Even these days Britain indulges in magic, filled with awe, and doing so with such remarkable rituals that you would think Persia learned magic from them! There is much that is common about magic amongst many nations, even though they fight about other things or do not even know that each other exists.

But, we all owe a debt beyond measure to the Romans because they destroyed these horrible activities in which human sacrifice was thought to please the gods, and eating the victim thought to be good for one's health. Pliny the Elder, *NH*, xxx.13

There is some confusion about the date when the Druids were suppressed in the rest of the Empire. Suetonius records that Claudius 'completely abolished the cruel and inhuman Druid religion in Gaul, which during Augustus' reign had only been forbidden to Roman citizens' (*Claudius* xxv). Neither Tiberius nor Claudius was particularly successful, as Druidism plainly continued to thrive in Britain. But it makes no difference to the fact that Pliny had no doubt about the validity of his moral judgement. More than a century before, Cicero acknowledged that in national characteristics the Romans would find they were no better than other peoples and sometimes were worse. But 'in a religious sense, meaning our reverence for the gods, we are far superior' (*DND*, ii.8). Even so, he deplored the decline of respect for the practise of soothsaying. Elsewhere, Cicero even recorded that his family knew a

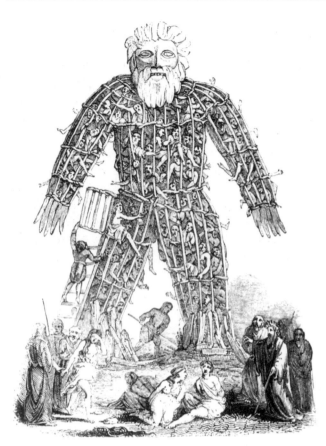

32 *An old engraving illustrates Strabo and Caesar's descriptions of the wicker effigy supposedly manufactured by Druids to contain their living victims (iv.4.5 and BG vi.16). Human sacrifice was regarded by the Romans as utterly intolerable*

Druid soothsayer from Gaul, called 'Divitiacus the Aeduan'. Divitiacus 'claimed to have that natural science, which the Greeks call "physiologia". He made predictions, using augury or just conjecture' (*DD* i.90).

What mattered to the Romans was not the soothsaying, but when Druids used human sacrifice to do it, or for any other reason (**32**). This Tacitus added as his final observation on the Druids and Paullinus' duty to destroy any such activity. However accommodating the reconstruction of Britain, the Druids could not be part of it (**33**). To us, there is more of a dilemma. The Roman world is easier to see as an oppressive organisation, which made an uncritical use of violence to achieve its ends and did away with anything it did not like. Today this is seen as only marginally less repellent than the idea of human sacrifice. But in antiquity the Druid way of things had come up against the Roman world, which had no means of accommodating them into an otherwise tolerant approach to religion. For Tacitus the well-established notoriety of the Druids made this a centrepiece of his account of the Boudican Revolt, which flared up as soon as Paullinus demolished the last grove and altar in Anglesey. Pliny and Tacitus wrote at second hand of course, but it is interesting that nowhere do they mention anything to do with severed heads in Anglesey. Much is often made of this Celtic preoccupation in modern accounts; considering its box office appeal, one might have expected Tacitus to make a meal of it, had he known anything about it happening in Britain. The well-known first-century tombstone of the Thracian cavalryman Longinus, found outside Colchester, is a classic case of how archaeological speculation about ritual beliefs can enter the canon of fact. Driven by the knowledge that a head cult existed in tribal society, it was assumed by excavators that irate rebels hacked off the face of Longinus in some sort of ritual beheading. In fact the face was recently recovered from the site. Builders or archaeologists had accidentally damaged the tombstone when it was discovered in 1928. The case is an object lesson in the dangers of inferring religious practice from archaeological evidence.

The destruction of the Druid spiritual headquarters had dramatic repercussions elsewhere in Britain. The Boudican Revolt had been sparked off by the harsh treatment of Boudica and her daughters following the death of her husband Prasutagus, king of the Iceni. But the scars ran deeper. The temple of Claudius at Colchester had already become a target of violent hatred, and symbolised more prosaic forms of oppression such as land seizures for the colonists.

The process of the Revolt is not relevant here apart from how it was described. Again, terrible omens propelled the story on: the statue of Victory at Colchester collapsed (**34**). Hysterical women screamed that destruction was imminent, and that strange cries had been heard in the senate house in Colchester. To add to the sense of theatricality, stories that the Thames had been seen to show an image of Colchester in ruins, while the sea itself had turned red. Positive signs for the rebels, the Romans naturally viewed them with horror. Tacitus of course exploited them to tell his story. The worse things looked, the greater the Roman achievement in turning the tide.

33 *London, tomb of Julius Classicianus, procurator of Britain. His work involved appeasing tribal sensibilities after the Boudican Revolt, including the damage done by the oppressive imperial cult at Colchester. RIB 12*

34 *A Roman Victory, here depicted on a silver denarius of Septimius Severus (struck 202-10). The Colchester statue will have resembled this winged figure, bearing the victor's crown*

Tacitus was relatively low-key in his description of the mayhem and death caused in the cities of Colchester, London and Verulamium as the rebels passed through. Dio was less restrained, though writing more than a century after Tacitus he may well have absorbed the embellishments of time. For Dio, the story turns into a more psychosexual tale of domination and sadism in which the women of the cities were horribly mutilated and killed, with the driving spiritual force being the British goddess of Victory, Andate (he also records Boudica appealing to the goddess Andraste – perhaps one and the same). Unmentioned by Tacitus, Andate, not surprisingly, makes no other appearance in the record.

Throughout this dramatic tale the literary association of native religious cult with the forces of utter barbarity is palpably clear. Sadly, we do not have the British point of view apart from the words put into Boudica's mouth by Tacitus and Dio. They recognised a legitimate sense of grievance, and an admiration for free-spirited resistance to oppression, which the Romans admired, but suppressed when it conflicted with their own power structures.

The reconstruction

The outcome of the Revolt was far from inevitable. The rebels nearly succeeded. More by luck than judgement Paullinus brought them to a set-piece battle (**35, colour plate 17**). The aftershock is really glossed over by Tacitus – the army remained 'under canvas' but there is no further mention of deliberate suppression of British cults. British Druids and Druids in general escape much further mention, apart from occasional retrospective observations made by later authors. Ammianus Marcellinus for example, writing in the fourth century, called them *Drysidae* and describes them as a kind of monastic intellectual élite. In the *Scriptores Historiae Augustae* Druids appear occasionally as prophets and seers (e.g. *Aurelian* xliv.4). Interestingly, in his description of the Anglesey campaign, Dio makes no mention of the Druids at all which suggests that either Tacitus had exaggerated their role for effect or that by the time Dio wrote, the Druids had been virtually forgotten. Even Tacitus omits them from the brief account of the Revolt in his *Agricola*, and leaves out any other religious topic in his description of the subsequent governorships up to Agricola (78-84). The decade following the Revolt was a turbulent one for Rome. Nero's reign spiralled into decline as the self-appointed singer, athlete and all-round artiste focused his attentions on grandiose projects and self-indulgence (**89**). Historians of the age relished in tales of his decadence, so that emperors like Vespasian, Trajan, Hadrian and Antoninus Pius seemed all the more outstanding. The Civil War of 68-9 involved some of the British garrison and it was not until the 70s that stability under Vespasian saw Britain developing into a Roman province at a feverish pace.

Vespasian's reign was manifested in Britain by a concerted effort at extending Roman dominion west and north, and by an explosion of imported Roman goods and urban development. It characterised a reign which began with Vespasian's restoration of temples and public buildings in Rome (Dio lxvi.10). Tacitus includes in his reference to the latter that Agricola encouraged the building of temples, amongst other things. It is likely that Agricola's predecessor, Sextus Julius Frontinus, played an instrumental if unspoken role in the work. The process demonstrates the further establishment of formal Roman religion in Roman Britain though it is feasible that private temples were also involved. It is interesting to note that

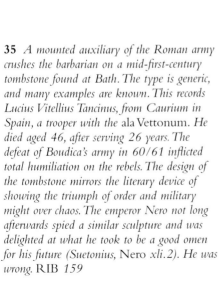

35 *A mounted auxiliary of the Roman army crushes the barbarian on a mid-first-century tombstone found at Bath. The type is generic, and many examples are known. This records Lucius Vitellius Tancinus, from Caurium in Spain, a trooper with the* ala *Vettonum. He died aged 46, after serving 26 years. The defeat of Boudica's army in 60/61 inflicted total humiliation on the rebels. The design of the tombstone mirrors the literary device of showing the triumph of order and military might over chaos. The emperor Nero not long afterwards spied a similar sculpture and was delighted at what he took to be a good omen for his future (Suetonius, Nero xli.2). He was wrong. RIB 159*

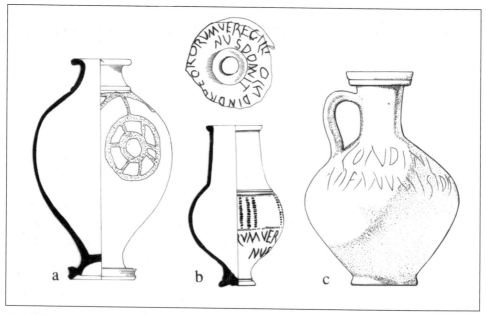

36 *Cult pottery.*
a) pottery jar with painted decoration of four wheel motifs. From the second-century shrine of Abandinus at Godmanchester (Cambs). Height 220mm. After H. Green.
b) colour-coat beaker from a grave at Dunstable (Beds), with an inscription meaning, 'Regillinus presented the pot of the dendrophori *['branch-bearers' associated with the worship of the eastern mother goddess Cybele] of Verulamium(?)'. Height 160mm. After Matthews.*
c) Late first-century flagon from Southwark bearing a graffito: Londinii ad fanum Isidis, *'London, at the temple of Isis'. Height 254mm*

the Fishbourne palace, for all its spectacular decoration, has yet to yield any sort of temple or shrine associated with the complex. The Verulamium forum inscription is tied to the governorship of Agricola, and the excavated ground-plan of the structure indicates the presence of three buildings in the south-west side of the forum colonnade. The forum-basilica at Verulamium is the only one firmly dated to the first century by epigraphy, but even that places it around 20 years after the Revolt. The three buildings were once thought to be temples, perhaps connected with the Capitoline Triad of Jupiter, Juno and Minerva, but opinion now seems in favour of their being used as the council chamber and flanking offices. But there is no evidence either way (**colour plate 2**).

Apart from the Chichester inscriptions, there are no other dated first-century religious dedications from Britain. The small first-century flagon from Southwark, London, which carries the celebrated inscribed reference to *Londinii, ad fanum Isidis*, 'the temple of Isis at London', is not really very helpful beyond telling us a temple to Isis existed at London (**36**). The inscription could post-date the flagon by several decades. Isis will be discussed later but in the next chapter we will start looking at the prolific archaeological evidence for the development of cult sites at around the same time as the Flavian civic public buildings started going up.

3 Sacred springs amid the groves

During the first century AD, sacred places in Britain began to experience radical changes. In the burgeoning towns new temples were built and consecrated. In the countryside new shrines grew up around natural phenomena like springs and trees that had been venerated for generations. Much of this activity is attributable from archaeological evidence to the Flavian period (69-96) during the reigns of Vespasian and his sons, Titus and Domitian. Vespasian and Titus were well known in Britain from their military careers. Circumstantial, and a little literary, evidence suggests their approach as emperors was positive and constructive, and that they enjoyed significant personal popularity in the new province. The changes to the sacred places reflect the tidal wave of Romanization that was spreading across Britain during the period.

Domitian seems to have been indifferent to Britain. His reign saw the cessation of sustained conquest and the abandonment of much of the territory captured by Agricola in the north. The province subsided into a place of marginal imperial concern. At any rate, this is the implication of Britain's virtual absence from any historical record until *c*.119. Germany was, for example, becoming a much more serious and long-term threat. Paradoxically, Domitian exercised his inclination to cruelty on enforcing a more rigorous approach to religion. Not only did he execute unchaste Vestal Virgins, but also punished examples of sacrilege (Suetonius, *Domitian* viii.3, 5). He thus effected a more traditional approach to Roman religious observations, reflecting the other side of his personality which retained an almost archaic sense of integrity and honour (*ibid* ix.1-2), and anticipated the trend to old values under Trajan (98-117).

Some obscure and remote woodland glades, or springs, were converted into places best compared with today's resorts or health farms. The process is plain enough from the archaeological evidence and illustrates perfectly the role in which cult and belief were linked with health, longevity, relaxation and even entertainment. Even in our secular age, this connection subsists at places like Lourdes in France. Miraculous cures are associated with visits to such holy places. In antiquity, despite the relatively high degree of medical competence and knowledge, cures for ailments were far from guaranteed. It was easy to resort to alternatives, not least because there were plenty of people then, as now, waiting to relieve the sick of their savings.

Pliny the Elder recorded his views on medicine around the time that some of Roman Britain's cult centres were being developed. He mused on the problems created by the fact that no two doctors ever produced the same diagnosis, and cursed the mercurial state of a profession that changed its claims daily. He was particularly critical of the 'vacant words of intellectual Greeks' (*NH* xxix.11), and noted that few Romans ever practised medicine. This left the way open to Greek doctors who totally dominated the profession and helped create the established requirement that anyone wishing to have medical authority had to publish his work in Greek (*ibid.* xxix.17). Pliny had plenty more to say but he ultimately blamed the prevalence of quackery on popular credulity, and the desire of people to place faith in something they did not understand.

Bath

One of Pliny's passing asides was noting the 'new fashion of using hot water for sicknesses' amongst doctors (*ibid.* xxix.22). Pliny wrote in the 70s, precisely the time that Roman engineers were in the throes of harnessing the mystical and commercial possibilities in a marshy area by a long bend in the river Avon in south-western England. The swampy ground boasted a fabulous natural phenomenon: a spring belching out more than 300,000 gallons of mineral water at 42°C every day. It cannot have gone without notice for all the time that men and women had passed through that way. But the pre-Roman visitors left no trace of their visits, and made nothing of the spring except, presumably, to tell stories about it. If there was a pre-Roman shrine, perhaps built of timber, it has vanished without trace.

By the AD 50s the trans-Britannia route of the Fosse Way had been built through the Bath area (**35**). The Romans called the settlement that grew up here *Aquae Sulis*, 'the waters of Sulis', though another of its names was *Fons Sulis*, 'the spring of Sulis'. At the time, this was still part of the military frontier, with at least two legions and their attendant auxiliaries in the region. The spring will have excited attention from the outset, but perhaps it was not until news of the medical fad for hot water cures that Pliny reported began to circulate that anyone thought seriously of developing the site (**37**).

What is immediately obvious is that anyone seeking to turn Bath into a usable settlement was confronted by a lot of water. The Romans may not have enjoyed sailing on water but they were accomplished at controlling it. Rome's own sewer and drainage systems were well-established by the late first century BC. The city was likened to one standing on stilts since there were so many tunnels underneath. The *Cloaca Maxima*, 'great sewer', was large enough for manned boats to sail up and down. Using the techniques that controlled Rome's waste, Bath's spring was drained and contained. The drain was a covered passage that channelled the gushing hot water out towards the river. This prevented it from saturating the land any longer, and was helped by lateral smaller drains that fed into it (**38**). Once the drain was operational, the land began to dry out. The engineers then started on controlling the spring by creating a walled pool around its outlet. Rammed timber piles consolidated the soil, and a retaining wall of stone in an irregular polygonal form provided the rigid framework for lead waterproofing.

The purpose of the wall was to create a stable pool of bubbling hot water that also fed the baths. When the reservoir level rose too high, a sluice gate flushed out the excess water along with any accumulating silt into the drain. When the natural supply

37 *Bath, looking north, as it might have appeared to a passer-by in the years before the Roman conquest, and around the time the army arrived in the vicinity. The hot spring gushed forth creating a marshy pool in the woodland near the river (the actual location is the Yellowstone National Park, Wyoming, but the resemblance is convenient)*

38 *Part of the drainage system at Bath for the spring and baths complex. The height of the arch is about 2m*

was reduced, the pool provided a reserve. It was rather like a hot water tank running permanently to supply a bath system, and an overflow outlet. The transformation was characteristically Roman and it contrasts radically with the earlier treatment of the site. What had been an entirely natural phenomenon had been converted into a manageable and maintainable facility. The bubbling spring could now be approached, and all the theatrical effects of the water's odour, colour, and energetic displays of heat and vapour appreciated. For the moment the spring remained an outdoor feature of Bath, overlooked by the new temple.

The only evidence for pre-Roman cult activity at Bath is the name of the god, Sul or Sulis. The name turns up on a number of inscriptions and in the ancient name for the place. But it is possible Sulis was a Roman invention. Writing *c*.125-50, Ptolemy called the place *Aquae Calidae*, 'Hot Waters'. Sulis is a marvellously ambivalent deity. She, or he, turns up conflated with Minerva on several inscriptions from the site. Minerva's presence is beyond dispute as the site has produced one of the finest busts, made of gilded bronze, of a classical deity from anywhere in Britain (**28**). The head has a fitting for a helmet, which makes her identification certain. The patron of arts and wisdom, Minerva was an appropriate spirit to link with a place that was embarking on a triumphant series of architectural achievements, and which also exuded a sense of mystery. Precisely how Sulis fitted in is more of a mystery. One suggestion is that the name is linked to the Suleviae, also known as the Matres Suleviae, 'The Mothers Suleviae' – known from a few inscriptions at Bath, Cirencester and in the far north at the fort of Binchester. That gets us no further with the meaning, but the Welsh *syllu* means 'to gaze'. Perhaps the name refers in some way to a god who overlooks, possibly in the sense of overseeing all acts good and bad.

If so, it would fit what Sulis-Minerva's pilgrims expected of her, and also the most prominent image in the shrine. The *templum Sulis*, as it is called on a curse tablet from the site, presented the visitor with a much more alarming sight than the refined elegance of the cult statue (**39**). The pediment sculpture depicts a male Gorgon with bulging eyes, swirling moustache, vividly swaying hair with wings and snakes, and is accompanied by Victories and even an owl to confirm the Minerva-Athena association (**colour plate 9**). In classical myth, Athena gave Perseus her shield so that he could kill the Gorgon Medusa by looking at her reflection in its highly-polished surface, to escape being turned to stone by not looking at her directly. Minerva is often depicted with Medusa on her breast-plate (**colour plate 18**). Even more specifically, the late Roman poet Claudian describes Minerva (under her other name Tritonia) armed with the Gorgon head motif on her breast (*Gigantomachia* 91ff) as her sole weapon in battle against Pallas. The subject was no great novelty in Britain. A coin issued by Cunobelinus of the Catuvellauni in the last two decades before the invasion of 43 had a sphinx on one side, and on the other what looks like Perseus carrying the Gorgon's head. Later, Medusa was a common mosaic motif in part because her head made a good image for placing in the middle (**colour plate 15**).

As the Bath gorgon is encircled by oak leaves, associated with Athena, it's hard to see how this might simply not be a symbol of Minerva's power. There is a problem in the fact that the face is male but as Medusa's defining characteristic was ugliness

39 *The façade of the temple of Sulis-Minerva at Bath as restored by Samuel Lysons in 1813. Late first century (see also **40**, **41**)*

this is perhaps less of a sexual definition than a decorative device. A very similar motif appears on the fourth-century Mildenhall 'Great Dish', where the moustache becomes a pair of dolphins, allowing it to be identified as Oceanus (**colour plate 30**). Some see the motif as a simple combination of the sea god with Medusa. Names apart, the decorative convenience and appeal of the image should not be overlooked in the rush to attach vast significance to minutiae.

A much less opaque (to us) statement was the temple that the sculpture formed part of (**colour plate 3**). Apart from the Gorgon it was entirely classical in its original form. The tetrastyle structure faced east and looked across the flagstone of the temple precinct immediately north of the sacred spring. In this early, open, phase the temple pediment would have seemed to shimmer in the waters of the spring to anyone looking across towards the temple. Although the temple remains buried, enough of its architectural features and parts of its plan have been recovered to make sense of its form. It stood on a 126-square-metre podium and was 9m wide and 14m long. Roofed, it towered some 13m above anyone standing on the precinct floor, the four columns alone being over 7m high. The temple was floridly decorated with sculptures of vegetation and fruit, many fragments of which survive. The focal point of all

40 *(left) Corner stone from the Bath precinct altar re-erected* in situ. *Two figures are depicted: Jupiter to the left, and Hercules to the right. More deities embellished the other corners. Two further stones survive (one built into a church at Compton Dando), the fourth is lost. Height 1.26m*

41 *(right) Statue base dedicated by the* haruspex *(soothsayer), Lucius Marcius Memor, at Bath. Weathering and damage has made the lettering difficult to read, but the first line names the goddess Sulis, the second Memor, and the third gives his office. The third line originally read* HAR, *but this seems to have caused confusion, perhaps because the post was unfamiliar in Britain. More letters were added to create* HARVSP(EX). *Height 90cm*

the activity was the sacrificial altar that stood as the centrepiece in the precinct, over-looked by the temple to its west and the sacred spring to the south (**40**). Its function is abundantly plain from the statue base found *in situ* nearby, naming the *haruspex* Lucius Marcius Memor and his dedication to Sulis (**41**). The *haruspex* was responsible for interpreting the entrails of sacrificial victims, laid out on the altar (see chapter 4 for a more detailed discussion of Romano-British priests).

Bath was obviously so significant a place that not knowing who was behind its development is particularly frustrating. The exploitation of the waters was as much a commercial or social undertaking as it was religious. This conflation of interests is a reminder that 'religious' facilities in antiquity often provided services that we now seek in more secular institutions. Bath ultimately belonged to the emperor. Britain was an imperial province (as opposed to a senatorial one) and as such constituted part of the emperor's personal estate. Naturally he could not run an imperial estate by himself, and nor could the senate manage senatorial ones. Just as in Rome herself, contracts were awarded to companies who undertook maintenance, and licences were granted to draw water. The Roman tradition of awarding state contracts for public facilities, their maintenance and the collection of revenues was well established and dated back into Republican times when the Senate supervised the distribution of contracts and their fulfilment. Sometimes the contracts were purchased, while other people had less direct involvement as guarantors or partners (Polybius, *Histories* vi.17). The process helped integrate the whole community in a shared interest.

Britain presents a problem when it comes to contracts. Apart from the army, and its veteran communities, it is unlikely that the necessary skills or funds were available to get Bath going. There is no surviving inscription that records the person or body responsible at Bath, and this opens the spa up to all sorts of well-intentioned speculation. One theory is that Togidubnus held the contract. The archaeology supports a late first-century date but Togidubnus happens to be one of the very few high-class philo-Roman Britons that we happen to know about, so consequently he invariably attracts a large amount of attention by default. There is no supporting evidence from Bath, leaving this as just an interesting possibility, unfortunately with nowhere to go.

In terms of general context, the army's patronage of spas is well-known on the continent. The dominant military sculpture from Bath in the form of tombstones and dedications makes this a distinct possibility, but it is also true that military sculpture always dominates the surviving record in Britain regardless of when or where (**35**). Military patronage does not guarantee that the army instigated development of Bath, and in any case some of the evidence names members of *VI Victrix*, which did not arrive in Britain until *c*.119. The source of the Clitumnus in Italy benefited the nearby people of *Hispellum* who had been given the site by Augustus. There they 'manage baths at civic expense and provide a hostelry' (Pliny the Younger, *Letters* viii.8.6). Bath might therefore have been donated to the local community by an emperor. Alternatively, if Bath was instead an official foundation, perhaps taxation was the reason. Vespasian is said to have introduced a number of new taxes, including one on public urinals (Dio lxvi.14.5), and substantially increased the tribute due from provinces (Suetonius, *Vespasian* xvi). Bath could have been either a means of directly raising taxes on the services, or of providing cash for the province's tribute payments. The latter does not preclude a possible involvement by a tribal leader, but certainly does not tie it to Togidubnus.

Sadly, none of Bath's extant inscriptions are precisely datable, bar one. *RIB* 172 is a small section of cornice citing the seventh consulship of Vespasian, which occurred in the year 76. Its find-spot is now unknown so it helps us only a little by pointing to building work under Vespasian, oddly the year before Agricola arrived. This illustrates Tacitus' ability to magnify his father-in-law's achievements at the expense of earlier governors, in this case Sextus Julius Frontinus. Frontinus was governor from *c*.74-7/8. In the year 97 he was made water commissioner in Rome, during which time he wrote a technical treatise on water management called *De Aquis*. The work survives. Although Frontinus makes no mention of Bath it seems rather too coincidental that his governorship of Britain coincides with the one datable inscription from Bath, unless he had some involvement in the new works. Perhaps Frontinus was the man who oversaw or commissioned the development of *Aquae Sulis*. He did, after all, prosecute a war against the Silures in south Wales and so must have come this way from London. *De Aquis* is written as a record of reforming abuses and supplying a public service, and Frontinus evidently took a keen interest in hydraulic technology.

42 *Tin votive plaque from the spring at Bath. Its symbolism is unknown but the facial design resembles those on face-pots* **(colour plate 4)***. Height 330mm*

Either way a local body, probably consisting of officials, architects, secretaries and others, will have been responsible for overseeing the Bath complex. Some or all are likely to have had military backgrounds. Amongst their duties will have been dealing with theft of spa water, and managing a task force of artisans and labourers who kept the spa going. That picture is entirely speculative but it draws on a general background of epigraphic and literary evidence for building and maintaining similar services elsewhere.

The substantial bath suite eventually became one of the most complex buildings in Roman Britain (**57**). Its structural integrity with the temple and its associated monuments makes it clear they belonged to the same institution, quite apart from the fact that the bubbling hot water supplied the baths as well as the sacred pool. From the very beginning, special windows in the bath walls allowed visitors to look across that pool and hurl their offerings in (**42, 166**). But it isn't clear from the archaeology that the baths were built at exactly the same time as the temple and pool. The circumstances of the period are a more reliable indicator, and it seems reasonable to link Bath's development with other public building projects of the late first century. The work will have taken a long time, and there were many alterations and embellishments lying ahead across the next 200 years.

However well-managed, Bath was nothing without its clientele and it is the evidence for them that helps us define the nature of the settlement. The inscriptions from the site that record people are effectively undatable. On the parallel of the general distribution of epigraphy of known date, most will belong to the second century and the first half of the third. So, while they take us beyond the period of the late first century they help create an image of Bath that endured throughout the rest of the pagan era. The majority refer directly to Bath's importance as a cult centre. The anonymous son of Novantius erected a monument for himself and his heirs as 'the result of a vision' (*RIB* 153). Dedications to Sulis and Sulis–Minerva dominate the record, but others commemorate a Genius, and Diana (*RIB* 139, 138), and one of the curse tablets from the spring records a temple of Mars, while another is dedicated to Mercury (Cunliffe 1988, nos. 53, 97). A number of military tombstones survive, raising the question of whether the soldiers died here having been sent to recover from an ailment, or were part of garrisons on the site during its military phase or throughout its later history.

Priscus, the stonemason from northern Gaul, is an interesting example because apart from the soldiers he is the only person at Bath to state that he came from elsewhere in the Empire (*RIB* 149). Even the soldiers all belong to units stationed in Britain and must have come from their bases rather than another province to make their offerings, or die. In some cases, soldiers' freedmen made the dedications, perhaps acting as proxy dedicants for their patrons such as Aufidius Eutuches, freedman of the *VI* legion centurion Marcus Aufidius Maximus (*RIB* 143). Not much has changed throughout the centuries. At Glenwood Springs, a spa town in the state of Colorado, is the grave of a hero from the Gunfight at the OK Corral, 'Doc' Holliday. He came to this American spa in search of relief from tuberculosis and here 'he died in bed' in 1887. His grave (or rather cenotaph, the exact location is unknown) overlooks the town and is regularly embellished with grave goods in the form of whisky bottles. Like the Bath inscriptions, there is no information about the cause of death on Holliday's tombstone and this does present us with a problem of interpretation. While we assume Bath was a healing cult, for very good reasons, there is no precise evidence of, or statements about, the illnesses involved. Nobody at Bath ever tells us why they came there, what cures they sought and for what diseases. Instead all we have are the petty feuds enshrined on the curse tablets and the gravestones of those whose cures, we may assume, were not forthcoming.

The most vivid glimpse of Bath's formal nature and administration comes from the altar erected by the centurion Gaius Severius Emeritus. Emeritus was 'centurion of the region' and thus was one of the myriad centurions detached from their units to manage zones throughout the Empire, as we use policemen. Emeritus' altar was found near the middle of Bath and it commemorated his repair and reconsecration of a *locum religiosum*, 'holy spot', after it had been vandalised 'by insolent hands' (*RIB* 152). The text is a vivid insight into Bath as a thoroughly human place, erected and enjoyed by the majority for their religious edification and trashed by an indifferent minority for a piece of selfish fun. The fact that it attracted vandalising emphasises Bath's totemic importance; vandals normally choose their targets carefully.

The rest of the clientele cannot have been entirely made up of malingering Hectors, genuine pilgrims, or people suffering from serious illnesses. Loiterers and malcontents, rakes, quacks and charlatans will have made as important a contribution to the colour of life at Bath, and at other temples everywhere in Roman Britain. Martial poured scorn on people falling for the 'dotard with staff and wallet' who, amongst other places, loitered on the threshold of either the Temple of the Divine Augustus or the Temple of Minerva in Rome. Here 'the crowd, as it meets him, gives him the scraps he barks for', believing that his wretched appearance meant he must be a philosopher from the school of Cynics (*Epigrams* iv.53). No, said Martial, he was 'a dog', playing on the fact that 'cynic' was derived from the Greek word for a dog. In his *Alexander*, the second-century satirist Lucian recounted how the oracle of Alexander of Abonuteichos cheated the credulous by pretending to be insane, and planting a goose egg in which he had placed a snake. Later he 'discovered' the egg and claimed thereby to have found the new-born Aesculapius. As far as Lucian was concerned those who fell for this were mentally-deficient and indistinguishable from sheep.

The well-known curse tablets from the sacred spring are often described as the most potent and vivid record of how the Romano-British used a cult centre. In some senses they are, but in others they are almost useless. We have virtually no idea what sort of person was responsible in any individual case, and that makes it impossible to analyse the sort of people using the establishment, or even exactly when. On the other hand they make it abundantly clear that pettiness, small-minded squabbles and trivial interests were at the top of the agenda. This is not a record of highbrow philo-sophical navel-gazing, but an insight into the narrow-minded self-interest Pliny the Elder thought dominated religious activity in his world. One of the tablets has been transcribed as follows:

> *[D]eae Suli donavi [arge-]*
> *ntiolos sex quos perd[idi]*
> *a nomin[ibus] infrascrip[tis]*
> *deae exactura est*
> *Senicia(n)us et Saturninus <sed>*
> *et Ann[i]ola carta picta persc[ripta]*
> (transcribed by RSO Tomlin; Cunliffe 1988, 118) (**43**)

It means, 'To the Goddess Sulis I have given the six silver pieces which I lost. It is up to the goddess to recover them from the names written below: Senicianus, Saturninus and Anniola. The daubed sheet has been transcribed.' The last line is particularly interesting. The words *carta picta*, 'daubed sheet', can mean coloured paintings, sketches, or pictorial representation. It is almost as if the would-be curser, who remains anonymous and known only to the goddess, had produced a sketch or jotting of what he or she wanted with a mixture of blundered words and images. Apparently a resident scribe had been commissioned to rewrite the curse into a form suitable for deposition in the spring. In one sense the subject is trivial, but on the other, six silver coins in the second century (though the curse is undated),

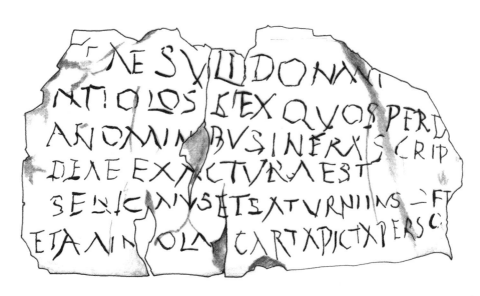

43 *'Curse' tablet on a sheet of lead, from the sacred spring at Bath. The message to the goddess Sulis concerns the theft of six coins. The text includes a reference to its having been copied out, presumably by a scribe who had been handed a draft or sketch. For a more detailed discussion, see text. Diameter 94mm. After Hassall, and Tomlin*

approximated to nearly a week's pay for an ordinary soldier (then 300 per annum). The nature of the 'curse' is a little opaque. Evidently, the curser has given up the coins for lost and merely hopes that Sulis will recover them from the guilty parties by whatever means she considers appropriate. There is no offer of a further gift or dedication. The basic format is familiar enough from many other examples, with the requested punishments often extending to death. At Ratcliffe-on-Soar (Notts) another curse tablet, this time an isolated find, employed a common device by being written backwards. This added to the sense of intimacy and exclusivity. Here the text records that the curser has already been to 'the temple of the god [unknown]' to dedicate a missing mule, and would like the thief or thieves to die at the hands of the god (*B* 1993, 310).

The Bath curse tablets form part of the colossal assemblage of artefacts and coins that were deposited in the sacred spring during its long life as the focal part of the temple and bathing complex. The spring lay directly between the temple and the baths and could be seen through three substantial openings in the north wall by the Great Bath. These, which survive today, provided pilgrims with a sight of the sacred spring and the opportunity to deposit their gifts (**166**). Coins, especially the worn and counterfeit examples found during the excavations, were the economy offerings here just as they were in shrines all over the Roman world. Of the 12,595 published coins recovered, just four were gold and two of those were almost certainly deposited together. Most of the rest were worn coins, or contemporary forgeries (**44**).

44 *Contemporary copies of Claudian coins. To make good a shortage of base metal coin under Claudius and Nero up to 64, large numbers of copies were produced, probably by the army. These were subsequently popular votive gifts, as well as worn official coins, because their low value and demonetised state made them useless. Clockwise from top left: copper as of Claudius, 41-54; brass dupondius of Claudius (41-54, possibly an official issue but worn to the point of uselessness); Minerva reverse of a Claudian as copy; degenerate, second-generation, Claudian as copy*

Cheapskate votives did not prevent Bath prospering from its late first-century religious beginnings. What mattered was the money spent on goods and services. Bath had two colossal advantages: a fabulous and unique natural phenomenon to exploit, with all the attendant spiritual associations; and, it was on a major highway. That meant resources and traffic could come in, and its reputation more widely disseminated. Bath's rapid integration into a mainstream Romanized cult centre is more likely to have been due to the presence of soldiers than anything else, though it might actually have been contracted to civilians for its operation. But not only did soldiers have the logistical skill to carry it out, but they also were the most literate and superstitious proponents of visible Roman religious culture in Britain. The epigraphic evidence points to them, and it does not point to any other source. That does not make the argument unequivocal, but on the basis of what we have it is the most likely.

Urban temples

Elsewhere in Britain other ancient rural sacred places were beginning to evolve into new forms. Tradition played a big part. Bath might have become a town, but in essence it was still a primeval sacred spot that had been Romanized. Bath does not seem to have had a structural or urban form before the Romans arrived, unlike some of the new regional capitals. Canterbury is a particularly enigmatic example, largely because the ravages caused by medieval and later activity have sunk countless pits and middens into the Roman deposits. Excavation in the city has been necessarily piecemeal and opportunistic. As so often with British urban archaeology it was only the devastation caused by German bombing in the Second World War, often exploited by cynical post-war developers, which made large-scale exploration possible.

Canterbury had a classical theatre by the late first century. Later on it was elaborated and rebuilt on a grander scale. The theatre was an integral part of classical religious complexes in a tradition that stretched back to ancient Greece. The construction of a contemporary theatre across the road from the Temple of Claudius at Colchester was a necessary requirement, as it eventually was at Verulamium (**45**).

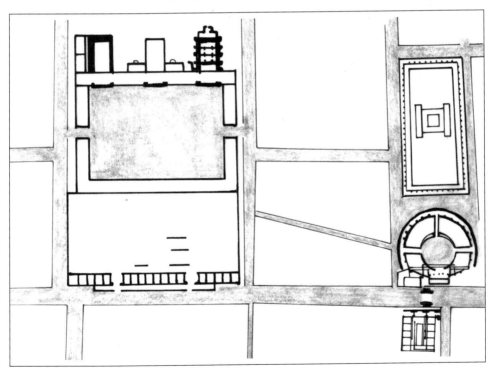

45 *Verulamium town centre (simplified plan, after Frere). To the left (south) is the forum and basilica complex. To the right (north), the Romano-Celtic temple in its rectangular precinct lies adjacent to the late second-century theatre (**53**). Note the arch foundations across the road beside the theatre (**49, 50**). The theatre was built in an area clearly set aside for it up to a century earlier, around the time the temple was built*

46 *Cupid gladiators spar on a fourth-century mosaic from the villa at Bignor (W. Sussex). Gladiatorial games were frequently linked to festivals that celebrated events in the religious calendar, though evidence for them in Britain is scarce*

The result was similar to the rural temple-theatre site at Champlieu in northern Gaul. The word 'theatre' is a pejorative one in English. To us it suggests entertainment, not religion. In the pagan Roman world the two were inextricably linked. Roman historians sometimes poured scorn on theatres, amphitheatres and circuses for their role in the unedifying indulgence of the rabble and the degradation to which the mob sank by their enthusiasm for mass entertainments. The image is so powerful that it is one we effortlessly associate with all Roman centres of popular entertainment. Writing around the beginning of the third century, the Christian apologist Tertullian slated the activities as generally idolatrous, frenzied and lustful:

> The pageantry is the same [as in the circus], to the extent that a procession is held from the theatre to the temples and altars, with that whole awful ritual of incense and blood. They march to the music of flutes and trumpets, directed by those two most decadent masters of ceremonies at funerals and sacrifices: the undertaker and the soothsayer.
> Tertullian, *de Spectaculis* x.2

Tertullian might have had a point. A curious find at Verulamium's theatre was a bronze knife handle depicting a copulating couple. It is conceivable that the displays on stage extended to performances of what we would call the obscene, but in a world given to public celebration of the phallus they were simply part of revelling in fertility rites. Several other similar knife handles are known, all found in Britain, perhaps sold as 'top-shelf' souvenirs of the occasion.

But in Rome games, such as the 'Games of Ceres' held every April, were linked to religious festivals, however loosely – or even apocryphally (**46, colour plate 12**). The Ceres games even included a suspension of races to accommodate a diversion when a fox was set loose with a burning torch tied to its tail. This was punishment for a legendary fox that had been caught after stealing chickens and set on fire. It escaped and set fire to crops as it raced away (Ovid, *Fasti* iv.679ff). Tertullian also explained how pagan games commemorated and celebrated idolatrous practices. One of these occasions, described by the grammarian Sextus Pompeius Festus, was on 15 October when a horse from a victorious chariot team was sacrificed to Mars for the sake of a good harvest, and his head lopped off (see the Loeb edition of Ovid's *Fasti*, p.414). Ostensibly held for religious reasons, the horse-sacrifice event also provided graphic entertainment that climaxed with a running street fight over the severed head.

Such accounts provide us with a convenient list of connections between games and traditional cults, though we have no way of knowing which or any were celebrated in Britain. But given the important status of London, and the 'Roman' role colonies like Colchester and Lincoln (**colour plate 12**) were supposed to publicise, we can safely assume that some similar annual events were arranged. Tertullian often relied on popular etymology for the links. This is not a problem because he was only reflecting contemporary beliefs in the connection. That Tertullian objected to them does not affect the point. 'The testimony of antiquity is confirmed by that of succeeding generations', he warned, 'for the name which the games go by today betray the nature of their origins' (*de Spectaculis* vi.1). He pointed out that the *Liberalia* games 'clearly proclaimed the honour of Father Liber', another name for Bacchus whose association with licentious drunken behaviour had already provoked official sanctions against Bacchic gatherings back in 186 BC during the more sober days of the Republic (Livy, xxxix.8ff). By Tertullian's time the same reason made Bacchus a popular target for Christian loathing though this probably focused on the extreme ends of Bacchic behaviour (*de Spectaculis* v.4). Ironically, the Christian use of wine in their own rites provoked exactly the same sorts of accusation amongst pagan critics. Tertullian proceeded to list the dedications to, and images of, the various 'unclean deities' in the circus and amphitheatre. Under Septimius Severus (193-211) 'we saw all types of different shows in every theatre at the same time. These included the all-night religious ceremonies that imitated the Mysteries' (Herodian iii.8.10).

A theatre, especially in the provinces, could also act as a gathering place for public assemblies and displays of ritual (see for example, Tacitus, *H* ii.80). The Great Theatre at Ephesus in Asia Minor was directly linked by a long road to the celebrated Temple of Diana/Artemis that lay to the north of the city (**47**). Along this road commemorative parades and pageants took place, joining the establishments. It was no coincidence that the silversmiths led the townsfolk into the theatre in the mid-first century to defend their economic interests against the preaching of Paul (*Acts* xix.24ff). They totally depended on trading in model shrines and statuettes of the goddess.

47 *This street in Ephesus is known from inscriptions to have been the route along which religious processions travelled between the theatre and the temple of Diana. In Britain, temples and theatres were also linked, sometimes being built as part of the same complex (see **45**)*

48 *Fragments of classical masonry from the 'temple' insula in Canterbury, making the presence of a classical temple here, as yet unlocated, highly likely*

Canterbury's first-century theatre lay across a road from a large courtyard surrounded by a colonnade. The belief that this was a temple precinct is sound. The location was central and substantial. There are many fragments of monumental classical masonry (**48**), including pieces of exotic imported stonework, and the remains of two small Romano-Celtic temples have been found (more than one temple in a precinct was not unusual).

The 'Romano-Celtic temple' was well known in the north-western provinces during the Roman period. A very small number of pre-Roman rectangular temples, like Heathrow, may be evidence that the type had begun its evolution long before the invasion. 'Romano-Celtic temples' is a modern name for a distinctive type of temple building found in the north-western provinces. The usual form is a central square *cella* with a concentric square ambulatory. The surviving remains of the Temple of Janus at Autun in Gaul show that the *cella* was tall and had putlog holes in its walls about halfway up to take the lean-to roof timbers of the ambulatory. The concept was similar to the classical temple in the sense that the gatherings, processions and ritual took place outside in the precinct, with the temple forming a backdrop to the centre of activity around the outdoor altar. Only the secret ceremonies and the cult statue were housed within. This does not mean all Romano-Celtic temples took the same form, but most classical temples conformed to basic conventions and so the Romano-Celtic temple probably did too. Recognition and familiarity are essential triggers in identifying a building's function, but there are likely to have been local variations, especially in whether the ambulatory was surrounded by an open colonnade, a half-colonnade, or solid walls.

Canterbury's 'main' temple probably belonged to as early a phase in the town's development as the theatre, and almost certainly lay on top of a pre-Roman religious focal point. Excavation in the precinct has produced a surprising number of Iron Age coins (evidence for minting them has also been found elsewhere in Canterbury). But the finds are not odd if this was once a pre-Roman tribal religious zone and administrative centre, forming part of the extensive Iron Age settlement known to have existed in the Canterbury area immediately before the conquest. The name of the settlement, *Durovernum Cantiacorum*, contains a vital clue. *Duro-* means nothing more than 'town' or 'settlement', but *verno-* survives in Welsh as *gwernen*, 'alder tree', and *gwern-*, a 'swamp' or 'alder grove'. The town name thus means something like 'town at the alder grove'. Alders are particularly associated with watery or boggy places, a theoretically favourite setting for water deities, but this also provides the wood with the enormous practical advantage that its tolerance of moisture made it extremely reliable for use in piles, foundations, and pipework – a fact noted by Vitruvius and recounted by him in detail (ii.9.11, see also Pliny *NH* xvi.218). So, even if the Canterbury alder swamp had special sacred properties it also had immense practical value. The two were probably related, a useful reminder that sacredness and usefulness in antiquity were often connected.

Across the road was an area believed to have accommodated the basilica and forum though there has been a fair amount of futile debate about the exact form these might have taken. What is reasonable is the suggestion that the zones were laid out as a single major scheme of public building. The archaeology from Canterbury is said to point to a Flavian date, but this might have been guessed anyway. On the evidence of other sites arches will have formed the principal entrances to the temple zone (**49, 50**). London has produced significant quantities of masonry from one arch (though this is thought not to have been built until the very late second century at the earliest), and more recently, the foundations of another around 12m wide have been found near the Old Bailey.

49 *(left) Brick arch at Pompeii. The marble cladding is lost, but the size and form of this example resembles the arches at Verulamium (**45**)*

50 *(below) One of the arches at Verulamium. This arch stood across Watling Street outside the theatre (**45**) and may have played a part in processions to and from the theatre and its adjacent temple (see **49**)*

51 *(opposite) Pipeclay figurine of 'Venus'. The head and right arm are missing (normally raised and holding the figure's hair). The statuettes were imported from Gaul in large numbers. Height 150mm*

No inscription from Canterbury survives to confirm a date or even a deity for the putative temple, but the town's identity as the civitas capital of the Cantiaci will have made some sort of central administrative and religious area a political necessity. The location in south-east Britain meant the town's early promotion was essential, and this might help explain the absence of epigraphy. The army and inscriptions go hand in hand. Places that were military bases before they became towns have usually yielded a number of inscriptions from the military phase, such as at Colchester or Cirencester. When inscriptions are virtually non-existent, this normally means that a military phase, if it occurred at all, was no more than fleeting. Canterbury is unlikely to have escaped the army's attention and a few military-style ditches have been identified. But Canterbury was rapidly left behind as the soldiers moved inland, making it a prime candidate for elevation to formal urban status in a part of Britain that was unlikely to have resisted conquest. It was too near, and familiar with, the Roman world to try and avoid the inevitable.

Meanwhile, London had rapidly become a major player in Romano-British urbanisation through sheer force of character. We have no formal reference to London's status. It is only in terms of its second-century scale and size of buildings that makes it beyond doubt that it had grown from the burgeoning commercial centre of the late 50s to become the premier city in Britain by the end of the first century. The burial there of the post-Boudican procurator, Classicianus (**33**), by the late 60s or 70s might mean it had become the administrative centre perhaps as early as the end of the reign of Nero (54-68). Under the Flavians a relatively modest forum and basilica were erected as soon as the early 70s with, alongside, what seems to have been a temple and precinct. The temple was probably classical but it was small (the *cella* was 8.5m square) and unprepossessing for a provincial capital. London was also an entry-point for imported religious goods. The wharfs have produced fragments of the well-known white 'pipe-clay' Venus and Dea Nutrix figurines manufactured in Gaul and the Rhineland (**51**). Such items served a growing market in Britain for deities in human form.

Roman town-planning was sometimes a protracted affair, falling foul of corruption, blundered lay-outs, unexpected fires, and a lack of funds. Such problems are amply recorded by Pliny the Younger's letters from his time as governor of Bithynia and Pontus. The picture is a familiar one in our own time, but unravelling the details of a piecemeal execution of ambitious building projects in the challenging environment of urban archaeology is impossible, especially without the information that could only come from written sources.

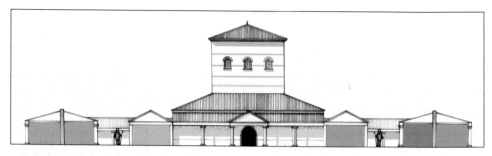

52 *Cross-section through the Romano-Celtic temple and precinct beside the Verulamium theatre (**53**)*

London's first forum and basilica were swallowed up under Hadrian by a new complex that consumed the old one and its temple companion. Perhaps this had always been intended, but whatever the truth we are still left without a major central London mainstream temple precinct thereafter. A theatre has yet to be located though the St Andrew's Hill area has been suggested as a possibility. If one is identified, a religious precinct is certain to have been associated with it though the known amphitheatre on the Guildhall site may have been all that London ever had. In the west of the city an octagonal temple may have been built *c.*170 but this is based purely on form – no votive goods were found which would confirm its function. At Verulamium (St Albans) we do have an instance of a fixed point: the Agricolan dedication of the forum. The town centre has also largely escaped later building. It was once thought that the forum was equipped with temples, but these are now thought to be stand-alone structures for the town council (*curia*) and offices, facilities normally accommodated within the basilica (**45**, **colour plate 2**). The sophisticated design of the complex sits oddly with the installation of a Romano-Celtic temple nearby (**52**).

The Verulamium temple may have been connected with the *macellum* (market place) across the road, recalling the sort of protection sought by the guild of smiths at Chichester from Neptune. But it is also likely that ceremonies and celebrations of whoever the god (or gods) at Verulamium was might have attracted commercially-exploitable gatherings. In any case, there is every possibility that the temple had much older origins than that. We don't know, but the subsequent elaboration of the Verulamium temple, and the erection of a theatre beside it in the second century, makes it very likely that the whole zone was planned from early in the town's history (**45, 53**). The theatre area was left clear until that project was executed, which has to mean that it was set aside from the outset for that purpose. There is nothing untoward about this. Military inscriptions from the north include texts that refer to the completion of buildings left unfinished for generations. Even in our own time central London building sites created by bombing in the Second World War have only really completely disappeared in the last 10 years. It may have been a question of funds, perhaps only forthcoming on the death of a local worthy who left the necessary cash (see for example Suetonius, *Tiberius* xxxi).

Verulamium shows us the clearest example of a British town centre instituted under the Flavian emperors with an integral religious complex, performing a funda-

53 *The theatre at Verulamium looking south. The church in the distance stands on the basilica. The temple* (**45, 52**) *lay to the right*

mental social and spiritual role in reinforcing a cohesive urban identity in a Roman idiom. It is unfortunate that we know nothing about the deity, but on the basis of other examples it is likely to have included several mainstream figures like Mercury and Minerva alongside the Spirits of the Emperors and local gods. The beaker from Dunstable connected with a Verulamium-based Cybele cult is of later date and does not help us here (**36**).

The only other large town with a similarly open centre is Silchester but here the absence of any major central temple complex is even more conspicuous, showing that we cannot assume the existence of one at other places without some evidence. The Flavian forum and basilica was timber, and even its replacement in stone by *c.*125-50 went without any sort of temple (at least, none has been found). Given that *Calleva* was a major Iron Age *oppidum* for the Atrebates, it is possible that a nearby religious zone similar to that at Gosbecks by Colchester remains to be discovered. But it has also been suggested that any urban cult centre was established in the basilica itself. If that is right, the Flavian timber predecessor may have been similarly equipped.

Even so, several Romano-Celtic temples are known at Silchester, with some of these conforming to the earlier street-grid, identified by its slightly off-set alignment with the later and more conspicuous lay-out. These temples may therefore belong to the first century. One of them is reasonably central and has produced some epigraphic and sculptural evidence for possible dedications to Pax, Victory and Mars by a *collegium peregrinorum*, 'guild of provincials' (*RIB* 69-71). Temple *collegia* resembled trusts, organi-

54 *Silchester's amphitheatre, looking from one of the entrances across the arena floor to one of the ringside shrines (see also **156**)*

zations to which even the most ordinary people contributed and which then looked after the funds, distributing them as alms or to pay for festivals and temple upkeep. Much later, Maximinus I (235-8) provoked widespread outrage when he appropriated temple wealth, probably including these savings (Herodian vii.3.5).

The Silchester temple date and *collegium* recall the Chichester inscription to Neptune and Minerva, which of course lay not far to the south. Further east, in a precinct later bordered by the Silchester city walls, at least two temples lie next to where the medieval church now stands. Also on the early alignment the precinct probably contained at least one more temple. However, the most important feature is that this precinct lies little more than 100m from the entrance to the town's amphitheatre (**54**). Here we have the only example in Roman Britain of a temple complex close to an urban amphitheatre. Given the illustrations from literary sources mentioned above it is difficult to avoid concluding that the two were built to work together, and probably belong to the earliest phase in the town's formal development. A road led directly from the forum to the precinct. The northernmost of the two is one of the largest Romano-Celtic temples known in Britain though no evidence has yet been found to confirm who or what was worshipped there.

The second century and beyond

There is then at any rate some tangible, albeit indirect, evidence for Tacitus' claim that Agricola would *hortari privatim, adiuvare publice,* 'urge individuals, encourage public bodies', to build temples (amongst other things), especially if we interpret that as a more broadly Flavian urban initiative (*Agr* 21). The statement implicitly avoids attributing the projects directly to the government, whether imperial or provincial. This is entirely borne out by later inscriptions that tend to record religious structures, or their embellishments, as gifts from individuals or groups. The Silchester *collegium* of provincials is a case in point. Donations such as theirs were an important part of social ritual through which allegiance to the community in its new Roman context was emphasised, renewed and confirmed. If government assistance was involved, perhaps it took the form of providing land or architects.

As the economy of Roman Britain developed, the towns benefited from the religious installations given by individuals from Britain or further afield who set out to express gratitude for commercial fortune and the privileges of status. In 221 at York, Lucius Viducius Placidus, a *negotiator* (trader) from Rouen, dedicated an arch and gateway to Neptune(?), the Genius Loci, and the Spirits of the Emperors (**55**). Neptune is a guess, restored in one reconstruction of the original text; another

55 *York. Dedication to Neptune(?), the Genius Loci ('of the Place'), and the Spirits of the Emperors by the trader Lucius Viducius Placidus of Rouen (his full name is known on another altar from Holland). It records his gift of an arch and shrine in the year 221. Diameter 63cm*

56 *Altar erected at Bordeaux to the goddess Tutela Boudiga by Marcus Aurelius Lunaris, sevir Augustalis (priest) of the colonies at York and Lincoln in the year 237, commemorating a voyage from York. The altar is made of Yorkshire millstone grit and must have been brought expressly for this purpose*

suggestion is Jupiter Optimus Maximus Dolichenus. This was an age when epigraphy in Roman Britain was at its most prolific, and the text has several interesting features. Placidus selected a suitable trinity of deities that reflected his own personal trading interests in the form of Neptune (if this is correct) and the Genius, and his lip-service to the regime in the form of the imperial spirits. The historical context of 221 was an age of mercurial, sometimes megalomaniac, emperors when it was wise for anyone with social prominence of whatever sort to cement his relationship with the state before any questions were asked. Under Caracalla (211–17) a governor of Gaul had been murdered under imperial orders and it is likely that Gaius Julius Marcus, governor of *Britannia Inferior* (equivalent to northern Britain) in about 216, was murdered too.

The altar erected by Marcus Aurelius Lunaris at Bordeaux in 237 provides a broader perspective on official religion and patronage in urban Roman Britain (**56**). Lunaris was a *sevir Augustalis* at York and Lincoln. At Bordeaux he thanked the goddess Boudig (probably for Bourdiga, the goddess of Bordeaux) for her protection during the voyage from Britain. Appropriately he had brought a slab of northern British millstone grit to use for the altar. Lunaris is likely to have been a freedman, the *seviri* normally were, and was probably engaged in commerce of some sort. Even at his modest level in society, Lunaris belonged to a class accustomed to moving about widely, and holding status in more than one city. As a *sevir Augustalis*, Lunaris served on a board of six men appointed to administer emperor worship at set locations.

These two men are exceptional in the record, but they almost certainly represent a much broader base of similar individuals who contributed to and managed aspects of official urban religion in Roman Britain from the late first century on. There is nothing similar for the second century in Britain apart from the theatre stage dedication at Brough (see below), but what we do see in the archaeology for the period is the much more significant elaboration of some of the conspicuous urban temples and shrines. This takes us back to Bath once more. The second century was an era of military consolidation in Britain, and the military side to religion is dealt with in chapter 5. But in the south urban development proceeded at a more leisurely pace once the principal public buildings had been erected. The temple at Bath had started out as a very largely classical building, in spite of the wildness of the pediment centrepiece (**colour plate 9**). It was substantially altered in the late second century in a rather curious way that resulted in a hybrid form. The podium was enlarged on the sides and back so that what seems to have been a covered ambulatory could be arranged around the three sides. At the front a pair of chapels seem to have terminated the ambulatory and flanked a new set of temple steps.

One suggestion is that the Bath alterations converted the temple into a sort of classical version of the Romano-Celtic style. This is quite plausible; a number of the more elaborate Romano-Celtic temples in Britain like Lamyatt Beacon (Somerset) had a pair of additional shrines flanking their entrances. Hybrids appear on the continent. At Champlieu in Gaul, where the temple was accompanied by a theatre, a classical-style podium supported a square temple with pilastered walls and porch. At the Altbachtal sanctuary near Trier a building very similar to the second-phase Temple of Sulis-Minerva at Bath stood. Here a classical-type temple was surrounded on the sides and back by a lean-to ambulatory of a type very similar to those used on Romano-Celtic temples. Bath's new form is a mark not only of changing fashions but also perhaps that the purely classical did not appeal in Britain. It perhaps represents a maturity of regional fashion in which the purely classical either now seemed archaic, or failed to fulfil all the functions required of a temple in Britain. But the other possibility is that the temple at Bath is not yet fully understood, thanks to so much being buried. There is, as yet, no certainty about the plan in detail. Nevertheless, the work surely shows that Bath was successful, and had continued to attract substantial investment.

It was probably at around this time that Bath's Great Bath was rebuilt (**57**); the sacred spring was transformed from an open-air bubbling pool into an artificial cavern. The temple alterations were more cosmetic, but this project was a considerable change in direction. A monumental vaulted structure was placed directly over the spring, accessed by a small door leading off the temple precinct. The intention can only have been theatrical – the spring had become an artificial manifestation of a religious fantasy, a grotto that lurked in the murky gloom of rising steam, enhanced

57 *The Great Bath at Bath. Almost all the superstructure here is modern, but it helps create a sense of the site's scale in antiquity. The reinforced piers for the Roman vault can be seen around the edge. Beneath the colonnade across the water is a large section of the vault, recovered from where it had fallen. All around, subsidiary baths and facilities opened off the Great Bath, as well as the sacred spring and the temple precinct*

by the growth of algae and other vegetation. The warm moist air encourages the exaggerated growth of some plants, seen today in cooling towers of power stations. Submerged plinths supported other features – long lost – that were perhaps statues or cod ruins.

One of the few other clues we have to Bath's theatrical religious elaboration was a carved screen now called the 'Façade of the Four Seasons'. Only fragments survive, but they show this was an elaborate classical lay-out probably designed to balance the three-dimensional architecture that surrounded other parts of the precinct. A small section of inscription survives to record that it was rebuilt after years of dereliction at the expense of one Claudius Ligur. The style of lettering is certainly not earlier than the late second century and maybe somewhat later. The text is tantalising but it reminds us once more of the importance of private investment in these public projects. A reconstruction of the scattered sculpture suggests that the screen was topped by a pediment depicting Luna, who looked across to a carving of Sol above the entrance to the spring (**9**).

The text also shows that Bath had been subjected to periods of neglect. The period of time is already a long one – at least a century – and at this distance it is not possible for us to identify phases of popularity. But Bath of all places knows about changes in fashion and the fluctuating commercial consequences. At the time of writing, Bath's tourist trade has experienced financial troubles in the wake of an economic downturn and terrorism in America, leading to a temporary collapse in numbers of US tourists. However central Sulis-Minerva and her shrine were to Bath's Roman identity, the reality was that Bath still depended on attracting visitors. Indeed, the whole restructuring of the temple and its precinct might have been to drum up more trade.

It is certain there was more to Bath's religious heart than the temple, spring and the baths. Fragments of a circular temple, a *tholos*, have been found amongst the rubble, and massive walls known to have started on the north-east side of the baths might have been part of its precinct (**153**). This Greek form of temple, character-ised by a circular colonnade surrounding an inner circular *cella*, might be linked to Hadrian's visit to Britain in *c*.119. Hadrian was a lover of Greek culture and promoted it throughout the Empire. That there was a *tholos* is not now in serious doubt but the other possibility for the walls is that they were part of a theatre. As we have already seen, the theatre was an integral part of major religious precincts. Even rural temples, such as Frilford (see chapter 4) had amphitheatres. We are unlikely to find out because the main candidate for the site is under Bath's abbey church.

By the late second century at Verulamium a theatre had been constructed alongside the first-century temple. A major fire, normally attributed to *c*.155, seems to have provided the stimulus to a major reconstruction of much of the city but it is very likely that the theatre had been planned for a long time. Something of an oddity, it almost parallels the redesigning of the Bath temple by being neither a purely classical theatre, nor an amphitheatre. The result was essentially an amphitheatre with one of the long sides partly shaved away and a stage placed there. Subsequent alterations extended the stage out into the orchestra. The theatre undoubtedly formed part of the temple complex, and must have been used for gatherings associated with religious festivals, though it was later used for additional seating. This may help explain the theatre stage erected in *Petuaria* (at or near Brough-on-Humber) at the expense of the aedile Marcus Ulpius Januarius between 140-61 (*RIB* 707). His dedication was more political than religious, composed as it was in honour of the *Domus Divina* of Antoninus Pius and the Spirits of the Emperors.

If there was a general movement to elaborating urban religious centres in the middle and later second century and on into the third, it is difficult now to find a more general context or explanation for it. Hadrian was known for his grants to cities for a variety of different projects across the Empire erecting 'countless buildings in all places' (*SHA* xix.9), but only the Wroxeter forum inscription of 130-3 seems to record his impact in Britain for certain. Antoninus Pius also assisted communities with new, or restored, public buildings (*SHA* viii.4). But this is not a period in which Britain features very much in extant historical sources apart from occasional notices of wars in the north. Imperial assistance might have played a part in the development of religious centres. But elaborating temples may also have been simply a product of growing affluence in the settled lowland zone and a preparedness to seek imperial contracts, or was stimulated by a growing interest in new and more exotic cults that made it difficult for traditional centres to attract pilgrims and therefore income.

The fact is that from the first century onwards a whole series of cults had begun to proliferate across the Roman Empire. During the second century they became more entrenched and widespread. Part of the reason was that the educated élite in Rome, including men like Tacitus, had identified a paradox in Roman society. Rome's astonishing tenacity, discipline and skill had earned her a fabulous Empire, but possession of that Empire was destroying the very basis of her power by encouraging decadence, laziness and indulgence. For some, the loss of meaning was compensated for in the mystery cults like Christianity, Mithraism, and other Eastern cults including Egyptian religion. Rome had embraced the parts of her world from where these religions originated and her communications systems and Empire-wide professional careers meant that they were liable to spread. By the late second century, Britain had been home to a substantial garrison for over a century, many soldiers of which had spent their working lives being transferred from one part of the Empire to another. Even private civilians living in London included men from the other end of the Mediterranean. But Britain was largely defined by her military population, and soldiers recorded their exceptional catholicity and curiosity in cults. Thus, in York at some point in the late second or very early third century Claudius Hieronymianus, commander of *VI Victrix*, built a temple to Serapis, contributing to the extraordinary image of a god from the shores of the River Nile in the damp and distant streets of northern Britain (**116**). In chapter 6 we will look further at the arrival of the exotic cults in Britain.

Death and burial

It is now only really possible to study Romano-British burial practices in towns and forts. Urban cemeteries produce enough remains for patterns to emerge, while sites with a military phase, as we have already seen, are far better sources of tombstones, providing details of origins, age at death and occupation. Rural sites of course produce graves but they are much more scattered and less well known. Isolated cremation burials, of which very many are known, are broadly speaking similar and provide no statistical data about age, disease or sex. The small cemetery in a small village-like settlement around half-a-mile east of the villa at Hucclecote (Glos), where perhaps some of the villa estate workers lived and were buried, is a rare instance of an identified rural burial ground. Some of the odder practices, perhaps more closely linked to ritual, are discussed in chapter 1, for example at Lankhills (Hants). Roman law required that burials took place outside areas of human settlement, though this

58 *Grave goods from a rich cremation burial at Welwyn (Herts) belonging to the period just before the Roman invasion*

apparently did not apply to infant burials, or in practice to the victims of murder. Cemeteries are found within Roman towns, but usually only because they belong to an earlier phase in the town's development and were subsequently covered by expansion. In exceptional cases, prominent burial under artificial mounds like the Bartlow Hills (Essex) preserved, or at any rate mirrored, older prehistoric traditions for the upper classes.

Whatever the evidence of graves, it has been recently stated that the total number of burials recorded from Roman Britain is less than 20,000, most from urban cemeteries (Jones 1996, 23). So there is an inherent bias in the record, and a very small sample compared to the total population, equal in fact to about a thousandth of one per cent of the population on an annual basis. As a very general observation, burials of the Roman period were normally cremation in the first and second centuries, giving way to inhumation in the third and fourth. The Hucclecote example, mentioned above, is one of the exceptions; here the dozen inhumation graves were of first- or second-century date. The Roman tradition was that cremation had become popular because it prevented the dead person being disinterred (Pliny, *NH* vii.187). But there are invariably exceptions, perhaps linked to a belief that the physical body's destruction might compromise the afterlife. A burial from Harper Road, Southwark, belonged to a woman from the mid-first century. She had been inhumed, together with a flagon and a neck-collar. Conversely, at Chichester St Pancras cemetery we find cremations running on well into the third century.

59 *Tombstone from Lincoln recording the death of Flavius Helius, 'a Greek by race', who died at the age of 40. It was erected by his wife, Flavia Ingenua. The formula* DM *for* Dis Manibus *appears at the top. However, the stone was evidently bought 'off the shelf'. The lower two-thirds of the panel (not shown) were left blank.* RIB *251*

Pagan burials usually included grave goods, depending on the wealth and inclination of the deceased. They represent shared Roman and Celtic traditions (**58, 60**). In general though grave goods were directly connected to pagan beliefs in the afterlife, and correspondingly inhumation graves without grave goods are normally interpreted as belonging to the Christian tradition. The souls of dead people were considered to be gods, the *Manes*. But there are grey areas throughout and there is no cut-and-dried rule, especially as the 'Christian' graves are almost by definition undatable by reference to grave goods, and we find from St Augustine that some (the 'less well instructed') Christians still brought meals to lay by tombs, a practice which clearly had its origins in pagan burial customs (*CG* viii.27) (**129**). Moreover – and this is important – not everyone subscribed to a belief in the afterlife. Pliny called such ideas 'juvenile gibberish' (*NH* vii.189), while at the same time others may have indulged in an almost hysterical terror of the dead coming back to haunt them. No wonder the range and types of graves vary enormously, and we can take it for granted that the cynics might have instructed their cremated remains to be scattered to the wind.

Tombstones are very rarely found in direct association with a grave, cremation or inhumation, and are only datable on style, military unit (if applicable), or the name of the deceased or kin where a citizen's name can be linked to a specific reign. A name beginning Marcus Ulpius, for example, would normally belong to someone who, or whose ancestor, had been awarded citizenship under Trajan (98-117). But tombstones are of limited value. Only a few hundred have been found in Britain and the

60 *Flagon from a late first-, early second-century cremation at Castleford (W.Yorks)*

majority belong to military sites reflecting both taste and the expense. Verulamium, for example, one of Britain's largest Roman cities, has produced not a single one. By definition we only have stone grave markers to work from. In all probability the vast majority were made of painted wooden panels and have simply been lost to the ages. In exceptional circumstances, stone tombs embellished with symbolic sculptures like sphinxes, or lions devouring victims, were erected within cemeteries or in their own enclosures (**colour plate 17**).

The formulae of the tombstone inscription conform to a fairly narrow set of parameters. In the early part of the period *Dis Manibus*, abbreviated to DM, and meaning 'To the Spirits of the Departed' (**33, 59**), was not widely used and instead we have texts naming the deceased, his father, his age at death and if we are lucky the city or nation of his birth, his position in life and details of his kin. Women were treated similarly but less frequently, sometimes with details of their husbands and children. But most were of soldiers, military families, officials or immigrants. Some do name indigenous Britons but they are very rare indeed.

The cremation burials of the first and second centuries vary enormously, usually in the range and type of grave goods. Typically the cremated remains were placed in a large kitchen jar or less usually a face-pot (**colour plate 4**), with a purpose-made lid or a samian bowl or something similar serving the same purpose. Indeed, Pliny the Elder observed that 'most of the human race uses pottery containers for this purpose' (*NH* xxxv.160). Alongside, the usual extras were vessels like flagons, beakers and

61 *Lead cremation urn from York. The inscription records the death of Ulpia Felicissima, aged eight years and 11 months, buried by her parents, Marcus Ulpius Felix and [...] Andronica. Height 360 mm.* RIB *691*

smaller jars, which will have contained liquid and other food gifts to sustain the dead person on the way to the Underworld (**60**). To help them on their way coins were provided to pay the 'ferryman' for the journey across the Styx, and a pair of shoes (surviving as hobnails) provided comfort – at Cirencester they may even have been manufactured for sale at the cemetery rather than waste a good pair of shoes. This is an interesting reflection of the way worn old coins, damaged *paterae*, and miniatures were utilised or even marketed as votive gifts. Some of the grave-good tradition survived right on into the third and fourth centuries, and are not unknown even in burials that might otherwise be interpreted as Christian.

The vessels were purpose-made (or bought), or were reused household goods. More expensive containers include glass jars, lead canisters (**61**) or wooden boxes with bronze or iron fittings. Wooden boxes survive normally only in the form of their fittings, and the same applies to any sort of frame into which the burial was placed unless this was made of tiles or bricks (**62**). This represents the simple hierarchy of

62 *Cremation grave from Colchester. The ashes have been buried in a face-pot, accompanied by a flagon, and protected by a framework of tiles. Late first or second century*

wealth and status in life. Affluent Romans went to their graves with gold and silver jewellery, unguents, favourite possessions and so on. Very few tombstones can be asso-ciated with any specific grave. The likelihood is that most were marked with painted wooden posts or panels, sometimes with tubes down which gifts could be sent to the burial. At Caerleon a cremation was found complete with a tube from the burial running all the way to the surface.

Whether grave goods really tell us anything about the dead person, burial ritual and symbolism is another matter. One of the more bizarre claims of recent years was that a lamp depicting gladiators accompanying a female burial in London (even the sex was a matter of dispute) was evidence that the deceased had been a woman gladiator. Setting aside the extremely limited evidence for women gladiators for a moment, this creates an interesting problem of interpretation when human graves contain lamps decorated with centaurs, rams or satyrs! Female gladiators are testified in the literary evidence but it is quite obvious from the context that they were highly

101

unusual (Suetonius, *Domitian* iv.1). On the other hand, archaeological finds of lamps or samian bowls depicting gladiators are not. Undoubtedly a reflection of our own politically-correct age, the so-called 'London gladiator girl' is the perfect example of spurious conjecture passed off as respectable scholarly deduction, which does nothing more than mislead the public in a facile attempt to drum up publicity. The critical point is that this woman (if a woman it was), or any other woman, could indeed have been a female gladiator, but being buried with a lamp depicting gladiators is not evidence for it.

The 'gladiator girl' was extremely successful in getting the intended publicity. A 90-minute television film promoting the interpretation was the result though it enjoyed limited respect in scholarly circles for its exaggeration and manipulation of the evidence. Another example burst onto the press in 2002 when a fourth-century Roman burial at Catterick found in 1981 was announced, as part of the effort to advertise the publication of excavations stretching back to 1958. The skeleton was wearing items of jet, shale and bronze jewellery and there were two stones in its mouth. The archaeological 'spin' machine galvanised the impressionable British media with the suggestion this might be the remains of one of Cybele's castrated adherents, the 'Galli'. The Galli undoubtedly existed, and there is some epigraphic evidence for them in Britain (see above, **36**, and below, p.181).

Of course, the archaeological reality is rather more opaque because of the difficulty of associating excavated evidence with that from written sources. The Catterick skeleton was interpreted as being that of a young man, but skeletons of young men and women are sometimes difficult to distinguish with absolute precision. The differences in skeletal form are not always absolute and there are some ambiguities until, for example, a woman has experienced childbirth. In any case, the jewellery is local material for northern Britain and scarcely unequivocal evidence for exotic eastern rites. It is certainly true that Cybele's adherents were considered by their opponents to have perverted sexual tastes but such accusations are commonplace in slanging matches and are not necessarily reflected in fact. It also ought to be obvious, to the most undiscerning critic, that even if this was a man, identifying a eunuch from skeletal remains is impossible. Yet the entire basis for interpreting the remains as that of one of the Galli depends on this. The stones inserted into the skull's mouth have been claimed as substitute testicles for the afterlife. But the practice is not testified as being something that happened to deceased Galli, and is not without precedent in other contexts, for example at Crowmarsh (Oxon). It might simply be an innocuous burial rite or even oral padding to prevent sunken cheeks during burial.

Both the 'gladiator girl' and the Catterick skeleton, presented to the world by some newspapers as 'Crossus Dressus', create the impression of certainty in archaeology that is simply misleading. The effort to pin 'box office' labels on these discoveries ends up telling us more about ourselves, and our preoccupations. The theories serve not only to gloss over the fact that there is more than one explanation for either instance, but also the unpalatable reality that archaeology is not necessarily the means to identifying the right one. This problem extends into other areas of Romano-British religion, particularly when it comes to the mosaics of the fourth-century villas (see p. 203ff).

4 Wayside shrines

Bath was the most conspicuous example of the wayside shrine, though its exceptional site and hot spring made it a special case. Bath was never awarded formal status as a regional centre, and nor was it ever apparently equipped with major administrative buildings like a forum and basilica, though it was eventually walled. The temple and baths complex lay right in the middle of the town and covered a substantial part of its total area. It was essentially a religious resort whose market and population was dependent on the shrine's location on a major route. Remote rural temples like Hayling Island or Wanborough were obviously also accessible in the sense that they could be reached at all but the new road system had an entirely different effect on places where through-traffic, or route intersections, guaranteed a flow of visitors and passers-by. The identity of these places was more ambiguous.

Roman roads were not necessarily virgin installations – many probably used existing sections of track or traditional paths, even if the new system was more integrated, contiguous and reliable. The difference between Roman Britain and before was that there was far more individual and official traffic across the island. This is most easily seen in the dispersal of soldiers from their units, for example on detachment to the governor's staff in London. But it is also apparent in some of the inscriptions recording private individuals too. As with the modern United States, a tradition of serving this mobile population developed, something that is easy to forget now that most of the British Isles can be crossed in a few hours. A traveller from Lincoln to London in the mid-second century would have found it hard to cover more than 20 miles a day, making the settlement at Ancaster a perfect first overnight stop (63).

Whether settlement or cult came first in any one place it is now impossible to say. Location was everything. Those on or close to the roads developed under Roman rule were liable to grow into more significant settlements, some to the extent that local cults were eventually subsumed and forgotten, or at any rate marginalised into the everyday throng of town life. In others, perhaps local cults just developed out of all proportion merely because the passing traffic meant they were bound to gain attention with local people utilising them as a means to make their settlement more attractive. This was particularly the case when the cult was associated with a natural phenomenon.

63 *Ermine Street, looking south from Lincoln towards Ancaster from near Navenby. Apart from the modern tarmac the road here has changed little. A traveller from Lincoln could hope to make Ancaster in a day where he would find the shrine to Viridios* **(colour plate 32)**

Pilgrims

Great importance could be placed in antiquity on making a journey expressly to visit a cult centre; in other words a pilgrimage. The evidence from places like Bath is that individuals had often come from some distance to visit the shrine though we lack the documentary evidence to attribute the vast bulk of the untraceable votive gifts found there. But the tradition of the wayside shrine endured in medieval Britain and Europe. The habit illustrates the pattern and the economic effects not only on the final destination but also on places along the way. Little Walsingham (Norfolk), close to the centre of what seems to have been a Roman-period cult, became the focus of a shrine to the Virgin Mary in the twelfth century. Thanks to the pilgrims who journeyed across medieval England to visit it, other places en route benefited, such as the Red Mount Chapel at King's Lynn where foreign pilgrims arrived by sea. Built in 1485, Red Mount Chapel provided facilities for pilgrims who wished to give thanks for arriving safely, and to prepare themselves for the journey ahead by road. Medieval Londoners headed for Walsingham came often by road the whole way, and found shrines and sustenance at various places including the chapel at Hilborough near Swaffham. Bigger places like Newmarket provided similar services, forming only part of that town's greater economy. As we will see later, these medieval shrines were the source of large quantities of religious badges and trinkets that followed a great tradition of souvenirs of pilgrimages to holy places stretching right back into Roman times and beyond.

A mark of how random the Roman record can be is the bronze feather-type votive plaque from Godmanchester (Cambs) dedicated by Vatiaucus to an otherwise completely unknown god called Abandinus (**36**). Vatiaucus' gift was found with three more bronze feather plaques, wrapped together, in late third-century rubbish clogging the redundant aqueduct that supplied the town's *mansio*. The *mansio*, or inn, was an integral part of how these small towns developed. Further south down Ermine Street from Ancaster, Godmanchester sat on the edge of the Fens and was a day's travel from Water Newton, *Durobrivae*, a town with a burgeoning pottery industry that dominated the third- and fourth-century markets in eastern Britain. It was a perfect location for a local economy partly built on the through-traffic to the north. Evidence for metalworking and pottery production has been found, as well as a bakery, though the truth is that it would be surprising if a small town had lacked these industries. Rather, it is limitations of survival in the archaeological record and the vicissitudes of time that tend to prevent them being found.

The Godmanchester *mansio*, or at least the building interpreted as one, lay in the north-west quadrant of the settlement immediately beside a small temple precinct, though another temple flanked Ermine Street in the southern part of the town. The *mansio*'s temple precinct lasted from the early second century to the late third, with the temple itself starting life as a timber building before being rebuilt in Romano-Celtic form. In the late third century the temple and *mansio* were demolished. The temple was replaced by a polygonal building of unknown function. The temple and *mansio* probably depended upon each other. One might compare it to the modern roadside motel with attendant restaurants, garages and other businesses. It is equally reasonable to suggest that the temple was dedicated to Abandinus, but the haphazard nature of the record means that his Latinized name survives not in the temple but in rubbish from an adjacent building. Without that plaque, Godmanchester's temple would join the ranks of urban and wayside temples where we have no idea who or what was worshipped. Unfortunately there is little more to go on though Abandinus is likely to be based on the well-known British prefix *Ab-*, 'river' – and indeed the Great Ouse flows north just to the west of the town. However, there is no evidence yet that Godmanchester existed in any form prior to the arrival of the Roman army. This may be a case where a god from slightly further afield was absorbed into the new settlement's traditions or even created when the *mansio* was built. The town's name, *Durovigutum*, offers no clues because it refers to no more than a walled town or fort.

The most likely explanation is that locations like Ancaster or Godmanchester, associated with specific deities, that happened to be close to or on roads, benefited because they were more likely to mutate into larger settlements. There is no doubt that travelling, and the passage from one place to another, represented an important spiritual experience. Godmanchester was also a significant Fenland road junction. The consequence was settlement growth, and also the roadside shrine centres. There were many examples, and some seem to have experienced a kind of parallel development from the

64 *The* mansio *baths at Wall,* Letocetum, *on Watling Street in Staffordshire. This small town depended on through-traffic for its existence. The inset (lower right) shows a crude carving of three heads, almost certainly a representation of an anonymous triplicated local deity which must have stood in a shrine on or near the* mansio. *Other carved stones found incorporated into buildings on the site suggest a pre-Roman shrine was demolished when the* mansio *was developed*

late first century and into the second, for example Wall, *Letocetum*, in Staffordshire (**64**). Interestingly the name itself seems to enshrine a reference to a wood. Chelmsford, on the main road from London to Colchester, was dominated by its *mansio*, with apparently one temple nearby and another just beyond the town walls.

Even the roads themselves were occasionally worthy of veneration in their own right. Titus Irdas, one of the governor's bodyguards, dedicated an altar at Catterick (N. Yorks) with a unique text 'to the god who devised roads and paths' (*RIB* 725). In the year 191 Quintus Varius Vitalis, on the governor's staff, restored it. Doubtless, Irdas was grateful for a successful journey and Vitalis, following in his footsteps, may have been just as keen to respect the spirits who had protected the lines of communication.

Springhead and Greenwich (Kent)

The principal road route into Roman Britain was Watling Street. It left Richborough in east Kent and ran along higher ground on the south side of the Thames Estuary, eventually diverting north to enter London near the present London Bridge. Several Roman towns grew up along its route, principally Canterbury and Rochester, along with several smaller settlements. The route very probably had pre-Roman origins and some of the settlements undoubtedly existed in some form prior to the conquest, for example at Canterbury. One of these was a place now known as Springhead. Today, the site is wholly unrecognisable beneath the dual carriageway of the A2, a redundant railway embankment and a garden centre.

Excavations in advance of the widened modern road made it possible to explore this strange little place where the Roman road crossed the Ebbsfleet. Watling Street turned out to have zig-zagged through the little town that grew up here. Alongside, though not in any regular enough way to explain the kink in the road, was a small temple precinct accommodating several shrines, and a pair of 'foundation burials' with decapitated bodies. The presence of babies' bodies in this context is difficult to attribute simply to the high death-rate amongst children at any time before the twentieth century, whereas infant burials at villas like Hambledon probably can be. But there is a huge leap between human sacrifice for an infant foundation deposit, and the utilisation of a child that died from natural causes for a foundation deposit. We cannot resolve that.

Two temples were reasonable-sized Romano-Celtic examples facing east and sitting beside one another. There was a good deal more to Springhead than the temples. Buildings and a cemetery lie scattered along and around the vicinity. These include once more a bakery, a facility that is a reminder that pilgrims and travellers used these places to rest, eat and recuperate as well as make offerings. The corner of a much larger building across the road escaped identification because not enough was explored. But it appeared to be big enough to be a *mansio*, or some other form of shrine accommodation. Wayside shrines were simply part of a broader economic infrastructure.

Unfortunately, the Springhead excavations were piecemeal and ill-recorded with some confusion of interpretation. It is now far from certain whether the temples overlay earlier buildings of similar function, but the one sensible synopsis of the work concluded a second-century date for construction of the extant temple remains. There is unfortunately no means of knowing the deity apart from a pipe-clay figurine of Venus found on the *cella* floor (**51**, **65**). But these items were common-place and turn up in a variety of mundane, commercial and domestic deposits. They were probably sold here to passers-by, and this is really the essence of a wayside shrine like Springhead. A traveller from the east would have approached on Watling Street, seeing the facades of the two temples from some distance away. To the west the land rises dramatically, providing the location with a theatrical and attractive setting.

If the traveller found Springhead an appealing place to lay his head, make an offering and spend some of his money, he will have found the approach to London even more inspiring. Watling Street ran down the west slope of Shooters Hill presenting traffic with a panorama stretching across the Thames basin. *Londinium* was readily visible, and between the traveller and the great city lay what is now Greenwich Park.

Greenwich has remained a favoured spot since the Middle Ages. Centuries of land-scaping and building have irretrievably altered its primeval appearance, but a Roman

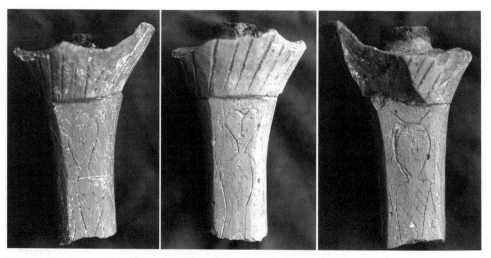

65 *Clay handle from north Kent (Springhead) apparently depicting deities: uncertain (left), Venus (centre), Mercury or a horned god (right). Perhaps a home-made incense burner*

building has been known in the Park since at least the nineteenth century. A return to the site in 1999 revealed that beneath the cropped grass, the remains of what was almost certainly a wayside shrine subsisted. The finds were unusual. Very little in the way of coarse wares turned up, but an unusual series of coins was found that matched the sequence from the excavations of a century before. Dating from the Flavian period onwards they were all characterised by being well-struck, large-flan, specimens, suggesting they had been specially selected. A tile stamped for the procurator of the province of Britannia at London means that an official connection is likely (**66**). This is borne out by an inscription recovered in 1999 most easily restored as a dedication to the Spirit of the Emperor, or Emperors (**67**). Several other inscriptions are also known though none can be as easily restored. There is no doubt that there are real problems with Greenwich. That there is a Roman building there is beyond doubt, but the absence of the usual pottery detritus means that some of the finds can be interpreted as the remains of an antiquarian collection, perhaps displayed in a garden grotto. There is no documentary evidence for that, but Greenwich was home to court hangers-on, the wealthy and educated élite, and naval officers for centuries.

On the other hand, Greenwich was a prime location for a temple. The hill overlooks the Thames and beyond to London. Watling Street passes here. It was the perfect place to stop and make an offering for a safe journey. Amongst these people will have been officials and soldiers en route on state business or to take up posts. Perhaps one of them was Olus Cordius, *st(rator) co(n)s(ularis)* 'governor's horse overseer', who built a shrine (*aedem*) to the Italian Mother Goddesses at Dover (*B* 1977, 426–7, no. 4), probably after arriving from Italy to take up a new posting. That is just a guess, but London's importance and expansion from the late first century onwards makes it inevitable that shrines like Springhead and perhaps Greenwich were destined to benefit from that kind of trade, at least so long as pagan worship was legitimate.

66 *Tile from the temple site at Greenwich, stamped* PP BR L[ON], *for* procurator provinciae Britanniae Londinii. *This makes it possible the temple was an official establishment, perhaps a wayside shrine for government officers, soldiers and the like, to make dedications en route to or from the Channel ports*

67 *Greenwich Park. Inscription probably forming part of a dedication 'to the Spirits of the Emperors',* Numinibus Augustorum, *or the singular equivalent*

Nettleton

A few miles north of Bath, along the Fosse Way, is the remote village of Nettleton (Wilts). Now a tumble of farms and cottages lurking behind hedgerows and trees, it is difficult to imagine this was once a major trans-Britannia route (**164**). Here the Fosse Way carried traffic between Cirencester, the second largest city in Roman Britain, and Bath. The road was in some sort of operation as a frontier communication route while Colchester, far to the east, was being made into the first Roman colony. Nettleton was equipped with a small ditched enclosure on the higher ground around that time which supplanted an earlier occupation site. Little more than a fortlet, its presence is most easily explained as a small military encampment built to oversee the little valley. A scatter of fragments of military equipment and a number of bronze brooches fit a military context, albeit an inconclusive one.

Quite why Nettleton should have merited a military post in the late 40s is not now apparent. But just over a century later a circular temple had been built on the north-facing slope of the valley by the river. A later inscription from the site, dedicated to Apollo Cunomaglos, makes a pre-Roman deity here extremely likely. The point here is not that the religious element needed military control, but that shrines attracted people. A shrine was a gathering place, a centre of trade, dissemination of news, and dissent. It was important to supervise such places, but the arrival of continuous administrative and military traffic meant that shrine centres stood to gain. The passing trade would always be in search of food and shelter. The soldiers, far from being repelled by a native cult, would have been attracted to it. Making sacrifices and dedications, or buying protective amulets, was simply a routine part of Romanized life. Nettleton would never become a Bath, perhaps because Bath itself was so close, but it was guaranteed a clientele of sorts and in succeeding decades would grow into a substantial and important shrine centre.

Cunomaglos, a 'Celtic' word, belongs to a well-known series of names based on *Cuno-*, 'a dog'. Together with *mag-* 'high' or 'noble', this gives a meaning of something like 'noble hound', though whether that means a deity literally perceived as a dog or simply one with qualities otherwise associated with a dog is unknown. Apollo's attributes included archery and care of flocks and herds, making him suitable for conflation with Cunomaglos (**68**). However, another relief from the site depicts Diana with a hunting dog, a handy reminder that these associations and conflations were fluid and almost limitless in their applications. In any case, other deities benefited at Nettleton, clear from finds recovered from across the settlement. Another altar was dedicated to Silvanus and the Spirit of the Emperor, and a relief of Mercury with Rosmerta was also recovered (**17**).

This proliferation of deities, many of whom are found elsewhere, shows that by our standards worship was something of a free-for-all. This is commonplace at Roman religious sites. At Lower Slaughter (Glos) further north along the Fosse Way, a well in the settlement produced a strange variety of religious carvings deposited in a well-shaft. They include Mars, Genii Cucullati, altars and other unidentifiable deities. It is impossible to say *why* they were cast into the well, but they were

68 *Bronze votive plaque, originally soldered to an iron backing, showing the head of Apollo and dedicated by Decianus. From the late third-century version of the shrine at Nettleton (Wilts). Height 107 mm.* After Wedlake

probably gathered up from nearby, perhaps from a shrine where travellers and locals made offerings to a variety of gods (**29**). Thanks to the later Roman development at Nettleton, the date of the circular temple can only be fixed from archaeological evidence to between 69 and 210. It was eventually successful enough to fund a vastly more ambitious building – one of the most exciting structures yet known in Roman Britain (see chapter 7).

Pre-Roman origins

Ancaster, on Ermine Street in Lincolnshire, was on another major military highway by the 60s (**63**). It has yet to produce evidence of a temple, but so far has yielded a large body of evidence not only for local cults but also an industry in manufacturing religious sculpture. Scattered evidence for Iron Age settlement lies alongside the presence of the army in the form of a large marching camp just north of the later Roman town. It is abundantly clear from a number of religious sculptures found here that cult activity was prominently displayed, and cult objects probably manufactured from local limestone (**69, 70, colour plates 32 & 33**). To date though, any temples

111

69 *The Ancaster Minerva. A comparatively recent find, this weathered relief is likely to have stood outdoors in a shrine. Height 240mm*

70 *Ancaster (Lincs). An inscription found in 1961 covering a 'medieval grave' and recording the gift of an arch (arcum), to the god Viridios. This must have been the entrance to the as yet unlocated temple precinct (see also **colour plate 32**)*

have escaped notice largely because the medieval church almost certainly lies on top of the remains. The recovery nearby of two inscriptions recording a god called Viridios or Viridius, a name which seems to have Latin and Celtic links with the concept of plant and vegetation fertility, makes it highly likely his shrine stood in the town and may have been a prominent part of it (**70, colour plate 32**).

The name Viridios is an interesting example of the problems presented by deities whose names are otherwise unknown. The word at first sight seems to have an obvious link to the Latin *viridis*, 'green', a word that easily evokes pastoral fertility. But this may only be a coincidence. The god is unknown anywhere else, which makes such a straightforward Latin connection unlikely. The Gaulish god Erriapus is depicted in association with tree foliage, and a statuette of him is known from Britain depicted as a bust with a tree-trunk body (**20**). Viridios has yet to be found in anything like so unequivocal an association, or indeed any representation at all. Alternatively his name may be a Latinized version of a local deity whose name was based on the Celtic prefix *Ver-* or *Vir-*, 'very' or 'mighty', producing a name resembling the old Roman *nomen*, Visidius (Cicero, *Philippics* vii.24), and itself probably based on the Latin word *vis*, 'strength'. Of the two Ancaster inscriptions, the second omits the first vowel altogether, suggesting a certain amount of doubt about its transcription or ambiguous pronunciation. A Germanic goddess called Viradecthis is known at Birrens (*RIB* 2108). The existence of several inscriptions in Germany giving her name with a different spelling each time, including Viroddi and Viradecdi, shows how unwise it is to make pedantic interpretations of such names from one or two instances. Antenociticus at Benwell (see chapter 5) presents similar problems.

Other temple excavations have shown that early Roman temples may even have succeeded pre-Roman sacred structures, rather than simple natural features like trees or springs. At Harlow (Essex) a small hill beside the river Stort had been venerated for a long time, though it formed part of a wider settlement in the vicinity. Bronze Age burials were followed by a round building in the Iron Age, surrounded by a scatter of Iron Age coinage and brooches of pre-Flavian date. Iron Age coins are more frequently found in quantity on religious sites than anywhere else (**71**).

Around the time that Bath was receiving its vast capital investments Harlow's round building was replaced by the first phase of a 'Romano-Celtic' temple. Regardless of the precise detail, Harlow is a good example for demonstrating that the second basic temple class found in Roman Britain was established by the late first century, often supplanting earlier temples. A theatre mask from here is a reminder of the part performance and parade played in pagan rituals, though if there was a theatre here it was probably only a timber auditorium. Another temple, not far to the west at Folly Lane, St Albans, seems to have accompanied rather than replaced a different kind of cult site. Here, a late first-century Romano-Celtic temple was built in an old Iron Age ditched enclosure that had contained a square-cut pit revetted with timber. The Iron Age pit had attracted the burial of an apparently prominent individual around the middle of the first century, accompanied by armour and horse-trappings. The new temple was built alongside, and the site seems to have remained in use until the third century with both temple and pit in use.

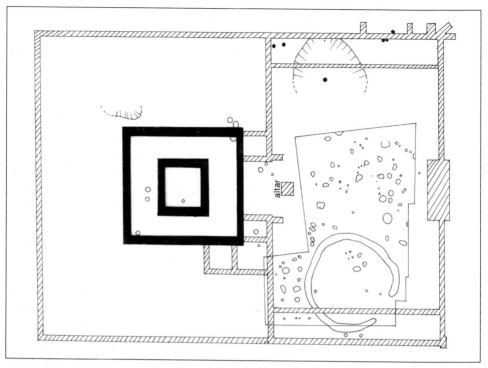

71 *Plan of the temple site at Harlow (Essex). The Iron Age round building is in the south-west corner at lower right; black spots mark cremations. The 16m-square Romano-Celtic temple was built a few yards away and was later embellished with the precinct wall and courtyard with altar pedestal which enclosed the pre-Roman structure.* After France, Gobel and Bartlett

Similarly, at Wanborough (Surrey) a circular temple of late first-century date turned up near to a conventional, square Romano-Celtic temple dated to the mid-second century (**16**). The site was already notorious thanks to a sustained campaign of illicit metal-detecting that had generated large numbers of Iron Age coins. In fact the early temple turned out to have been built in the last two decades of the first century, clearly much later than some of the finds, and overlaid a sequence of ditches and gullies containing tribal coinage and other material. At Hayling Island (Hants) it was aerial photography that in the first instance identified the presence of a circular building nearly 14m in diameter, lying within a piazza enclosed by a pair of concentric square walls.

Hayling Island is a significant location; it seems to have been part of the territory associated with the philo-Roman king Togidubnus in the first century. On excavation it was established that the east-facing circular building, with its tiled roof, wall-plaster and porch, was first- or second-century in date, but had succeeded a similar arrangement of the first century BC built in timber. The tribal affiliations in this area fluctuated throughout this time so it is difficult to know exactly how to interpret the structure. Similarities to Gaulish temples like the Tour de Vesone at Périgueux suggest that the new temple represented a conflation of local tradition with new Roman-type building techniques and materials. Enough of the latter, incidentally, survives to show that the building was a tower in form. The proximity of the remarkable 'palace' at Fishbourne at least demonstrates the presence of advanced Roman architectural skill in the vicinity.

In some respects this transition to building parallels what is often found on rural house sites. Typically, the rural farm or settlement changes in the latter part from the first century form a pre-Roman type of timber round house into a masonry structure characterised by stone walls and right-angled corners. The change is one of the most radical seen at any time in British history and represents a complete change in habits and standards. Given this, it is not so surprising that sacred sites should have been treated in a similar way. Like so many other temple sites, Wanborough underwent a further change in the second century and was turned into a more elaborate structure.

Great Walsingham

Great Walsingham's temple, like Ancaster's, exists only as a theory and is based on the fact that numerous examples of artefacts normally interpreted as being votive have been found in and around the small Roman settlement here. Unlike Ancaster though, Great Walsingham was, and is, somewhat off the beaten track in a relatively remote part of north Norfolk. This does not prevent it being a religious site. After all the medieval shrine nearby at Little Walsingham was in the same position, but it does mean it was probably a different type of religious site. East Anglia has produced a remarkable amount of Roman material in recent years thanks both to the intensive large-scale agriculture of the region, building development in and around the area's modern towns like Thetford, and also the use of the metal-detector. This of itself is a reminder how our perception of the ancient record is inevitably distorted by modern influences. The great fourth-century treasure hoards, like Mildenhall, Thetford and Hoxne, are entirely at odds with the virtually total absence of evidence for the wealthy villa culture of the period in the area (**colour plates 24 & 30**).

Great Walsingham lies some 30 miles (50km) north-west of the nearest civitas capital, Caistor St Edmund, *Venta Icenorum*, and about 13 miles (19km) east-south-east of the fort at Brancaster, *Branodunum*. The civitas capital was in existence for most of the Roman period, but the fort is not known to have existed before the end of the second century or the beginning of the third. A network of roads and minor settlements linked the three places, but villas of any classification are rare compared to most other parts of southern Britain. Around 20 miles (30km) from Great Walsingham is another Romano-British shrine site at Felmingham Hall (**122**).

Great Walsingham's votive finds include representations of deities, and the so-called 'miniature' tools. Jupiter, or at any rate a bearded head which looks as if it could be Jupiter, appears as does Mercury, known to have been one of the most popular gods in the north-western provinces, represented by several cast bronze figurines. The style is variable. One statuette is a reasonably competent, well-proportioned figure with a posture that shows that whoever produced the archetype (from which the cast was made) understood how to represent a realistic stance. The other two are much heavier and stockier in posture. In other words, they represent the products of more than one workshop or at least more than one sculptor. Minerva appears twice, as an appliqué bust and as a figurine. An anonymous deity appears in the form of a small bronze bust of a three-horned man (**4**).

Horned or antlered gods turn up in a variety of religious contexts in Britain, drawn from a long-established tradition of depicting horned men and beasts, for example the enigmatic Antenociticus of Benwell on Hadrian's Wall (**5**). Cookham (Berks) has produced a three-horned bull on a 45mm-diameter bronze plaque with holes and fittings for attachment, though there is some dispute about its date, which may be medieval – itself a mark of how uncertain this subject can be. Tripling a feature or a figure seems to be a particularly popular feature of art in the north-west, especially Britain and Gaul, and is normally applied to figures who are undoubtedly gods like the Genii Cucullati or Mothers (**112**, **113**, **colour plate 33**), or animals with particular symbolic or aesthetic importance. It is impossible to know who the Great Walsingham three-horned god is. None of his features ties him to anyone in particular, though it is quite likely that the object has closer connections to the Iron Age than the Roman period. An iron bowl from Iron Age deposits on the later site of the fourth-century temple at Lydney, for example, had bull-head fittings with knobbed horns. It was quite normal for a multiplicity of gods to turn up in any one place and there is no need to struggle to, say, interpret him as some sort of local version of Mercury. The bronzesmith who made him may have done so for a specific commission, or simply as his own design utilising various traditions.

This multiplicity is amply represented by the array of additional objects that include several cupids, satyrs, Mercury's familiars – the cock and the goat, rings inscribed for the Mother Goddesses, Mercury and one with the letters TOT. The latter is well known from a number of examples, several from Lincolnshire, and now widely believed to represent the Celtic deity Toutatis (**72**, and see p.127 below for the problems with this interpretation). Several rings from Great Walsingham with gemstones depicting gods such as Ceres, Mars and Neptune add to the list. Neptune is not necessarily out of place; as creator also of the horse his appeal was wider than just purely maritime interests. The number of different deities is really not a problem. Many temple sites produce evidence for more than one cult, though it is worth bearing in mind that we may also be looking at a settlement that also produced religious artefacts for distribution or sale in other places, or which were brought here from other places.

The miniatures generally belong to a range of 'votive' goods found at many temple sites in Britain. They include model spoked wheels, tools and weapons (**73**, **74**, **122**). There were also many seal-boxes, little bronze containers, usually with enamelled lids that were used to protect the wax seals on documents. They divide into an easily identifiable range of shapes: diamond, square, circular and teardrop. The document was secured with a knotted cord. The opened seal-box was placed under the cord that fitted into slots on either side of the box. The softened wax was then poured in and stamped with the owner's engraved device on a ring, and closed. This kept the seal

72 *Silver ring inscribed* TOT, *for Toutatis(?). See p.127 for problems interpreting this abbreviation. From Lincolnshire. Diameter 22mm*

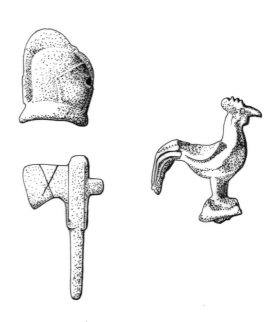

73 *Miniature votives. Left: helmet and axe from Kirmington (Lincs). Right: cockerel from Chelmsford (Essex). Height of the cockerel is 41mm.* After Leahy, Drury and Wickenden

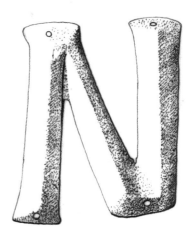

74 *Votive gifts. Left: 'horse-and-rider' brooch from Hayling Island (Hants), diameter 30mm. Right: bronze letter 'N' from Wood Eaton (Oxon), with holes for suspension on a wall. Height 62mm*

secure and safe, in theory. Lucian's *Alexander* describes how dishonest cult-operators had various methods of breaking open such seals. That way appropriate answers could be supplied to gullible punters, who were consequently impressed at the god's perceptiveness.

The assumption is that there was a cult centre at Great Walsingham primarily dedicated to Mercury. This is very possible but it is also true that once a site starts to 'produce' metal artefacts, this news rapidly spreads amongst those who use metal-detectors and attracts progressively more and more attention. Metal-detector use invariably results in metal finds, usually in much larger numbers, and certainly in larger proportions, than in conventional excavations that are not only more restricted in their coverage but are also more likely to miss some. At least some of the Great Walsingham finds could belong to the normal run of quasi-religious artefacts that embellished both home and the individual, without any particular significance for the function of the site. This makes it hard to accept the theory that seal-boxes have a particular association in a votive context – the argument is that they were used to seal the vows made to a deity. But if so, Great Walsingham has produced no inscriptions that record the fulfilment of those vows. Vow-fulfilling altars are best-known from the northern frontier in Britain, as scattered finds or in bulk from cult sites such as Coventina's Well. Their wholesale absence, and that of bronze plaques serving a similar function from Great Walsingham is a problem. It is also the case that none of the vows themselves are known – it was common, but not universal, for these to be recorded on lead tablets (**43**). The shrine of Mercury at Uley (Glos) has produced many of these, and given the successful metal-detecting at Great Walsingham it might have been expected that one or two would have been found by now. Seal-boxes are no less likely to have played a part in the transmission of estate and contract business.

Nevertheless, Great Walsingham has produced a distinct concentration of brooches and a large number of coins. This sort of feature is often assumed to represent a cult centre – but the 4700-odd coins represent only an average of 13 per annum for the whole Roman period, and were not found all in one place like the Bath spring. Not all the dates of the coins are available but a histogram published in 1991 shows the usual Romano-British settlement pattern with a late third-century peak and again between 330-48, and 364-78 (Davies and Gregory 1991, 73). While that might be taken to be evidence for a late pagan-revival shrine (see chapter 7), it is a well-known fact that later Roman coins dominate site finds as a matter of routine simply because they were available in large numbers and were readily discarded, thanks to a very low unit value, on the occasions when the coinage system was reorganised. The Great Walsingham coin pattern matches other ordinary settlements, but specifically differs from the pattern found at a temple in Caistor-by-Norwich and at other cult sites like Bath and Coventina's Well (see chapter 6). Equally, the significance of most of the brooches and seal-boxes being of second-century date is rather limited by the fact that this was when most of these were made and used, whatever the nature of the site. Brooches are invariably the most frequent find on Roman sites after pottery and coins, in that order, whether the place is a town, fort, villa or temple.

The fact is that prolific metal-detecting has produced a particular range and type of find, and that in the absence of excavation or any inscription which might genuinely reflect the process of cult activity the result has perhaps been to distort our perception. A published discussion of the finds from Great Walsingham has included the suggestion that the coins and brooches represent gifts by 'the poor', and the statues gifts by 'the élite'. The abstraction of this sort of judgement from the evidence is a mark of how much archaeologists strive to fabricate some sort of coherent but unsupportable story from a very inadequate source of information. We have no idea what sort of organic gifts were deposited, for example. It also shows an elementary misunderstanding of the pattern of numismatic evidence from cult sites.

If Great Walsingham did have a temple or cult centre, it need have been no more than a small and normal part of a settlement that also had an everyday identity as a farming and manufacturing village. To be fair there is no evidence for actual manufacturing like the unfinished brooches found not far to the south at Old Buckenham (Norfolk). It is, in the absence of any recorded pattern or context of the finds, difficult to make any worthwhile judgement. In fact the single most interesting aspect of the whole site is the existence of the medieval shrine of 'Our Lady' at Little Walsingham, a few miles away. This may be one of the most significant pieces of evidence for a Roman cult site nearby at Great Walsingham, preserving a tradition from antiquity right into the Middle Ages and beyond.

Fair temples

Being on a major route was not the only way for a cult to reflect and benefit from a special location. The temple sites at Frilford and Wood Eaton (Oxon) have long been recognised to lie close to the 'boundary' between Dobunni and Catuvellaunian territory. During the Roman period this will have been of no more than symbolic importance, but the tradition of spiritual neutrality as a commercial and social meeting place, oriented around annual religious festivals may have once softened much more violent rivalries. These are perhaps better considered as fairs, a tradition which survived long into the medieval period and up until relatively recently, by which time they were normally fixed around saint's days, such as the St Anthony's fair, held in Padua in Italy for a week before and after the saint's day on 13 June. Thus *nominally* religious festivals they were also times for fun, games, contests, freak shows and commerce. 'I saw in Southwark at St Margarites faire, a monstrous birth of Twinns, both females and most perfectly shaped, save that they were joyn'd from breast to breast' noted the diarist John Evelyn who proceeds to list various other freaks of nature on display (*Diary* 13 September 1660). At St Bartholomew's Fair at Smithfield in London, Samuel Pepys watched an intriguing array of Christian and pagan performances including episodes in the Bible, as well as 'the Sea, with Neptune, Venus, mermaids, and Cupid on a dolphin, the sea rolling; so well done' (*Diary* 4 September 1663).

Frilford's possession of an amphitheatre is a timely reminder that these facilities were not necessarily the exclusive preserve of gladiatorial impresarios. Amphitheatres provided places where ceremonies and displays could be conducted in front of a mass audience. As we saw earlier, Silchester's amphitheatre was a stone's throw from a temple precinct. No amphitheatre in Britain has yet yielded a piece of gladiatorial equipment. At Champlieu in northern Gaul, a temple precinct abutted the stage wall of a theatre, beyond which was a baths building. The temple was of unusual form – a classical-style podium, but the building itself was square, with pilasters around the edge, and a porch on one side (bearing some relation to the curious hybrid structure created at Bath; see chapter 3). Here the theatre and temple, despite not being on exactly the same alignment, were evidently part of the same complex. The site was a rural one, but it reflects extremely similar arrangements at Canterbury.

The closest settlements to the two sites are the small towns of Alchester and Dorchester-on-Thames. But both lie several miles away. The two temples were certainly accessible by road, but it was a minor route that ran north-east to south-west across the Thames valley. On the basis of what we know at present about the Romano-British landscape it would be impossible to make a good case for the stimulation of either site by constant passing traffic. Instead, the two places must have depended on specific visits by individuals or on special occasions when crowds gathered. Wood Eaton has produced some strange epigraphic evidence. An enigmatic fragment of gold leaf bearing Greek lettering seems to refer to a 'Lord' but otherwise relies on the force of repeating several other letters (*RIB* 2430.2). Several fragments of similar bronze plates, equally incoherent to us, are likely to represent the remains of 'spells' or communications with the resident deity, posted or buried at the temple site. A variety of single letters found nearby are relatively common from temple sites (**74**). Today, these are interpreted as letters sold at the shrine to pilgrims who then posted their messages in abbreviated form on the temple building or walls set aside for the purpose. This is not spurious. In the Roman world, abbreviated message formulae were entirely normal, and appear on coins, public inscriptions and private dedications (**163**). Pliny the Younger added to his account of the Clitumnus shrine in Italy that 'you can scan the many inscriptions of many hands on all the columns and all the walls, with which the spring and that god are celebrated' (*Letters* viii.8.7). It is unfortunate that we know so little more about the cults here, but a fragment of a tombstone recording one Decimus Malusius might mean that there was a graveyard for pilgrims who died (*RIB* 240). It is hard to say, though the stone itself is very casual in its execution, and uses letter forms closer to handwriting that suggests an informal burial.

Minor shrines

In addition to the more prominent shrines which formed integral parts of towns and villages, it was also common for much smaller shrines to be sited at various spots in the countryside, by streams and waterfalls, special trees, road junctions, bridges and

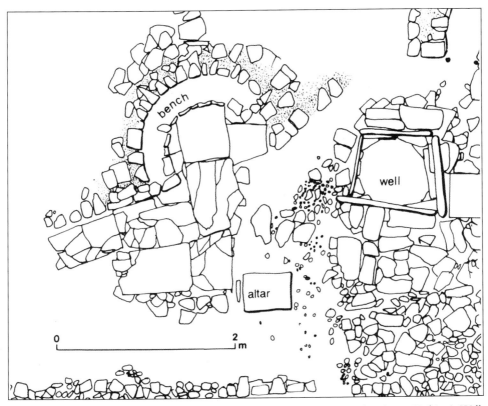

75 *Outdoor shrine of the Nymphs and Genius of the Place at Carrawburgh on Hadrian's Wall, consisting of just a small paved area, a seat and an altar. Probably typical of thousands of little shrines across Britain.* After Smith

so on. By their very nature such places hardly ever survive in a recognisable form. They were almost bound to be demolished or cleared away in the centuries after the Roman occupation. Their 'idolatrous' content was not going to endear them the church authorities and handy lumps of stone were utilised whenever possible.

At Carrawburgh, a fort on Hadrian's Wall, is a rare instance of the kind of shrine that probably once existed in much larger numbers across Britain. Its survival here is due to the waterlogged and silty conditions of the little valley it lay in, and its discovery to the fact that it lay just outside the entrance to the fort mithraeum (see chapter 6, and **102**). Otherwise, it would have gone completely unnoticed. The shrine was extremely simple and consisted of nothing more than a small paved area next to a small well (**75**). A semi-circular bench provided seating, and in the middle a single altar was dedicated to the Genius of the Place and his Nymph companions, dedicated by the prefect of *cohors I Batavorum*, the fort garrison.

The isolated altars, reliefs and other dedications which turn up reused in places like modern field walls probably originated in little shrines such as this one (**colour plate 10**). At Custom Scrubs, Bisley (Glos), a pair of carved reliefs, one to Romulus and the other Mars Olludius, were found during quarrying (*RIB* 131-2). Of broadly similar style, they were probably produced by the same man, perhaps the Juventinus who tells us he made the Romulus slab, for display in a small shrine near where they were found. The area is particularly apposite because the Cotswold limestone is so easy to carve – this helps explain the large number of isolated pieces from the area that might otherwise have been carved in wood. A relief of Mercury and Minerva turned up recently at Aldsworth (also Glos), in an area with many scattered traces of Romano-British settlement. The slab retains two pierced holes, probably used to suspend the sculpture on a wall in a now-lost shrine (*B* 2000, 362-3). The medieval church at Tockenham (Wilts) now has a carved gabled relief of a Genius built into one of its outside walls – its source is now unknown. Easton Grey (Wilts) seems to have been a Roman site of sorts, probably a villa. This yielded a small gabled stone panel depicting three figures attending a man in military costume. Curiously it was inscribed, but only to the effect that 'Civilis made this' (*RIB* 99). Perhaps it depicts a ceremony at a shrine on the estate by senior men of the family.

There are so many examples of this kind of work that the potential list is almost endless (**17**). Perhaps the closest parallel is the manner in which Mediterranean countries and the Republic of Ireland today often display small shrines to the Virgin Mary outside houses, beside the road or at junctions. Some immigrant communities, usually of southern European origin, in the United States have carried the tradition there. Maintained by local people, and enjoyed or visited by travellers they preserve an ancient habit which was once displayed across the Roman Empire and in Britain, leading to Tertullian's lament that the whole world seemed to be smothered in pagan shrines (*de Spectaculis*, viii.9). Since we only have survivors in stone, and then almost always out of context, we will never have any real idea how common they were in Britain, and the extent to which wooden examples and paintings on plastered walls made up the numbers.

Priests and regalia

By the second century and into the third, the priesthood was an integral part of Romano-British society. Broadly speaking, in the Roman world priestly duties were all part of the portfolio of duties carried out by the senior man in whatever context was relevant. Neglecting religious responsibilities was readily seen as the cause of military and natural disasters. The father of a household officiated over domestic religious rites. In towns the city elders, councillors and so on, acted as priests in the course of their official duties. In the army, the officers took care of these and at the top, the emperor was the supreme priest – *pontifex maximus*. There were professional priests but they did not form an exclusive caste. If anything, professional priests aroused suspicion and the destruction meted out on the Druids illustrates that. Only with the advent of the mystery religions did the position begin to revert.

Serving as a religious official could be a part-time activity. Pliny the Younger was delighted when he was made an *augur*, another form of omen-interpreter, because it was an honour to benefit from the emperor's choice in his favour, and also 'because the priesthood is an old-established religious office and has a particular sanctity by being held for life' (*Letters* iv.8.1). Pliny was a member of the senatorial class, which also produced Britain's governors and legionary legates. Most, if not all, will have served as a priest at some point in their careers. In other words, the prestige and honour trickled right down from the top, though we know very little about how more regional or local appointments were made. In Pompeii, the prominent landowner and businesswoman Eumachia served as a priestess, and was depicted as one in a statue in the building named for her by the city forum. No example of a woman holding such a position in Britain is known, but the businessman Marcus Aurelius Lunaris as a *sevir Augustalis* (see above, p.92) served in a similar role, as did Marcus Verecundius Diogenes at York whose personal origins were the Bituriges Cubi tribe of Bourges in Gaul (*RIB* 678). Such men were organised into *collegia*, with six men apiece. Normally freedmen, their status cemented their own loyalty to the state and provided them with the opportunity to be seen to do in public. They and their families benefited. At Colchester, in the early years of the province, it is likely that the disgruntled staff at the Temple of Claudius included local worthies press-ganged into a similar role. Togidubnus will have officiated over some of the religious dedications made in his territory, though in his case he clearly welcomed the privilege.

We have already met the *haruspex* who plied his trade at Bath: Lucius Marcius Memor (**41**). Although he was a Roman citizen, his name really tells us nothing about his origins. As a soothsayer he will have played an important role in religious practice by predicting the future. There were two techniques. The augurer interpreted natural phenomena like storms or animal activity. The other skill, *extispicium*, was interpreting the entrails of sacrificial animals. Ovid describes a sacrifice that shows just how revolting this could be, at least from our perspective. On 15 April were rites that celebrated the sprouting seeds in the ground, and the pregnancy of cows. The calves were ripped from the stomachs of their mothers, their entrails cut out for soothsaying and the bodies burned (*Fasti* iv.629ff).

The essence of reading entrails was the 'omen' – those signs and clues to the shape of things to come, and which the wise could look back to, nod sagely, and say, 'ah, well, the omens were there'. Memor harked back to a remote Roman, and before that Etruscan, past but his skills were entirely in accordance with local tradition and the powers of priests like the Druids. Memor, however, examined the entrails of sacrificed animals rather than the guts of executed prisoners. A *haruspex* who found 'a cleft in the lung of a victim' could cause some undertaking, whatever it was, to be 'postponed to another day' (Cicero, *DD* i.39.85). Cicero had his doubts about the validity of these interpretations, echoed later in Benedick's question, 'is it not strange that sheep's guts should hale souls out of men's bodies?' (*Much Ado About Nothing* ii.3.57).

Martial, writing towards the end of the first century AD, recorded what he thought was a hilarious story about a soothsayer. A billy-goat was to be sacrificed to Bacchus by a Tuscan *haruspex*. While engaged in cutting the animal's throat he asked a handy yokel to slice off the animal's testicles at the same time. The *haruspex* then concentrated on the job in hand when the yokel was shocked to see 'a huge hernia revealed, to the scandal of the rites' emerge from the goat's body – or so he thought. Anxious to live up to the occasion and observe the religious requirements by removing this offensive sight, the yokel sliced off the hernia only to discover that in fact he had accidentally castrated the *haruspex* (*Epigrams* iii.24). The story is a reminder that the pomposity of the *haruspices* was as much a source of fun in antiquity as John Cleese's ludicrously self-important Pharisee in the film *Life of Brian*.

Memor is one of several religious officials known from Roman Britain. Of the three inscriptions that mention a priest, *sacerdos*, two are from Hadrian's Wall, which is not surprising considering this area's quantity of religious inscriptions of all kinds. One from the Newcastle area names Julius Maximus on a dedication to a god perhaps called Digenis. The other, from a now-unknown location along the Wall, names Apollonius on a dedication to Nemesis (Fate) (*RIB* 1314, 2065). Bath is the source of the third. A tombstone records G. Calpurnius [R]eceptus, *sacerdos deae Sulis*, 'priest of the goddess Sulis', perhaps a man or his descendant who had been awarded his citizenship under the governorship of Agricola (*RIB* 155). In addition, at Greetland (W. Yorks) was Titus Aurelius Aurelianus, the only Romano-British instance of a *magister sacrorum*, 'master of sacred ceremonies', mentioned on an altar to Victoria Brigantia and the Spirits of the Emperors (*RIB* 627). This might seem a small number of priests for Roman Britain, considering the way religious dedications dominate the epigraphic record, but in fact priests are better represented than many other professions and the numbers compare well with other provinces.

We have a reasonable idea of how some of these priests dressed up to fulfil their roles (**76-8**). One of the Antonine Wall dedication slabs erected by *II Augusta* around 142-3 includes a panel showing a sacrifice. Four soldiers watch the officiating toga-clad priest, while he pours an offering over an altar. A pig, sheep and bull wait nearby while the priest's assistant, the *victimarius*, encourages them to approach (**colour plate 8**). The scene is thought to represent a ritual that prepared soldiers for the work ahead. But as the inscription on the slab commemorates the completion of a major stretch of Wall curtain, it may record the fulfilment of a vow.

The Antonine Wall priest was positively underdressed if the *equipage* found at temple sites further afield in southern Britain can be believed. An inscription from Brougham (Cumbria) seems to provide the word *instrumento* for temple paraphernalia (*RIB* 783). The regalia included the priestly crowns; the crown was so synonymous with pagan worship that Christian writers singled it out as particularly symbolic of idolatrous acts (for example, Tertullian, *de Corona Militis* x.9). A bronze crown from Hockwold-cum-Wilton (Norfolk) consisted of a round band decorated with medallions, and another pair of bands over the head, capped with a little finial (**76**). The crown was adjustable for head size that suggests it was a temple heirloom, used by whoever the incumbent was. At Wanborough, a similar effect was achieved with chains (**77**), while at Lydney a *repoussé* diadem depicting a sun god in a chariot represents a different style (**78**). But there is a possibility that these crowns were actually worn at wedding ceremonies (*ibid.* xiii.4-5). We cannot be certain to whom they belonged. The priests seem also to have carried staffs or sceptres, capped with little bronze heads. It has sometimes been claimed that these represent specific emperors but this is normally based on nothing more than generalized features like beards. In this sense they belong to the style of

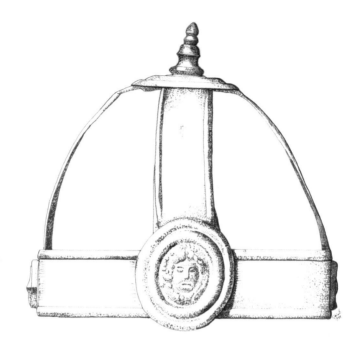

76 *Hockwold-cum-Wilton (Norfolk). Bronze priest crown with repoussé medallions. Adjustable for head size. Height 159mm*

77 *Priestly regalia, based on finds from the temple at Wanborough (Surrey)*

78 *Lydney Park (Glos). Bronze diadem from the temple of Nodons. Diameter 190mm*

an age as the Lullingstone marble busts do, and there is no reason to assume they are emperors any more than they might be wealthy benefactors or their ancestors. One from Aldworth (W. Berks) has three faces, each with a female head-and-shoulders. Perhaps an example of triplicated Mother Goddesses, they might preserve an image of the deities worshipped at the nearby temple on Lowbury Hill.

Dressed in their ritual costume, the priests in Cicero's ideal republic would make offerings to the gods 'according to prescribed rites and on the prescribed days . . . so that no violation of these customs shall take place, the priests shall determine the manner and annual round of such offerings. They shall prescribe the victims that are proper and pleasing to each of the gods' (*de Legibus* ii.8.20). For the priests alone there was access to the temple *cella* where they could be infused with the perfume of flowers and incense (Columella, *DRR* x263-4). So, we can imagine a great deal of serious observation of dress, accessories, and pride, as the priests at cult centres up and down in Britain undertook their ponderous rituals. But, as in all human societies, personal dedication will have varied with self-interest, pomposity and factionalism. There can be no doubt that charlatans, opportunists and cynics played their own parts in seeking to add to their personal fortunes through the contacts and contracts obtained by virtue of position, and others who relieved willing pilgrims of their cash for votive goods and offerings.

Votive goods, TOT rings, personal talismans and decoration

Religious or sacred charms carried about, or worn on, the person form one of the most important types of artefact from Britain. What we mean by these is objects like rings that bear some sort of religious motif, or inscription, like the TOT rings discussed in detail below (**72**). They are also amongst the hardest to interpret. If the interpretation of these as abbreviations for Toutatis, a Celtic deity sometimes conflated with Mars, is right does that mean the wearer was a devotee? Not necessarily, because rings also serve as decorative items and are also passed down, or re-sold. The same applies to small bronze busts of gods and animals, with attachments for steelyards or furniture. It is extremely important to remember that in antiquity religious subjects dominated iconography, and this does not necessarily denote votive intent on the part of the maker or owner.

This is even more of a problem when it comes to gemstones. Gemstones could be installed in new settings almost *ad infinitum*. The Thetford Treasure possibly consisted in part of a jeweller's work-in-progress, as well as the silver and gold material associated with the cult of Faunus (**colour plate 24**). The rings themselves were of fourth-century date but the gems were much older. The Snettisham hoard belonged to the late second century or early third and included more than a hundred loose gemstones as well as a large number of silver and bronze coins clearly selected for melting down to make new rings. The gemstones depicted a variety of subjects, some of which were depictions of gods like Ceres (20 examples), Minerva (six), and Mercury (five) (**colour plate 14**). But interpreting these designs as overtly 'religious' is a very simplistic interpretation. Gemstones also acted as identity cards, passwords and PIN numbers do today. The device and the individual carving identified the seal as the authentic property of the owner – in other words, it validated documents and messages. Motifs were chosen as allusions to names, background and experiences, or simply out of taste. Augustus used sphinxes to begin with, but gravitated to his own likeness. Galba (68-9) revived a device his ancestors had used: a dog on a ship's prow (Dio li.3.6-7). There is no convincing instance of gemstones being used commonly as votives. The finds from the sacred spring at Bath, and the drains at Caerleon, are best interpreted as casual losses owing to the settings loosening on bathers' fingers.

Small bronze or silver cubes engraved with designs have yet to have their purpose identified but may be connected with gemstones. One found at Kingscote (Glos) was decorated with images of Sol (two), Roma, Mars, Concord's hands, and a running horse. Another, found in Shropshire, has imperial portraits and standing figures clearly taken from silver coins of the reigns of Antoninus Pius and Marcus Aurelius. That one had religious figures, and the other not (apart from the coin reverse types of Fortuna and Mars), makes it unlikely the purpose was anything to do with religion. Instead, they more likely served as seal-dies instead of rings, or as gaming pieces.

Rings without gemstones occasionally bear inscriptions. The TOT rings are one of the classes where a case for a religious connection can be made, albeit rather a tenuous one, by expanding the letters to read Toutatis. The rings are broadly speaking concentrated in the Lincolnshire/East Anglia area. Toutatis appears conflated as Mars-Toutatis on a plaque from Barkway (Herts), and on another from the Hadrian's Wall area (*RIB* 219; *B* 2001, 392, no. 20). The god is also named on a graffito from Kelvedon (Essex, *RIB* 2503.131). So, there is no obvious consistency between the distribution of the rings and other references. But we need to be careful. The Hadrian's Wall plaque was found more than 50 years ago, but has only just been brought to the attention of scholars. This is a mark of the random nature of the record.

Moreover, there is no unequivocal verification of the expansion on the rings, especially as the name in full always appears as TOUT- on other inscriptions. Moreover, Lucan calls him as the Gaulish god *Teutates horrens*, 'dreadful Teutates', associating his worship with human sacrifice as does Lactantius who called him 'Teutas' (*Pharsalia* i.445, *DI* I.21). So, it is not instantly obvious that TOT- automatically must mean Toutatis/Teutates, as there is clearly a phonetic discrepancy. One exceptional example seems to read DLO / TOT, with DLO probably a blundered DEO. This provides the only approximate confirmation of the expansion though the item has escaped formal publication (Mills, 105).

The design of the TOT rings involved differs widely, and no other deity seems to be so frequently referred to in this way, making it equally likely that the letters actually stand for a phrase or slogan which is now lost to us. Possibilities include *terras obscura teneret*, 'darkness holds the land', and *tonat omne tumultu*, 'it [heaven] thunders with the tumult' (*Aeneid* iv.461, xii.757). It might alternatively represent *totius orbis terrarum*, a conventional expression meaning 'of the whole world', which appears in a variety of forms in Latin. Any one of these phrases is possible, each of which could easily have had a meaning as a slogan or significance to a group or cult which we now know nothing about. On the other hand, the most frequent use of *totus* is with *domus divina*, 'the whole Divine House', so this is also a conceivable possibility (for example *RIB* 897). Compressing phrases this way was normal. For example, the exhortation *utere felix*, 'be happy', well-known from the full version on brooches, appears on one ring compressed to VTF (*RIB* 2423.28). But there is no such unequivocal expansion for TOT. Finally, it is worth noting that early Anglo-Saxon coins imitating late Roman issues frequently and strangely featured the letters TOT, instead of the correct VOT (for *votum*). While there is no suggestion of any direct connection, there must be a possibility of some sort of phonetic aspect to TOT that obscures the real word meant.

Whatever the truth about the TOT rings, it is plain that interpreting this kind of device is not always straightforward. More commonly inscriptions, either formed as part of the design, or scratched in, make exhortations of wishing the owner a long life, or just name the owner. Some are more specific, though interpreting them relies on expanding brief slogans like MER as *Mer(curio)*, 'to Mercury'. A lost ring from Carrawburgh bore the text MATRES, for the Mother Goddesses. These are casual references though compare to the ring from Wendens Ambo (Essex) with the letters COL / DEI / SIL, which can only mean *Col(legium) dei Sil(vani)*, 'guild of the god Silvanus'. Evidently the ring was manufactured originally for the guild, but they are as likely to have been a hunting fraternity as anything else (see *RIB* 2422.30, 28, 52).

1 *Omens. This exceptional sky appeared after a bout of very heavy rain. In antiquity its colour would have been interpreted as a sign of foreboding, influencing political and military decisions*

2 *The forum at Sbeitla (Sufetula) Tunisia. The west side of the forum at Verulamium, erected in the late first century, was similar in appearance – the temple-like buildings were probably used for administration, but the scene still provides a good idea of the scale of town-centre classical temples in Britain that probably existed at places like London and Canterbury*

3 *Bath, temple of Sulis-Minerva as it might have appeared in the late first century*

4 *Colchester (Essex). Face-pots of various types. The purpose of these vessels and the significance of the faces are unknown – some were used for cremations but it is not clear if this was their primary function*

5 *Gods on coins (all silver* denarii *unless otherwise stated; dates are for strikings, not reigns). See also* **colour plate 6***.*
Top row: *Salus (health) on an* aureus *of Nero (c.65-6); eagle (symbol of Jupiter), Vespasian (76); Ceres (corn, harvests), Titus (79).*
Second row: *Minerva (wisdom), Domitian (92-3); Securitas (safety), on a* dupondius *of Nero (64-8);Venus (love), Titus (79).*
Third row: *Serapis, Caracalla (212); Providentia (forethought), Hadrian (119-38);Victory, Hadrian (119-38).*
Bottom row: *Laetitia (Joy), Elagabalus (218-22); Uberitas (fertility), on an* antoninianus *of Trajan Decius (249-51); emperor holding the banner of Christ,* solidus *of Valentinian I (364-75)*

6 *Roma, as depicted on a brass sestertius of Nero, struck 64-8, at the mint of Rome. This was one of the first base-metal coins of imperial date to depict the personification of Rome in divine form and similar examples were soon in circulation in Britain*

7 *Asthall (Oxon). Ritually-broken votive gifts or scrap? This small settlement has produced no evidence for a cult centre, but such broken pieces of brooches, spoons and a larger object, found on or near a temple site would probably be immediately called ritual gifts*

8 *Bridgeness (West Lothian). Distance slab commemorating 4652 paces completed on the Antonine Wall – painting based on the right-hand panel of this relief, depicting a sacrifice. Four priests officiate over the altar below a vexillum of* II Augusta, *one pouring a libation from a bowl. To the lower left a fifth man beckons on the sacrificial animals while a flute player pipes them along to their fate. The colours are included simply for clarity, and two of the faces are restored – however the original may well have been similarly coloured. Note the griffin head at upper left. Probably c.139-44. Painting: author*

9 *Part of the pediment sculpture from the temple at Bath showing the Gorgon sculpture*

10 *(above left)* Dea Regina, 'Queen Goddess', on a crudely-carved and inscribed little relief found at Lemington, near Moreton-in-Marsh (Glos). The sculpture was probably the do-it-yourself product of an ordinary person who made it for a household or roadside shrine. Height 267mm. RIB 125

11 *(above right)* Lincoln. Altar to the Parcæ, 'Fates', and Spirits of the Emperors, dedicated by Gaius Antistius Frontinus, curator (probably of a guild). RIB 247

12 *(left)* Lincoln, carved relief of a charioteer. Theatre and circus festivals were inextricably linked with the religious calendar. Perhaps from the tomb of a performer

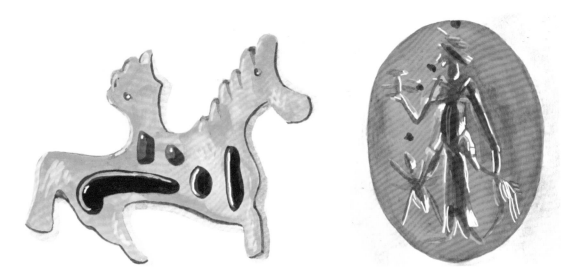

13 *(above left) Horse-and-rider brooch. This type is especially associated with sacred sites, though the identity of the figure is unknown. They may have simply been souvenirs, or also had some sort of protective or amulet function. This painting, based on an example found in Norfolk (Hattatt 1175), restores the original appearance of a shiny bronze plate with red and blue enamel inlays. Actual diameter 32mm. See also **79**.* Painting: author

14 *(above right) Snettisham (Norfolk), unmounted gemstone depicting the rural goddess Ceres, seen here clutching ears of corn, holding a tray of fruit and is accompanied by an ant (often associated with Ceres). Ceres was a popular choice for gemstones and may be linked to the sculptures usually described as Mother Goddesses. Height 15mm.* Painting: author

15 *(below) The Medusa mosaic from the villa at Bignor (W. Sussex). Medusa was a popular subject in Romano-British art and frequently appears as a convenient mosaic device*

16 *Maryport (Cumbria). This painting is based on one of the parade ground altars dedicated to Jupiter, and attempts to reconstruct something of the garish original whitewashed and painted appearance though the exact colours used are not known. Dedicated by Gaius Caballius Priscus, tribune of* cohors I Hispanorum. *RIB 817. Painting: author*

17 *Wotton, Gloucester, tombstone of Rufus Sita, trooper with* cohors VI Thracum. *He died aged 40, after 22 years' service. A sphinx and two lions, traditional symbols of death and the afterlife, overlook the panel depicting Sita as he would have liked to be remembered. The red paint is modern. Probably c.50-70. RIB 121*

18 *Bath, carved relief of Minerva. Appropriately enough, this carving was found in the Great Bath (57). On her breast she wears the Gorgon's mask. Height 69cm*

19 *Marble figure of Bacchus from the villa at Spoonley Wood (Glos). Although classical in style the figure could very well be fourth-century in date and belong to the late aesthetic interest in classical art. Height 400mm*

20 (above) Water Newton (Cambs). Part of the Christian hoard. The feathers are a pagan device, pinned up outside shrines, but here bear the unequivocal Christian Chi-Rho. Length of longest 157mm

21 (below) Icklingham (Suffolk). Lead Christian baptismal font with the Chi-Rho, flanked by W (Omega) and A (Alpha). Diameter 81.3cm

22 *Brading (Isle of Wight). Panel depicting griffins, a cock-headed man and a kiosk. Whether this floor represents cryptic references to exotic mystery religions involving Iao, or has a more straightforward meaning is a moot point (see text and* **144***)*

23 *Littlecote (Wilts). The restored Orphic floor of the triconch hall*

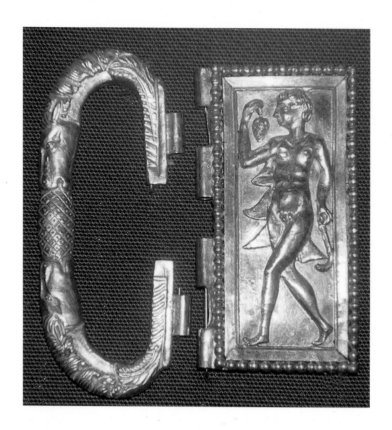

24 *Thetford (Norfolk), gold buckle. Forming part of the remarkable late-Roman treasure hoard associated with a cult of Faunus, the buckle plate depicts a satyr holding a small crook (pedum) and a bunch of grapes. Height of buckle 59mm. Fourth century*

25 *Brading (Isle of Wight). The Medusa floor. Medusa forms the centrepiece but around her a series of scenes depict divine and mythical figures (see **15**) as well as the Four Winds. Is this purely decorative, or symbolic of deeper interests?*

26 *Hinton St Mary (Dorset).*
The central panel depicting the earliest
known representation of Christ (see **152***)*

27 *Uley (Glos), lifesize head of Mercury. Probably*
from the cult statue once placed in the temple

28 Brading (Isle of Wight).
The 'philosopher' panel. The
figure is unknown, but his
equipment suggests someone
symbolic of learning with interests
in science and astronomy

29 Lydney (Glos). Temple
of Nodons, the façade as
it might have appeared.
Painting: author

30 *Mildenhall (Suffolk). The fourth-century Great Dish with its central image of Oceanus, recalling the Bath pediment (**41**). Replete with references to pagan myth, and even Christianity, the treasure is a classic example of how impossible it is to deduce the owner's religious interests from the iconography*

31 *Uley (Glos), temple of Mercury. The original form of this temple is very uncertain but the cella seems to have been open, with the cult statue in the rear ambulatory. The painting is based on the plan for the period c.353-80.* Painting: author

32 *Ancaster (Lincs). Inscription dedicated to 'the holy god Viridios' (see **9**, **70**). Width 52cm*

33 *'Mother Goddesses' from Ancaster (Lincs). This trio was found on the site of the medieval church, near to which two inscriptions recording a god called Viridios have been found (**70**, **colour plate 32**). As they are holding food rather than babies, it may be that they are triplication of a fertility deity like Ceres. Width 47cm*

*79 Horse-and-rider brooch from Nottinghamshire. Note the recesses for enamel, now lost. As is common, the brooch has suffered damage. Compare with **colour plate 13** for its original appearance. Diameter 25mm*

Christian exhortations are known on several different rings. They range from the Chi-Rho (X P – the first two letters of Christ's name in Greek), sometimes reversed to act as a seal, to variations on *Vivas in Deo*, 'live in God' (**colour plates 21 & 26**). This formula is associated with Christianity by implication, and specifically when the Chi-Rho is included as it was on a ring from Richborough. Here a name was included to produce the text *IVSTINE VIVAS IN DEO XP*, 'Justinus, live in God. Christ' (*RIB* 2422.70). But adapting existing exhortations like *utere felix* shows that well-known sentiments were also just appropriated – a lead casket from East Stoke (Northants) includes *utere felix* with a Chi-Rho and a pair of figures identified as angels (see *RIB* 2422.70, 2416.8).

In general, though rings were simply devices that were used for religious references, so were they also used for simple marks of ownership and more importantly as symbols of marriage, friendship and loyalty. Many more rings have designs with no possible religious connotation, or even have no device at all, which is a reminder that religious motifs also belonged to the broader general canon of decorative subjects. This of course applies to the vast bulk of other jewellery, the most common of which are brooches. That these were sometimes deposited as votive gifts has already been discussed, but it is worth considering whether any were manufactured from the outset as talismans. For a start, decorated brooches virtually never depict human beings either as part of the design, or as the shape of the brooch, except the very stylized 'horse-and-rider' brooches which form part of a class based mainly on certain animals.

Horse-and-rider brooches are best known in any quantity from a few temple sites perhaps being sold as souvenirs of a warrior or mounted god, though it is interesting that the god goes unnamed. They also turn up as isolated single finds (**79, colour plate 13**). The motif is known in other forms, for example a carved relief of a horse-and-rider god found at Stragglethorpe (Lincs), but more often as bronze statuettes. The Stragglethorpe relief is 740mm high but only 65mm deep, thin enough to be

80 *Asthall (Oxon). Bronze zoomorphic swimming duck brooch. The feathers were emulated by enamel inlays, now lost. There is no known link with a deity, such as the cockerel with Mercury, and it is impossible to say whether such brooches were primarily decorative or 'votive'. Length 46mm*

mounted as wall decoration in a shrine. With several dedications and references to Mars known from the area, including a shrine to Mars Rigonemetos at Nettleham (Lincs), this horse-and-rider, and perhaps others too, might be a Romano-British version of Mars. But it is equally possible that the brooches simply represent the process of making a journey or pilgrimage to a shrine, rather than a deity. Rather curiously, the Stragglethorpe rider is shown spearing what looks like a long-tailed marine monster of uncertain form. As a matter of passing interest the general region down as far as north-west Cambridgeshire is well known for its fossils of the Jurassic age (*c.*180 million years ago), extending even to articulated skeletons of the plesiosaur, a substantial marine reptile with a long neck and tail and four flippers (see chapter 7 for the discussion about griffins). It is quite possible such remains served as physical manifestations of myth and helped stimulate their representation, though there is absolutely no verification of this apart from a fair number of literary references. They make it plain fossil remains of epic creatures did not go unnoticed in antiquity and were perceived as evidence for gods and their works (for example Pliny the Elder, *NH*, ix.10–11).

Most of the other zoomorphic brooches are horses, hares, hounds and ducks (**80**). Other animals are known, like lions, bulls and eagles but these are relatively rare compared to the core groups. It is impossible to know whether there was a genuine religious aspect to these brooches. The possibility that some were bought for, and worn by, children purely for decoration in connection with perhaps some long-lost tale or favourite story is one worth considering. Cockerels are most likely to be linked with Mercury.

One of the problems of interpretation is that we lack the knowledge to pick up on the iconographic significance of some of these items. If we recall Tacitus' comment that the German Aestii tribe used the boar as a symbol of a mother goddess (*Germania* 44) we can see how impossible it is to know what these animals symbolize without that sort of reference. At medieval shrines like Great Walsingham and Canterbury, a vast array of badges and trinkets were sold as souvenirs of pilgrimages. The difference is that the connection is usually a good deal more obvious to us. Perhaps the best-known examples are those sold as souvenirs of Thomas à Becket, such as those depicting the saint's bust in his bishop's regalia within a representation of Canterbury cathedral. Such badges were often cast in pewter, which made mass-production of identical pieces easy. En route to Canterbury to visit the place where Becket was murdered, pilgrims could pick up souvenirs of wayside shrines. The church of SS Peter and Paul at Charing (Kent), for example, sold little six-sided frame badges with a head of John the Baptist in the middle. In other words, it is entirely plausible to see some Romano-British goods like the horse-and-rider, and other zoomorphic brooches, as an ancient pagan equivalent of this long-established tradition.

As we will see in chapter 7 even members of the Christian community in the fourth and fifth centuries still utilised pagan imagery in their surroundings and writings. This usage affected practically every part of Roman daily life at all times, including all sorts of the smaller artefacts regularly found on Roman sites. Small bronze busts of gods and emperors, or figures of animals, were also manufactured for straightforward daily use as steelyard weights – a fact made perfectly obvious by the suspension loops on their heads or bodies. Others, of similar design and size, were produced as fittings for furniture or even clothing. Typically they still have traces of the rivets that attached them to the furniture. Even knife handles could be treated this way, with some having purely decorative motifs and others figures or busts.

Some of the animals, like the hare, represented on zoomorphic brooches or mounts, drew on a regional tradition of favourite subjects. The phallus, however, was not something that existed in Celtic art or religion, despite the preoccupation with other symbols of fertility, virility and strength. Conversely, the phallus played a prominent role in Roman and Greek religion. As so often, it is the revulsion felt by a Christian writer who recorded his feelings that provides us with some of our evidence. Augustine was particularly disgusted by the god Bacchus in his guise as Liber, the deity slated earlier by Tertullian for the games dedicated to him and marked by licence and indulgence. As we saw earlier, a knife handle from Verulamium's theatre depicts a copulating couple. Augustine cited Varro's account of ancient Italian rites celebrated 'with such obscene licence that male phalluses were made the objects of worship in Liber's honour' (*CG* vii.21). To Augustine's horror the phalluses were traditionally mounted on carts and wheeled around. In the city of *Lavinium* (Lavinio) a month was set aside for the celebrations. Everyone used foul language and innuendo, and the events climaxed with the phallus being displayed in the forum where matrons could place flowers on it.

Augustine, like most of the more uncompromising Christian teachers, had an almost paralyzing dread of anything that alluded to the natural physical fertility of the world and may well have exaggerated some of what he was reporting. This was an instinctive response by diehard Christians who probably had even more trouble dealing with the activities associated with phallic worship. Indulgence, loss of control, and orgiastic behaviour became synonymous in the Christian mind with certain types of pagan worship and festivals. Augustine's description of the phallic festivals shows how much he feared the power of the phallus, illustrating its popularity amongst the wider pagan public. The phallus was also a more general symbol of good luck, and was

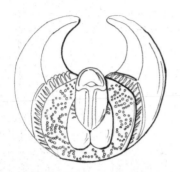

81 *Little Waldingfield (Suffolk), bronze phallus amulet. The phallus projects from what looks like a pair of horns. Diameter 43mm. After Plouviez*

82 *Carved phallus relief from Chesters on Hadrian's Wall (see also colour plate 17)*

used as an amulet to resist the forces of evil like perhaps the personal bronze phallic medallion with suspension loop found at Little Waldingfield (Suffolk) (**81**). It was often depicted on door lintels, to mark the passage from one zone to another, but also appeared as a comic device. In Roman Britain the phallus appears in a variety of wider settings, including reliefs from Hadrian's Wall and decorative motifs on pottery (**82**). In one curious instance at Maryport, an altar shaft had a phallus-shaped top embellished with a carved face on one side, and a serpent on the other.

The phallus was also a symbol of Priapus, a Roman god of procreation, usually depicted as a figure with a prominent phallus and regarded as a protector of gardens (see for example Horace, *Satires*, i.8.2ff). Priapus makes a single appearance by name in Britain, on a relief found probably at the fort of Birrens to the north-west of Hadrian's Wall. The relief depicts the head of a horned god and the inscriptions *[P]riapi m(entula)*, 'the phallus of Priapus', and was perhaps displayed as a guardian wall ornament (*RIB* 2106). With his 'mighty member' and reaping hook he was also supposed to scare off garden thieves (Columella, *DRR* x.33-5).

These categories are all fairly well defined. The horse-and-rider brooches, for example, are very similar to one another and turn up quite frequently. But 'one-offs' still turn up, providing the archaeologist with a perplexing problem of interpretation.

83 *Malton (N. Yorks). Crude relief with a dedication to the Genius Loci ('of the Place'), and exhorting the resident young slave (servule) to make the most of his good fortune 'in this goldsmith's shop'. Diameter 330mm. RIB 712*

A recent find from north Kent, probably from in or near the settlement at Springhead, is what seems to be a handle made fired in red clay. On each of the three sides of the handle is a crudely-engraved figure. One, with a face in the shape of a heart is probably Venus, and another with horns or wings on his heads is perhaps Mercury or a horned god, while the third is less easy to identify (**65**). Perhaps a home-made incense burner, its purpose can now only be guessed at.

Household cults

In chapter 7 we will look at the contentious subject of whether some of the most impressive fourth-century villas of Roman Britain were, first and foremost, cult centres. Religion played a part in every Roman house but it is rare that we find much detailed evidence for what went on. It was routine for the Roman house to have a *lararium* or *aedicula*, shrines where the household gods and ancestors could be venerated much as in the same way people entering a Roman Catholic church will wash their hands in holy water. Every little workplace and home had its own protectors (**83**). The *tazza*, normally a pottery cup on a pedestal with frilled edges, was used for burning incense and is found both in domestic and temple contexts (**84**).

It was also possible to have a shrine on one's land, close by, or even to take on the care of an ancient cult that pre-dated the estate. Pliny the Younger took care of a

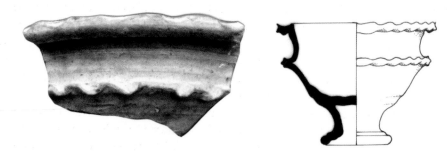

84 *The* tazza, *or incense cup. These vessels were used in shrines and homes as open lamps or for burning incense (see also* **65**). *The sherd is from London, the drawing of a complete example found at Verulamium (after Frere). Height of the complete* tazza, *106mm*

temple of Ceres on his land. He was mindful of the fact that the annual feast day, on 13 September, attracted crowds from far and wide. Here they attended services, made vows to the goddess or recorded the fulfilment of those vows. Pliny had problems though – the visitors had nowhere to shelter from the sun or the wet, and the wooden cult statue was rotting away. He commissioned a friend to help him source building materials and a new statue (*Letters* ix.39).

Pliny was writing around the beginning of the second century. By then a number of rural houses in Britain had begun to adopt a more Romanised form. Lullingstone (Kent) presents a fascinatingly complex building sequence to which we will return because of the celebrated Christian wall-paintings of the late fourth century. But in many ways its earlier history is as interesting. During the second century Lullingstone became a winged-corridor villa overlooking the river Darenth a few yards to the east. In its earlier phase a room with a sunken cellar had probably served as a grain store. Now it was converted. A niche was cut into the wall, a well was dug into the floor, and the niche was painted with nymphs. A new room was built alongside, at a higher level, which looks (in plan) like a Romano-Celtic temple though its function is unknown. A small circular building a little way to the north may have been a garden shrine. The nymph room had become an internal cellar water shrine. At Verulamium one of the townhouses had a subterranean corridor, fitted with niches for lighting, which ended in a statue-sized apse. This, too, was probably a household shrine, though in this case access seems only to have been from outside rather than from within the house. The south wing of the Great Witcombe (Glos) house included a chamber fitted with a font and three niches. Apparently some sort of internal water feature room, it perhaps functioned as a domestic shrine but that does not mean it was the house's primary function.

At some point during the third century the Lullingstone house seems to have been abandoned. This would explain a radical conversion of the nymph room. Two exceptional marble portrait busts, one of which had already been damaged and trimmed down, were deposited on the old steps (**85**). Two pottery vessels were placed in holes cut in the floor for them. One was a small third-century beaker from the

Rhineland with the painted inscription SVAVIS, 'Sweet', placed in there with them. The other was an ordinary kitchenware jar. The beaker had a sheep rib in it, and both were so sited that food and drink could still be placed in them. The assemblage was clearly deliberate, not casual.

The two Lullingstone busts are of critical significance but ascribing motive to their burial with any confidence is extremely difficult. Made of Mediterranean marble at a high level of competence, they are extremely unusual survivals in Britain. They would have passed muster in an upper-class household anywhere in the Roman world. They are clearly portraits, and in a style that fixes them firmly to the middle and second half of the third century. The most likely explanation is that they had been displayed in the house in former times, probably as part of a family's ancestor cult. A few other instances of marble portrait busts found in Britain have also been interpreted as ancestor sculptures (**85**). As genuine individuals, and therefore someone's ancestors, being put in a cellar is strange unless those doing the sealing had no personal connection, but wished to respect them. The excavator's theory that new owners of Lullingstone found the busts – which of itself is strange – and deposited them so that they remained in their 'home' but not in a context which might offend the *feng-shui*, for want of a better term, of the new family but could be visited from time to time. They remained there for the rest of the house's life, though during in the middle of the fourth century new clay flooring covered the votive pots but left the well accessible.

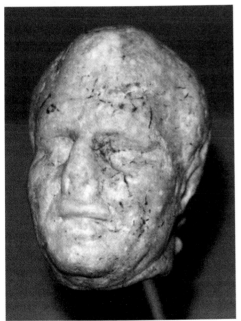

85 *Left: Exeter. Marble bust of an elderly man in the style common in the later first century, though it was found in fourth-century rubble. Probably from a statue of an ancestor once displayed in a household shrine. Height 65mm*
Right: one of the Lullingstone marble busts, of Hadrianic date. Found deposited on steps in the 'Deep Room'. Height 75cm

Around the year 300 the so-called 'temple-mausoleum' was built on the higher ground immediately behind the house. A man and woman, in their early twenties, were buried in lead coffins placed at the bottom of a pit within a wooden chamber. Various grave goods were deposited, including a disc with an image of Medusa, and the pit filled in. A mausoleum with a ground-plan like that of a Romano-Celtic temple's was placed over the top. Villa burials are unusual anyway, but finding them this close and in such an unusually elaborate form is exceptional. One of Martial's *Epigrams* paints a picture of a scene that provides a poetic backdrop to these anonymous remains, and illustrates the enduring importance of a grave to a family and household.

> Faenius consecrated this grove and the pretty acres of cultivated soil,
> to the eternal honour of those turned to ash.
> Antulla is shut in this sepulchre, taken from her family with unseemly haste.
> The ashes of her parents will be mingled in this tomb.
> I'm warning anybody with his eyes on this little plot to give up hope,
> The field will lie subject to its masters till the end of time.
> (*Epigrams* i.116).

It is impossible to know what lay behind the Lullingstone burials – perhaps the unexpected deaths of the owner's eldest son and daughter-in-law from disease? His children? Who knows – but the event was considered important enough to create this unusual architectural feature that will have dominated the villa house throughout much of the fourth century. It would go on to leave a remarkable legacy (**158**).

Lullingstone was, and is, an unusual place. The house was never very big, but the exceptional busts point to ownership in the second century by a man who is likely to have had a connection with provincial administration. London was, after all, only a day's ride away. If so, he will probably have had family origins in Italy, Gaul or Spain. In general it is very difficult to have any idea at all about who owned a villa at any time in Britain, which makes it impossible to know whether evidence of cult is a family of local origin carrying on local traditions or indulging in more classicised tastes, or a family of immigrants bringing classicised tastes with them or indulging in a little local colour. In the military zone though, the love of display and epigraphy provides us with a vast array of evidence for what was worshipped and who by.

5 This seat of Mars

It is often said that Roman Britain can be roughly divided into a military north and west, and a civilian south. That is broadly true but Roman Britain was really a military province throughout, with civilian settlements dotted in and around the military installations. Even then, Roman soldiers were a defining part of all of Roman Britain at all times, discussed in detail in the author's *Eagles over Britannia* (Tempus 2001). Their religious interests are manifested not only in the widespread appearance of gods associated with war and loyalty to the state, but also in the fact that the vast bulk of all religious dedications and imagery from Roman Britain are associated with soldiers and turn up on military and civilian sites (**86**). In spite of this there is little one can do to date the rise and fall of different cults with any meaningful accuracy. Private or military unit inscriptions do occasionally carry dating information and, together with inscriptions referring to incumbent emperors, show that the practice peaked in the middle of the second century and again from the 190s through to the 240s. Undated, crude carvings of gods like the Yardhope shrine in Northumberland could belong to any time Roman occupation is known to have occurred.

These soldiers never numbered more than about 40,000 in Britain, a tiny proportion of the overall population, but to us easily its most conspicuous feature. Soldiers, 'full of strange oaths', are notorious for their superstition and capricious loyalties. In a world where state religion was inextricably linked with the personality, psyche and symbolism of the emperor, military loyalty to the state was expressed in a variety of community and individual ways. The focal point of the Roman fort was the head-quarters building, and its focal point was the *sacellum*, 'the temple where the standard and images of the soldiers are worshipped' (Herodian iv.4.5). Here the unit's political and religious loyalties and identities were merged into one.

Some of these statements were obligatory, others were personal and instinctive. As we saw at the beginning of this book, the invading army of 43 viewed the prospect of crossing the Channel with awe, fear and a terrible sense of foreboding. The progression of the campaign is not of interest here, apart from to bear in mind that as the army fanned out across the landscape, the soldiers found themselves confronted with a variety of new gods and spirits for example at Nettleton (see above, chapter 4). Propitiating, in fact appropriating, these new gods was an essential part of the conquest and was supposed to transfer their protective powers to the Romans. It is very easy to focus on the building of forts and roads and see this as the framework on which taking Britain was based. Of course that was true, but in the Roman military mind there was an intense awareness that coming to terms, and making a pact, with the deities of the new territories was as fundamental a part of success as holding a difficult mountain pass.

86 *A modern re-enactment group recreate the appearance of Roman legionaries in a display at Castleford (W.Yorks), once Roman fort and town of* Lagentium, *'fort of the swordsmen(?)'. The centurion to the left displays* phalerae *on his chest. Each of these plaques was decorated, often with the images of gods and protective spirits. The others bear shields embellished with thunder-bolts, symbols of Jupiter's power. Much of the rest of their equipment, especially parade gear, was decorated with images from Roman religion and myth*

The early years

For the early years of the conquest the visible evidence we have for the troops and their religious sensibilities is really confined to the tombstones, mainly those of legionaries and the auxiliary cavalry units (**35, colour plate 17**), and decorative fragments of military equipment. None of these is dated, but those that belong to units later removed from Britain like *VIIII Hispana* and *XIIII Gemina* must belong to the first century. In *XIIII*'s case they cannot post-date 70, which was when the legion was permanently withdrawn. Gaius Mannius Secundus was a member of the *XX* legion, serving on the governor's staff (*RIB* 293). His burial at Wroxeter is undated and his detachment does not inevitably mean the rest of *XX* was there at all. It is likely that it belonged to the time when this was a fortress of *XIIII*, or perhaps as a base for vexillations of other legions in the late first century. The tombstone bears stereotypical Roman symbols of death and the afterlife. Two lions ride on the top of the stone, flanking a pinecone. Pinecones were common gravestone devices. In myth Atys (see chapter 6) had 'exchanged for this his human form and stiffened in its trunk' (Ovid, *Metamorphoses* x.103). Thus Atys escaped the oblivion of death and lived on. Whether Mannius Secundus gave this much thought before he died, or whether the stone was prefabricated and carved with his names to order, does not matter much. The stone projected a visible form of classical mythical symbolism into the wilds of western Britain, but it remains a rare survival of the period. Most of the others, particularly those from Lincoln, are plain. In common with the period even the exhortation *Dis Manibus*, 'To the Spirits of the Departed', is absent though it does appear on the early tomb of Classicianus at London (**33**).

87 *Kingsholm (Glos). Decorative copper cheekpiece from an auxiliary cavalryman's helmet, decorated with a seated figure of Jupiter. The iron backing has corroded away. Mid-first century. Height 160mm*

Military equipment, by its very nature, is hard to date but a number of examples survive on which gods and heroes drawn from the classical pantheon and myth cycles are depicted. These are unlikely to be really symbolic of individual belief, any more than the similar range of topics found on decorated samian ware. Instead they represent the canon of artistic motifs that soldiers preferred. The military love of decoration was particularly well-expressed by the auxiliary units, reflecting the same tastes which manifested themselves in the cavalry tombstones (**35, colour plate 17**). The decoration was probably the most important factor, at least in designing the equipment in the first place. That the subjects could include a Cupid, on a cheekpiece found in Leicester, the Heavenly Twins (perhaps denoting the owner's birthday) on examples found at Brough (Notts) and South Shields, and Jupiter, on a cheekpiece from the mid-first-century legionary fortress at Kingsholm (Glos), shows a fairly diverse range (**87**). What perhaps is more interesting is whether they were simply discarded when damaged, were awaiting repair or recycling, or whether their decoration had led to a subsequent reuse as votive objects.

In size and imagery these examples bear comparison with the plaques found at sacred sites but none of the contexts would bear this out. An exception is the remarkable legionary shield boss recovered from the Tyne at Newcastle. Originally the property of Junius Dubitatus, centurion with *VIII Augusta*, the boss is a rectangular panel with projecting central boss (**88**). The boss has an image of an eagle and panels on either side have legionary standards in them. Above and below two rows of three smaller panels depict the Four Seasons, a bull, and Mars. The subject matter is a mixture of myth, the Zodiac, militaria and gods. It is possible the boss was designed from the outset as a one-off, for being deposited in the river to give

88 *Bronze shield boss of Junius Dubitatus, of* VIII *Augusta. The decoration is punched in, but shown as solid lines here for clarity. The various figures include Mars, the Four Seasons, and military symbols. Found in the Tyne at Newcastle, and likely to be a practical item later selected by its owner as a votive gift. Height 280mm*

thanks for a safe journey or victory, or was hurled in almost on impulse. *VIII Augusta* was never stationed in Britain long enough for any significant record to survive, but it is known to have contributed to the invasion in 43, and also provided a vexillation for an expedition to Britain under Hadrian. Unfortunately as this kind of item is extremely rare, and virtually unknown from a 'normal' context, it is impossible to know if the decoration was unrepresentative. However, it is becoming increasingly clear that Roman soldiers had considerably more freedom to choose their own favoured motifs for embellishing their equipment, so it is perfectly possible that Dubitatus had commissioned the piece out of taste first and then decided to use it in a votive context. However, there is no certainty that Dubitatus was still its owner when it was thrown into the river because military equipment was often handed on or reused.

The votive context, the provision of a gift to the gods that survives well into our own time in the unconscious habit of hurling coins into pools and wells, lies behind the deposit of almost all the Roman religious artefacts in Britain. At least, that is, the goods deliberately deposited in, or created for, ritual. But it is not until the Roman army began to put down permanent roots in Britain from the end of the first century on that more unequivocal evidence for its religious practices start to appear. Being a creature of routine and habit, the Roman army operated a calendar of religious festivals and holidays, sometimes commemorating events from centuries before like the annual celebration of the birthday of Germanicus on 23 June. These operated as much as ritual declarations of loyalty to the imperial state as they did any kind of private sense of belief. Indeed, it is almost certainly wrong to see the festivals as representing 'belief' as we would understand the word. These public rituals had far more in

89 *Left: Nero, on a gold* aureus *struck in 65-6. Nero came to power with military support but his self-indulgence and consummate failure to fill the role of a supreme commander excluded him from the Roman military religious calendar of deified emperors.*
Right: Hadrian on a gold aureus *of 117-38. Deified after his death, Hadrian was commemorated by the Roman army annually on 24 January as part of their year-round cycle of sacrifices and dedications. His attention to military discipline and his tour of the frontier garrisons helped perpetuate loyalty to him*

common with the kind of church services arranged for, and attended by, institutions like schools or the armed forces in our own time. Failure to fulfil the schedule of appropriate sacrifices and festivals was regarded as a sure path to punishment on the battlefield.

A copy of the Roman military religious calendar survives from Dura–Europos in Syria. The find was exceptional and reflects special arid environmental conditions. Although it is dated to the reign of Severus Alexander (222-35), the list will have been broadly representative of similar examples used throughout the Empire. The list was a mixture of the traditional and additions incorporated to take account of deceased deified emperors and military victories. For example, 7 January was payday and also the day when honourable discharge of veterans took place. Various sacrifices were made to the senior members of the Roman pantheon: Jupiter received an ox, Juno and Minerva cows, and Mars the Victorious, a bull. 24 January was the celebration of the deified Hadrian, to whom an ox was sacrificed, and more sacrifices followed four days later to celebrate not only the day Trajan had become emperor more than a century before in 98 but also the military victories won by Septimius Severus (**32**). Emperors who had failed the army and state in leadership and prestige were excluded from such honours, even though their images continued to circulate on coins (**89**). The year proceeded with a variety of commemorations based around members of the imperial family, past and present, and the state gods. The calendar helped impose structure and homogenise the Roman military community, with all its disparate ethnic members.

90 *Caerleon (Newport), the legionary fortress amphitheatre. The arena was used for entertainment, but also for ceremonial display and the performance of unit rituals, with the resident part of the legion (in this case* II Augusta*) and its auxiliaries in attendance*

The amphitheatres

Just as the urban theatres and amphitheatres played a part in religious celebrations, so did the military arenas. Two of the legionary fortresses in Britain, Chester and Caerleon, are known to have had operational amphitheatres by the late first century (**90, 91**). In fact they differ slightly from urban equivalents in having proportionately larger arenas, and were normally called *ludi*. London also had an amphitheatre by this time, and its location immediately beside the corner of the Cripplegate fort makes it very likely this was built in the first instance for the army though it must have been used by civilians as well.

The Roman army derived much of its sense of purpose and destiny from historical and mythical battles. This is best evoked on what we call their 'sports' or 'parade' armour, particularly beloved of the auxiliary troops. Each legion had its own auxiliary wings attached to it, and garrisoned with it as required. The auxiliary cavalry units excelled at tour-de-force demonstrations of their skill in mock battles that re-enacted great moments from the mythical past, and not even necessarily a Roman one. Equipped with highly decorative armour which allowed the soldiers to pose as legendary foes, such as Amazons, and which also adorned the horses, they engaged in displays of riding and weaponry.

91 *Caerleon, legionary amphitheatre shrine incorporated into the eastern entrance. The niche probably housed a statue of Nemesis (Fate), and a dedication to her*

Whether these events were staged in part in the arenas is not known for certain, but they played an important role in contributing to the spiritual unity of the army. The events are also likely to have included soldiers set against one another in trials of strength and skill, much as modern armies organise regimental boxing matches. If so, soldiers knew who decided their destinies. At Chester, a centurion called Sextius Marcianus set up an altar to Nemesis ('Fate') in the amphitheatre, stating that this had followed a vision (*JRS* lvii, 203). Nemesis also turns up at Caerleon, but in a rather more extreme context. A lead plate names her as Domina Nemesis, 'The Lady Nemesis'. There is no doubt about its connection with the arena as it was found in the amphitheatre. The text reads, 'Lady Nemesis, I give to you a cloak and boots. Let he who brought them not redeem them except with the living matter of his blood' (*RIB* 323). The meaning is not precisely clear and there are other ways of translating it, but it seems to suggest that one competitor is cursing another, by granting the goddess his opponent's clothing, only redeemable by the opponent in the event of his death.

Chester's fortress was unusually big, partly to accommodate an exceptional structure now known as the Elliptical Building. Apparently begun in the late first century, the project was not fully executed and it was more than a century before a different version of the same was completed on the site. Its purpose is entirely unknown though one suggestion it that it was possibly some sort of facility for displaying statues of gods and goddesses. If so, that would be extremely unusual for a fort or fortress. Religion normally played a comparatively minor role within the actual ramparts and was confined to the headquarters buildings. Barracks, granaries and other functional structures took up the rest of the space. Cult activities therefore normally turn up beyond the fort itself like the parade ground and the *vici*.

The northern frontier

The most prominent surviving evidence for military cults comes from the development of the northern frontier region from the early years of the second century. This is also the time from which Roman military religious activity of any sort finds its greatest expression, leading to an exceptional body of material lasting right up to around the middle of the third century.

Maryport, *Alauna*, was an auxiliary fort on the coast of Cumbria. It held a commanding position which allowed it views across the northern Irish Sea towards the Isle of Man and in the opposite direction north towards Scotland. For the moment the fort is only known to have existed from Hadrian's time on, and at least in its first phase as a stone fort belongs to the sequence of military installations that formed part of the Hadrian's Wall system. Archaeologists, particularly those given to exploring Roman military facilities, are normally drawn to the obvious physical remains of the actual forts of the north. Maryport is one of few places where the associated parade ground can not only be identified to this day, but which has also had that parade ground explored. The result was a series of pits, filled with a sequence of about 16 broadly similar altars dedicated to Jupiter Optimus Maximus (hereafter IOM). In almost every case the formula is practically the same. The following text is typical:

I.O.M.

COH I HIS

CUI PRAE

M MAENI

US AGRIP

TRIBU POS

This is an abbreviation for *Iovi Optimo Maximo cohors I Hispanorum cui praeest Marcus Maenius Agrippa tribunus posuit*, 'The First Cohort of Hispanians, commanded by the tribune Marcus Maenius Agrippa, erected this altar to Jupiter Optimus Maximus' (*RIB* 823). The formula only really varies on the others in the name of the commanding officer, who sometimes appears as prefect instead, and in the amount of abbreviation (see also **colour plate 16**). Although to Jupiter, these dedications were as much statements of loyalty to the incumbent regime as to any deity, a kind of Roman equivalent to 'God for Harry! England and St George!' and this is where we see the upper tier in the hierarchy of Roman gods. There might have been an element of choice in the target god. Mars Militarus, 'Military Mars', appears on two Maryport altars similar to the Jupiter series but in both cases dedicated by *cohors I Baetasiorum* (*RIB* 838, 842). Neither is dated and apart from a sojourn on the Antonine Wall between 139-61, and a reappearance at Reculver in the fourth century, little is known about the unit's bases in Britain. It may have been at Maryport only briefly, leaving these altars to stand side-by-side with the Jupiter examples.

Marcus Maenius Agrippa is an important individual in Romano-British history because his career was recorded on an inscription at his home town of Camerinum in Italy (*ILS* 2735). This links his time to the reign of Hadrian, with his tribuneship at Maryport being an early part of a series of posts culminating in the procuratorship of Britain. From this we can deduce that the other similar altars roughly precede and follow the one set up under Maenius Agrippa. The procedure may have been connected with Hadrian's policy of improving military discipline that included regulating duties – this extended specifically to reforming abuses in Britain (*SHA Hadrian* x.3, xi.2). It was later said in the same work that Hadrian 'had contempt for provincial cults, [but] he observed Roman ones with great diligence' (*ibid.* xxii.10).

The Hispanians were not an unusual unit at all – at the time this was a *cohors equitata*, which means six centuries of 80 foot soldiers, and four units of 32 cavalry making a nominal strength of just over 600 men plus officers. The occasion of the altar dedication was probably 3 January, the date on which soldiers swore a vow of allegiance to the incumbent emperor and prayed for his safety and health in the new year, or 11 August, the date of Hadrian's accession. The altars are mostly remarkable for the absence of any weathering that makes it possible to picture the annual ceremony when the new altar was dedicated, and its predecessor buried. Subsequently the site was built over by the fort *vicus*, guaranteeing the altars' preservation until they were excavated in 1870. Unfortunately, little attention was paid to what the altars were buried with, which might have given us some idea of what else went on in the ceremony.

Altars of this type have turned up at many other sites (**92**), but only Housesteads and Birdoswald on Hadrian's Wall have produced similarly large sequences. They show that the ritual continued in the mid-third century. At Birdoswald an IOM altar was dedicated by the resident *cohors I Aelia Dacorum* between 259-68 by the tribune Marcius Gallicus during the reign of Postumus, first ruler of the breakaway Gallic Empire (*RIB* 1882). The last precisely dated altar from Roman Britain is another from the same fort, dedicated in 270-3 by the tribune Pomponius Desideratus (*RIB* 1885). By then the practice of epigraphy was rapidly dying out in Britain and we have few examples of any inscriptions at all apart from milestones after that date. Of course, as we shall see, official paganism had little more than 40 years left anyway.

Jupiter, as king of the gods, was a natural symbol for military religion and allegiance. He appears in many variations across the military north. One of the Maryport sequence names him as IOM Capitolinus, alluding directly to the Capitoline hill in Rome where his temple was (*RIB* 832). The most popular variant was IOM Dolichenus (**93**) though there is no example from Maryport. Dolichenus was an old

92 *(above left) Vindolanda (Northumberland). Altar from the fort dedicated to Jupiter Optimus Maximus, 'other immortal gods', and the Genius of the commandant's house, by Quintus Petronius Urbicus, prefect of cohors IIII Gallorum. The deleted section of text would have carried an imperial title for Caracalla, Elagabalus or Severus Alexander, and thus must belong to the period 211-35. Height 1.37m.* RIB *1686*

93 *(above right) Jupiter Dolichenus at Piercebridge (Durham). Cut down in the Middle Ages for reuse in a church pillar, this was once an altar dedicated by a centurion from Upper Germany called Julius Valentinus. The last line carries the consular date for 217 in the reign of Caracalla.* RIB *1022*

94 *(opposite) Arch pillar from the shrine of Mars Thincsus, Housesteads (Hadrian's Wall). Dedicated to Mars Thincsus, the two Alaisiagae, Beda and Fimmilena, and the Spirit of the Emperor by the 'Germans, citizens of Twenthe'. The pillar probably supported a decorated arch (105). Height 1.82m.* RIB *1593*

eastern sky-god from the Hittite Empire who seems to have been easily conflated by Roman soldiers with Jupiter. He became popular under Septimius Severus (193-211) and especially amongst soldiers from Danube provinces. But it seems from the dedications made in Britain that his appeal easily extended to units from the German frontier legions on detachment at Piercebridge under Caracalla (*RIB* 1022-3) (**93**), legionary legates and centurions as well as more mundane auxiliary units. At Bewcastle, one inscription records a temple to him, the only one known specifically to have been dedicated to Jupiter in Britain (*RIB* 992), while another from Benwell shows that he was being venerated in Britain at least as early as the reign of Antoninus Pius (*RIB* 1330). But Dolichenus seems to have been more susceptible to dedication by individuals. At Greatchesters on the Wall, two altars record the god, one by a centurion of *XX*, and another for a woman whose name is lost, by a man of unnamed status (*RIB* 1725-6). The Sun association emerges in a different way at Carvoran where Julius Pollio set up an altar to IOM Heliopolitanus (*RIB* 1783).

The same seems true of Mars, one of the most popular of all the classical pantheon in the military zone – hardly surprising, but he made little inroad as the subject of dedications by or for whole units. Although he was the god of war he was more generally associated with any sort of active individual military or male pursuit, together with a more ancient association with agriculture. Mars is in fact known to have been worshipped at Wood Eaton, to have had a temple in or near Bath on the basis of a reference on a curse tablet, a probable shrine at or near Stony Stratford (Bucks) and perhaps a *collegium* of worshippers at Silchester, but by far and away his greatest appeal lay in the frontier world. He was particularly popular at Housesteads where a variety of dedications by units or individuals record him. But it was in one of the longest series of conflated identities that the Roman god of war found his public (**94**). Not all of these were demonstrably military in association. Nettleham, east of Lincoln, has produced a slab recording an arch dedicated to Mars Rigonemetos, 'Mars, King of the Grove'. Incongruously, Colchester is the source of a plaque dedicated to Mars Medocius Campesium, 'Mars Medocius of the parade ground' (*RIB* 191). Although Colchester began its life as a legionary fortress the dedication includes a reference to the Victory of Severus Alexander. The most likely explanation is that a soldier on detachment on police or government duties, or a retired veteran, placed the plaque in an urban temple precinct.

In the frontier zone, Mars was associated with a variety of deities whose nature and background is not really known at all, such as the enigmatic Mars Barrex recorded on an altar from Carlisle, perhaps meaning something like 'King of Adversity' by adapting the Latin for King and the Celtic for anger or adversity. Mars appears more frequently in association with Belatucadrus, 'the Fair Killer', though Belatucadrus is even better-known on his own. Cocidius was a warrior god exceptional in being associated with a site with such prominence that it took his name. The fort at Bewcastle, an outpost to the north-west of Hadrian's Wall, seems to have been called *Fanum Cocidi*, 'The

95 *Cocidius. Silver plaque found in the headquarters' strongroom at Bewcastle,* Fanum Cocidi, *'Shrine of Cocidius' (Cumbria). Height 110mm*

96 *(opposite) Altar said to be from Netherby, but probably from Bewcastle, to Cocidius. The dedication is by Paternius Maternus, tribune of cohors I Nervana Germanorum milliaria equitata (an infantry cohort with a cavalry component).* RIB 966

Shrine of Cocidius', a name that only appears once in antiquity in the Ravenna Cosmography. The Ravenna list was drawn up in the eighth century from what seems to have been, by then, old maps. Rivet and Smith (1979) believe that the area north of Hadrian's Wall was based on a Flavian map of the region that had been amended in the interim to incorporate new forts and settlements. *Fanum Cocidi* is unlikely to have been Bewcastle's official name – but if that it is the case, no other name is known. More likely is that this is the name by which the place became popularly known, either because the shrine existed on or near where the fort was built, or the shrine developed afterwards and was later adopted for the fort.

Although IOM makes an appearance at the fort, built originally at least as early as Hadrianic times, it is the discovery of several references to Cocidius, and Mars Cocidius, which makes it certain Bewcastle was once *Fanum Cocidi*. Two silver plaques depicting and naming Cocidius were found in the strongroom of the third-century headquarters building (*RIB 986-7*) (**95**). Given the fort's location on a small plateau, which the eccentric third-century plan covers, it is quite likely that any pre-Roman cult centre lay here and is now undetectable (**96**). The fact that there seems also to have been a temple to Jupiter Dolichenus makes it possible the site's identity was rather blurred in antiquity between being a functional fort and a cult centre. The two plaques portray and name Cocidius as a martial figure armed with shield and spear, which made him naturally similar to Mars though only one altar from Bewcastle does identify him as Mars Cocidius, dedicated by Aelius Vitalianus (*RIB* 993). One suggestion is that the name itself translates partially from an ancient British word for red, *cocc-*, and thus reinforces the connection with Mars. Rivet and Smith refute this on the grounds that the double *cc* never appears on Roman inscriptions mentioning the god (1979, 363). This is a strangely pedantic objection seeing as every inscription we have is a Roman, that is Latinised, transcription of a word previously heard only orally. Under such circumstances it simply isn't credible to make such a point as we have no idea how the name was precisely pronounced or how it was heard at the time.

The Bewcastle plaques were part of a cache of goods sealed in the strongroom cellar that also included traces of an imperial statue, and part of a flagpole display. They were probably once posted on the walls of the headquarters *sacellum*, perhaps along with the bronze letters that were also recovered. Mars Cocidius turns up in several other places in the military zone, most of which are on or near the western sector of the Wall. The Bewcastle dedications are from a variety of sources, but the most interesting is probably Quintus Peltrasius Maximus the tribune. He recorded the fulfilment of his vow after being promoted from the post of *cornicularius* (clerk) (*RIB* 989). Pliny the Elder's remarks on the self-interest that fuelled religious activity echoed down the centuries.

Cocidius was presumably a local warrior god who found his first visual manifestation in a Roman idiom when the army arrived in this part of Britain. By being adopted and absorbed into an association not only with the soldiers, but also their beloved Mars, Cocidius and all he represented was integrated into the protection of Rome's interests rather than her enemies. Mars was merged with other deities in the north. At Bowes, Piercebridge and Chester-le-Street to the east he appears as Mars Condates (*RIB* 731, 1024, 1045). Condates was perhaps an equivalent to Cocidius from the other side of the Pennines, exported by his new fans to the fort on the Antonine Wall at Cramond (*B* ix, 475).

Mars had a peculiar ability to be adapted by the soldiers of the north in a way the other major classical figures did not. Minerva appears at several forts along the Wall, in its vicinity and even at the legionary fortress far to the south at Caerleon, but never conflated with any of the local goddesses who might have shared her interests. Mercury, despite his enormous popularity in the north-western provinces, was little better-off. Well-represented in statuette form throughout Britain, he had a temple in Uley (Glos) and a guild of worshippers at Lincoln (*RIB* 270). He turns up at several

97 *Lead shrine from Wallsend (Hadrian's Wall). Found in a fourth-century context, the figure is thought to be Mercury, though he is accompanied by a dolphin and at the top, a sun god. A pair of doors swung on pivots to close the shrine, which was probably carried as a personal talisman. Height 75mm*

places in the north – at Wallsend, for example, a statuette was dedicated to him by *cohors II Nerviorum*, and the same site has produced a portable little lead shrine of the god (**97**). This makes it likely there was a temple to him somewhere near the fort. Mercury of course was not a warlike god, and this is a reminder that gentler deities also had interests here. Apollo turns up on at a variety of locations in the north, often conflated with other figures. Several altars are known from Corbridge and also one from Ribchester. The latter is datable to 238-44 and shows him as Apollo Maponus, 'the Divine Youth', adopting a British deity.

Although such mainstream figures are not the only ones in the frontier area, and form a significant part of the record, they are easily outnumbered by the very large number of deities which had a specific local identity or which seem to have been brought in from somewhere else. Two gods, undoubtedly being worshipped after Hadrian's Wall was brought into commission, were Antenociticus at Benwell and Coventina at Carrawburgh. The cults were quite different in their practice and focus, but neither had had any visible manifestation – that we can recognise – before the Roman army adopted them. This is crucial to understanding the bias in the record. It is quite conceivable that other deities, whose sacred places were more remote, never entered the Roman military consciousness and so are just absent from what we have to hand. Antenociticus and Coventina only emerge from the primeval mists through the Roman inscriptions that record them, and the reliefs and statues that depicted them. With the passage of the Roman world they disappear once more.

98 *The temple of Antenociticus at Benwell (Hadrian's Wall). Length of the temple is approximately 8.8m. The altars are replicas. The fort of* Condercum *lay to the right and beyond*

Antenociticus was worshipped in a tiny one-room temple just outside the south-east corner of the cavalry fort at Benwell, *Condercum* (**5, 98**). He is known from nowhere else in Britain or any other part of the Roman world. Benwell sat on top of a prominent hill overlooking the land in all directions. We can only speculate now, but perhaps a tree or some other natural feature here was once the object of his veneration. We cannot even be clear about his name. One of the three altars from the temple which name him calls the god 'Anociticus', and is conveniently datable to the period 177-80, a time associated with the full recommissioning of the Wall after the Antonine Wall was finally given up. It seems very likely that the other two altars belong to roughly the same time because one is also dedicated to the Numina Augustorum, which cannot pre-date the joint rule as Augusti of Marcus Aurelius and Commodus, starting in 177. The three soldiers responsible were relatively high-ranking. Two were prefects, and one was a legionary centurion. Tineius Longus, who abbreviated his god's name, was prefect of cavalry, Cassianus (his full name is lost) was prefect of *cohors I Vangionum*, and Aelius Vibius was centurion of *XX*. None of the men is out of context. It has long been recognised that the constant ebb and flow of detachments of units, and individuals, meant there was a procession of different men all the time along the Wall, its forts, and its service roads. It is possible they combined their interests to fund the little shrine, and the statue of the god, whose head survives. But the cult apparently did not last very long. The preservation of the altars of roughly the same period, and the cult head, suggest it was abandoned in relatively short order.

There is no straightforward interpretation of the name Antenociticus. Indeed the 'abbreviated' form, Anociticus, might be the more original. A Quintus Pompeius Anicetus dedicated an altar at Bath (*RIB* 148), raising the possibility that Antenociticus was fabricated on Celtic lines in a Roman idiom out of existing syllables. The name Anicetus is not rare and resembles Anociticus. The American state of Idaho bears a name invented by a US senator to 'sound' Red Indian in origin, and indeed it does. Equally, it is easy to see how Anicetus or Anociticus bear some resemblance to the imperial name Antoninus, perhaps leading to adaptation. Antoninus became part of the imperial name from the reign of Antoninus Pius (138-61) and lasted right into the third century. The altar with the Numina Augustorum text shows that the obscure god was being associated with imperial interests. But the bust shows a clean-shaven male head sporting a pair of horns. The device is known elsewhere in Britain, for example a relief of a stag-headed god found at Cirencester, usually called Cernunnos from a Gaulish inscription.

But busts of unnamed horned gods turn up elsewhere, such as the bust from Moresby (Cumbria). It is quite possible the deity represented is Antenociticus as Cernunnos himself is not recorded in any written form in Britain at all. Having said that, the horn device seems to be one that appears quite commonly in Britain as an addition to a god's features, perhaps as little more than a totemic symbol of fertility and strength. Chesters Museum, not far to the west, for example houses a horned male bust probably from the fort there or nearby. Either way, Antenociticus was not the only god worshipped at Benwell, though his is the only temple. Mars turns up twice, once as Mars the Victorious, and in even more practical vein 'the three Mother Goddesses of the Parade Ground'. A bronze ansate plaque, apparently found nearby, was dedicated by Marus, a tribune of *XX Valeria Victrix* to Hercules. Pierced for suspension it was probably hung outside a shrine or statue near or in the fort (*B* 2001, 392) (**99**).

Carrawburgh is a more remote location than Benwell today but in antiquity the two places were probably little different. Unlike the Antenociticus cult though, Coventina was worshipped outdoors beside the spring that was sacred to her. Coventina's 'Well' was noted as early as 1732, though no one had any idea at the time that it was more than just a source of water which rose a few yards north of the fort and bubbled along the little valley to the south. It was not until nearby lead mining drained the spring in the mid-1800s that it became possible to explore the valley more easily. Lead miners came this way searching for a new source of ore, and exposed the springhead. Happily they left it thus, allowing the local antiquarians to quench their curiosity. The results were dramatic and in short order the well was cleared of its extraordinary contents. Like the spring of Sulis-Minerva far to the south, the well had been the recipient of a tumble of gifts ranging from reliefs and altars to coins and brooches. The reliefs and altars made it certain that the water was sacred to a goddess or nymph called Coventina, or Covetina. A little over 20 altars were found, but the coins are known to have numbered at least 14,000 – had it not been for the locals enthusiastically helping themselves to souvenirs the recorded numbers would have been higher (**100**).

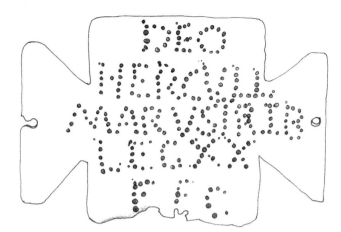

99 *Bronze ansate plaque from near Benwell (Hadrian's Wall). Made for Hercules by Marus, tribune with the XX legion. Diameter 71mm*

100 *Coventina, the Carrawburgh nymph, on a relief from her sacred well by Hadrian's Wall, dedicated by Titus D(omitius?) Cosconianus, prefect of* cohors I Batavorum. *Height 0.74m.* RIB *1534*

101 As of Antoninus Pius, struck in 154 with a reverse depicting Britannia. Although about 16,000 coins were recovered in 1876 from Coventina's Well, around 327 were of this single type, making it likely they were deliberately selected as votive gifts. Many of the coins were dispersed after the find and only around 70 of this type have survived to the present day. The patina of this coin and its general condition make it highly possible it came originally from the Well. Actual diameter 25mm

The surviving finds do a good job of illustrating the range of trouble and expense the pilgrims of the Roman military frontier were prepared to go to (of course we can only guess at the range of gifts of food and drink that might have been thrown in). Those who selected coins generally took care to select worn copper or bronze pieces – the same pattern is found at Bath. Indeed, at Bath the appearance of counterfeit and demonetised pieces suggests that either people kept hold of redundant money for this purpose or there was a trade in bad old money for votive gifts. The 327 instances of Britannia coins struck under Antoninus Pius in 154 and found in Coventina's Well must be linked to an element of selection (**101**). If they were deliberately chosen, that could be either because of the Britannia reverse, or because the issue is notable for its generally poor style and ragged flans making it coin to be spent or disposed of rather than retained. Usage of old or bad coins makes it difficult to use them to build up a chronology of activity on either site. At Bath the list runs right back to a series of largely illegible first-century issues, but this is typical for second-century coin groups which normally included much older coins still in circulation.

Hadrian's coins outnumber those of his predecessors from Coventina's Well, which would be typical for coins circulating in the middle of the second century and later. Late third-century coins are relatively poorly represented. This is known to be unrepresentative of long-period sites, where coins of the Gallic Empire rulers from *c.*259-73 dominate thanks to their vast availability and the speed with which they were discarded in later years (see Great Walsingham in chapter 4). Fourth-century coins are well-represented and, conversely, this is normal for long-period sites. So, on the basis of the coins the spring seems to have been popular in the later second century and on and off thereafter until the end of the fourth century. The latest coin is from the decade 378-88, which could have been deposited at any point up to 40 or 50 years later. Interestingly, coins from the reign of Charles II (1660-85) seem to mark a casual resurgence in the habit of visiting the well from the late seventeenth or early eighteenth century, though it is highly unlikely that any specific knowledge of Coventina had survived.

The site could not be more different from the Antenociticus shrine. Coventina's spring was evidently a place to visit throughout virtually the whole time that Hadrian's Wall was a functioning military installation, and apparently by all and sundry. The objects chosen as 'gifts' range from bronze miniature animals, brooches, buckles, to studs and a handle that might have been originally designed for furniture. The carved stones give us a little idea of the clientele. They included a relief of Coventina dedicated by Titus Cosconianus, prefect of *cohors I Batavorum* (**100**). The unit is testified at only this fort on a number of altars and other inscriptions. But the inscriptions from the well show that soldiers from a variety of other units made offerings here, generally all fulfilling their vows in return for favours apparently granted by Coventina. Crotus, the German, was evidently so impressed with the results that he returned to supply her with another altar. Most of the lettering is crude and together with the variable spelling of the name, and the series of uninscribed altars, probably means that some were made by the dedicants themselves. Two ceramic incense burners were undoubtedly home-made. The text on one translates as 'Saturninus Gabinius made this votive gift for Covetina Augusta with his own hands', and this man was also responsible for the other. Very few of the gifts could really be described as high value apart from a pair of gold rings.

Carrawburgh had several other shrines in the *vicus*. A mithraeum (see chapter 6) was built a little way to the south of the Coventina spring, and just outside its entrance stood a small outdoor shrine to the Nymphs and the Genius Loci, 'Genius of the Place' (**75**). The shrines and temples were simply part of everyday life in the Roman military settlement (**102**). The very large number of inscriptions found at other forts along the Wall and elsewhere in the north show that by and large similar cult activities were probably to be found at most of them. Some were apparently little personal shrines. At Bowness-on-Solway, one [Ant]onianus dedicated a shrine – the god concerned is not known though the metrical nature of the inscription has been utilised to suggest that the missing line referred to the Mother Goddesses. Antonianus promised that if his *fetura quaestus*, literally 'profit-making scheme bore fruit', he would return to gild the letters of his inscription (*RIB* 2059).

Few fort *vici* have been explored in any significant detail but Birdoswald is now known to have had a much more extensive one than previously thought. Buildings stretch out to the east and west of the fort filling much of the land between the Wall curtain to the north, and the steep hillside to the river Irthing on the south. Aerial photography at Old Carlisle, a fort to the south-west of the Wall in Cumbria, has shown up a large and straggling roadside settlement beside the fort. Perhaps this was where a temple, restored by the prefect Lucius Vaterius Marcellus, stood, dedicated to a goddess whose name we only know began with A. At Castlesteads on the Wall

102 *Shrines at Carrawburgh (Hadrian's Wall). The view is east. The road runs directly on top of Hadrian's Wall. The left arrow marks the site of Coventina's Well. The right arrow, further down the valley, marks the site of the mithraeum (117). The slope between them was occupied by the fort vicus, while the fort's west rampart can be discerned as the dark ridge running from left to right behind*

itself, a centurion called Gaius Julius Capitianus restored a temple to the generously all-encompassing Matres Omnium Gentium, 'Mother Goddesses of All Races'. Here too, a recent geophysical survey has exposed a substantial settled area to the south of the fort that this inscription probably comes from.

This process of temple restoration is an interesting one in itself and it helps give us an idea of the history of frontier religion. When the Wall was built soldiers on detachment, and in the new garrisons, will have established shrines and temples almost everywhere. One such established place might have been the probable temple built at or near Wallsend by Gaius Julius Maximinus, centurion of *VI Victrix* (RIB 1305). The statue base which records it is impossible to date, but *VI Victrix* played a major part in building the Wall and the structure might well belong to the first few decades of the frontier's life. Over the succeeding century, the forts and their attendant buildings suffered periods of abandonment and dilapidation. Some were not completed for generations. The early third century was a time when the army in Britain seems to have been ordered to renew and repair its facilities. Part of the reason was undoubtedly the Severan expedition of 208-11, but force of circumstance might have been just as important. Neither of the two temple restoration examples cited above dates itself, but an inscription from Netherby records another temple restoration following its collapse. The unit calls itself *Severiana [Alexandriani]*. This epithet dates the inscription to the reign of Severus Alexander (222-35), and can be associated with a very large number of building inscriptions of all types that belong to roughly 190-240 (*RIB* 979). This was of course quite a long time, but it fits a picture of well-established places now coming up for repair and renewal. Another example of a restored temple is the one at Ribchester (Lancs). Again, the deity's name is lost, but it too can be dated to the years 222-35 (*RIB* 587). Finally, at Old Penrith (Cumbria), a unit probably called the *vexillatio Marsacorum* restored a shrine to the Matres Tramarinae, 'Mother Goddesses from Overseas', at this time as well.

Importing gods

The Old Penrith Marsaci (above) were serving as a vexillation, and are otherwise unknown in Britain. Tacitus mentions them as a hostile tribe somewhere in northern Gaul (*H* iv.56) during the Civil War of 69. Evidently, like so many other former enemies, they eventually capitulated and contributed troops to the Roman forces. The adoption by them of a shrine to the Mother Goddesses from Overseas perhaps reflected a need in their hearts to think of home and how they had come to Britain. We cannot know. In many other cases, the auxiliaries and legionaries of Britain's frontier simply imported their own gods. At the more exotic end, a Greek doctor called Antiochos set up an altar at Chester to Aesculapius and his daughter Hygiaea, Greek god and goddess of health (**103**). Aesculapius was a comparatively common deity in the military world, not surprisingly as the army employed many Greek doctors, but these individual dedications are usually found in the fort headquarters building (*principia*) or commandant's house (*praetorium*) when found in their original

103 *Aesculapius at Binchester (Durham). An altar dedicated by Marcus Aurelius [...]ocomas, medicus (doctor), for ala Vettonum. Aesculapius appears on the right, the figure to the left may be his daughter Hygiaea.* RIB *1028*

157

locations as opposed to having been reused. Caracalla (211-17), for example, sought treatment for his ailments at a shrine of Aesculapius at Pergamum in Asia (Herodian iv.8.3). Dedications to him at the forts of Lanchester (Durham) and Maryport had Greek texts. Another, found recently at Carlisle, only preserves the name of the god but is likely to have been dedicated by a doctor (**15**).

Hercules, of Greek origin as Heracles, was also popular but amongst a wider public (**99**). He was one subject of a dedication by the remarkably generous Marcus Cocceius Firmus, centurion of *II Augusta*. His dedication to Hercules at Auchendavy on the Antonine Wall covered almost all possibilities by adding Mars, Minerva, Victoria, the Campestres and even the rare Celtic goddess Epona (*RIB* 2177). The altar must belong roughly to the period *c*.139-61, but Cocceius Firmus also commissioned three altars dedicated to a variety of other gods, including the 'Genius of the land of Britannia' (*RIB* 2175). Near Mumrills, also on the Antonine Wall, Hercules appears conflated with what must be a local hero deity, Magusanus (*RIB* 2140). Elsewhere in Scotland we find other mainstream classical deities like Diana, to whom an appeal at Newstead yielded *prosperos eventus*, 'favourable results' and was rewarded with an altar (*RIB* 2122).

But the majority of these imported deities are considerably more obscure – to us, at any rate. At Chester the Soteres, Greek saviour gods, were commemorated by the doctor Hermogenes (*RIB* 461). A vexillation of Suebians at Lanchester, during the reign of Gordian III (238-44), took the opportunity to engage a skilled but unnamed sculptor at the fort to make for them a large and imposing altar to their goddess, Garmangabis (**104**). The Suebi is an umbrella name for several German tribes, described in some detail by Tacitus as having a powerful and distinctive sense of identity (*Germania* 38ff). The altar's style is an interesting combination of traditions. The text is conventional and includes a joint dedication to the spirit of Gordian III. By this time it had become acceptable to refer to the spirit of a *living* emperor, and in the case of a military unit it was unwise *not* to; but the altar's capital is an abstracted version of the normal volutes.

104 *Lanchester (Durham), altar to Garmangabis and Gordian III (238-44). Dedicated by the* vexillatio Sueborum *of the fort of* Longovicium. RIB *1074*

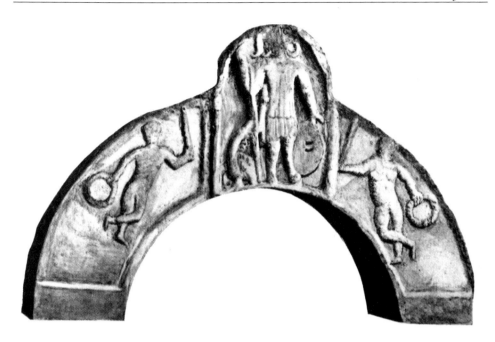

105 *Housesteads (Hadrian's Wall), arch of Mars Thincsus from a shrine in the fort vicus. Mars Thincsus in military garb is flanked by a pair of male companions of unknown identity. The arch is thought to have formed part of the niche that contained the shrine's cult statue. Probably third century. See also* **94**. *Diameter 1.7m*

These are implied, but only just, by creating a pattern from triangles and spoked wheels. Several inscriptions from the fort are dated to the reign and they all conform to the same style of lettering, suggesting that there was a particularly accomplished sculptor in the resident unit, *cohors I Lingonum*. The altar was found about 250m north-west of the fort where it perhaps formed part of a shrine. Garmangabis was naturally not the only deity at Lanchester. A little gold ansate plaque, found on the other side of the fort, was given as a gift to Imperial Mars and is likely to have been attached to a statue or a shrine wall – at least four more altars also record Mars. Other inscriptions from Lanchester record a more conventional array of Aesculapius, Fortuna, IOM, Mithras, Silvanus, various Geniuses and even the rare Regina ('Queen Goddess').

Garmangabis had a particularly unforgettable name, but she was just one of several strange figures who arrived with the forces stationed here. At Housesteads Mars Thincsus appears in a dedication on a square pillar from a temple. He was a German variant on Mars, with Thincsus meaning something connected with the people's assembly of representatives. Appropriately he received the gift from 'the Germans, citizens of Twenthe', and was depicted on a one-piece arch from the fort in association with a pair of male companions (**94, 105**). Mars Thincsus had two female companions Beda and Fimmilena, known as the Alaisiagae, also recorded on the inscription. This makes interpretation of the two male figures rather inconclusive. The temple probably stood in the vicus to the south of the fort. The *cohors II*

106 *Housesteads (Hadrian's Wall). Altar to the god Hvitris, dedicated by Aspuanis or Aspuansis for himself and his family. Height 330mm.* RIB *1603*

Tungrorum at Birrens included men drawn from the German tribe called Condrusi. They set up an altar to Viradecthis, known from several inscriptions found in the Rhineland in the vicinity of where Caesar places the tribe in the *Gallic War* (vi.32). There seems to be no doubt about the Birrens text but, as we have seen already, other continental inscriptions provide different spellings.

The variation in spelling reflects the obscure origins of this kind of deity but none more so than the remarkable variations on Hvitris/Veter. This spirit appears in singular or plural form, and even as male or female. Spellings include Hueeteris, Vheteris, Votris and even include a conflation with a much rarer god called Mogons, thought to mean something like 'Great One'. The Veteres turn up at various places in the north but seem to have been particularly attractive to soldiers at Carvoran, Housesteads (**106**) and Vindolanda. Almost invariably recorded on poorly-carved altars, they seem to be prime examples of spirits attractive to individual soldiers, rather than ones popular amongst units. Few of the Veteres' fans name themselves and even fewer specify their status in life. Julius Pastor, an *imaginifer* with *cohors II Delmatarum* is the only man to provide us with all this. In just one instance the deity appears further south, on a plaque found at Thistleton (Rutland), interestingly dedicated by a woman called Mocuxsoma, a name likely to be of Germanic origin. The virtual restriction of the variations to the military frontier, in spite of the very large number of dedications must mean that these amorphous deities were either imported or belonged to the local landscape.

The Veteres illustrate the enthusiasm that some frontier troops had for making and dedicating these offerings and dotting them about the landscape. Find-spots suggest that almost any place would do if the circumstances were right. Mars Cocidius received an altar from a centurion in *cohors I Batavorum*, erected near milecastle 59 on Hadrian's Wall. The Mother Goddesses were commemorated on an altar near milecastle 79. Perhaps these followed special experiences though we hardly ever hear about these. At Kirkby Thore, a woman called Antonia Stratonis also had a vision and set up an altar to Fortuna Servatrix, 'Fortuna the Deliverer' (*RIB* 760). At Risingham an unnamed woman erected an altar to the Nymphs, having been told to do so by a soldier. The soldier had had a dream in which he was instructed to tell her to do this (*RIB* 1228, and see also 153). We can only imagine what personal experiences, tragic or happy, which had led to such cryptic dedications.

Hunters

Some remote altars have simple explanations. On the banks of a stream at Eastgate three miles (5km) from Stanhope (Durham), Aurelius Quirinus dedicated an altar to Silvanus (**3**). Quirinus is known from dedications at Lanchester some 12 miles (15km) to the north-east to have commanded *cohors I Lingonum* there under Gordian III (*RIB* 1091-2). We know from the Vindolanda letters of the late 90s that hunting was a popular pastime for officers and, as a woodland god, Silvanus was a popular subject for officers away from base. The altar was perhaps just a nod at a pleasant setting, but Quirinus may well have been on a hunting expedition. Perhaps he knew about the *collegium Silvanianorum*, 'guild of Silvanians', made up of men from *II Augusta* and recorded on an altar at Corbridge (*RIB* 1136, reread in *RIB95*, p.780).

Silvanus was an ancient Italian god of all trees and woodland, his name being an expansion of the Latin for forests and woods, *silva*. An inscription from Gaul names Tiberius Claudius Chrestus, prison jailer at *Lugdunum* (Lyons), who had dedicated an altar and image (*aram et signum*) of the god appropriately *inter duos arbores*, 'between two trees', in an *aediculam*, 'little shrine' (*ILS* 3549). This text is a rare instance of being more descriptive of an altar's context and is a reminder that isolated altars were originally erected in locations which now bear no relation to their ancient appearance, obscuring their original purpose. Silvanus is also called by Virgil the 'god of fields and flock' (*Aeneid* viii.600), and in some contexts he was regarded as a rural version of Mars. This explains his association with one of the other Mars alter-egos, Cocidius, on an altar from Risingham and the conflation of the two on another at Housesteads (*RIB* 1207, 1578). These are examples of our inclination to distinguish spiritual identities, which misses the reality that the people who made the dedications were simply using different labels for broadly the same things.

In an even more remote and windswept location some miles to the south, and still difficult to reach today, is the Eller Beck on Scargill Moor. Only two miles from the fort at Bowes, the stream trickles through bleak moorland that was once ideal hunting territory for the officers of the fort known as *Lavatris* (**107**). Several altars have been recovered from a shrine set up here, two giving the unit name of *cohors I Thracum*, erected by two prefects, one centurion, and an individual whose name and rank is lost. The god was clearly a local deity, unknown anywhere else. He was called Vinotonus and conflated with Silvanus on two of the altars, one as Vinotonus

107 *Scargill Moor (Durham), near the fort at Bowes,* Lavatris. *The view is to the south across the Eller Beck up the East Black Sike where the little shrine to Vinotonus Silvanus was built and embellished with altars left by visiting soldiers (inset lower right, as displayed today at Bowes Museum, Barnard Castle). Remote and windswept, there is nothing to see at the site now but it retains a remarkable sense of ancient wilderness*

Silvanus Augustus (*RIB* 732, *B* xix, 491). Vinotonus may be derived from the word *vin-* found at the beginning of numerous Romano-British place-names and which means something like 'mountain' or 'hill'. One of the men responsible was Lucius Caesius Frontinus, prefect of *cohors I Thracum*, adding that he was from Parma in Italy (*RIB* 733). This had perhaps provoked his interest in Silvanus and perhaps establishing the shrine.

The Genius

One of the most flexible of all Roman religious concepts imported to Britain, and which found its broadest expression in the military north, is the Genius. The Genius was essentially a guardian spirit that Horace described as the 'companion who rules our birth star, the god of human nature, but mortal for each single life' (*Epistles* ii.2.187). The Genius was thus a different kind of god whose existence was tied to the life of the individual it protected. It resembles the Christian concept of the 'guardian angel'. But a Genius could be associated with almost any entity, including inanimate objects or places. The Genius Loci, 'Genius of the Place', is perhaps the most abstract, and draws on the concept of creating a named deity out of the spiritual identity of a location or area like Brigantia. Equally, the name may really be a synonym for the unknown name of a local deity, a catch-all term which satisfied the pagan mind-set. St Paul criticised the Athenians for their superstitious belief in *Agnosto Theo*, 'the unknown god', recorded on an altar there (*Acts* xxvii.23). One exceptional instance of a possible candidate still in situ is the sculptured relief apparently depicting a Genius at Eagle Rock, West Lothian, close to the Antonine Wall fort at Cramond. It was presumably carved at the behest of a soldier, or unit, based on the Wall in the middle of the second century.

The Roman army was very flexible in its use of the Genius, for example the Genius Centuriae, 'Genius of the Century', found at Carlisle and Chester (*RIB* 944, 446-7) (**108**). Other inscriptions show it applied to specific units like the Genius *alae primae Hispanorum Asturum,* 'Genius of the first cavalry wing of Hispanian Asturians' at Benwell (*RIB* 1334) and we can take it for granted that every unit will have at some time seen a similar dedication. Many of those that can be dated seem to belong to the third century, for example the Genius *legionis II Augustae* at Caerleon in 244, and the Genius *legionis XX Valeria Victrix D[eciana?]* probably for 249-51. Even the less rigorously organised auxiliary units had their own Genius. At Burgh-by-Sands, a *numerus* of Aurelian Moors included their Genius on an altar and provided the imperial epithets of Valerian and Gallienus that dates the text to 253-8. It was common for the Genius, in whatever guise, to appear as a subsidiary or associate beneficiary with one or more other gods. On an altar at Housesteads soldiers of *II Augusta*, serving as *agentes in praesidio,* 'the powers in the camp' (i.e. garrison duty) included the Genius huius Loci, 'Genius of this Place' alongside IOM and Cocidius (*RIB* 1583).

108 *Vindolanda (Northumberland). Altar to the Genius of the* Praetorium *(commandant's house), dedicated by Pituanius Secundus, prefect of cohors* IIII Gallorum. RIB *1685*

Genii Cucullati, warriors and wheels

Altars like those dedicated to Silvanus at least give us some idea of the religious purpose of the dedication. We can infer something from the god's properties and powers, and the setting in which he or she was worshipped. The northern frontier has also produced vast quantities of anonymous religious sculpture, often of types found elsewhere in Britain, but found here in large quantities. A very few survive in their original settings. A figure of Minerva is still visible at Edgar's Field, Chester, in what was once the fortress *canabae* (extra-mural settlement). The enigmatic armed figure known today as 'Rob of Risingham', clearly a hunter god, may be a representation of Cocidius who, as we saw above, appears on an altar from the fort (**109**). Another similar relief, perhaps removed from the vicinity, survives further to the east of the fort now built into a farmhouse. At Yardhope (Northumberland), a modest little rock shrine preserves a relief of warrior god with shield and spear. It probably represents Mars or Cocidius, or both, since it resembles the Bewcastle plaques but it is entirely possible another, unknown, god is depicted. At Corbridge yet another variant on this theme appears in the form of a pottery mould that was used to make plaques depicting a warrior god onto jars (**110**).

The spoked wheel is a motif that appears in a variety of contexts. Sometimes the spoked wheel was held by a god, or simply included as a feature — for example on a variety of altars dedicated to Jupiter, the Garmangabis altar (**11**, **104**), roof antefixes at the legionary fortress of Caerleon, or even on a tombstone from the same site (*B* 1997, 458). A niche in the fort bathhouse at Castlecary (Stirlingshire) on the Antonine Wall produced a small and crude relief of Fortuna with cornucopia, rudder, and spoked wheel. It also appears as a votive miniature from temple sites further south, and on head-dresses from the temple at Wanborough (**77**).

109 *Rob of Risingham. The surviving part of the relief near the fort at Risingham (Northumberland) shows a warrior god, perhaps Cocidius. Old engravings show that he was equipped with a quiver and bow. The original figure was around a metre in height*

110 *Pottery mould from the military supply-base and town at Corbridge (Northumberland). A warrior god, identified as Taranis, is depicted with club and shield, alongside the spoked wheel motif, considered to be a sun symbol. The drawing shows what the mould produced. Height 120mm*

The wheel motif had fairly simple and obvious associations as a solar symbol, often described as being somehow an exclusively 'Celtic' item, usually in a mystical and reverential fashion. In classical lore the spoked wheel was linked directly to the sun god's chariot wheels, made for him by Vulcan, while the circus itself in popular etymology had been linked to Circe, daughter of the Sun, as the first circus impresario in honour of her father (Tertullian, *de Spectaculis* viii.2). In myth, Phaethon was the son of Apollo. When allowed to ride Apollo's chariot, Phaethon lost control and was brought down by Jupiter with a thunderbolt. This neatly links Jupiter to the wheel symbol that not only appears as a decorative feature on some of the Maryport Jupiter altars, but also might explain an altar from Chester, dedicated to IOM Tanaris (sic) (*RIB* 452). This is probably the Taranis sky-god deity that appears on several inscriptions from Gaul and in Lucan's *Pharsalia* (*ILS* 4623-5; i.446). The Corbridge pottery-plaque figure has been identified as Taranis, though it is not exactly clear whether nothing more than a circular argument is in operation. Coinage struck by the Atrebates in the years preceding the Roman invasion includes several examples where the spoked wheel is part of the decoration, but usually alongside a horse. This rather suggests that the wheel symbolizes the chariot as well as the sun – especially as these coins have a bust on the other side identified as Apollo. The basic coin design can be traced easily to Roman Republican silver denominations, and ultimately Greek issues. Even so, the tradition goes back much further than that. The Trundholm 'sun-chariot', found in Denmark, dates to the fourteenth century BC. The bronze group consists of a horse, itself mounted on two axles with spoked wheels on either side, towing a chariot, containing a gilded solar disk, also with spoked wheels.

In the *Metamorphoses*, Ovid provides a version of Phaethon's catastrophic joy-ride and describes 'the wheel rims with a golden curve, and an array of silver spokes' (ii.107-8). There is no reason to doubt that this was also drawn from an older and more primeval tradition that contributed to both Roman and 'Celtic' canons. Equally, the sun's resemblance to a spoked wheel hardly needs a genius to see, and parallel development and use of the same symbol is just as possible. The Corbridge pottery-plaque figure is an interesting example of the kind of religious motif that attracts modern attention about its significance. The imagery is real enough, but whether it ever really amounted to anything more potent than something like a St Christopher key-ring is just beyond us to tell. Equally, the spoked wheel was also aesthetically pleasing and its presence need not invoke anything more potent at all – a bracelet from the Backworth (Northumberland) treasure includes a fastener in the form of a spoked wheel, repeated on necklaces from the hoard. In this sense, the use of the device marked the group as a cohesive matching collection or set.

But by far and away the greater part of surviving religious sculpture and other imagery from the frontier area comes from components of demolished buildings, and statuary or reliefs that once embellished shrines. There are so many examples of these that it would be impossible to even start to describe them in detail. The more compe-tently executed carvings, like a relief of Victory in a niche from Housesteads, are the easiest to interpret. Found within the fort, the Victory is large enough to have decorated one of the administrative buildings or one of the forts. Victory was a common subject for dedications on altars, including one from Housesteads, given by an anonymous *custos armorum*. She may have been the subject of the astonishing building at Carron, just north of the Antonine Wall. The beehive-shaped stone building survived until the eighteenth century so there is no real doubt about its shape and dimensions, and it was reputed to have contained a statue of Victory. A similar building was depicted on a relief from Hadrian's Wall, accompanied by a Victory (**111**).

At the other end of the scale are the far more enigmatic and spectral figures of the Genii Cucullati, 'the hooded geniuses' – though in fact no inscription from Britain ever accompanies them. But carvings of these diffident cloaked gods are well known on the continent, and in Britain turn up principally on the Wall area and around Cirencester way to the south. The latter is probably connected with the easily-carved local stone which has contributed to a large body of local sculpture – we cannot estimate how many wooden versions might have been in use elsewhere. Conclusions drawn about this kind of distribution pattern tend to overlook this aspect. One other pocket of religious sculpture in Lincolnshire is centred on the Ancaster stone area – the same Jurassic limestone as Cotswold stone.

Triplication was a common 'Celtic' theme, which has of course survived into Christianity in the form of the Holy Trinity, and was a common stylistic feature applied

111 *Relief from
Gilsland (Cumbria)
near Hadrian's Wall.
This relief shows a
building similar to
the Carron 'temple',
accompanied by a flying
Victory. Although this
is an old engraving,
the piece is extant and
probably formed part of a
dedication slab. Diameter
1.1m*

112 *Nymphs from the Shrine of Coventina, Carrawburgh on Hadrian's Wall. The figures represent
Coventina and two attendants, a triplication of Coventina herself, or just three generic nymphs.
Diameter 0.95m*

to certain other deities. It also appears in the trio of nymphs found in Coventina's
Well (**112**), and amongst representations of Mother or Fertility Goddesses. On rare
occasions, quadrupling occurred – a group of four of these female deities was found
at Blackfriars, London. However, tripling the Genii Cucullati seems to have been a
peculiarly British phenomenon. A Housesteads set of the so-called Genii Cucullati
were found built into a niche of a vicus building, and over a small hoard of coins said
to terminate in 229. Despite the crudity of the carving a ludicrous amount of significance has been read into the features of these individual figures. One theory claims
that the middle figure is distinguishable as a male and the others as possible females to
act as fertility symbols partly on the basis of relative size. One of the more subjective
observations about crude Romano-British sculptures, this totally ignores the sheer

167

113 *Genii Cucullati. Note that the figure on the right is slightly smaller than the other two. That this was entirely a consequence of the sculptor's incompetence and right-handedness rather than any deeper significance is certain, as the sculptor is the author of this book. It was produced from a slab of Cotswold limestone in 50 minutes though he had never done anything like this before. Further experiments also showed that hooded figures were far easier to produce than anything else. The result is a reminder that many low-grade sculptures were probably the one-off products of amateurs and that assuming symbolism in marginal differences in size and treatment is unwarranted*

simplicity of the execution and the hit-and-miss consequences of carving at this level of skill. It is impossible to tell what sex an amorphous hooded figure represents, if it represents either sex at all. The erratic nature of this kind of elementary carving is shown especially well by the mismatched sizes of the three figures. The right-hand figure is small because not enough room was left for it after producing the other two (**113**). This is a normal consequence of the sculptor being right-handed, or vice-versa for a left-handed sculptor. Even the powers of the Genii were only vaguely linked to fertility in the way that some are portrayed carrying eggs, and a seated woman accompanies the trio from Daglingworth (Glos).

The Roman army's accommodation of gods and spirits is really a measure of the tolerance, or cynical appropriation, exhibited by the Roman Empire. Our own capacity to measure the extent of cult in the northern wilderness is limited to the material which bears enough lettering or features to allow us to work out some of who was being worshipped and how. The series of unidentified male heads found at various locations along the Wall, for example, could represent innocuous statues of individuals or gods about whom we know nothing. Others would have it that they were linked to some sort of Celtic 'head' cult – plausible but, frankly, quite beyond us to tell. What we have scarcely touched on here though was the welcome the military world showed to the exotic gods from the East. The military record, once more, provides us with more evidence for them (apart from Christianity) than any other part of Roman Britain.

6 Stewards of the Mysteries

By the early third century, Rome's political stability and military success was on the wane. Even Britain's garrison became involved in political machinations against Commodus during the 180s, and soon afterwards sponsored the disastrous attempt of Clodius Albinus to become emperor in the civil war of 193-7. Conventional religion was regimented, and primarily concerned with the rigid performance of ritual. That process began to look flawed as imperial prestige was debased and the frontiers came under increasing pressure. It also offered very little in the form of emotional involvement, escapism through ecstasy, and the chance of a glorious afterlife.

The exotic mystery gods of the East offered an alternative to people who felt existing religions had let them or the state down, but interest in them had been already growing for a long time. In the mid-first century BC, Cleopatra's relationships with Caesar and Mark Antony were as notorious for where she came from as for her personality. Egypt was a special place in the Roman world, retained as a private imperial possession. Here dark and brooding religion was trawled and explored by Roman tourists and soldiers stationed along the Nile and into the desert. But Egypt was just one source of exotic novelty. There were other cults to choose from in the East but a common theme was some sort of posthumous resurrection, redemption usually through the acts of some Earth-bound intermediary, and a challenging regime of initiation and rites that offered disciples the secret of an afterlife. During the second and third centuries they became increasingly popular, especially amongst the soldiers, but they had been a part of Roman life from as far back as the third century BC.

These religions included Mithraism, and of course that based around the executed radical from Palestine, Jesus Christ. There are some about which we know practically nothing. Ancasta, for example, recorded on a single altar from Bitterne (Hants), is a unique record of a goddess unheard of anywhere else (*RIB* 97). The name is not obviously Celtic, but there is no easy solution to what she stood for or where she came from. Bitterne was a port town but the dedicator's name, Geminus son of Manius, tells us nothing more though a Caius Manius is known from North Africa (*ILS* 9395). Ancasta was perhaps an exotic, but very parochial, import brought to Britain by a man who made landfall at Bitterne.

Exotic cults had a number of important differences from mainstream Roman religion. Some were based more on congregations, made up of adherents who had been admitted to the religion through some sort of initiation or teaching ceremony and were the only ones party to the rites. In the mystery religions ritual, carried out by the congregation, was more likely to be conducted in private inside the temple or church, rather than outside as was the custom with classical or Celtic cults. This was partly to do with being discreet and avoiding discovery, but in the long-term this would become the norm.

The deification of the emperors, a process called *apotheosis*, had also become more ambiguous. This was inextricably linked with eastern influence where the concept of the ruler as a living god was widespread. As we saw earlier, the posthumous deification of an emperor was a privilege he had to earn. But by the third century it had become much more routine, and some incumbents like Elagabalus (see below) were reluctant to wait until death to enjoy the status, blurring their identities with other gods. It also provoked increasing tensions with mystery cults, particularly Christianity, which were not prepared to acknowledge divine rulers. Herodian called *apotheosis* 'normal practice' on the death of an emperor. A model of the deceased was created and laid on a sham death-bed. The final illness and death was then re-enacted, followed by an elaborate series of ceremonies and a cremation of the model in a pyre from which an eagle was released as a symbol of the emperor's soul rising up to the gods (Herodian iv.2, describing the burial of Septimius Severus in 211). Trajan Decius (249-51), an opportunist soldier-emperor with an insecure power base, issued a long series of coins in the names of his deified predecessors. Despite his own modest military origins, he thereby sought to link his own fly-by-night dynasty with a dynasty of spirits of the past.

Egyptian gods

Today, ancient Egypt is celebrated as the most exotic and mysterious part of the ancient world. The Egyptians' obsession with death and the afterlife, manifested in their strange temples, pyramids and tombs, goes hand-in-hand with tales of weird beast-like gods, tomb-robbers, warrior pharaohs and mystics. In many ways, the beguiling nature of Egypt's bewildering antiquity is one of the oldest phenomena in western history. The Greeks and Romans were just as fascinated by this remarkable country, strung out along the Nile, as we are. Herodotus' fifth-century BC account of the country's history and monuments publicised Egypt's idiosyncrasies. Over succeeding centuries, as Egypt was brought into the Mediterranean orbit when it was conquered by Alexander the Great and later the Romans, a succession of wide-eyed tourists made their way up the Nile. To this day, some of the pharaonic tombs of the Valley of the Kings bear the graffiti of their classical visitors. Roman emperors were portrayed as Egyptian rulers in reliefs that, apart from their names, are all but indistinguishable from Egypt's mighty pharaonic past (**114**).

In the year 19, Germanicus, brother to the future emperor Claudius, toured Egypt. Tacitus described how Germanicus was transfixed by the stone 'colossi of Memnon' which stand to this day beside the road to the funerary temples of Western Thebes. The cracked stone of one made sounds as the sun rose, and was consid-ered a wonder worth travelling to see. Germanicus was a man of major political significance but in the cosmopolitan Roman world, military and civil careers at

114 *Egypt, the Temple of Hathor at Dendarah. Far from being a product of ancient Egypt, the relief is of early second-century date. The 'pharaoh' to the right is the Emperor Trajan (98-117), and the work reflects the awareness of Egypt's remote past, its gods and traditions in the Roman world*

any level could involve a posting in Egypt. The first mounted cohort of Thracians (*cohors I Thracum equitata*) is testified in Britain on several occasions in the second and early third century, for example 122, 158, 178, 197-202, and 205-8. But the same unit also seems to have spent time in Egypt (Alston, 183). The same applies to *cohors II Thracum*. Likewise, Egyptians themselves were recruited into the Roman armed forces, though we have no instance of an individual in Britain. At Cadder in Scotland, a prefect of an auxiliary unit called Lucius Tanicius Verus made a dedication (*RIB* 2187). His unusual name allows a possible ancestor of his to be identified in Egypt (*ILS* 8759b).

Part of this cultural contact included the adoption by the Roman peoples of Egyptian gods. As early as the third century BC, the cult of Isis had reached the Greek colonies of southern Italy and in 105 BC the port town of Pozzuoli, near to where the Roman fleet was based at Misenum, had a Serapeum (*CIL* i.2.698). She continued to have appeal in spite of her association in early imperial times with Cleopatra. Isis was closely linked to fertility and rebirth of the land through the annual inundation of the Nile, but her protection of marriage and navigation meant that her appeal became more universal, spreading even to Britain.

The third-century lawyer and Christian apologist Minucius Felix found the worship of Isis difficult to understand. He could not see what pleasure or solace

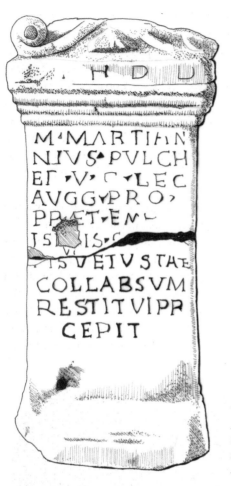

M·MARTIAN
NIVS·PVLCH
EГ·V·С·LEC
AVGGYPRO›
PPAЄT·ЄNᴸ
JS[ ]IS·
TSVETVSTAᴱ
COLLABSVM
RESTITVIPR
CEPIT

115 *London. Altar naming the governor Marcus Martiannius Pulcher and his restoration of a temple of Isis. Pulcher was probably a third-century incumbent and is otherwise unknown. Height 1.22m*

there was to have in a cult where Isis annually bemoaned the loss of her son Horus, and then celebrated his discovery. As far as he was concerned it was ridiculous to spend time mourning a god, or worshipping a god who was being mourned. 'Yet', he reluctantly concluded, 'these ancient Egyptian rites have now turned up in Rome so anyone can dance like an idiot to the sistrum of Isis . . .' (*Octavius* 23).

During the first century AD, the worship of Isis grew in the Roman world. Her relatively early arrival in Britain is testified on the remarkable London flagon graffito (**36**). Found in Southwark, the vessel states clearly an address in Latin that means, 'at London, by the temple of Isis'. Of course, the text could significantly post-date the flagon's late first-century date, but the evidence of a temple seems to be beyond doubt. Astonishingly, the temple's continued existence, or that of another in London, was confirmed by the discovery of an altar built into London's late riverside wall (**115**). It names Marcus Martiannius Pulcher, and tells us he was the governor. The text cannot be precisely dated, but the early third century is likely. Pulcher commemorated his rebuilding of a temple to Isis (*B* 1976, 378-9, no. 2). It fits the broader context: Isis worship reached an Empire-wide peak of popularity in the third century.

Thanks to an account by Apuleius in the *Golden Ass*, we know what took place in the principal Isis festival. London will have been home to the sacred procession of Isis in which her devotees scattered the road with flowers and perfume. Meanwhile music and trumpets heralded the approach of the gods, apparently men and women with appropriate head-dresses. The centrepiece was the sacred boat of Isis, bearing its written vow of a new and prosperous sailing season. The boat was then sent out to sea, and the procession returned to the temple to store all the holy images until the next time. The ceremony was closed with a vow of loyalty to the Roman state and emperor, and to ships across the Roman world. Several iron rattles found in Moorgate Street might conceivably be *sistra* from an Isis cult, but it is as likely that they are children's toys.

In the fourth century the legitimisation of Christianity displaced the worship of Isis along with other pagan cults (though there were revivals). But some of her attributes, and even imagery, were effortlessly absorbed or paralleled by Christianity. Representations of Isis suckling the infant Horus are almost indistinguishable from images of Mary with the infant Jesus. Isis was perceived a saviour. She had after all reunited the dismembered parts of her dead husband Osiris and achieved a sort of quasi-immaculate conception through her fabrication of his missing penis. For all her exotica, Isis ultimately was something close to a conventional mother goddess and it is very easy to be distracted by the minutiae of the cult and overlook this basic appeal.

116 *York. Dedication of a temple to Serapis by Claudius Hieronymianus, legate of* VI *Victrix. Probably very late second century or the first few years of the third.* RIB *658*

Inscriptions from elsewhere in the Roman provinces link the worship of Isis variously to other Egyptian gods like Serapis, and the messenger god Anubis as well as the existence of *collegia* of worshippers. Serapis was a late Egyptian deity created as a hybrid under the Ptolemaic Greek rulers of Egypt and based on the bull god Apis. Amongst his properties he was believed to have healing powers, sometimes transmitted through the emperor's hand (Suetonius, *Vespasian*, vii.2-3). Hadrian's biographer states that during the reign Apis underwent a revival in Egypt (*SHA* xii.1) and Septimius Severus then worshipped Serapis during a visit there (xxvii.4). Caracalla made a special point of worshipping Serapis in Alexandria (**colour plate 5**). As Caracalla was murderously intolerant of any dissent, the York temple dedicated around this date might have been a statement of appropriate allegiance (Herodian iv.8.6-7), though it could have been to please Septimius Severus who based himself here during his campaign of 208-11 (**116**). At Kirkby Thore (Cumbria), Serapis and Jupiter were commemorated side by side on an altar by Lucius Alfenus Pa(...) (*RIB* 758). Either of these men might perhaps have spent time in Egypt, but it is no less possible that they developed an interest elsewhere.

Persia and the East

Astarte, a Persian equivalent of Venus, appears on an altar inscribed in Greek at Corbridge (*RIB* 1124). She was a rare visitor to Britain but the Persian god Mithras enjoyed considerable popularity amongst soldiers, in ports and major towns. Britain, being maritime and with a substantial military population, provided a number of opportunities for this curious religion to find new homes. From an archaeological point of view the temples, or *mithraea*, are remarkably well-defined.

Mithraism developed from Persian Zoroastrianism, a religion that had its origins in the teachings of a Babylonian king called Zoroaster (dates are uncertain but not later than the sixth century BC). Renowned for his qualities as a leader, Zoroaster was attributed with having invented magic. He believed that the symbol of the supreme being was fire. Under the Sassanids in the third century AD, Zoroastrianism became the dominant religion in Persia, though Mithraism had already reached Rome in the mid-first century BC. With Persian influence through trade and war steadily increasing in the east, it was not surprising that religions moved across too. Mithraism was open only to men and required its adherents to conform to strict codes of practice, endurance and discipline, which made it attractive to soldiers and other like-minded men. It offered a passage to rebirth and renewal — a characteristic that it shared with Christianity, and an increasingly popular theme in the Roman world. Indeed, Christianity and Mithraism initially functioned almost as rivals. Unlike traditional religions that placed great emphasis on location, Mithraism also shared with Christianity an infinite portability. We can see this contrast quite clearly with the native British cults, like Apollo Cunomaglos at Nettleton, or Viridios at Ancaster. These were the homes of those particular gods and we do not find them anywhere else.

117 *Carrawburgh (Hadrian's Wall), the mithraeum looking north. At the far end of the little hall, altars stood beneath the reredos that housed the now-destroyed scene of Mithras slaying the sacred bull. The posts are concrete casts of the timber roof-supports. The shrine of the Nymphs (75) lay in the foreground. See also* **102**

A mithraeum could be built anywhere so long as running water was available. The priority was creating the right setting for the commemoration of the central episodes in the myth and ritual. Another difference was providing facilities for the cult members to take part because Mithraism, like Christianity, was a congregational religion. The basilican form of building was perfect for this purpose (**117**). Mithraic beliefs held that Mithras had been engaged in a fight to the death with a bull created at the dawn of time. Mithras killed the bull in a cave, thus releasing the blood that contained the essence of life. A mithraeum had no windows in order to recreate the mystery and symbolism of the cave, and the devotees all faced a large relief depicting the sacred killing, the 'tauroctony' where they participated in the meal that formed a pivotal role in the rites. Theatrical props enhanced the sense of being in a special place with, for example, perforated altars through which lamps cast eerie pools of light and shadow across the congregation. Statues of Mithras's associates Cautes and Cautopates stood in the nave (**118**). It is these features that make the mithraea so easy to identify, even in the absence of any epigraphic confirmation, though in fact Britain's examples do provide this.

Becoming a member of a Mithraic sect was not straightforward. It was an exclusive religion and only accepted men who were willing and capable of enduring extreme physical tests. In this way they could demonstrate that they were of a mettle

STATUE OF CAUTES,
A COMPANION OF MITHRAS

STATUE OF CAUTOPATES
A COMPANION OF MITHRAS

118 *Housesteads (Hadrian's Wall). Mithras' associates, Cautes and Cautopates, found together in the fort mithraeum. Both figures had been smashed. Height of Cautes, 98cm*

119 *(opposite) Tauroctony sculpture from the London mithraeum, dedicated by a veteran of II Augusta. Diameter 55cm. RIB 3*

equal to the cult's eponymous hero. At Carrawburgh, on Hadrian's Wall, a trench was dug inside the mithraeum and covered with flagstones. It was probably some sort of endurance pit for an initiation exercise, though in a later phase of the building's history the trench was filled in. The routine was partly theatrical. Commodus (180-92) was said to have desecrated Mithraic rites by murdering people 'even though normal Mithraic ritual involved saying or pretending something to create an impression of terror' (*SHA Commodus* ix.6). The tolerance of pain and the significance of bloodshed as a means of eternal life was of course shared with other mystery religions, and provoked Christian outrage. Jerome provides us with the stages of Mithraic initiation, and Tertullian with a description of the climax:

> The monstrous images there by which [Mithraic] worshippers were initiated as Raven, Bridegroom, Soldier, Lion, Perseus, Sun Runner, and Father.
>
> Jerome, *Letters* cvii

> Deep in a cave, in the very camp of darkness, a crown is presented to the candidate at the point of a sword, as if in a mimicry of martyrdom, and placed upon his head. Then, he is admonished to resist and throw it off, perhaps slipping it on the shoulder of the god, saying 'Mithras is my crown'. He is immediately acknowledged as a soldier of Mithras if he throws the crown away, saying that in his god he has his crown. Thereafter he never places a crown on his head, and uses that to identify himself, if anywhere he is tested on his oath of initiation.
>
> Tertullian, *De Corona* xv.3-4

All of Britain's mithraea have turned up in military contexts. Three are known on Hadrian's Wall, a natural context for the cult, at the forts of Rudchester, Carrawburgh and Housesteads. Another is known at Caernarfon fort in north Wales. Even London's mithraeum is really military in context, despite lying in the heart of the provincial capital (**9**). Nearby was found the finest surviving piece of Mithraic sculpture from Britain, dedicated by a veteran of *II Augusta* (**119**). In any case, London was a garrison town where soldiers of various units were detached to the governor's bodyguard, though its prominence as a port of entry would have played a part. There is little significance in the exact distribution – we can be almost certain that mithraea would have existed at Chester, York, and most other major and minor forts at some time. Mithraic sculpture and inscriptions have turned up at Caerleon, Carlisle, High Rochester, and Lanchester amongst other places though occasionally figures of Atys are mistaken for Cautes or Cautopates. A Mithraic token, made from a *denarius* of Augustus struck in 18 BC, was found with late second-century material at Verulamium (*RIB* 2408.2). It may indicate there was a mithraeum there too, but such a portable item could have found its way there through casual loss.

Mithras was often mentioned in one breath with Sol Invictus, 'the Unconquered Sun', though he also appears under the even more ambiguous name Deus, 'God'. At this distance it is difficult to be clear about the precise significance, but Mithras was undoubtedly part of an increased interest in the concept of a single deity, rather than the unlimited bit-part players of the Roman pantheon whose appeal so intrigued people like Pliny the Elder. The concept of a sun god had always existed but his popularity increased during the second and third centuries (**120**) – Hadrian remodelled and rededicated the colossal statue of Nero in Rome as the

120 *(above) Corbridge (Northumberland). Part of a relief from a temple of Jupiter Dolichenus. Sol rides on a winged horse (left) towards one of the Heavenly Twins under a temple pediment. Further to the right was a figure of Apollo(?), perhaps a collection of deities, and then a balancing Twin and a final figure. Third century. Height 54.5cm*

121 *(left) Housesteads (Hadrian's Wall). Altar dedicated to Sol by Herion, and found in the mithraeum. Unusually for an altar an image of the god was included. Third-century style. Height 53.4cm.* RIB 1601

122 *(below) Felmingham Hall (Norfolk). Bronze spoked wheel from a hoard of religious material (see also **11**). Diameter 78mm*

Sun (*SHA* xix.13). The temple of the sun god Baal at Emesa in Syria was a focal point of the eastern cult, though the first dated appearance of an imported sun god in Britain is at Corbridge between *c*.163-6 on a slab dedicated by *VI Victrix*, and appeared in association with Mithras at Housesteads (**121**), Lanchester, Rudchester and London. However, it is equally plain from the recurrence of the wheel motif in cults associated more specifically with Britain that worshipping the sun was scarcely a radical theme (**122**).

The Corbridge dedication occurred during the governorship of Sextus Calpurnius Agricola, interestingly also a period when a dedication was made to the Dea Suria ('the Syrian Goddess' – Cybele, see below) at Carvoran by a Syrian unit called *cohors I Hamiorum sagittaria* during the governorship of Sextus Calpurnius Agricola around 163-6 (*RIB* 1792). At Castlesteads and Housesteads he was conflated with Mithras altogether. The Hamian archers had been in Britain at least on and off since 122, and had perhaps played an important role in importing eastern deities. But given that we know auxiliary units were not necessarily made up of nationals from the regions whose names they bore, we should not assume this to be a fact. However, we do have individuals who tell us they were from the area – the best-known being Barates from Palmyra, recorded on his wife's tombstone from South Shields (*RIB* 1065).

It took outright eccentrics like Elagabalus (reigned 218-22) to bring the Sun forward to more general Roman consciousness (**26**). Elagabalus, nephew of Septimius Severus by marriage, had been brought up in the service of the sun god Baal, or Elagabalus, at Emesa in Syria. His family connections and wealth made him an attractive prospect to the opportunistic soldiers of the day, especially when, with an eye to the main chance, his mother told them he was Caracalla's son (he wasn't). Elagabalus was made emperor by the Eastern army against Macrinus, who was toppled in 218. Elagabalus dressed and posed as the sun god priest he was from the outset of his reign. Herodian – probably an eyewitness – said he looked like a cross between a Phoenician and a Persian. Thereafter Elagabalus indulged 'his ecstatic rites . . . and appeared to spend all his time

123 *Chesters (Hadrian's Wall). Statue of uncertain identity but variously described as Cybele, Julia Domna or Julia Mamaea as Cybele, or Juno Regina. The female figure is shown standing on a heifer. The quality is unusually high for Britain. Height 1.61m*

124 *Figure identified as Atys, found in Bevis Marks, near Aldgate, London in 1849. Height 61cm*

dancing and performing sacrifices' (Herodian v.5.3, 6). After a short reign of self-indulgent mayhem he was murdered and replaced by his more sober cousin, Severus Alexander (222-35).

From Republican times, the Phrygian mother goddess Cybele, also known as *Magna Mater* ('Great Mother') enjoyed a great deal of popularity in the Roman world. This was particularly so from the time of Claudius when the worship of Cybele was integrated into the official Roman pantheon. Nero despised most cults but made a temporary exception when it came to her (Suetonius, *Nero* xlvi). Cybele's powers over fertility equated her easily enough with Roman Ceres and also Juno (**123**). It is in this guise that she appears in the remarkable poem inscribed on an altar from Carvoran by the acting prefect Marcus Caecilius Donatianus (*RIB* 1791). Called by him *Ceres dea Suria*, 'Ceres the Syrian Goddess', he accredited this heavenly 'virgin' with powers over corn, law, cities, apparently in direct gratitude for his position. Severus and his wife were in Britain from 208 until his death at York in 211 so it is likely the inscription belongs to that period, possibly resulting from a visit in person.

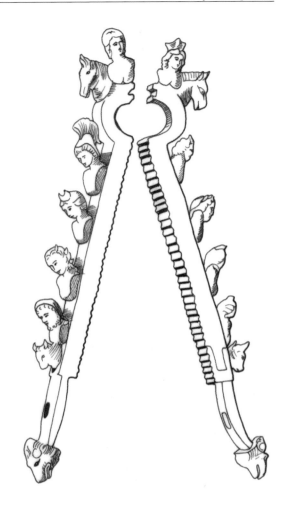

125 *The Thames, London. Castration clamps, probably used in rites associated with Cybele and Atys. Length 290mm*

The Cybele rites included a role for her lover Atys (**124**). Unfaithful to Cybele, he was consumed with remorse. In the ultimate act of self-imposed punishment, he castrated himself. Cybele's most fanatical male adherents, known as the Galli, engaged in an orgiastic once-only rite of dedication by castrating themselves. This earned them the unedifying label *semiviro Cybeles*, 'Cybele's company of half-men' (Martial, *Epigrams* iii.91). The theory was that Cybele rewarded the act of castration by enhancing the virility of the Romans (Augustine, *CG*, vii.26). The origin of the name Galli is variously attributed to the river Gallos near Mount Berecynthus and tribes who settled in Galatia (see Ovid, *Fasti* iv.361ff), but in practice Roman humourists like Martial never missed a chance to make a pun on the name – a 'Gaul' was often used as a euphemism for a eunuch. The 'half-men of Cybele' seem to have existed in Britain – a set of castration clamps decorated with images of Cybele and Atys was dumped in the Thames, either to protect it or dispose of it (**125**).

St Augustine, and other Christians, predictably considered the Cybele rites to be little more than an excuse for obscene displays of licentious behaviour allowing him to engage in lascivious accounts of self-righteous disgust (*CG* ii.26, and see also vii.24). But even the normally tolerant Roman state was disturbed by the frenzied carryings-on of Cybele worshippers, which included rowdy parades to the sound of cymbals and raucous horns, as well as arm–slashing, and controls were instituted to prevent public disorder. As a passing matter of interest, Lucretius' account of their activities contains a rare instance of evidence for the role of coins in religious worship. During the entry of a figure of Cybele into a city 'they shower her whole route with copper and silver coins' (*DRN* ii.626). One might speculate how many urban coin finds in roadside ditches, or embedded in the metalling, were the consequences of such events rather than casual loss.

Near Verulamium a *collegium* of Atys worshippers seem to have circulated. That they are only known from a beaker found in a grave at Dunstable (Beds) is a mark of the tenuous links that have transmitted Romano-British religious activity to us (but see above p.102). The beaker is painted with a graffito stating that 'Regillinus presented the vessel of the *dendrophori* of Verulamium' (**36**). However, even that depends on expanding 'VE' as *Verulamiensium* (*RIB* 2503.114). The *dendrophori*, 'branch-bearers', were so named for their practice of bearing a pine tree during re-enactments of Atys' funeral procession annually on 22 March. It was suggested that the so-called Triangular Temple at Verulamium was home to the Cybele cult but nothing exists from the site to confirm it, other than pine cones.

Christianity

We instinctively treat Christianity in the Roman world as a special subject for obvious reasons. But the new religion existed at many different levels in Roman society. At the most extreme end it was regarded by officialdom as a subversive and dangerous rejection of Rome's political and social foundations. At the other, it simply added another god to the pantheon and was treated as a matter of curiosity. To committed Christians, following their religion was a personal right. Today the traditional image of a universal religious conflict between the Christians and everyone else throughout the Roman world has largely dissipated in favour of a more complex picture. Christianity presented the Roman world with a paradox. The concept of another god was no problem, and many people were happy to integrate Christ into their pantheon of favourite deities (**126**).

But diehard Christians, and that was not all of them by any means, took a more uncompromising view. The literary rants of Christian writers and thinkers give us some idea of how ubiquitous the pagan shrines and statues were. 'There is nowhere that is entirely free of idols', moaned the Christian apologist Tertullian at the beginning of the third century. The Devil and his angels have filled the whole world' (*de Spectaculis*, viii.9). For people like Tertullian, it was all or nothing. The supremacy of Christ was all-consuming, and that meant rejecting out of hand the idea that one would make any sort of dedication to a pagan god, and condemning all other religious practices as a highway to spiritual oblivion. Normally, the crux of the matter was the imperial cult. There was an inherent problem of interpretation. For

126 *Water Newton (Cambs). Part of the hoard of Christian plate was made up of silver plaques or 'feathers' that combined a pagan object with Christian labelling. Left: plaque with Chi-Rho and Alpha-and-Omega symbols, height 157mm; right: damaged plaque with similar Chi-Rho and an embossed inscription translated as 'Anicilla fulfilled the vow she promised', diameter 100mm. Anicilla had evidently made the vow-transaction traditionally associated with pagan deities. The hoard is exceptional, and the earliest such group from the whole Empire. See also* **colour plate 20**. *Probably third century*

the Roman authorities the imperial cult was closer to a statement of political loyalty. It was the rejection of this that mattered more than anything else. For the dedicated Christians any sort of alternative ritual was simply blasphemous. Not only that, there was undoubtedly a desire amongst some to provoke confrontations which would lead to their martyrdom, because that was perceived as the quickest and most glorious path to Heaven. It was also encouraged by elements of the leadership. Influential Christian fathers like Jerome later idolised and celebrated martyrs in their writings, and took an almost indecent pleasure in recounting the agonies endured by some. The phenomenon sounds all too familiar in our own time.

Tracking Christianity in Britain is extremely difficult because there is very little documentary information to work from. Portable artefacts are exceptionally scarce, and none have ever been found in Romano-British buildings that could otherwise be passed off as churches. Indeed, an absence of artefacts is almost a definition of Christian features, graves in particular. There is not a single monumental inscription from Britain that helps us either, yet it is precisely this class of artefact that provides most of our evidence for all the other cult activity. So, we are hamstrung from the outset.

The legend of the martyrdom of Alban in the Roman city of *Verulamium*, which now bears his name, is one of the few surviving tales that preserves an authentic-sounding incident of the experience of Christianity in Roman Britain. The story is undated but is normally attributed to the early third century when Septimius Severus (193-211) campaigned in northern Britain and left his younger son, Geta, in charge of Britain's administration. However, another theory places it almost a century later under Diocletian. Alban sheltered a Christian priest during a bout of persecution and was converted. He proceeded to refuse to make a vow or offering to a pagan idol in or near the forum – a crucial challenge to Roman authority. For this he was tortured and executed against, so the story goes, a background of miraculous events which included a river drying up to let him pass to his death. The theory that the entire story, including Alban's existence, is a Christian fabrication that actually masks the appropriation of a pagan cult, flies in the face of a tradition that is actually remarkably well documented (by comparison) for the period. There is no good reason to doubt the basic veracity, even if Alban's role was perhaps exaggerated in time or perhaps conflated with tales of other martyrs.

Another story commemorates the soldiers Aaron and Julius from the 'City of the Legions', perhaps Caerleon, base of *II Augusta*, who were put to death for being Christians (Gildas *DEB*, x-xi). Aaron's name is a reminder that Christians were often Jewish converts; Judaism is practically invisible in Roman Britain and this may help explain the limited evidence for Christianity at this time. An interesting connection might be the small chapel identified within the walls of the late Roman fort at Richborough (Kent), by then said to be *II Augusta's* base. It is possible that the army harboured a significant Christian component that 'came out' when Christianity was legitimised, but it is no less likely that Richborough was then indistinguishable from a town. During the fourth century, Christianity found itself in an entirely different position. It was no longer a sect that attracted the dispossessed, the morally destitute and those in search of new meaning. It had superseded Jupiter himself but it found new challenges too. In Britain the pagan backlash was more active than in many other parts of the Empire.

Death and burial in the third century and beyond

During the third century, inhumation became the norm. Coffins were made of wood, lead or stone, sometimes with lead coffins placed in stone sarcophagi but these are obviously the wealthiest burials (**127**). Although this provides the archaeologist with more to work from in the form of human remains, few are inscribed in any way. The decline in use of grave goods once Christianity was legitimised makes analysis more difficult though there are many transitional cases, such as the grave of a young girl found at 15-23 Southwark Street. Her remains were packed in chalk, a preservative associated with Christianity, but she was still accompanied by grave-goods such as bracelets and pins.

127 *Carved stone sarcophagus from the Minories, London. Only 1.52m (5ft) in length, when found the sarcophagus contained a lead coffin with bones of a boy aged about 10-12 years, together with a quantity of lime. Typically for more elaborate coffins the decoration includes scallop shells and astragalus, as well as in this case a rare instance (for Britain) of a portrait. The coffin may have been designed for display in a mausoleum rather than burial. The grave was evidently that of a child from a wealthy family. The iron clamps securing the lid are original. Probably third or fourth century*

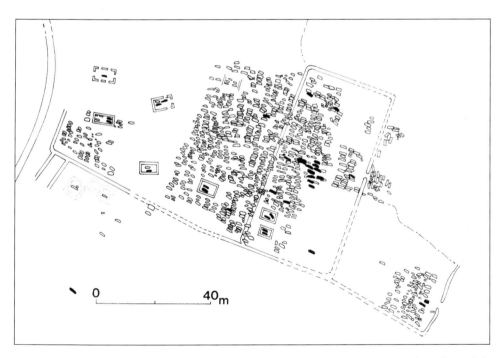

128 *Poundbury, Dorchester (Dorset), the late-Roman cemetery. Open graves are wooden coffins, solid are stone coffins. Note the common orientation. North to top. After C.J.S. Green*

185

129 *Makhthar, Tunisia.
Although not from
Britain, this late-Roman
tombstone shows perfectly
the ambiguities current in
religious consciousness in the
Roman world. Although the
Chi-Rho monogram heads
the stone, the pagan formula
DMS for Dis Manibus has
been added. It shows that
making assumptions about
the religion practised on the
basis of grave orientation is
far too simplistic (see also
33, 59, and 128)*

Whatever the difficulties of interpreting individual graves, the lack of detailed, extensive and fully-published cemetery excavations is the main problem. Poundbury, by Dorchester (Dorset), is one of the few instances. Here the inhumation cemetery shows the arrival of the 'Christian'-type layout to good effect during the fourth century (**128**). The typical burial consisted of a body placed in a wooden coffin and laid out with the head to the west (and thus oriented to greet the 'Second Coming'). Some, as at York, had been filled with gypsum, possibly an attempt to preserve the body for resurrection. A small proportion of the burials were in stone coffins and even fewer were contained within mausolea. Does this automatically mean a Christian community? As we have already seen from comments by St Augustine in chapter 3, that interpretation is far too simplistic to draw from what may be essentially a fashion, regardless of its origins (**129**). Indeed, paganism was about to experience a Romano-British Indian summer.

7 Ancient Gods

The fourth century in Roman Britain is its strangest period. The halcyon years of the second century, when the Empire enjoyed relative political stability, had disappeared. The turbulent third century had given way to an entirely new form of imperial government established by Diocletian (284-305), in which multiple tiers of regional civil and military commands oversaw provincial government and defence. Britain, now divided into four provinces, was even more marginalised from the imperial centre stage than she had ever been as the Empire became preoccupied with the waves of barbarian incursions, and ideological and theological struggles between Christian factions.

The physical remains of this period are amongst the most dramatic and impressive in Britain (**colour plate 15**). Paradoxically they include some of the most conspicuous military remains, and the greatest displays of rural domestic wealth. The great forts of the Saxon Shore, built on and off throughout the third century and into the fourth, dominated the south and eastern coasts. Most of the significant towns were now equipped with major defences, often the only visible remnants of these places today. York had evolved from a legionary fortress into an imposing administrative and military command centre. Across the countryside, many of the villa houses of the wealthy were transformed into showpieces of art and ostentation. Even in Cirencester, around this time, Jupiter columns still stood in the town centre (**130**). Conversely, public building in towns had all but ceased.

As far as religion was concerned, the legal and spiritual ground rules had been transformed forever. Under Constantine the Great (**131**), Christianity was legitimised in new laws in 313 that saw membership of the church become an essential qualification to mainstream civil and military status. This itself created a whole new dynamic of tension between the old and new. Some families were ousted from centuries of status to make way for Constantine's new men, while some committed Christians struggled to reconcile their beliefs with the practical obligations of government and war. Rome's secret had once been its capacity to absorb people, regardless of cult or creed. Now that was changed into a new way. That new way would define the politics of the Middle Ages and provide the basis of the religious wars of the epochs to come. For the moment it provoked factionalism and frustrated exclusion. The state remained schizophrenic for a while yet. Constantine continued to issue abundant coins with a reverse depicting 'The Sun, the Unconquered Companion'.

Over the rest of the fourth century Britain, along with everywhere else, faced a raft of new proscriptions that gradually banned pagan worship and temples from towns and ultimately even the countryside. This might explain the fate of

130 *Cirencester, column capital from a late Jupiter column (probably not the same one whose restoration is recorded on an inscription). This face depicts Bacchus with his drinking horn*

131 *Constantine I, the Great (306/7-37). His legitimisation of Christianity transformed the Empire but created a whole new raft of religious and social tensions. Monumental bust found in York, where he was declared emperor in 306. Height 42cm*

132 *Verulamium. Bronze figurine of Venus found in the debris of a fourth-century metalworker's shop. Height 200mm*

the Verulamium Venus statuette, found in a fourth-century context in a building associated with metalwork but made in a first- or second-century style. Perhaps it once stood in a townhouse *lararium*, but the new laws and a change in beliefs led a family to throw it out for melting down, though in truth it could have happened at any time (**132**). Britain saw her great urban pagan temples begin to crumble into decay, and sporadic instances of probable churches emerge into the archaeological and literary record we possess (**153**). Verulamium's theatre fell into disuse, presumably made redundant by the end of publicly-celebrated pagan festivals. Some of the decay might have already begun. Ancaster (Lincs) was walled in the late third or early fourth century, reducing the town's area. What had been settlement became cemetery areas. The shrine of Viridios has never been found and probably lies beneath the new western rampart, itself now below the medieval church (**70, colour plate 32**). This part of the town was severely altered when the new ramparts were thrown up. Evidently the temple was either derelict already, or was a matter of no concern, by the time the late defences were erected.

133 *London. Fragment of carved stonework from the monumental arch demolished and reused in the fourth-century riverside wall. Left: Mars. Right: purse and shoulder of Mercury. The arch probably stood as an entrance to a temple precinct*

In London the remains of an arch decorated in late second- or early third-century style with reliefs depicting various gods, and possibly once having served as the entrance to a temple precinct, were built into a new part of the city wall around the early part of the fourth century (**133**). Along with it went the remains of a carved screen of gods, and other religious sculptures. Given that these monuments can have been little more than a century old, the most likely context for their reuse this way could well have been new laws that saw prominent city-centre religious complexes, or simply anything that depicted pagan subjects, being cleared away or collapsing (**153**).

Yet simultaneously the countryside, particularly in the west, saw a distinct increase in pagan temples. The phenomenon was not entirely restricted to the countryside. Caerwent, the remote civitas capital *Venta Silurum*, lay close to the legionary fortress of Caerleon in south Wales. Still comparatively removed from modern centres of population, some of its buildings have survived particularly well. This little settlement had pretensions, and enjoyed many of the attributes of the larger civitas capitals to the east. That included a substantial Romano-Celtic temple with precinct by the town's main street in the late third century (**134**). Clearly designed as a coherent whole, the precinct occupied a rectangular *insula* with the temple placed neatly in the centre and approached from the main street through an entranceway flanked by halls. The whole site replaced earlier structures that included an ordinary house and a building with a deep circular pit, perhaps an earlier temple.

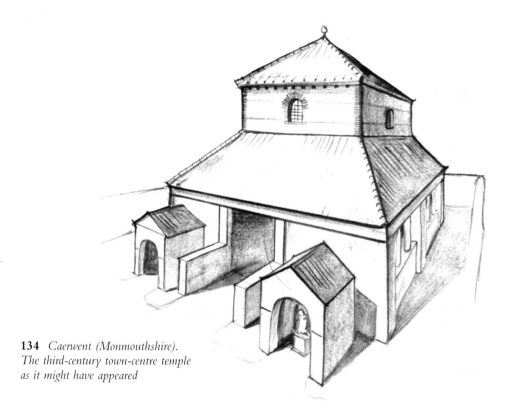

134 *Caerwent (Monmouthshire).*
The third-century town-centre temple
as it might have appeared

The new Caerwent temple is all the more remarkable because this was a time when public building of any sort in towns across Britain had practically ceased. Who or what was worshipped here is unknown, but the entrance part was enlarged during the fourth century. Apparently the proscription of urban paganism had no immediate impact out here. It is a mark of the haphazard enforcement of law in the increasingly authoritarian fourth-century Empire. Caerwent's proximity to the fortress at Caerleon makes it likely some of its residents were veteran soldiers, a traditionally conservative group. Christian influence and power simply could not demolish centuries of tradition overnight, particularly where local interest groups identified their futures in a pagan idiom.

St Augustine in *The City of God* confronted the pagan revivalism that he saw as being handed down by a 'secret religious tradition' and castigated the cults for engaging in nothing more than 'lewd utterances . . . and every kind of depravity' (ii.6). Violent resistance to the laws against paganism happened at a number of cities in North Africa. The focus of resentment was often some symbolic feature of the city, such as a favourite statue of a god associated with the settlement's mythical origins. Here it was not so much the religious side to any cult, as its link with tradition and also with established patterns of power and influence that provoked the confrontations. Christianity was a medium through which 'new men', and this included priests, found an avenue to political and social status that supplanted the old order.

So, it is hardly surprising that paganism became the banner under which the forces of conservatism fought to hold on to power. But the revival was distinctly mainstream and conservative. Interestingly, the references to pagan gods in the literature of the period generally make much more of the traditional gods like Mars and Mercury. For example, Ausonius the fourth-century Gallo-Roman poet and tutor peppered his writings with references to classical gods. The ancient local Gaulish deities like Teutas/Teutates/Toutatis, Taranis and Epona pass without mention, yet in the early imperial period it was precisely these that had fascinated a poet like Lucan. Lactantius, a Christian writer who died *c*.325, said that Roman civilisation had debased itself with its fascination for barbaric provincial gods like 'Teutas'. As far as he was concerned barbaric gods and barbaric practices were what one should expect of barbarians, but asked 'are not our countrymen, who have always claimed for themselves the glory of gentleness and civilization, found to be more inhuman by these sacrilegious rites?' (*DI* I.24). Perhaps the average fourth-century pagan revivalist sympathized with this approach and was generally inclined to more polite, classical forms of ancient cults, and their association with Rome's great days.

In the fourth century Cirencester was the capital city of one of the four provinces Britain had been divided into, in this case *Britannia Prima*, roughly equivalent to the south-west quadrant. The name provides a *terminus post quem* for the inscription recording the restoration of a Jupiter column and statue by Lucius Septimius [...], *rector primae provinciae*, 'governor of Prima province' (*RIB* 103). In other words, at around the time, or after, that Christianity was coming to the fore, a governor of a Romano-British province was restoring a major symbol of the pagan divine backing for secular power. Perhaps Septimius was consolidating his control by accepting and fostering a committed pagan élite. If so, it certainly fits with the popularity of pagan myth as a subject for the mosaics of the great houses of the fourth century dotted around Cirencester's hinterland. Cirencester is, incidentally, the only one of the four regional capitals for which there is no literary evidence of a resident bishop in the fourth century.

This might have been a genuine 'revival' or simply continuity of paganism removed to the isolation of more discrete locations, but in an age when investment in public building was almost non-existent, rural temples and villas underwent a virtual explosion in new investment. The Cirencester Jupiter column is an exceptional instance of spending on an urban monument in this period. The explanation almost certainly lies in the fact that in the ancient world, as now, it was one thing to draft and initiate new legislation, and quite another to enforce it. The Roman state, as all states, was no more effective an executive force than the level of corruption, indifference or opposition in any one place allowed it to be. Compliance was all, and it was not always forthcoming. Throughout the fourth century, emperors found themselves confronted by cities and communities that remained adamantly pagan. Perhaps this explains the lead curse found in the Hamble estuary and addressed to Neptune. The author of the curse is concerned about the loss of coins and uses the term *argentiolus* for the silver coins concerned. This is a denomination used from the end of the third century and throughout the fourth. It must date the curse to about that time (*B* 1997, 455-7).

It would be delightful if we really knew for a fact what was going on in Britain. But the historical sources for the period are fairly limited in detail even for the basic chronology of events, let alone the spiritual interests of the Romano-British population. Add to that the virtual disappearance of any kind of epigraphic record, and the frustrating reluctance of Christians to include datable grave goods in their cemeteries, and the result is a very thin body of evidence for understanding who was financing the new temples, and to what extent the traditional cults and the new mystery cults had survived into the last century of Roman Britain.

During this time in the north there was a curious mix of casual dereliction with outright iconoclastic destruction, though the latter is hard to date. It is hard to see how else the remains at the mithraea of London and Carrawburgh can be interpreted, though ascribing motive under such circumstances is a thoroughly suspect process. Carrawburgh and Rudchester seem to have had their mithraic tauroctony reliefs shattered, apparently deliberately, in targeted acts that left the other altars undamaged. London's mithraeum was also damaged but not before the devotees had had the wit to bury their valuable statues in and around the temple. The coin list from the nearby Coventina's Well runs right up to the end of the fourth century, admittedly in reduced quantities. However, offerings were evidently still being made at the same time as some believe the theoretical iconoclasts were wreaking havoc on Mithras a few metres away. The damage to these and other pagan monuments could have taken place long after the Roman period. Bede records the conversion of King Edwin of Northumbria in 627 and the immediate offer by his chief priest, Coifi, to destroy 'the altars and shrines of the idols' at a place called Goodmanham near York (*EH* ii.13). This was an Anglo-Saxon pagan site but so much of the Roman pagan past must have remained visible in the north that it is very possible that some of the demolition of temples and statues belonged to a different age, by which time altars were buried under debris and earth.

New temples

In the late third and fourth centuries a number of new pagan temples were installed in rural locations, generally in the south and west. The phenomenon is an important one because there is a geographical connection with the elaborate villas of the period, and also a geographic distinction from areas associated with military activity or a military presence, typically the forts of the north and the new-phase forts of the Saxon Shore. It would be wrong though to suggest that this revival followed a hiatus in temple-building or maintenance. Bath had been thoroughly remodelled by the third century, as had Harlow, far to the east. A precinct enclosed by a palisade went up at Harlow in the early second century, followed in the early third century by a pair of chapels flanking the entrance, and a new courtyard in front of the temple (**71**). Pagan activity at Harlow continued. A pit on another site about 600m to the north-west of the temple, with third- or fourth-century pottery also contained a curse tablet addressed to Mercury on both sides. The writer, with the

135 *Nettleton (Wilts). The late third-century octagonal shrine of Apollo Cunomaglos as it might have appeared in elevation from the east. The central lantern was not adequately buttressed and eventually the temple collapsed in spite of attempts to remedy the structural shortcomings*

votary's customary interest in pursuing selfish concerns, was apparently seeking protection during his adulterous affair with a woman called Eterna (*B* 1972, 325). It may have originated in the known temple, or belonged to another religious site on the settlement.

Meanwhile, Nettleton reached its most elaborate octagonal form in the late third century (**135**). The temple became an exceptional example of experimental architecture. An octagonal podium surrounded the old circular temple in the early 200s but within a couple of generations the temple had been replaced by its great octagonal successor. In many ways this was one of the most reckless architectural indulgences in Roman Britain. The plan shows that it was an early version of a building type that later took its finest form in the extant sixth-century Church of St Vitale in Ravenna. Unfortunately, Nettleton's architect lacked the benefit of experience and omitted the vital buttresses to inhibit the pressures caused by the central lantern. Oddly, the architect of a similar temple at Chelmsford (Essex) seems to have been aware of the dangers, and incorporated thickened wall joints. It, too, seems to have supplanted an earlier and simpler version. Reinforcements installed at Nettleton in the beginning of the fourth century failed to prevent collapse and the temple soon became derelict. Even so, the design may have had wider influences especially as it lay beside an important road. Similar structures appeared in bathhouses attached to villas at Holcombe and Lufton. The temple at Pagans Hill (Somerset), built around 300, was also octagonal though less elaborate.

Nettleton had clearly done extremely well out of its location on the Fosse Way. The improvements roughly coincide with the elaboration of Bath's facilities. Perhaps the revamped Bath attracted a new wave of pilgrims, bringing more money to the economy of certain rural wayside shrines en route to the spa religious resort. By the late third century Nettleton's temple had become the focal point of a complex of structures in the narrow valley, including a rectangular building immediately next to the temple. This seems to have been built out across the river, supported on piers, perhaps either as a sheltered landing spot for pilgrims or a place to deposit gifts in the water (or both).

At West Hill, Uley (Glos), a cult site with a long history of religious activity stretching right back into the Iron Age, the temple was significantly altered in the mid-fourth century. Superficially the temple resembled the Romano-Celtic form but the outer corridor or ambulatory only surrounded three sides, and contained the cult statue. The *cella* may even have been open to the elements, the cobbled flooring found in the ambulatory was absent from the *cella*, though this is difficult to reconcile with the absence of any drainage provision. A pit in the middle contained hundreds of coins. Presumably, visitors were able to access the *cella*, perhaps with a view of the cult statue through a window. The revised plan (**colour plate 31**) installed a portico with steps. In excess of 200 'curse' tablets have been found on the site which, together with the surviving cult head and two altars, make it clear that Mercury was the principal deity, and probably had been from the outset (**colour plate 27**). The vast quantities of bones of sheep, goat, and fowl found on the site must be evidence for sacrifice of these animals, well known as Mercury's familiars. Uley, in the heart of villa territory, was clearly geared up for receiving visitors to a pagan shrine at a time when pagan worship was under legal pressure to cease. The temple even seems to have survived structural damage in the late fourth century and remained in use.

The existing temples, even in their elaborated forms, were evidently either not enough, or sometimes inappropriate, for the fourth-century market. The fact that Nettleton, in ruins in the mid-fourth century from structural failure, was never rebuilt suggests that the pagan revival had specific tastes rather than outright growth. On a narrow hilltop called Lamyatt Beacon (near Bruton, Somerset) a new Romano-Celtic temple was built in the late third century (**136**). There is no doubt that the Lamyatt spot was carefully chosen, though it is interesting that it had not apparently been utilised before. Reaching a height of around 220m, the ridge is not only a prominent landmark but also enjoys a panoramic view all around. But it was not entirely isolated. The Fosse Way is around three miles (5km) to the west, and parish boundaries appear to preserve the branch road that led to the temple, making Lamyatt Beacon around a day's journey from Bath to the north and Ilchester to the south. The location meant that the temple's structure was not well preserved because by being perched on the ridge the outer walls had to be built up to where a level

136 *The Romano-Celtic temple astride the 220m-high ridge at Lamyatt Beacon (Somerset) as it may have appeared in the fourth century. Built in the late third century, the temple seems to have been a place where a variety of mainly classical deities, for example Mars and Mercury, were worshipped. The view is from the south*

floor platform could be created, at around 2m above the foundations. Natural erosion and weathering had severely denuded the ruins, but a remarkable amount of information was recovered during the comprehensive excavation of the site in 1973.

Lamyatt Beacon's plan shows that although it consisted of the usual two concentric squares, the outer 'ambulatory' looks as if it was actually divided into rooms, with the inner walls helping to buttress the *cella* walls against the steep banks of the hill. Anyone entering the temple from the east did so between a pair of projecting wing rooms, not unlike the projecting 'chapels' built onto Harlow's temple or the façade of the temple at Bath. But Lamyatt resembles even more closely a Romano-Celtic temple at Brean Down, built some 30-50 years later (see below). Thanks to the latter's similarly prominent location just over 30 miles (50km) to the north-west both temples were theoretically visible from each other. On the south side at Lamyatt there seems to have been another annexe, a small room built on with steps leading down to a sunken floor. Apart from a single small, unaligned, building almost abutting the temple's north wall, there was nothing more to the site. This matches Brean Down, and Maiden Castle, an important distinction that makes it unlikely these temples, unlike Lydney Park, Pagans Hill or Uley, were an attraction for overnight stays. Instead they seem more like private, isolated, garden temples frequented only briefly by passers-by or members of small family or social groups. Being rural and remote, enough survived on the site to show that a variety of mainstream classical deities were worshipped here: Mars, Minerva, Mercury, Jupiter, Hercules, and a Genius, reflecting the pagan interests in literature of the period. Not only did fragments of stone carvings survive but also a number of bronze figurines that could have been votives deposited by pilgrims, or goods sold on the site to visitors (**137**).

The discovery of antlers, known at a number of other temple sites such as Maiden Castle, means a Celtic deity like Cernunnos may also have been worshipped, either in his own right or conflated with Mars. The figures are interesting because of the temple's late date and because there are enough of them to see that the manufacturer(s) were well versed in conventional pagan imagery and iconography. They highlight the problem of dating on the grounds of style. The marble classical figures of Diana Luna and Bacchus from, respectively, the villas at Woodchester and Spoonley Wood (Glos) are a case in point (**colour plate 19**). There was a marked revival of interest in classical style during the fourth century. It matches the interest in mythical imagery used on fourth-century villa mosaics, the new temples, and

137 *Bronze statuettes of Mercury at Lamyatt Beacon. Other statuettes found on the site represent Hercules, Mars and Minerva. Height of large figure 106mm*

even the language and metaphors used by the educated Christian élite in Gaul and beyond. These factors make a direct connection with the villa owners possible. This is discussed in more detail below.

The Temple of Nodons at Lydney Park (Glos) is one of the clearest instances (apparently) of a rural pagan religious revival, though in this case the god concerned was a Celtic one. Lydney began life as an Iron Age promontory hillfort, but a number of ornate metal fittings and an iron bowl decorated with three bull heads sporting knobbed horns show that the pre-Roman occupants had access to high-quality manufactured goods, decorated in the quasi-religious symbolism of the period (**4**). But little seems to have happened at Lydney apart from finding a new use in the Roman period as a place to extract iron ore. This lasted at least as late as the end of the third century, but might have gone on a little longer. There is no evidence from the site for any kind of cult activity before this date, in spite of the Iron Age finds. Therefore it differs from places like Hayling Island, where cult activity stretched back before the Roman period, or Nettleton, where cult activity began probably by the end of the first century. Even so, excavations at Lydney in 1981 did produce a little evidence that the precinct wall of the new temple complex might have been begun in the late third century. But given that this hinges on the relatively ill-dated pottery of the period and a single copy of a coin of Tetricus it is scarcely definitive proof.

Lydney almost seems to have been selected by the equivalent of a religious property developer. Its transformation in the early fourth century was so comprehensive and dramatic that it had to represent heavy investment and planning in relatively short order. It is possible that some sort of sleepy local tradition of a local god had persisted but we have no way of knowing. There is no evidence that one had ever been actively worshipped here, until the fourth-century development. The deity concerned was Nodons, conflated here also as Mars Nodens/Nodons. The only other place where he turns up is Cockersand Moss (Lancs), recorded on two statuettes which have long since been lost (*RIB* 616-17). The Cockersand Moss examples were found together, and in isolation, making it quite possible they were bought or acquired in antiquity from somewhere else. Lydney is the obvious candidate but there is no way to verify that.

Lydney was developed as a compound on the promontory, complete with walls and gate. The centrepiece was the curious temple, and around it were rows of chambers, a bathhouse and a structure resembling a *mansio* or inn. There is no temple quite like Lydney's (**colour plate 29**). In basic form it resembled a hybrid made of the classical, basilican and Romano-Celtic styles. Like a classical temple it stood on a podium and was approached by a set of stairs. It was rectangular and had a nave and aisles. However, the aisles continued round the back of the nave to create a continuous corridor. The exterior wall of the aisles had recesses in it, projecting as bays outside. These may have provided structural strength by acting as buttresses, but they were also probably places where benches and beds were installed for pilgrims to sleep on in the presence of the god. The building suffered a catastrophic internal collapse when a ground fault gave way by *c.*375. It was rebuilt, with the walls between the columns being filled in, and thus separating the two areas into an internal *cella* with surrounding corridor.

The purpose of the Lydney temple becomes clearer with the information provided by a mosaic, now lost, from the floor. It featured sea monsters, geometric motifs, and an inscription. The text read:

D M N T FLAVIVS SENILIS PR REL EX STIPIBVS POSSVIT
O[PITV]LANTE VICTORINO INTERP(R)[E]TIANTE
(*RIB* 2448.3)

The suggested translation in *RIB* is 'To the god Mars Nodons, Titus Flavius Senilis, *pr(aepositus?) rel(igionis?)* ['superintendent of the cult'], had [this mosaic] laid out of the offerings, with the help of Victorinus, interpreter (of dreams)'. There is no parallel for the text, or even precisely of the offices mentioned on it, in this form. Interpreters of dreams were also known as *vates* (Cicero, *DND* i.20.55). But bearing in mind Lucian's account of the crooked oracular activities of Alexander of Abonuteichos we might amuse ourselves with the possibility that successful dream interpretation at Lydney could have been assisted by an element of sharp practice.

The former expansion of PR REL into *praepositus reliquationis*, 'fleet supply-depot superintendent', seems bizarre now though it was readily accepted for a long time when experts in Roman Britain tended to interpret everything possible as military. At any rate, the currently-accepted translation fits the context rather than trying to fit a quartermaster into a cathedral. The expansion of N into Nodens, Nodons or Nudens is beyond doubt because he appears in all these forms in full on metal tablets found at Lydney (*RIB* 305-7). Mars is equally certain thanks to one of the Cockersand statuettes on which the name was recorded in full (*RIB* 616). Strangely, the dedicant of this statuette was one Aurelius [...]cinus, a name that matches the Aurelius Ursicinus on the Hoxne (Norfolk) early fifth-century hoard of coins, spoons and jewellery. There is absolutely no demonstrable connection between the two, but if the pagan revival was a product of the wealthy villa-owning élite, it would not be surprising if they were one and the same man, or from the same family.

The curse tablets tell us a little about Nodons' functions as a god. Silvianus sought help in recovering his lost ring, apparently stolen by someone called Senicianus. The text is instantly reminiscent of the trivial pursuits that choked Bath's sacred spring. If Nodons had been revived from a primeval sleep to grace the pagan revival, he must have been disappointed to find what was waiting for him. Flavius Blandinus, the *armatura*, 'drill instructor', fulfilled his vow, and Pectillus supplied the gift he had promised the god.

If nothing else, the votive tablets showed that old habits died hard. In the hills of Gloucestershire, overlooking the Severn Estuary from the Welsh side, vows to pagan gods were being fulfilled much as they had been for centuries. If the dream interpretation really was going on, it helps explain the temple's design. The recesses in the walls were probably places for pilgrims to lie, perhaps in a state of tipsy or drunken restless ecstasy, where they could borrow the night to sleep the affliction of terrible dreams they hoped would explain the fitful fever of their lives, their illnesses, and their fates. The individual chambers in the range that lay near the temple were probably the economy chalets.

Alcohol and narcotics assisted the dreamers in getting to sleep. Columella reminded his readers of the poppy's power to help people nod off (*DRR* x.107). Today the drugs sourced from the poppy are amongst the most notorious and potent available. In antiquity drunkenness enjoyed a pagan veneration matched only now by artists of certain persuasions who argue that narcotics provide them with the mental state in which their creativity is unmatched. Certainly there are numerous pieces of modern popular music and their attendant lyrics that are easier to explain this way, though the sober critic might query the level of achievement. Perhaps it was also a reactionary response to the more extreme Christians who saw any level of indulgence through food, drink or sex as the devil's work. St Augustine reminded his readers of the preacher who warned that 'it is better to go into a house of mourning than into a house of drinking' (*CG* xxvii.20).

The secluded woodland setting must have made Lydney a convivial place to visit. The installation of baths shows that if offered more than just the services of dream interpreters. It is likely there was a healing component to Nodons' powers. A miniature of a dog is an important clue, because dogs were considered to help in healing by licking affected wounds (**138**). But we have no inscriptions like tomb-stones that might confirm the fact. That Lydney acted as a sort of health farm resort is a possibility we have to consider. Somewhat off the beaten track it was not far either from the town at Caerwent, or the villas of the Mendips and Cotswolds. This of itself raises the question of who built the place. One distinct possibility is that Lydney was built by the same people who owned villas in the area. As we know nothing about them that isn't particularly helpful. It mounts to no more than saying that people we know nothing about built something and might also have built something else. However, given some of the wilder speculations the average reader might come to the conclusion that some of the experts in the field were creaking under the weight of definitive evidence.

Well, they aren't. But what we can say is that the overall number of people involved in the great villas numbered no more than several thousand. Compared to a population that ran into several million, they amounted to a very small proportion.

138 *Lydney (Glos). Bronze dog statuette. Dogs were associated with healing cults, but were also sacrificed on occasions in the Roman religious calendar. Length 82mm*

139 *Brading (Isle of Wight). Panel from the Medusa floor depicting a mythological scene, perhaps Paris and the water nymph Oenone, or Atys and the water nymph Sangaritis. Fourth century (see* **colour plate 25***)*

What we also know from their mosaics is that the owners had at least an aesthetic interest in pagan mythology, and that they had money (**139, colour plates 22 & 23**). Dropping back to the end of the first century we know from Pliny the Younger's letters that owning and maintaining temples on one's estates was a routine part of Roman *noblesse oblige*. That is as far as we can take it, but the speculation that Lydney and some of the other new pagan foundations were semi-private initiatives is at least founded on a credible basis.

140 *Maiden Castle (Dorset). The fourth-century Romano-Celtic temple as it survives today within the ramparts of the Iron Age hill-fort*

Around 340, a new Romano-Celtic temple was built with a similar eye to an aesthetically pleasing and natural setting on a sea promontory across the water at Brean Down (Somerset). Maiden Castle, that long-defunct Iron Age hillfort in Dorset, was no more than a grass-covered curiosity from yesteryear in the fourth century. Until that is someone decided to build a nice new Romano-Celtic temple on its northern slope where it could be seen from nearby Dorchester. The installation was a good deal less sophisticated than Lydney – the building was simple, and apart from an attendant rectangular chamber and an oval building, the temple amounted to no more than a hillside kiosk (**140**). Whoever ran the place was far from fussy – the artefacts excavated included a local bull-god now known as Taurus Trigaranus, Diana and Minerva. The rectangular building produced coins, fragments of a votive statue, a steelyard and pottery. Perhaps the sales arm of the project, this was where the pilgrims bought their gifts and souvenirs on a pleasant walk across the ancient fort to fantasise about the past, and cock a snook at the anti-pagan laws of the age.

Orpheus, Bacchus and the Underworld

The eastern mystery cults of Isis, Mithras and Cybele stretched back a long way in imperial history and played modest roles in Roman Britain's religious world from early times. They were also, by and large, associated with people and units from abroad, though this is to a large extent thanks to the fact that we know about them from inscriptions. Inscriptions in Britain are generally military, and so the circular argument goes around. If the indigenous population took part in Isis processions they did not mention the fact and thus permanently absent themselves from the record we have.

The picture in the fourth century is a very much more complex one, largely because the epigraphic record on the whole disappears. The army, with its well-defined units and bases, retreats to a much more opaque profile. Instead we are confronted with the more conspicuous record of the enigmatic villas and their mosaics that parallel to some extent the 'pagan revival' of temple building. Although mosaics were being laid in exceptional circumstances in first-century Britain, and in the towns in the second (**27**), they scarcely ever appear in forts. During the later third and into the fourth centuries they became an integral part of the country houses but scarcely ever turn up in temples, an interesting point in its own right (above p.199). The bigger the house, the more mosaics and so on. The quality varies, and so does the content, but it is plain enough that in the south the quantity and quality was generally better, with regional variations in style and subject matter. The mosaics, more than anything else, have contributed to the school of thought that some of these more elaborate late houses were, as their prime function, cult centres.

That the villas and the mosaics of the late third and fourth centuries excite so much comment is to a large degree due to the fact that there is not much else for some archaeologists to talk, or at any rate speculate, about. Whether the pictograms and motifs that lay under sandalled feet ever excited any more attention or notice in antiquity than the carpets under our feet excite us is a moot point. What is beyond doubt is that ever since mosaics were uncovered in Britain, a debate has raged about the significance of images from religion and myth. The assumption is that the iconography of a mosaic floor carries specific information about the owner's religious beliefs. Recently Martin Henig has said that the owner of the villa at Bignor was 'clearly not a Christian', a view based on the pagan iconography of the magnificent series of mosaics (**colour plate 15**). Others take the presence of Orpheus on a mosaic, for example, to be evidence of an Orphic cult cell. The problem is that no ancient authority ever makes a reference to the religious iconography of mosaic floors. So there is no verification that they served any prominent function reflecting or embellishing cult interests on the part of the owner. The one place that might suggest otherwise is Ravenna in northern Italy. Here, a series of magnificent churches, baptisteries and tombs from the fifth century and later survive, many with spectacular mosaics. However, the nature of the Ravenna buildings makes their religious function beyond doubt, and the mosaics concerned are on the walls and ceilings. The floors are positively bare by comparison. That ought to remind us that scarcely any villa (or temple) from Roman Britain has produced significant traces of wall decoration of myth cycles or depictions of gods, thanks to the destruction of superstructures. Without them, we have no hope of making a balanced assessment of what rooms or suites were used for.

Most importantly, while we have no evidence for *temples* dedicated to Orpheus or Bacchus in Britain, there is plenty of unequivocal evidence from the period for

141 *Brading (Isle of Wight). The Orpheus floor, showing Orpheus in the centre with his lyre and Phrygian cap, and accompanied by various animals charmed by his playing (see also **colour plate 23**)*

how pagan imagery was a conventional part of artistic expression in both Christian and pagan contexts. Myth served Christians just as well when allegorical settings, or descriptive terms, were needed which would have universal currency. This is self-evident from contemporary literature. This writer therefore takes the view that while one owner might have used pagan iconography in a literal sense, another might have seen it as an allegory. As we are not in a position to distinguish either motive or interpretation, or to distinguish a series of owners with different views, we have to accept that we are too far separated from the minds of these men to conclude anything definitive about their motives or beliefs.

Since we know nothing about the ownership of any Romano-British villa, anything we 'infer' about function and purpose is entirely our invention unless it can be tied, however loosely, to corroborating information from elsewhere in the Empire. The Orphic mosaics appear as far apart as Brading in the Isle of Wight, and Cirencester in Gloucestershire (**141, colour plate 23**). They must reflect the shift in taste towards a sort of antiquarian interest in ancient myth and tradition, but whether the Orphic mosaics necessarily mean that a 'villa' is more correctly a cult centre seems to be an unnecessarily monochrome way of looking at things. However, Orpheus had symbolic significance in his visit to, and return from, the Underworld. He thus transcended life and death, a theme that played a common role amongst many of the mystery cults, including Christianity. As an aesthetic device the Orpheus mosaic generally features a circle of animals parading around Orpheus with his lyre. In the most basic sense it avoided the problem of mosaic panels that constantly presented a would-be viewer with upside-down or side-on images. The Littlecote villa complex, with its Orphic triconch hall, has been the most popular candidate for an Orphic cult centre largely because the hall seems to be an oddly extravagant building for anything else. But elaborate *triclinia* – dining rooms – were common features in villas. Triconch rooms appear at several examples on the continent, for example Löffelbach and Piazza Armerina, without an Orphic association. At Lullingstone (Kent), the largest room in the house seems to have served this function and had the only mosaic floor replete with a scene from myth. Here, because the scene is Europa being abducted by Jupiter there is no serious issue of a religious connotation apart from those who have tried to find hidden Christian messages in the Latin couplet which forms part of the scene.

A ring from Piercebridge with a gemstone depicting a lyre is probably alluding to Orpheus, and might even have belonged to someone with an interest in the cult. But in Rome an inscription records a man called Tiberius Julius Orpheus (*ILS* 8060). The gemstone could as easily be a motif playing on a man's name and acting as his seal. The gemstones from the sacred spring at Bath were originally interpreted as votive deposits. Re-examination showed that while most seem to have originated from the same workshop (though even this is a thoroughly subjective claim as no one making it has any expertise in engraving gemstones), the different rates of wear and damage suggest they were individual casual losses by bathers as the water loosened the stones from their settings. At the legionary bathhouse at Caerleon gemstones from the drain had obviously found their way into the water the same way. It is a mark of how divorced we are from knowing all we need to know to interpret these things that the possibilities are so broad.

The Orphic mosaics prey on the minds of many modern commentators but Orpheus was not so controversial in antiquity. St Augustine, happy to curse plenty of pagan cults and not a few variants on Christianity, makes no mention of him in the *City of God*. Even St Jerome, a bigot of unparalleled bile who makes Augustine seem open-minded and imaginatively tolerant, could only concern himself with how Orphic lyre music might dull one's 'chastity' (*Letters* cxvii.6). Jerome was of course subscribing to figures of speech – and this is really where much Orphic imagery belongs.

It is very easy to adopt a medieval Spanish-Inquisition-style mindset and assume that anything pagan was invariably idolatrous to Christians. But in the world of late antiquity, Orpheus and other mythical figures also acted as figures of speech, providing metaphors for mood and settings. Pagans and Christians alike engaged in this, as is entirely plain from the literature of the period. But in an age when it is common for 'experts' in Roman civilisation and archaeology to have little or no knowledge of Latin, and also to have never read ancient literature in any detail, it is not odd that this use of mythology for universal metaphor seems to come so frequently as a surprise. But it is also true that classicists of whatever persuasion often take little interest in archaeology, and prefer a pedantic isolation. Thus our contemporary fixation with specialised disciplines sometimes serves to do no more than annihilate creative, or more expansive, thought.

The fourth-century Gallo-Roman poet and imperial tutor Ausonius cited the *Orpheos tripodes*, 'Orpheus' Tripod' – apparently the label applied to the three core elements of earth, water and fire (see the Loeb edition, I, p.367). Ausonius was only three years old in the year of the Edict of Milan, and therefore grew up in an age of Christian emperors and even became tutor to Gratian. Yet his writings throughout show a consummate familiarity with all the verbal imagery and allusions of pagan myth and religion. Ausonius' personal religious persuasion is not certain but the fifth-century Gallo-Roman priest Sidonius simply used Orpheus, and other figures, as metaphorical symbols for branches of learning – in this case *tenere . . . cum Orpheo plectrum*, 'to hold the quill with Orpheus' (*Letters* iv.3.5). On that basis, an Orphic mosaic might just as easily serve as evidence for a library.

Ausonius and Sidonius were submerged in the pagan classical tradition that coloured the manner in which people expressed themselves. It reappeared in the Renaissance when prominent persons had themselves painted as figures from myth or posed as ancient heroes. In other words, the figure of Orpheus – or, frankly, anyone else – is not the basis of a case for a cult centre in what would otherwise be happily interpreted as a villa. Nevertheless, this has not stopped a good deal of speculation in recent years about some of the villa houses. Any villa judged (subjectively) to have a surfeit of baths or large baths, or which has produced cult items of practically any sort, now often leads to the claim that instead of being villas, these were the centres of healing cults.

Part of the problem is the question of emphasis. For a start, the functions are not incompatible. Chedworth was a villa that grew into a large complex in the fourth century (**142**). It had mosaics, and a variety of rooms in several wings in an elegant location on an east-facing slope not far from Cirencester. That it had two large bath suites, a garden shrine and another nearby temple, together with some small and mostly crude reliefs of deities, has led to the suggestion that this was a cult centre of Lenus-Mars, a deity whose principal sanctuary was at Trier. The basis for the claim seems to be that one of the reliefs, of execrable quality, is inscribed ...ENM... (*RIB* 126). Those letters are indeed expandable as *Len(o) M(arti)* but even if there was a shrine to Lenus-Mars here there is no reason why it was not just a part of the estate, rather than the prime basis for its existence. Reliefs depicting Mars and other classical gods are well known in the Cotswolds, thanks to the easily-carved stone. Material like this was a commonplace part of the Roman world (**143**). In any case the Chedworth residents were fairly relaxed in their choice of subjects for epigraphy. Of the two other examples from the house, one is inscribed with the name of the Green faction in the Circus, and the other with a Chi-Rho – an eclectic series if ever there was, and equally good 'evidence' for Chedworth being simultaneously the headquarters of a circus supporters' club and a church.

Chedworth's ensemble of artefacts and architectural features though draw us back to the idea that some of the same people who financed these domestic improvements were also embellishing their estates with new pagan temples, or in some cases patro-

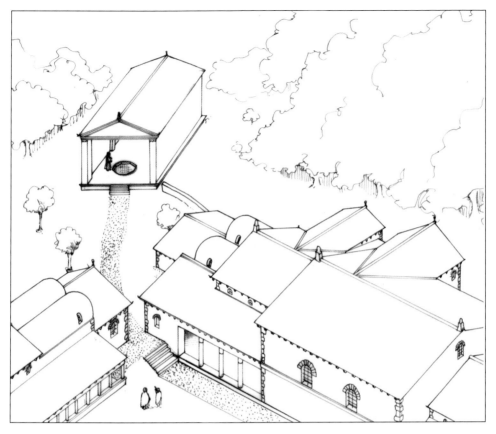

142 *Chedworth (Glos). The north-west corner of the villa. A gap in the wings between two bath-suites allows access to the small garden shrine. Such features were normal villa embellishments and not necessarily evidence that this was the site's prime function*

nising existing ones. At Wycomb, about $4\frac{1}{2}$ miles (7km) from Chedworth and even closer to two other villa houses, a poorly understood settlement seems to have been built around a central temple precinct, possibly even with a theatre like Gosbecks and Wycomb. There is no specific evidence for such a connection here or anywhere else, but the houses are good evidence for increased concentrations of wealth. That might be linked to greater control over larger estates and the idea of modelling themselves on the golden days of early imperial Rome when the Italian villa owners like Pliny the Younger took care of the ancient temples on their estates. The sheer conservatism of the figurines from Lamyatt Beacon (**137**) looks like a very traditional and reactionary approach and a search for comfortable and reliable icons of better times. The explicit references to Virgilian literature, and lines taken from it, on the coinage of the British usurper Carausius (286-93) is ample proof that there was a well-versed public to appeal to this way.

143 *King's Stanley (Glos). Altar of Mars, depicting the god in his normal Roman martial pose. This is one of several altars of Mars from the site, which was probably a rural shrine to the god playing an integral part in the cycle of rural agricultural life*

Philosophers and griffins

Brading villa on the Isle of Wight possesses a series of mosaic floors that have proved a particularly fertile source of speculation about their purpose and the owner's motivation. Like so many other villas it grew from modest late first-century AD beginnings, though there may well have been a late Iron Age house on the site. It was not until the fourth century that the original house was entirely incorporated into a much larger building that looked out over a courtyard flanked by other structures. The main house was embellished with mosaics in several of the rooms, enhanced by wall-paintings though only fragments of the latter survive. The Orpheus floor was not an elaborate version and consisted of just a medallion depicting Orpheus inserted into a simple square border, possibly overlooked by the Four Seasons. The figure greeted anyone entering the house from the east. In the northern wing the most interesting floors show a variety of mythological scenes involving pagan deities and heroes. One of these is Perseus, armed with the Gorgon's head and rescuing Andromeda from being consumed by sea monsters. Other panels depict Ceres, perhaps Achilles, Lycurgus chasing the nymph Ambrosia, and figures that may represent Paris and the nymph Oenone, or Atys and the nymph Sangaritis (**141, colour plate 25**). Various other motifs integrated into the overall design include the Four Winds and various sea monsters.

At the most basic level there is no need to see any of these features as more than artistic decorations appropriate to a rural villa in a maritime setting. Brading once overlooked a natural harbour that cut off the south-east corner of the Isle of Wight. Even today it is only a short walk to the sea. Brading's villa economy benefited from trade across the water, as the finds of imported pottery demonstrate. The philosopher panel portrays a man with the accessories appropriate to interests in science, astronomy and time (**colour plate 28**). The theme is known from floors in Italy. In Roman villa culture, it was normal for educated men to engage in philosophical social gatherings. In the late Roman world there was a self-conscious emulation of this tradition, reflected in the literature of the period and stimulated by Epicurean philosophy. Does the figure represent the owner, or reflect the tone he wanted to set? Given that we do not know the room's function, the speculation is a little futile. We do not know who the figure represents.

The most bizarre floor at Brading lies on the other side of the house. A house or hut with a staircase is flanked by a pair of griffins on one side, and on the other a cock-headed man (**144, colour plate 22**). Several of the attempts to interpret the panel have focused on the Latin for a cock, *gallus*, and possible allusions to emperors like Gallienus (253-68), or Constantius Gallus (351-3). Other possibilities are further puns on *gallus* where the word means a Gaul, or the *Galli*, the priests of Cybele. The other, and rather more esoteric, interpretation is that the cock-headed man is the god Iao.

Iao, also known as Abrasax or Abraxas, is rare in Britain, but turns up on a lead dedication found at West Deeping (Lincs – see *B* 1996, 443-5), and gemstones from Thetford and Silchester (*RIB* 2423.15-16). Both the latter name Iao and illustrate him as a cock-headed figure with serpents for legs. Macrobius, a fifth-century writer, records in his *Saturnalia* that Iao was identified with Zeus, Helios (i.e. Apollo), Hades and Dionysus, using information from the oracle of Colophon:

> When Clarian Apollo was asked which of the gods should be regarded as the god Iao, he replied: 'the unsearchable secrets should be hidden by those who have learned the mysteries'. However, for those with limited understanding and feeble minds, think about this: Iao is the supreme god over all the gods. In winter, Hades; at the start of spring, Zeus; in the summer, Helios; and, in the autumn, splendid Iao.
> Macrobius, *Saturnalia* i.18.19-20.

Griffins were legendary creatures of the east that pulled Apollo's chariot (Sidonius, *Carmina* xxii.66-7). One is depicted in association with Apollo on a fourth-century silver lanx from Corbridge. Griffins were reputed to live in the hills on the route across Asia where they guarded gold (Herodotus, *Histories* iii.114; Pliny, *NH* vii.10).

144 *Brading (Isle of Wight). Cock-headed figure (Iao?) and kiosk (see **colour plate22**). See the text for the complex possibilities surrounding this strange image*

They also entered general classical iconography as decorative fabulous beasts, appearing even on the distance slab from the Antonine Wall (**colour plate 8**) and on the Orpheus mosaic at Woodchester.

Moreover, Sidonius and Macrobius are late sources and wrote not much later than when the Brading floor itself was laid, perhaps drawing on a common source. Diodorus Siculus, writing in the first century BC, suggested that Iao was to be identified with the Jewish Jah (i.94). Finally, it takes only a small leap of imagination to realise that the Egyptian sun-god Horus was commonly depicted as a falcon-headed man; the Brading figure might very easily represent a conflation of supreme sun-god imagery, perhaps composed by someone who had seen various images of Iao (who normally appears with serpent legs), Horus and others, but not understood them fully. It is very easy to concentrate too much on the individual names and attributes and forget that Jah, Iao, Horus, Helios, Apollo and so on were all really variations of the same thing. Long before, Cicero had pondered on this very problem. If he found it difficult, the idea that a Romano-British mosaic could carry a definitive allusion to any one myth or god is exposed for the unresolvable pursuit it is.

> The sun's name, being Sol, you can work out from the fact that there is only one, the sole example, of his kind, but theologians have even come up with several Suns! One is the son of Jupiter, and grandson of Aether, another one was fathered by Hyperion, and the third was fathered by Vulcan, the son of the River Nile ... The fourth is reputed to be the one whom Acanthe gave birth to on Rhodes and the fifth is said to have sired Aeetes and Circe at Colchi.
>
> Cicero, *DND*, iii.53, 54

145 *A* Protoceratops *of the Gobi Desert guards its nest. These Cretaceous dinosaurs are found in large numbers and have been plausibly linked to the griffin myth. Note the skull shape and the frill that resembles the griffins' wings (see* **colour plate 22**). *Displayed in the American Museum of Natural History, New York City*

This scarcely explains why griffins should appear at Brading. It has been recently pointed out that the griffin myths can be convincingly linked to the fossil remains of a herbivorous dinosaur called *Protoceratops*, of the Cretaceous period (Mayor 2000). The remains are well known and studied from a very large number of well-preserved, prominent and conspicuous fossils in the Gobi Desert (**145**). The skulls and frills closely resemble the mythical griffin beaked head and wings, and the remains are frequently found in their nests. No one has ever commented before, including Mayor, on the fact that Brading lies around one mile from the only place in the former Roman Empire where dinosaur bones are to this day common and conspicuous finds (**146**). Yaverland beach produces on every tide scattered traces of disarticulated vertebrae, skull and limb bones of the herbivorous dinosaur *Iguanodon*. The same shore has significant quantities of visible and distinctive dinosaur footprints. It is inconceivable that the residents at Roman Brading were unaware of this. Indeed an excavation at Bembridge in 2001 close to the Brading villa produced a stratified fragment of fossiliferous rock that can only have come from the beach.

Obviously, no connection can be proved but we might at least ask ourselves whether the owner of Brading villa had an interest in myth reinforced by discoveries nearby. Considering that the Iguanodon skull is beaked too, and the floor panels include one depicting Perseus rescuing Andromeda from sea monsters, and another with sea tritons and a merman, the idea seems less harebrained and more of an elementary observation of the obvious. It is, at any rate, certainly no more off-beam than some of the theories already published on the subject, and has the advantage that the mosaic's figures are facts, and so are the dinosaur bones.

Whether or not the Brading owner was stimulated by finds from near his house, he was still making a choice of subject matter from a broadly conventional canon of

146 *Isle of Wight. Iguanodon skeleton now displayed at Sandown Dinosaur Museum. Bones and footprints from these large Cretaceous herbivores abound on the shore near Brading villa and may have contributed to the villa owner's interest in the mythical beasts displayed on his floors*

topics. The links and relationships, and shared identities, between mythical figures are impossibly complex for us to unravel completely. It was just as difficult for people in antiquity. There was, and is, no simple and straightforward explanation, and nor should there be. We are totally dependent on the literary sources we have. They show that educated men used and manipulated mythological allusion and imagery as the mood took them. That Sidonius, a Christian bishop, wrote a poem about myth shows that we cannot assume anything at all about the personal religious beliefs of the owner of Brading, Bignor, or anywhere else.

Mythical figures and scenes could be used for a variety of purposes, the most paradoxical of which was the use of pagan and mythical figures as Christian allegories. For example, even Anglo-Saxon literature preserved the idea of the panther as Christ, 'peaceful, kind and loving', rising on the third day to issue the 'most lovely of songs' and a 'fragrant' breath (Crossley-Holland 1984, 286). The episode of Bellerophon killing the Chimaera was seen as the triumph of good over evil and was utilised even by Christian writers of the fourth and fifth centuries. It appears on the mosaic at Frampton (Dorset), alongside a Chi-Rho and an image of Neptune. If this seems strange, one need only remember the character of Aslan in the *Narnia* books by C.S. Lewis to see how the allegorical tradition of representing Christ in animal form has endured. Interpreting such imagery as automatically pagan or Christian is, on the whole, a very simplistic way of looking at things.

Pagan treasure

The same principles that lay behind the literary topics adopted by men like Ausonius and Sidonius ought to apply to the great fourth-century silver plate hoard from Mildenhall in Suffolk (**colour plate 30**). Typically for the late Roman world it showed a generous accommodation of motifs and figures on some of the dishes, drawn from the general canon of Bacchic myth. The Great Dish, a stupendous platter over 60cm wide, features two concentric parades of figures. The outer shows a Bacchic revel, including a drunken Hercules and Bacchus himself. The inner features Nereids and, in preparation for the centrepiece, marine beasts. The central motif is Oceanus himself, functioning in decorative terms exactly as the Gorgon head on the pediment at Bath. The circularity of the motion and layout reflects a similar treatment at Bath, and in the perambulating circularity of some of the Orphic mosaics. Indeed, Oceanus even appears as a motif in one of the wreaths on the Woodchester Orphic floor. The Corbridge lanx, mentioned above, depicts a variety of pagan deities like Apollo, Artemis, and Leto in what seems to be a scene set in the island of Delos. While it might recall the visit to the island by the pagan revivalist emperor Julian II (360-3), it might also have just been treated as a work of decorative art in an idiom appreciated by an owner of whatever religious persuasion. We know from Pliny the Elder that master craftsmen adopted particular mythological scenes and subjects as their personal trademarks. It helped identify their work and encouraged fads (*NH* xxxiii.139).

If the Mildenhall hoard was not evidence for a late Roman mystery cult, then is there any real evidence for late pagan religion in Britain beyond the physical evidence of places like Lydney? The answer here ought to be the Thetford Treasure. A lucky strike has preserved for us the burial of goods that were at some point in their history used in the cult of an obscure Republican god called Faunus. That it was only found by a metal-detector user *after* a genuine archaeological investigation had taken place goes to show just how much serendipity has played a part in what we have to talk about at all.

Coins believed to have been recovered in the Thetford hoard (but dispersed before its existence was revealed), as well as the style of the artefacts, show that its burial cannot have occurred before the very end of the fourth century. It may actually have been deposited well into the fifth. The hoard included a number of pieces of jewellery, apparently being made up of new gold settings for somewhat older gemstones. The inclusion of the jewellery means that the hoard might not have been deposited by its original owners. The 33 silver spoons included references to the god Faunus, an associate of Bacchus, in conjunction with other cryptic Celtic-style names which appear to allude to a reverence for wine and produce (**147**). One suggestion is that these were characters in the Faunus rituals, individually adopted by participants. 'Medugenus', possibly meaning 'mead-begotten', recalls the subject matter of an ode by Horace in which he describes the Faunus cult (iii.18). Perhaps the Thetford Faunus sect used a vernacular version, now lost to us, of the same story, and which provided the names. Most of these, like 'Andi Crose', have evaded

147 *Silver duck-handled spoon from the Thetford treasure. The bowl is inscribed:* dei Fauni Crani, *'(property) of the god Faunus Cranus'. The meaning of the epithet* Cranus *is not certain but may either have a Celtic origin, as several of the other epithets found on the treasure are, in this case perhaps linked to the word which survives in Welsh as* crand, *'grand'. Or it may be derived from the Greek* kranos, *'helmet'. In other words, no one knows. Length 92mm*

understanding. The alcohol associations suggest this was a cult that celebrated the enlightenment found in intoxication or narcotic stupours. In Ovid's *Fasti*, Faunus appears as a vision in dreams during sleep induced by poppies, and demanded a sacrifice of two cows (iv.663).

Of course the burial of the Thetford hoard might be easily taken to mean that it was buried for safety from some sort of iconoclastic gang of Christian vigilantes. But it is also possible the hoard was long since defunct and the jeweller had bought them as stock-in-trade. That does not affect the point that somewhere in Roman Britain there seems to have been a Faunus cult – though the spoons might have been imported. Even so, Faunus had not really made any sort of public appearance in Roman life since the first century BC when Horace wrote.

Apparently some sort of pagan revival, the Faunus sect perhaps drew their inspiration from an artistic backdrop that found more mundane manifestations in the floor designs of the mosaic-laying classes. But even in this apparently clear-cut case there was that blurring of tradition found elsewhere. The Mildenhall hoard included several spoons with Christian exhortations and motifs. These are similar in content to the exhortations already noted for rings (see chapter 4). The range of known types shows how flexible the formulae were. The Mildenhall spoons included examples with the explicitly Christian A XP W (Alpha Chi-Rho Omega, from *Revelation* i.8), alongside others with the *vivas* type, for example *Pascentia vivas*, 'Pascentia, long life to you' (*RIB* 2420.34). Even the Thetford treasure, with its unambiguous references to the cult of Faunus on some of the spoons (see below), also included the *vivas* type, for example *Silviola vivas*, 'Silviola, long life to you' (*RIB* 2420.40). The Thetford duck-handled spoons with their Faunus legends have a parallel in a very similar spoon from Canterbury with the XP motif (*RIB* 2420.61).

What we have then is a range of expensive silver tableware drawn from the same aesthetic tradition and generally belonging to the same level of social class, taste and style, but variably inscribed or decorated with motifs and exhortations drawn from what seems to us superficially like mutually exclusive sources. In fact the combination and range easily fit a social and literary taste context matching a man like Ausonius, educated in the classical pagan tradition but thoroughly integrated into the Christian hierarchy of the late Empire. The context would equally match a man with genuinely broad religious tastes, or none at all, and just a man with taste befitting the age he lived in and with respect for magnificent works of art. And, of course, we have no way of knowing whether the man who used or buried any of these hoard was its legitimate owner, a later owner (that is, not the one who bought them in the first place), a thief, or whether any of these hoards was made up from several different sources, or only one. Attempting to define the hoarder by the iconography of the hoard is potentially as simplistic as attempting to define a thief by the contents of his cache of stolen goods, or the twenty-first-century collector of Georgian silver spoons.

Christianity in the fourth century

By the same token it is impossible to know if artefacts of Roman date found in Britain and marked with Christian symbols or slogans belonged to, or were deposited by, committed Christians. The earliest certain Christian material from Britain is the celebrated collection of plate from the town at Water Newton (Cambs), thought to belong to the late third or fourth century (**126, 148, colour plate 20**). The earliest such collection from the entire Roman Empire, it consisted of material which included items more familiar from pagan contexts, such as the silver feathers. We can only guess at why such a valuable group should have been buried and abandoned. Perhaps the plate belonged to a shrine frequented by an underground sect that buried it during a time of persecution. But it is no less likely that it had been stolen – or perhaps even buried precisely because its pagan component was no longer acceptable to more orthodox Christian authorities. Unfortunately there is no way of knowing if the shrine it belonged to was in Water Newton or somewhere else entirely.

House churches did exist in the Empire. Based in private homes, they consisted of congregations that gathered in rooms set aside by loyal Christians. One of the few physical examples seems to have been at the Roman villa at Lullingstone (Kent) but was only identified because the wall-paintings depicting Christians at prayer and the Chi-Rho symbol were recovered from where they had fallen into a ground-floor room (**149**). There is no artefactual evidence to confirm its function but it seems impossible that it had been used for anything else.

Lullingstone and Water Newton are fairly unequivocal in their use of Christian symbols. In a world where certainty of any sort is hard to come by, the two are close to being as good as it gets. If these cannot be interpreted as secure evidence for active Christian communities it is hard to know what could be, but at the most they can hardly represent more than few dozen people. The sporadic instance of artefacts with Christian symbols is altogether a different matter because the Chi-Rho had also become a badge of power. Coins were repeatedly issued in the fourth century with reverses depicting heroic imperial figures waving the *labarum* with its Chi-Rho

215

148 *Water Newton (Cambs). Vase from the hoard of Christian plate (see also **126**, and **colour plate 20**). Height 203mm*

symbol (**colour plate 5**). It was no more or less a statement of legitimate victorious power than the issues of centuries before which showed military standards and Victories. Finding an artefact with the symbol is *not* an automatic and reliable means of identifying a cell of Christian worshippers. The word-square from Cirencester is a prime instance. The letters are arranged to form a five-word sentence in which the letters read the same backwards as forwards, thus:

R	O	T	A	S
O	P	E	R	A
T	E	N	E	T
A	R	E	P	O
S	A	T	O	R

The meaning, 'Arepo the sower holds the wheels with care', is entirely innocuous. The 'significance' is in two forms. Firstly, the fact that it reads the same in whichever direction one reads is either a source of amusement or deeper magical meaning, depending on one's point of view. Secondly, the letters can be *rearranged* to read PATER NOSTER AO, 'Our Father – the Alpha and the Omega', a distinctly Christian formula. However, the word square was in use from at least the first century before 79 (it has been found at Pompeii) and other such reversing sentences are

149 *Lullingstone (Kent). Wall-painting depicting the Chi-Rho monogram. From the upstairs suite on the east side of the villa interpreted as the late fourth-century house church*

known. It is not known really whether the Christian usage was primary or simply adapted an existing word-square. In antiquity, coding messages into letter sequences was certainly well known but the prospect of unravelling such hidden messages today sometimes relies too much on invention and manipulation. One recent work has attempted to uncover Christian messages by analysing inscriptions, such as the rhyming couplet on the mosaic floor at Lullingstone, and basing the interpretations on numerical sequences (Thomas 1998, but see Handley 2000 for the problems and flaws in the theory).

All Christian communities represented a diversion of resources. In times past, men like Marcus Aurelius Lunaris (see chapter 3), had endowed their communities and homes with monuments and facilities. In this way they linked their power and status to the traditional religions and repaid some of their wealth to the communities. In the fourth century, the pressure on Christians from their priests and bishops to divert their resources to the Church steadily increased. The amounts varied but in a spiritual climate which promulgated the theme that riches brought no path to eternal joy, it was comparatively easy for a vestment-clad Svengali to convince Christians to bequeath their estates to the church, and also even to 'help' them write their wills. Back in 197 the Christian apologist Tertullian said 'if we reflect that it is the very world which is more truly a prison, we shall realise that you have left a prison rather than entered one' (*Ad Martyras* ii.1). Such attitudes were common amongst the more zealous Christians. The result was that they had little interest in investing money, time or emotions in a temporal future when there was so much more wonderful a future waiting for them as soon as they were dead. Those who had made temporal commitments and gestures, whether in Rome herself or her provincial cities, did so because they had a vision for themselves and their families in a Roman future in this life. This embodies the abrupt difference between traditional pagan communities, of whatever shade, and the more committed Christians.

Despite the legalisation of Christianity there remained a host of situations in which a Christian might find him or herself with divided loyalties. Killing by a Christian, even in the army, was punishable by excommunication. The church resisted the idea that a Christian could serve the state and also be a communicant. This might seem strange to us, but to the Roman world it had potentially catastrophic consequences. At the most basic level, this attitude meant money was far less likely to be spent on public projects. At a more sophisticated level, the diverting of belief into Christianity necessarily began to separate the close identification of religious with political allegiance to the incumbent state. At the most extreme, given that Christians eagerly awaited the Second Coming and the end of the world, it is hardly surprising that they had little concern in investing in civic futures and the kind of religious monuments that had as much to do with keeping the Roman administrative system functioning as they had with worshipping the ancient gods.

But Britain seems to have experienced only a limited amount of this diversion of resources into Christianity. In 314 the Council of Arles makes it clear that an episcopal system existed. In 343 British bishops attended the Council of Sardica. London had a bishop, *episcopus*, called Restitutus. York had one called Eborius (presumably a local man, with a name derived from his city's), and Adelfius was bishop of what was probably Lincoln though the text is slightly corrupt at that point. The undated Risley Park silver lanx mentions the bishop Exsuperius – a modest name that seems to mean something like 'from heaven' – of an unknown place called *Bogium*, possibly not even in Britain. Funnily enough another Exsuperius contributed a curse tablet to the sacred spring at Bath so the name is not even necessarily Christian (Cunliffe 1988, no. 66). Less likely to have been imported are the sheet lead fragments from Shavington (Cheshire) labelled as the property of the bishop Viventius. No matter. The fact is that Britain had a Christian ecclesiastical hierarchy shortly after Constantine the Great legitimised the church in 313. Occasional glimpses show us a little more of the ecclesiastical system. Thus we have St Patrick (*c*.369-461) telling us that his father Calpornius was a deacon, and his grandfather a presbyter from 'Bannavem' (*Confessio* i). *Bannavem* may be *Banna* (Birdoswald) on Hadrian's Wall, a place that has produced a considerable amount of evidence for extensive civilian-type settlement beside the fort platform.

The limited literary evidence suggests British bishops resisted the financial attractions of being part of the new establishment. The Council of Rimini in 360 was also attended by Gaulish and British bishops, but they spurned government money to cover their costs, except three British bishops who had no funds at all. Interestingly those three preferred the state subsidy to a whip-round. That suggests they believed

150 *The 'church' at Silchester (Hants) – reconstruction drawing based on the work by S.D. Ford, which postulates a timber extension from the narthex over what has been interpreted as the baptistery (right). The view is from the south and thus it is evident that this 'church' is reversed from the normal orientation. Together with the lack of any artefacts, this has made it impossible to be certain if it was a Christian place of worship. Length about 21m*

the church was regarded as an onerous imposition in Britain, compared to the funds being spent on new pagan temples in Britain during the fourth century. The well-known Silchester 'church' was little bigger than a modern cemetery chapel at about 21m in length. It would have had trouble accommodating a flock larger than 40 or 50. In any case it was derelict by *c.*370. It has never produced any proof that it was a church and the possibility remains that it served another function, perhaps as the headquarters of a *collegium*, or even in some administrative capacity given that the basilica here had long since fallen out of use for its original purpose and had become occupied by light industry. However, a recent revision of the excavated evidence together with parallels from elsewhere has resulted in a very convincing reconstruction of its possible original appearance (**150**). In this new form, the Silchester church emerges as an extended and carelessly-executed building, though using plans based on carefully-computed dimensions and patterns. A timber roof took the narthex out and over what was once thought to be an outdoor baptistery.

The church at Colchester is less doubtful, because at least it has the correct orientation for a church. But the building is extra-mural and lies within a cemetery. It is therefore more likely to be a martyrium than anything else, and certainly not a mainstream and prominent urban church. A martyrium was a chapel built on or over the grave of a martyr. That made it effectively a shrine though St Augustine denied the resemblance to pagan shrines (*CG* viii.27). Lincoln's forum piazza contained the church of St Paul-in-the-Bail. It survived even into a Victorian form but it is uncertain if it existed in the Roman period (see chapter 8, and **162-3**). On the continent, the civilian basilican form became the blueprint for the new breed of Christian churches but Britain has yet to produce anything as convincing (**151**). There is a slim possibility that some of the surviving Romano-British urban basilicas were used as churches but there is nothing whatsoever to corroborate that. The only piece of evidence we really

151 *Santa Sabina, Rome. This remarkable building, erected c.425 and still in use, shows how the civilian basilica design was utilised for churches. Despite the existence of many such buildings in the regional capitals, which were virtually identical, no known late-Roman church was built on this scale in Britain*

have is the place name 'Eccles' which preserves the Latin for church, *ecclesia*. But in such instances without physical evidence of a Roman-period structure we cannot be certain whether there really was a Roman church, or whether it refers to a Saxon building. Lullingstone, which as we shall see is one of the very few places where tenuous continuity of a sort is likely, is demonstrably *not* called 'Eccles'.

Unlike most pagan cults, Christianity was more inherently mobile. Sacredness was enshrined in the person of the priest and the performance of sacraments, rather than in places and things. A number of lead tanks have been found in Britain, most of which have Christian symbols on them. One of the three tanks found at Icklingham (**colour plate 21**) is circular, with a flat bottom and vertical sides, was made from sheets soldered together to make it watertight, and has two Chi-Rho symbols on it, one accompanied by the Alpha and the Omega. The other two are similar but not identical, and several others are known from Wigginholt (W. Sussex), Ashton (Northants), Walesby (Lincs), and Brough (Notts). They were almost certainly baptismal fonts but it is difficult to explain why Icklingham should have yielded several unless this is just chance. Lead tanks, being infinitely reusable, were unlikely to be abandoned unnecessarily though they could only have been used for baptism when a bishop was there to officiate. But two of the Icklingham tanks are known to have been associated with a cemetery that included what may have been a small chapel.

So, there is no evidence for major churches of the type that had appeared in Rome and elsewhere. Likewise there is no Christian tradition of significant church figures proselytising the faith in Britain. Christian traditions, records and myths of these activities were, and remain, widespread and well recorded, as well as being independent of the places referred to. If there had been such a figure in Britain we would almost certainly know about him. For example, in Gaul St Martin of Tours (315-97) served as a founding member of religious communities, beginning with Ligugé, Gaul's first monastery. Not only did Martin prove a resilient missionary, undaunted by tough terrain, but also engaged in suppressing pagan shrines and temples, even using troops from time to time to help out. Like Martin, Victricius of Rouen (330-407) left the Roman army when he became a Christian. In 385 he was made bishop of Rouen, and such was his reputation as an influential power in developing the northern Gaulish church that it was said he was invited to Britain *c*.395 to sort out problems though the nature of these and his success are unknown.

It is the very conspicuousness of people like Martin of Tours that makes their absence in Britain all the more noticeable. Had there been such a figure, it might not have been necessary to invite Martin to deal with difficulties. What we might imagine is that Britain had too durable a pagan tradition amongst its ruling classes to attract men like him. Writing in the sixth century, Gildas, a chronicler who saw the past almost entirely as a series of moral episodes with appropriate punishments and rewards, said that the Britons received Christianity 'with no enthusiasm' (*DE* ix.1). Although Gildas reassured his readers that Christianity was adopted properly by the truly committed, he believed that the eager uptake of Arianism proved how the Britons were excessively inclined to adopt almost any novel heresy. Religious orthodoxy was synonymous with loyalty to the state: that explained why Britain had sent up one usurper after another during the fourth century. Her challenges to the secular state reflected her resistance to the orthodox religion.

In reality, the church itself was severely compromised by schisms, of which Arianism was the most potentially disastrous. Arians disputed the divinity of Christ, and even the emperors took sides. Just to complicate the message the Empire displayed a sudden lurch into reactionary revivalism under the pagan emperor Julian II (360-3). Perhaps Britain simply 'suffered' from being far enough from the centre to escape the worst excesses and became almost a refuge for paganism, at least outside the major towns. The Pelagian heresy in the fifth century shows that the Romano-British church had the potential to split between sides. It would not be surprising that paganism proved more influential with its inherent inability to fragment. Interestingly, in 363 Julian recruited 'Alypius of Antioch, one-time prefect of the British provinces' to restore the temple at Jerusalem (Ammianus Marcellinus xxiii.1.2-3). The project foundered, not least because Julian's brief experiment collapsed with the accession of Valentinian I and Valens in 364. Even then the return to state Christianity was not only less oppressive, but coincided with a time when Britain was being steadily severed from the Empire. The 'barbarian conspiracy' of 367 was just one in a series of disruptive incidents that absolved imperial authorities, secular or religious, from concerning themselves with a place that seemed increasingly irrelevant.

If paganism had proved a formidable barrier to Christianity in Britain this would at least explain why we have such limited evidence for its existence. But there were

152 *Hinton St Mary (Dorset). Figure of Christ (detail) from the middle of the large mosaic floor (see also* **colour plate 26***)*

Christian communities, and there was also something of a grey area in between. The Water Newton treasure, as we saw, is not unequivocally Christian. Much of it resembles pagan cult goods, literally rebadged as 'Christian'. The same applied to the so-called Christian mosaics at Hinton St Mary and Frampton (Dorset). The Hinton pavement carries what is usually regarded as the earliest image of Christ – a clean-shaven man with the Chi-Rho behind him (**152, colour plate 26**). But like the Chi-Rho at Frampton, this is only one small component of a much larger floor. Hinton's floor is easier to see as an adaptation of existing designs. Where a pagan floor might have had the Four Seasons in the corner, Hinton's has four men who are generally identified as the Four Evangelists. The overall result is something that resembles the ceiling decoration in churches of the fourth century and later in the Eastern Empire.

We tend to look for black-and-white distinctions when we seek out Christianity. The reality was that Christianity might have made inroads into Britain but this was a place where the impact was rarely more than superficial. The physical evidence of the pagan 'revival' is very much more considerable than the evidence for churches, and this is in spite of the fact that Christianity was now central to the imperial identity. It is impossible to measure how much people only paid lip-service to the new religion. Even amongst the élite in Roman Britain, paganism and its association with a former and greater age was more conspicuous. In a remote and unsophisticated part of the Empire, the Romano-British were probably inclined always to look back over their shoulders, forever aware of the remote spirits that had once flitted across the primeval woodlands and glades of prehistoric Britain. Even in more sophisticated parts of the Roman world, pagan cults continued to find patronage, especially in rural areas.

8 A World by itself

For all its great monuments like the villas, the new temples and the forts of the Saxon Shore, late Roman Britain is a relatively silent period. Yes, we have the accounts by historians like Aurelius Victor, Ammianus Marcellinus, and Libanius, but the individuals of Roman Britain are almost entirely missing. Britain makes only sporadic appearances in the texts, portrayed as a recalcitrant place that provided the empire with a constant source of problems. Monumental inscriptions had all but ceased production at any level, and while some inscribed religious votives belong to this period they are hard to fix.

The archaeological record shows that all the buildings and settlements integral to what made Britain Roman, and what defines it as this to us, simply dissipated into the fifth century. What matters here is the tenuous evidence for how Roman Britain's religious monuments and paraphernalia endured in the consciousness of the people who lived after Roman power had been withdrawn. Britain was a world by itself, at least from our perspective. The broad picture seems to be that the temples fell into disrepair and even the small number of churches of Roman date have extremely little evidence either for significant continuity into the fifth century, or for revival of their sites later on (**153**). In cases where pagan sites re-

153 *Bath, slab of curved entablature, probably from a tholos (a round temple of Greek design). Found at the east end of the Great Bath and most likely to have come from a sacred building now beneath the medieval abbey church. Height 460mm*

154 *Escomb (Durham), church of St John the Baptist. Probably built in the eighth century, the church is largely constructed of masonry taken from the nearby ruined Roman fort at Binchester. There is no evidence for an earlier, Roman, ecclesiastical foundation here*

emerged with Christian monuments, this was usually only after a lapse of two centuries or more. Instead, new churches started to appear with the revival of Christianity in the seventh century. Their locations seem to have had as much to do with convenient sites, habit, and available building material as any religious continuity (**154**).

Some of the temples remained focuses of attention, though at this distance it is almost impossible to know what form this really took other than that eventually they all ceased to function as shrines. Elsewhere in the Roman Empire some temples were physically converted into churches during antiquity but this is normally only evident from the sort of upstanding remains that are absent from Britain. At Aphrodisias in Asia Minor, the Temple of Aphrodite was adapted in the 400s for this purpose, though the rectangular layout made it easier to tranform a classical temple into a church than it would have been for a Romano-Celtic temple (**155**). It has been suggested that Uley (Glos) stopped being a shrine to Mercury, and was then rebuilt as a late Roman church. After *c.*380 the temple (**colour plate 31**) suffered partial collapse leaving just two sides of the ambulatory in use. But during the fifth century the remains seem to have been covered over by a church-like building with attendant baptistery. This 'church' was also eventually demolished and was replaced

155 *Aphrodisias, Asia Minor, temple of Aphrodite. The first-century BC classical temple was converted into a Christian basilica in the fifth century. The cella was demolished and the exterior columns were moved inside to create a nave and aisles. A new exterior wall and eastern apse completed the work. View west along the south aisle with one of the relocated columns to the right. Conversion work, now leaving no trace, could also have been undertaken in Britain*

by a small chapel to the east, which left the baptistery as a freestanding structure. There can be no doubt that Uley's old function was known: the cult statue head of Mercury was found in a pit by this seventh- or eighth-century chapel where it must have been deliberately buried.

The Hebron shrine described in chapter 1 is a reminder that even what might seem to us an overtly *pagan* site could attract a wide public, which even included the less discerning (or more open-minded) part of the Christian community. If Uley did become a church that might have been because a component of the Christian Romano-British had already started to visit the place for their own complex personal reasons way back in the fourth century. We could not possibly hope to unravel whether this really happened or why, but the Hebron case, and the ambiguous nature of the Water Newton treasure, illustrates that it was possible. At Silchester today, the only building within the city's ruined walls is the church of St Mary, lying in what was once the largest temple precinct in the settlement (**156**). The area under the church cannot be excavated but here we might have either continuity of basic use as a religious area, or continuity of Christian practice stretching back to the Roman period.

Bath was so monumental a complex, and on a main route, that it must have continued to attract the sort of attention that the wreckage of medieval monas-

156 *Silchester (Hants), the south-eastern part of the city walls. In the left centre the church of St Mary lies nestled in a corner of the old Roman settlement, once the largest temple precinct at Silchester and close to the short track leading to the amphitheatre (54)*

teries does today. Bath required heavy maintenance to keep functioning. The new architectural works like the vaulted cover building over the spring had already required vast additional buttresses to prop it up. Once attention to this sort of repair ceased, everything else started to go wrong. The spring pool was no longer cleaned out through its sluice gate and the result was that as the buildings them-selves started to fall down, the debris was flooded on a regular basis. That gradually buried the temple precinct and the rest of the complex under silt, reduced to tumbledown dereliction in a swamp (**157**). Attempts at restoring a semblance of order involved using architectural fragments from buildings as paving stones, including parts of the temple. This can probably be linked with the foundation of a monastery here in 675. Eventually, wholesale collapse followed with the wreckage being scoured for metal components to reuse. An oft-cited poem of the eighth century, apparently referring to Bath, describes the scene as one of fallen arches, collapsed roofs, and ruined towers – 'the buildings raised by giants are crumbling'. There is no sense of who was worshipped here, though in the twelfth century the chronicler Geoffrey of Monmouth included Bath in his semi-mythical history of Britain. He claimed that, centuries before the Roman occupation, one Bladud had founded Bath and built the hot baths there, choosing 'the goddess Minerva as the tutelary deity of the baths' (ii.10). Unless this was coincidental, Geoffrey must have either tapped into local lore or information gleaned from inscriptions uncovered there.

Dereliction was widespread, sometimes with evidence that this was deliberate though usually the evidence is far more ambiguous. If that seems rather dramatic, there is no getting away from the fact that existing buildings were no longer maintained and new ones were not built of durable materials. As well as the decay of buildings, in an island where paganism seems to have proved extremely resilient in the face of anti-pagan laws, paganism disappeared as quickly as the Christianity from the archaeological record we can recognise. The literature shows that Christianity and paganism continued. This is a classic instance of archaeology's fundamental weakness: a lack of evidence is not a reliable basis for a conclusion.

The curious temple on Lamyatt Beacon, a hilltop ridge in Somerset, has already been discussed in some detail above (see chapter 7). A late foundation, Lamyatt Beacon seems to have been demolished in the early fifth century, apparently with enough care to leave roof-tiles in stacks beside the walls. Interpreting this is impossible. The demolition could have been part of deliberate policy to erase pagan monuments, or just opportunistic acquisition of building materials by people who knew the temple had decayed from indifference. It could just as well be the remains of an interrupted major maintenance programme. But whatever happened, like the house church at Lullingstone, the site was not forgotten. A small cemetery was found north of the temple. At least 16 people were buried here, and most of them were women. Carbon-14 dates put one in the middle of the sixth century and one in the late eighth. Even

157 *Not Bath, but Miletus. Once one of the greatest port cities in Asia Minor, Miletus is now land-locked and half drowned in silt and marshy farmland. In the fifth and sixth centuries, Bath's abandoned temple precinct resembled this scene*

227

allowing for the normal statistical margin of error, the earlier burial could have had no connection with the temple in an operational state. This is not surprising because the burials are oriented east-west and are thus, by normal definition, in the Christian tradition. Perhaps the temple site had become a burial ground for a community of unknown identity some distance away. Another suggestion has been that the detached northern building on the site significantly post-dated the temple and was in fact a small oratory. An oratory is a small private chapel, and one might speculate that if the original temple was connected to a villa estate then the oratory might have belonged to the villa family's descendants, continuing the tradition but now in a Christian idiom. However, there is no means of connecting the two periods at all.

Lamyatt Beacon is not unique in this association of Christian-type burials with an earlier pagan temple. At Henley Wood (Yatton, Somerset) a temple site began life *c.*225-50, underwent a major rebuild in Romano-Celtic form at some point but fell out of use at the end of the Roman period. An inhumation cemetery of uncertain post-Roman date followed, with some of the 50-plus graves cutting into the causeway that carried a roadway into the former precinct. Maiden Castle's derelict temple precinct accommodated four similar inhumations. But it is also true that the Roman structures attract investigation and excavation, and most of the late temples are sited in prominent locations which might have provoked an entirely coincidental later use for burials without there being any connection between the two. As excavations rarely take place in similar rural settings *without* evidence for structural remains having already been identified, the apparent connection might just be an illusion. It is very easy to draw potentially fallacious conclusions based on a self-selecting sample. The problem is much more widespread. Silchester was comprehensively excavated in the 1800s and is now being re-excavated by the University of Reading. Its open fields and extant city walls define the settlement and focus archaeological attention. But scarcely anyone has touched the city's hinterland – little or nothing is known about Silchester's extra-mural suburbs and cemeteries apart from what aerial photography and field-walking has shown up.

In some cases, there is evidence for deliberate destruction. The case of the Hebron shrine mentioned in chapter 1 is a clear instance of what could happen when the Christian emperors managed to effect their anti-pagan proscriptions. Here Constantine issued 'directions for the demolition, from the foundations, of the altar formerly erected there, the destruction of the carved images by fire, and the erection of a church worthy of so ancient and so holy a place' (Sozomen, *Ecclesiastical History* ii.4). The mithraea at London and Carrawburgh seem to have been subjected to violent destruction during the Roman period. It is reasonable to suggest that Christian iconoclasts, citing imperial law as an excuse, were behind the mayhem. But the effect was also sometimes to damage temples and shrines so much that we are left with even less evidence to understand them from. The temple at Brean Down, together with the adjacent 'priest house', were in ruins at the beginning of the fifth century. The general lack of votive finds, apart from coins, found on the site has been explained as possible evidence that the site was deliberately cleared as part of the anti-pagan legislation of the fourth century, giving way to a period of use for

Fig.3. South West View of the Ruins of Lulling Hane Chapel. p. 128.

Samuel Walsh Esq. *Contributes this Plate.*

158 *The ruins of the Saxon church at Lullingstone (Kent), as recorded in 1769. The foundations of this structure were found to lie across the late Roman 'Temple-Mausoleum' close to the villa house*

industry. As at Lamyatt Beacon, a non-aligned structure was built within the ruins, reusing rubble, and including coins struck by 392 and 394. This may be contemporary with a grave built on the other side of the temple ruins. Whether there is any possible connection in function is a moot point. The site was a prominent look-out spot across the Bristol Channel. Given the very real risks from seaborne raiders, it would have made perfect sense for local communities to install a small hut here as an early-warning post. The temple might even have been demolished to prevent it acting as a landmark for raiders, rather than having anything to do with wanton iconoclasts.

More striking are the places where stories about their former importance must have circulated for generations. Lullingstone villa in Kent is remarkable for three reasons. Firstly, it seems to have had a late fourth-century house church. Secondly, it was accompanied by a mausoleum built in a form similar to the Romano-Celtic temple, dating from nearly a century before. Thirdly, the house itself seems to have contained an even earlier water shrine to nymphs. In the eighteenth century, the ruins of the Saxon church of 'Lullingstane', partly built from Roman rubble and tile, still stood on the site of the 'temple-mausoleum' (**158**). There is no documentary evidence to link the phases but it must have been the case that after Christianity was restored to Kent at the very end of the sixth century, the site was chosen for a church because of its history. The memory that Lullingstone had once been a place of religious significance must have continued to circulate, even once the house and temple were in ruins. The little ruined medieval church at Faversham (also Kent) incorporated a Roman mausoleum into its chancel. On one hand this might have been a simple case of practical reuse, but the other possibility is that the tomb had contained a prominent Christian and a memory of this had endured (**159**).

Some forts of the Saxon Shore, and a few of the other walled remains of Romano-British towns, later became homes to churches. The question here is whether that was a matter of convenience or whether there was some direct continuity of tradition. Richborough is now known to have had what was probably a late fourth- or fifth-century Roman church within its walls, though nothing survived excavation work apart from what seems to have been a baptismal font outside a timber and daub church. What makes this doubly interesting is that Richborough has produced an exceptionally large series of coins from the first decade of the fifth century. This is very unusual in Britain. Official coin supplies seem largely to have dried up by this date, with most places producing very little after the 370s and 380s. Richborough must have remained in contact with the continent for longer than other settlements, perhaps acting as an important commercial and communications centre thanks to the easy contact across the Channel.

But even if Richborough's late church played an important part in the fort's latter days in the first few decades of the fifth century, it had no lasting importance or enduring tradition. After the year 664 a nunnery was founded nearby at Sandwich by Queen Sexburga of Kent, rather than at the fort. Richborough's church escaped the notice of the excavators of the site, but their records made it possible to identify the stone supports for its timber piers next to the stone baptismal font on its tiled floor and

159 *Faversham (Kent). The ruins of the medieval chapel with a Roman mausoleum, perhaps the grave of a martyr or prominent Christian, in the centre*

160 *Reculver (Kent). The remains of the seventh-century church with later additions, built within the ruined walls of the third-century Roman shore fort of* Regulbium

flint foundation. This construction of the baptistery in a separate building was typical for the day and is well-known from other examples in late-Roman military settings on the continent. Even so, interpreting Richborough means taking a lot on trust. Just two sides of the putative 'church' can be traced from excavation records and there were no artefacts that would confirm its function, although this is normal.

A few miles north-west, at the other end of the channel that then separated the Isle of Thanet from the rest of Kent, is the Saxon Shore fort of Reculver (**160**). Reculver had been built as a fort in the early third century, around 50 years before Richborough was converted into one. By the end of the seventh century there was a monastery here (Bede, *HEGA* v.8). In fact the site had been given to a priest called Bass in 669 (*ASC* 669). Unlike Richborough, Reculver presents a different problem of interpretation. Was a church built here because there was a local tradition of a Roman-period church in the late fort? This is unknown. The other possibility is that the ruined fort was probably unsuitable for other uses, and the derelict walls and buildings provided ample raw materials for the Anglo-Saxon church, some of which are still evident today in the remains.

The same applies to Canterbury, just to the south. Here the semi-derelict remains of the cantonal capital *Durovernum Cantiacorum* bore no resemblance to the elegant first- and second-century town centre with its temple precinct and adjacent theatre. The first major buildings of the post-Roman period belong to the Christian conversion of Ethelbert of Kent by Augustine at the end of the sixth century, and consist mainly of the complex of three seventh-century churches centred on the main one dedicated to SS Peter and Paul. However, Ethelbert's queen, Bertha, was already using an old Roman church in the east part of Canterbury that Bede says was 'built in honour of St Martin during the Roman occupation of Britain' (*op. cit.* i.26). This may

161 *Canterbury, St Martin's (Kent). This church may include parts of the Roman church Bede says was still in use in the early seventh century. Although heavily repaired, Roman tile is clearly visible on the right*

in fact be the present-day church of St Martin, which stands about half-a-mile east of the city, and seems to have sections of actual Roman wall as well as reused tile incorporated into the structure (**161**).

Lincoln has produced what seems to be the only instance so far of a possible Roman-date church erected in a central urban location, and which continued to be used for that role thereafter. Excavations in the forum piazza on the site of the Victorian church of St Paul-in-the-Bail produced traces of a series of earlier churches underneath, the oldest of which was timber-framed and associated with graves (**162, 163**). A few of the graves produced radiocarbon dates of the fifth and sixth centuries but with statistical deviations of plus or minus 80 years. This 'church' (if it was) may have had origins in the Roman period, perhaps as the seat of the bishop of Lincoln, but that is difficult to accept if the forum was still operational. Moreover, it even overlay another earlier timber building, but only a squared corner was found making it impossible to know what it was. The only piece of dating evidence from the putative late-Roman 'church' was a coin of 388-402 found on the first church's floor, either from its first phase, or from the last phase of the forum piazza. Bede tells us that St Paulinus effected conversions here around the year 628 and erected a church of 'remarkable workmanship'. The remains found here hardly match that description but the building was in ruins by Bede's time and could have been that built by Paulinus. The radiocarbon dates do not preclude that possibility but the position is obviously far from settled.

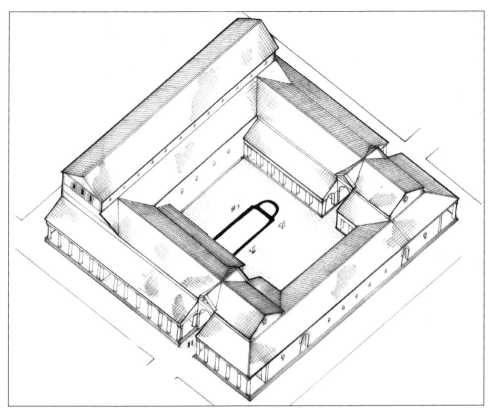

162 *Lincoln. The forum-and-basilica complex in their second-century heyday with the later plan of the first St Paul-in-the-Bail overlaid on the piazza. The church may have been Roman or post-Roman, with the forum remains providing boundaries to the consecrated ground (see also **163**)*

Roman or sub-Roman, Lincoln's forum church was a very simple type, with rectangular nave and eastern apse. The derelict forum might simply have provided it with a secure definition of consecrated ground, just as the Saxon Shore forts did. It is this physical convenience that probably played a larger part in the choice of location for religious settlement than anything else. The Saxon Shore fort at Bradwell-on-Sea (Essex), Roman *Othona*, is now half lost to the water and is a low-lying, windswept and bleak place. Bede describes St Cedd, Bishop of the East Saxons, actively pros-elytising the faith in 653 at 'the city the Saxons call *Ythancaestir*' (*HEGA* iii.22). *Ythancaestir* can be confidently identified as *Othona-castra*. The church, which must belong to around this date or the next few decades, was built over the west wall of the Roman fort, using rubble from the ruins. There is no sense here of any religious continuity of tradition, and even in the far north at Escomb near Bishop Auckland (Durham) is a late eighth-century church built from Roman masonry scavenged from the fort at Binchester (**154**). Hexham Abbey (Northumberland) also made use of stone from the fort and town at Corbridge. In most of these cases redundant Roman sites provided ready-prepared masonry for church building. During the

163 *Lincoln, St Paul-in-the-Bail. The site today, with the foundations of the church laid out in modern materials in what was once the forum piazza. As is patently obvious, the principal centre of Christian worship in Lincoln is now on a different site though a church remained on this site until modern times*

centuries after the Roman occupation there was little *original* stone and tile building work. In almost every instance recycled Roman material was used from wherever it was available.

There are few places where this recycling is less overt than the abbey church of St Albans. But St Albans is also one of the few places where a case for religious continuity from the Roman period can be made. The martyrdom of Alban can be attributed to the third century simply because this is when most of the testified periods of persecution took place. Until Christianity was legitimised imperial policy fluctuated wildly from silent accommodation to occasional episodes of outright violence. Alban is known from the literary traditions to have been put to death outside the city walls of Verulamium in the 'arena' (Bede, *HEGA* i.7). As this involved crossing the river, the location can be fixed to the east of the city where the abbey church is now. Bede adds that a church commemorating the martyrdom was built 'when the peace of Christian times was restored', which must mean some time in the seventh century. But that would only have been possible if the martyr's place of death had endured in local tradition and had probably been venerated in some form throughout. Either way there was evidently religious continuity of a sort at St Albans that has lasted to the present time though there is no means of verifying the connection archaeologically. The evidence cited for late- and post-Roman continuity in the old city itself is very thinly based on excavations from a single zone, and relies almost entirely on relative dating. This has been frequently cited as cast-iron evidence not just for continued occupation but also for a functioning civic organisation. However, the fate of the Roman settlement need not have affected interest in, or settlement gravitating to, the original martyrium which now must lie deep beneath the Norman abbey church, itself conspicuously built of rubble and tile taken from the ruins of Verulamium.

Alban's was an exceptional story for the time, and exceptional enough for a fairly detailed record of the events surrounding his excavation to survive several hundred years before it was written down. In fact, the story is one of the few episodes to record a snapshot picture of urban life in Roman Britain. There is nothing comparable for anywhere else in Roman or post-Roman Britain. The extra-mural church on the Butt Road site at Colchester stood in a cemetery and it is very reasonable to suggest that, like the first abbey church at St Albans, it lay close to the grave of a local martyr, though we have no idea who that might have been. There was no prior grave underneath though two people were buried within the church. Equally the church may have been a repository of some special relic associated with a martyr. The practice was common in early church history and is very similar to the pagan sense of special places. Essentially, the idea that a tree, spring or hill might be venerated had really been transferred to the spiritual power associated with someone who had exhibited extra holiness in his or her lifetime. Worshipping there or being buried nearby was a way of absorbing some of those properties by association.

But if this was what made St Albans so important, it had no lasting effects at Colchester even though the church lasted long enough to go through several alterations. It was certainly still functioning at the beginning of the fifth century though the lack of easily-datable evidence from after that date obscures just how long it remained in use. However, no later church succeeded it on the site and there is no surviving evidence for another until the church of Holy Trinity was built within the city walls in the tenth or eleventh century.

A case has been made for a very major reconstruction during the fourth century of the Temple of Claudius site in Colchester. The details are too complex to go into here, but essentially a number of late additions to the site make sense if a basilican hall oriented north-south was built across the old temple podium, entered by a wider vestibule on the south side with an apse on the vestibule's east end. The plan relies on assuming quite a lot, but the transverse vestibule and its apse seem to be beyond doubt. One possibility is that this was a church but the orientation is wrong, and its form bears a closer resemblance to known imperial audience halls of the period, for example at Trier.

Pelagius

Pelagius was perhaps the most remarkable and notorious religious legacy that Britain left to the late Roman Empire, though as a Briton he was truly exceptional in being notorious or significant for anything at all. The story of his heretical teachings caused a colossal crisis in the fifth-century church and resonated across the Empire. Its continued impact in Britain meant that historians and writers of the period provide us with a little backdrop to the enigmatic archaeology.

Born in Britain or Ireland, Pelagius did not arrive in Rome until the end of the fourth century. He was a learned man who, once he had reached Rome, engaged in one of the most controversial theological debates of the age. Pelagius believed that men had some control over whether they sought divine salvation. He found a direct contradiction to this in the words of St Augustine whose *Confessions* included the phrase, referring to God, 'give what you command, and command what you want' (x.29), based on the idea that men were fundamentally sinful. Pelagius took this to mean Augustine was claiming men had no choice and it was all up to God, a concept known as predestination. Pelagius utterly rejected this. A vicious row between the two men ensued, with Pelagius conducting his campaign from North Africa and the Near East. In 417, Pelagius was excommunicated for spreading 'far and wide his nauseating and abominable teaching that man had no need for God's grace' (Bede, *HEGA* i.10).

Although Pelagius disappeared after his excommunication, the crisis continued to resonate in the Christian world for a number of years. Pelagianism remained popular in Britain and Gaul, which of itself is useful evidence for an enduring church administration in Britain. Bede reported that before 429, Pelagianism had been introduced to Britain by Agricola, son of a Pelagian prelate called Severianus. According to Bede, Pelagianism was rejected in Britain but, rather cryptically, he tells us that the Britons 'were unable to refute its plausible arguments by controversial methods' (*op. cit* i.17). In other words, he is apologising for the take-up of Pelagianism. This rather makes it look that, far from being rejected, Pelagianism took a significant hold in Britain but, at any rate, the Britons sought help from the Gaulish church. This seems to describe an established Christian community in post-Roman Britain but not one that had many of its own resources. In 476 Sidonius Apollinaris wrote to his friend Faustus, bishop of Reiz, mentioning *antistes ac monachus*, 'a bishop and monk', called Riochatus then carrying the works of Principius, bishop of Soissons, to 'your dear Britons' (Sidonius, *Letters* ix.9.6). Riochatus may be the man later commemorated as St Riochatus of Wales, while Sidonius' reference to the Britons makes it sound as if Faustus might have been a Briton too. Even so, the episcopal structure which attended the Council of Arles in 314, if it still existed, can have had little more than nominal links with the towns like Lincoln and London, which in the 400s were shadows of their former selves.

Two Gaulish bishops, Germanus of Auxerre and Lupus of Troyes, were despatched to help throw out Pelagianism in Britain. They fought off storms sent by 'devils' to stop them, and then equipped with those indefatigable armaments, 'eloquence' and the scriptures, argued their case. Their future adventures included a visit to the martyrium of Alban, and Germanus was unlucky enough to have his leg broken by a 'devil', though such was his holiness that a fire that broke out where he was convalescing did not harm him. Shortly afterwards the bishops led the Christian Britons to victory in a battle against the Saxons and Picts, reputedly in 429. In 435 Germanus had to return to fight off a Pelagian revival, but his miraculous powers that healed a chieftain's son saw off this renewed threat.

Or so the story goes. Of course the tale of Germanus and Lupus was essentially a moral yarn which served to show how the devil did his work, using 'plausible arguments' to deceive the gullible folk of Britain. Bede wanted to show how his heroes, at the vanguard of legitimacy and orthodoxy, not only brought healing but also victory in battle against the heathen hoard. But it also projects an image where Christianity was functioning as some sort of administrative power, at least in the sense of being part of the Britons' identity. There was clearly some contact with the continent, and an active ecclesiastical relationship with the Gaulish church in the early fifth century. There is no easy way to link this with the archaeological record of the period, not least because the archaeology is so fragmentary, epigraphically silent and poorly recorded. It is difficult to see how the little church at Richborough for example could have been linked to the kind of ecclesiastical hierarchy described.

Only at Wroxeter, where a large timber complex was built in the ruins of the baths-basilica, do we have an urban context of the type in which some of these figures can be set – though, it must be said, without the slightest piece of corroborating evidence. Could the timber house or palace, call it what you will, which stood on the baths-basilica site here be the seat of a bishop? In other words had urban and regional government in fifth-century Britain passed effectively to the religious government structure, held together by a common need to confront external threats? Bede's account would not be out of context with that, though the rise of Pelagianism illustrates a tendency in the British ecclesiastical hierarchy, like the rest of the Church, to schism.

It is also possible that Pelagius, as a Briton, was influenced by the more pagan idea that human beings had a hand in their spiritual destinies. It was, after all, fundamental to the pagan process that men and women could engage in a relationship with a deity, make a vow and fulfil it. In this sense, Pelagius turns the world full circle and reminds us of Pliny's account of pagan religion four centuries before. Had pagans subscribed to Augustine's idea of fatalistic predetermination there would have been little point in hurling curses into the spring at Bath or fabricating an altar and setting it up in a woodland glade.

The Augustinian view might be taken as proof that Britain's fall was somehow predetermined and a decision of God's. Pelagianism, on the other hand, was a theology that could also be a theme for stimulating men and women to rise up and resist the political and social fragmentation of Britain once the Roman government had ceased direct control. Attractive though the idea is there is no proof that Pelagianism provided a foundation for resistance to decline. In any case, Pelagius himself seems not to have come up with his reaction to Augustinian predetermination until after he had left Britain, a place he apparently never returned to.

164 *Nettleton (Wilts). The site today. The temple of Apollo Cunomaglos (see **135**) lay on a hillside where the copse in the middle is. Nothing whatsoever remains visible on the surface*

Epilogue

In the end Britain was as irrelevant to Pelagius as it was to the rest of the Empire. In a religious sense the island retreated to the prehistoric world – at least from our perspective. The Romano-Celtic temples of the fourth-century pagan revival faded into oblivion, joining the demolished, collapsed and forgotten temples of the towns (**164**). The Thetford hoarder never returned to collect the cult objects of the Faunus sect. Of course the material that was valued and protected is by its very nature normally absent from the record. Without the Christian chroniclers and moralists we would have even less to go on. For example, we are told that Germanus returned in 447 to help lead the resistance against Pictish and Saxon incursions. We cannot now know to what extent pagan and Christian traditions really survived amongst the silent masses in Britain in the fifth and sixth centuries, and how much the surviving pagan monuments of the Roman period were later destroyed by iconoclasts from Christianised Anglo-Saxon communities.

The likelihood is that many Romano-British gods endured in an oral tradition until they gradually merged imperceptibly into the new traditions of Anglo-Saxon pagan beliefs, the revival of Christianity, Norse beliefs and finally the medieval church. Ancaster's medieval church almost certainly stands on top of the Roman town's temple precinct, marking at once some sort of disjointed continuity and suppression of the old order, like Constantine's church at Hebron. It is just one of

165 *Exeter Cathedral, 2002. At this stand, visitors to the church can write and post prayers, messages and requests to the Christian God recalling how, in similar ways, the men and women of Roman Britain sought pagan divine intervention in their lives (see 43)*

many such instances. Occasional glimpses of surviving pagan traditions mark the resilient association between ancient deities and the landscape. Ceres, for example, appeared depicted as a decorative finial on medieval thatched roofs. The association of churches, monasteries and cathedrals, with places that turn out to have had pagan origins shows that much medieval religious activity and significance was, to borrow a modern term, 'rebadged' paganism. In this way the Church exploited existing habits and traditions and perpetuated them in a different form.

While there is no demonstrable direct connection between the medieval shrine of the Virgin Mary at Little Walsingham and the Roman religious activity nearby at Great Walsingham, the later pilgrims mirrored in many ways the journeys and en-route cults of their Roman counterparts. Medieval priories and wayside chapels serviced their needs as the wayside shrines and inns of places like Nettleton and Godmanchester had provided food, lodging and temples for Roman Britain's travellers. Sales of pilgrim badges preserved the ancient tradition of religious souvenirs, to be taken home and cherished. Right up until early modern times the holy wells of Wales preserved antiquity's fascination with special sacred places, though by then they were almost invariably linked to saints. This cast a thin Christian veneer over a pagan approach to the propitiation of the spirits of the landscape. Even today we can still find practices that have links with the ancient past (**165**).

Today, Bath's temple precinct is the only Roman one in Britain that a visitor can still walk through. But now it lies deep beneath modern streets and it is difficult to appre-

166 *Bath. The visitors at centre right are looking out of one of the Roman openings through which ancient pilgrims threw votive offerings into the sacred spring. That spring now lies beneath the medieval King's Bath in the foreground*

167 *Ancaster (Lincs). A shattered relief depicting a hunter god, recently brought to light by the plough. Anonymous and battered, he bears witness to the prolific remains of religion in Roman Britain that disappeared in the fifth century. Height 298mm*

168 *Ancaster. Excavation in 2001 of a late- or post-Roman grave revealed that an inscription referring to the god Viridios had been reused to make a cist-like box around the body.* See **colour plate 32**

ciate what this place must have looked like once (**166**). Rob of Risingham is one of the very few carvings of a god to remain where it was carved into the living rock (**109**). In that sense the physical legacy of Romano-British religion is almost non-existent. The rest consists of buried temples, shattered and demolished shrines, and the scattered votive gifts (**167**). The cache that was Coventina's Well by the fort of Carrawburgh was emptied in a few hours in the nineteenth century. The Thetford and Water Newton treasures were found only by chance, and yet were recognised immediately to be pivotal discoveries in our hunt for the religious life of Roman Britain.

Our picture of religious life in Roman Britain is therefore unavoidably dependent on a patchwork of fortuitous discoveries, occasional historical references, inscriptions, curse tablets, and the broader panorama of evidence from across the Roman Empire. It is hopelessly incomplete, but there is enough to show that the weakest link of all is our speculative rambling to fill in gaps. The story, for all its blanks, is quite remarkable enough on its own. Some of the evidence cited in this book has been included to illustrate the commonality of the human spiritual experience, whether in Monument Valley or Exeter Cathedral. Most of what plagued the Romano-British were concerns that preoccupy all of us: health, death, a sense of injustice, a fear of the unknown, and a need to explain the world around us from fossils to thunderstorms. We all find our own ways of dealing with these issues. The truth is that one man's god is another man's demon, a source of treasure, an archaeological find, a metal-detector discovery or just a matter of indifference. With no one left to believe in them, the gods of Roman Britain now belong to the ages, only to be revived when the soil falls from an uncovered inscription and we can read their names again (**168, colour plate 32**).

> You'd be no goddess, Fortuna, if there was any sense.
> *We* made you a spirit and set you in the sky.
> Juvenal, *Satires* x.365-6

Appendix

This list has been compiled from all epigraphic references to gods and goddesses found in Roman Britain, and literary references by contemporary authorities. It does not include uninscribed statues. The list was previously published in *Companion to Roman Britain* (Tempus 1999) but I have taken the opportunity here to make some corrections, and introduce some additions and new discoveries.

Abandinus
Godmanchester: bronze plaque by Vatiaucus. *RIB* 2432.4

Aesculapius/Asklepios
Binchester: altar to [Aesc]ulapius by M. Aurelius [...]ocomas, *medicus*, for welfare of *ala Vettonum*. *RIB* 1028 (with Salus)
Burrow-in-Lonsdale (Overborough): altar by Julius Saturninus. *RIB* 609 (with Hygiaea (sic))
Carlisle: altar. *B* xxxii (2001), 390, no. 15
Chester: altar by Antiochos, *hiatros* (in Greek). *JRS* lix (1969), 235, no. 3 (with Hygiaea and Panakeia)
Chester: altar by the legate T. Pomponius Mamilianus. *RIB* 445 (with Fortuna Redux, and Salus)
Lanchester: altar to [Aescula]pius by the tribune T. Flavius Titianus with parallel Greek text (known from *RIB* 1083, Ebchester, to have been tribune of *cohors I Vardullorum* during the governorship of Antistius Adventus, c. 175-8). *RIB* 1072
Maryport: slab by A. Egnatius Pastor (in Greek). *RIB* 808
South Shields: altar to Esculap(ius) by P. Viboleius Secundus. *RIB* 1052

Alaisiagae, see also **Beda, Baudihillia, Fimmilena, and Friagabis**
Housesteads altar by 'the Germans' of *cuneus Frisiorum Ver(covicianorum) Se(v)e(riani) Alexandriani* between 222-35. *RIB* 1594 (with Mars and Numen Augusti)

Ammilla Augusta Felix
London: miniature bronze warship prow. Identification uncertain, possibly the personification of a named ship. *RIB* 2432.1

Ancasta
Bitterne: altar by Geminus. *RIB* 97

Andate ('Victory')
Unlocated: referred to as the 'grave of Andate' by Dio and a place where the members of the Boudican Revolt conducted various sacrificial acts. Dio lxii.7

Andescociuoucus, see **Mercury**

Anicetus, see **Mithras**

Anociticus, see **Antenociticus**

Antenociticus, also **Anociticus**
Benwell: altar by Aelius Vibius, centurion of *XX Valeria Victrix*. *RIB* 1327 (with Numina Augustorum)
Benwell: altar by *cohors I Vangionum* under the prefect [...]c(ius) Cassi[anus]. *RIB* 1328
Benwell: altar to Anociticus by Tineius Longus, prefect of cavalry, between 177-80. *RIB* 1329

Apollo, see also **Genius collegii Apollinis**
Auchendavy: altar by M. Cocceius Firmus, centurion of *II Augusta*. *RIB* 2174 (with Diana)
Bar Hill: altar to [Apoll]in[i]. *RIB* 2165
Chester-le-Street: altar by Tertius. *RIB* 1043
Hadrian's Wall (near mc 42): altar by Melonius Senilis, *duplicarius* from Germania Superior. *RIB* 1665
Nettleton: bronze plaque by Decimius. *RIB* 2432.3
Newstead: altar by L. Maximius Gaetulicus, legionary centurion. *RIB* 2120
Scarcroft: altar. *JRS* lv (1965), 221, no. 6 (with Numen)
Whitley Castle: altar by Gaius [...]ius of *cohors [II] Nerviorum*. *RIB* 1198

Apollo Anextiomarus
South Shields: bronze patera by Marcus A[...] Sab(inus). *RIB* 2415.55

Apollo Anicetus, see **Sol Apollo Anicetus**

Apollo Clarius, see **Clarian Apollo**

Apollo Cunomaglos
Nettleton: altar by Corotica, son or daughter of Iutus. *JRS* lii (1962), 191, no. 4 (and Wedlake 1982, 135-6, no. 1)

Apollo Grannus
Inveresk: altar by Q. Lusius Sabinianus, *procurator Augusti*. *RIB* 2132 (see also *ILS* 4649)

Apollo Maponus
Corbridge: altar by Q. Terentius Firmus, *praefectus castrorum* of *VI Victrix*. *RIB* 1120
Corbridge: altar by [Calp]urnius [...], tribune. *RIB* 1121
Corbridge: altar by Publius Aelius [...], centurion of *VI Victrix*. *RIB* 1122
Ribchester: shaft by Aelius Antoninus, centurion of *VI Victrix* and commander of *n(umerus) eq(uitum) Sar[m(atarum)] Bremetenn(acensium) [G]ordiani* between 238-44. *RIB* 583

Arciaco (with Numen Augusti)
York: altar by Mat...Vitalis, centurion. *RIB* 640 (with Numen Augusti). But note the variant on Mercury (next entry) which may possibly explain this otherwise-unknown deity

Arecurius, see **Corbridge**; under **Mercury** as **Arecurio**

Arimanes
York: statue by Volusius Irenaeus. *RIB* 641

Arnomecta
Brough-on-Noe: altar by Aelius Motio. *RIB* 281

Astarte
Corbridge: altar by Pulcher (in Greek). *RIB* 1124

Atys, see **Cybele** and **Atys**

Balatucadrus, see **Belatucadrus**

Barrax, see **Mars Barrax**

Baudihillia et Friagabis (Alaisiagae)
Housesteads: altar by numerus Hnaudifridi. *RIB* 1576 (with Numen Augusti)

Beda et Fimmilena (Alaisiagae)
Housesteads: shrine door jam by 'Germans, citizens of Twenthe'. *RIB* 1593 (with Mars Thincsus, and Numen Augusti)

Belatucadrus and variants, see also **Mars Belatucadrus**
Bowness-on-Solway: altar to Belatocairo by Peisius, *m(iles)*. *RIB* 2056
Brougham: altar to B[a]latu(cadrus). *RIB* 772
Brougham: altar to Balatucairus by Baculo. *RIB* 773
Brougham: altar to Blatucairus by Audagus. *RIB* 774
Brougham: altar to Belatu[ca]drus by Julianus. *RIB* 775
Brougham: altar to Belatucadrus. *RIB* 776
Brougham: statue to Belatucadrus. *RIB* 777
Brougham: altar to Belatucabrous. *JRS* lix (1969), 237, no. 7
Burgh-by-Sands: altar to Belatucadrus. *RIB* 2038
Burgh-by-Sands: altar to Belatocadrus by Antr(onius) Auf(idianus?). *RIB* 2039
Burgh-by-Sands: altar to Belatucadrus. *RIB* 2044
Carlisle: altar to Belatucadrus. *RIB* 948
Carrawburgh: altar to Belleticaurus by Lunaris. *RIB* 1521
Carvoran: altar to Baliticaurus. *RIB* 1775
Carvoran: altar to Blatucadrus. *RIB* 1776
Castlesteads: altar to Belatugagrus by Minervalis. *RIB* 1976
Castlesteads: altar to Be[l]atuca[dr]us by Ullinus. *RIB* 1977 (and *Brit.* v (1974), 463, no. 10)
Kirkby Thore: altar to Belatucadrus by [...]iolus. *RIB* 759
Maryport: altar to Belatucadrus by Julius Civilis, optio. *RIB* 809
Old Carlisle: altar to Belatucadrus by Aurelius Tasulus, *vet(eranus)*. *RIB* 887
Old Carlisle: altar to Belatucadrus by Aurelius Diatova. *RIB* 888
Old Carlisle: altar to Belatucaurus. *RIB* 889
Old Penrith: altar to Bel[a]tuca[drus]. *RIB* 914
Old Penrith: altar to Balatocadrus. *Brit.* ix (1977), 474, no. 7
Old Penrith: altar to Belatucairus. *Brit.* ix (1977), 474, no. 8

Bellona
Old Carlisle: altar by Rufinus, prefect of *ala Augusta*, and his son Latinianus. *RIB* 890

Bona Dea Regina Caelestis (the Good Goddess, Queen, Caelestis), see also **Regina Caelestis** and **Virgo Caelestis**
Chesters: altar. *RIB* 1448

Bona Fortuna (Good Fortune)
Corbridge: altar to B(ona) F(ortuna). RIB 1135 (with Panthea)

Bonus Eventus et Fortuna
Caerleon: slab by Cornelius Castus and his wife Julia Belismicus. *RIB* 318
York: slab to [Bono Eventu]i et F[ortunae]? *RIB* 642 (*RIB* 703 is part of the same)

Braciaca, see **Mars Braciaca**

Bregans
Slack: altar by T. Aurelius Quintus. *RIB* 623 (and Numen Augusti)

Brigantia see also **Caelestis Brigantia, Nympha Brigantia, Brigantia Augusta**, and
Victoria Brigantia
Adel: altar by Cingetissa. *RIB* 630
Birrens: figure in gabled relief by Amandus *arcitectus*. *RIB* 2091
South Shields: altar by Congeniccus. *RIB* 1053

Britannia
Balmuildy: altar by Q. Pisentius Justus, prefect of *cohors IIII Gallorum* between 138-61.
RIB 2195 (with Campestres)
London: lead sealing naming *Brit(annia) Sanc(ta)*. *RIB* 2411.33
York: altar by Nikomedes, imperial *libertus*. *RIB* 643

Caelestis Brigantia
Corbridge: altar by G. Julius Apolinaris, centurion of *VI Victrix*, his name, rank and unit
replacing someone else's or else recarved to make a correction. *RIB* 1131 (with Jupiter
Aeternus Dolichenus and Salus). See also *Brit.* xxvi (1995), 380, no. 7 for another
possibility

Campestres (Goddesses of the Parade Ground), see also **Matres Campestres**
Auchendavy: altar by M. Cocceius Firmus, centurion of *II Augusta*. *RIB* 2177 (with Mars,
Minerva, Hercules, Epona and Victoria)
Balmuildy: altar by Q. Pisentius Justus, prefect of *cohors IIII Gallorum* between 138-61.
RIB 2195 (with *Britannia*)
Gloster Hill: altar by *cohors I [...]*. *RIB* 1206
Newstead: altar by Aelius Marcus, *decurio* of *ala Augusta Vocontiorum*. *RIB* 2121

Camulus, see **Mars Camulus**

Capitolinus, see **Jupiter Optimus Maximus Capitolinus**

Cautes (associate of Mithras)
Carlisle: altar by Julius Archietus. *RIB* 943

Cautopates (associate of Mithras)
Lanchester: altar to C(auto)p(ates). *RIB* 1082 (with Mithras and Sol Invictus)

Ceres Dea Suria (Ceres, the Syrian Goddess)
Carvoran: altar by M. Caecilius Donatianus, serving as tribune in the post of prefect,
between 197-217. *RIB* 1791 (with Mater, Pax, and Virgo Caelestis)

Christos (represented by the XP 'Chi–Rho' monogram and/or A W 'Alpha' and 'Omega'), see also **Deus** (see also *RIB* vol II, fascicule 2 for items bearing Christian-style exhortations e.g. 2416.4)

Appleshaw: pewter dish. *RIB* 2417.36

Ashton: lead tank bearing XP. *RIB* 2416.13

Biddulph: silver spoon bearing A XP W. *RIB* 2420.56

Brough: lead tank bearing IX, for Iesus Xristus. *Brit.* xxvi (1995), 318–22

Caerwent: pewter bowl. *RIB* 2417.38

Canterbury: silver spoons bearing XP. *RIB* 2420.60–1

Colchester: pottery graffito. *RIB* 2503.133

East Stoke: lead tank bearing XP. *RIB* 2416.8

Exeter: pottery graffito. *RIB* 2503.134

Gatcombe: pottery graffito. *RIB* 2503.136

Hinton St Mary: mosaic with figure of Christ and XP. *RIB* 2448.14

Icklingham: lead tanks bearing W XP A. *RIB* 2416.9

Icklingham: lead tanks bearing XP. *RIB* 2416.10

London: pewter bowl. *RIB* 2417.40

London (Battersea): pewter ingot stamped XP. *B* 1998, 438 no. 24

Lullingstone: wall-paintings bearing A XP W and images of people praying. *RIB* 2447.6–8

Maryport: stone plaque inscribed XP. *RIB* 856

Mildenhall: silver spoons bearing A XP W. *RIB* 2420.53–5

Monmouthshire: silver spoon bearing A XP W. *RIB* 2420.57

Richborough: pottery graffito. *RIB* 2503.135

Silchester: lead sealing. *RIB* 2411.38

Stamford: pewter plate. *RIB* 2417.41

Sutton (Cambs): pewter bowl. *RIB* 2417.29

Traprain Law: silver items bearing XP. *RIB* 2414.20–1, 2420.58–9

Walesby: lead tank bearing XP. *RIB* 2416.14

Water Newton: silver bowl by Innocentia and Viventia, bearing A XP W. *RIB* 2414.1

Water Newton: silver bowl/cup bearing A XP W, and naming a sacred sanctuary. *RIB* 2414.2

Water Newton: silver strainers bearing A XP W. *RIB* 2414.3

Water Newton: silver strainers bearing XP and Iesus Xristus. *RIB* 2414.21

Water Newton: silver pan bearing XP W. *RIB* 2414.4

Water Newton: gold disc bearing A XP W. *RIB* 2430.3

Water Newton: silver plaque bearing W XP A. *RIB* 2431.1

Water Newton: silver plaques bearing A XP W. *RIB* 2431.4–11

Welney: pewter dish. *RIB* 2417.39

Wigginholt: lead tank bearing XP. *RIB* 2416.12

Winchester: floor tile inscribed with XP. *Brit.* xxiv (1993), 316–17, no. 18

Clarian Apollo

Housesteads: altar recording the oracle of Clarian Apollo in Ionia by *cohors I Tungrorum*. There are various references in classical texts, for example Ovid, *Fasti* I.20. *RIB* 1579

Claudius Divus (the deified Emperor Claudius)

Colchester: *templum divo Claudio* in use by the year 60. Tacitus, *Annals* xiv.31

Cocidius, see also Mars Cocidius, Silvanus Cocidius and Vernostonus Cocidius

Bewcastle: altar by Annius Victor, legionary centurion. *RIB* 985

Bewcastle: silver plaque. *RIB* 986

Bewcastle: silver plaque by Aventinus. *RIB* 987

Bewcastle: altar by Aurunceius Felicessemus, tribune promoted from *evocatus*. *RIB* 988

Bewcastle: altar by Q. Peltrasius Maximus, tribune, promoted from *cornicularius* to the Praetorian Prefects. *RIB* 989

Birdoswald: altar by [Tere]ntius Valerianus, commanding *cohors I Aelia [Dacorum]*. *RIB* 1872

Birdoswald: primary dedication on an altar with secondary, and probably unrelated, dedication to Jupiter Optimus Maximus by Pomponius Desideratus, tribune commanding *cohors I Aelia Dacorum* between 270-3. *RIB* 1885

Hadrian's Wall (near milecastle 37): altar by Vabrius. *RIB* 1633

Hadrian's Wall (milecastle 52): altar by *II Augusta*. *RIB* 1955

Hadrian's Wall (milecastle 52): altar by *XX Valeria Victrix* between 262-6. *RIB* 1956

Hadrian's Wall (near milecastle 55): altar by a vexillation from *VI Victrix*. *RIB* 1961

Hadrian's Wall (near milecastle 55): altar to Co[cidius]. *RIB* 1963

Hadrian's Wall (near milecastle 60): altar by *VI Victrix*. *RIB* 2020

Housesteads: altar by Valerius, soldier with *VI Victrix*. *RIB* 1577 (with Genius praesidii)

Housesteads: altar by *II Augusta*. *RIB* 1583 (with Genius huius loci and Jupiter Optimus Maximus)

Netherby (or Bewcastle?): altar by Paternius Maternus, tribune commanding *cohors I Nervina* and promoted from *evocatus Palatinus* (recorded at Netherby, probably erroneously). *RIB* 966

Risingham: altar. *RIB* 1207 (with Silvanus)

Vindolanda: altar by D. Caerellius Victor, prefect of *cohors II Nerviorum*. *RIB* 1683

Concordia legionis II Augusta et legionis XX (The Concord of *II Augusta* and *XX*)
Carlisle: base of sculptured relief. *Brit.* xx (1989), 331, no. 4

Concordia legionis VI Victrix Pia Fidelis et legionis XX (The Concord of *VI Victrix Pia Fidelis* and *XX Valeria Victrix*)
Corbridge: slab. *RIB* 1125

Condates, see **Mars Condates**

Conservatores (the Preservers-of-welfare Gods)
South Shields: altar dedicated 211-12. *RIB* 1054

Contrebis, see also **Ialonus Contrebis**
Burrow-in-Lonsdale (Overborough): altar by Vatta. *RIB* 610

Coventina, see also **Coventina Augusta**, and **Nympha Coventina**
Carrawburgh: altar to Conventina (sic) by Bellicus. *RIB* 1522

Carrawburgh: altar to Conveti(na) by Mausaeus, *optio* of *cohors I Frixiavonum*. *RIB* 1523

Carrawburgh: altar to Coventina by Aurelius Campester for *cohors I Cubernorum*. *RIB* 1524

Carrawburgh: altar to Coventina by Aurelius Crotus, a German. *RIB* 1525

Carrawburgh: altar to Coven(tina) by Vinomathus. *RIB* 1528

Carrawburgh: altar to Coventina by P[...]anus, *miles*. *RIB* 1529

Carrawburgh: altar to Covetine by Crotus. *RIB* 1532

Carrawburgh: altar to Covontina by Vincentius. *RIB* 1533

Carrawburgh: gabled relief to Covventina by Titus D(...) Cosconianus, prefect of *cohors I Batavorum*. *RIB* 1534

Carrawburgh: relief to Covven[ti(na)] by Aelius [...]pius, prefect of *cohors I Batavorum*. *RIB* 1535

Coventina Augusta
Carrawburgh: clay incense burner to Cove(n)tina Augusta made by Saturninus Gabinius. *RIB* 1530 and (revised) *RIB* 2457.2

Cuda(?)
Daglingworth: relief. *RIB* 129

Cultores (Gods of this Place)
Risingham: altar by Julius Victor, tribune (of *cohors I Vangionum*; see *RIB* 1217 under Jupiter Optimus Maximus below). *RIB* 1208

Custodes (Guardian Gods)
Vindolanda: altar by *cohors II[II] Gallorum* and Ve[...] Caecil[...]. *RIB* 1687 (with Jupiter Optimus Maximus and Genius)

Cybele and Atys
Dunstable: pottery graffito referring to the *dendrophori* ('branch-bearers') of Verulamium. The association with Atys is inferred. *RIB* 2503.114

Deus, see also Mithras, and Mithras Invictus
Caistor St Edmund: silver spoon bearing *Vivas in Deo*, in this case implicitly Christian in the phrasing of the exhortation. *RIB* 2420.49

Carvoran: pedestal or perhaps an unfinished altar recording the gift of a bracelet (*armilum*) from Binius. *RIB* 1806

Old Carlisle: altar to [D]eo by Flavius Aventinus. *RIB* 904

Rudchester: altar by L. Sentius Castus, (centurion?) of *VI Victrix*. In this case, the findspot in the fort mithraeum makes it certain that Mithras is meant. *RIB* 1398

Deus qui vias et semitas commentus est (God who devised roads and paths)
Catterick: altar by Titus Irdas, *singularis consularis*, and restored by Q. Varius Vitalis, *beneficiarius consularis*, in 191. *RIB* 725

Diana
Auchendavy: altar by M. Cocceius Firmus, centurion of *II Augusta*. *RIB* 2174 (with Apollo)

Bath: altar by Vettius B[e]nignus, *lib(ertus)*. *RIB* 138

Caerleon: slab recording restoration of a temple of Diana by T. Flavius Postumius [V]arus, senator and (legionary) legate, probably mid-third century if this is the man who was *praefectus urbi* in Rome in 271 (see *RIB*). *RIB* 316

Corbridge: altar by N[...]. *RIB* 1126

Risingham: altar by Aelia Timo. *RIB* 1209

Diana Regina (Queen Diana)
Newstead: altar by G. Arrius Domitianus, centurion of *XX Valeria Victrix*. *RIB* 2122 (see this man again at Newstead under Jupiter Optimus Maximus and Silvanus)

Digenis/Digenus?
Chester-le-Street: altar to Dig(enus?). *RIB* 1044

Hadrian's Wall (between Wallsend and Newcastle): altar to Di[genus?] (reading very doubtful). *RIB* 1314

Dis (The Underworld/Hades)
Lincoln: on a tombstone of a nine-year-old girl. *RIB* 265

Disciplina/Discipulina Augusti/Augustorum (Discipline of the Emperor/Emperors)
Bertha: slab to Discipulinae Augusti. *JRS* xlix (1959), 136-7, no. 6
Bewcastle: altar to Discip(linae) Aug(usti) (secondary text). *RIB* 990
Birrens: altar by *cohors II Tungrorum c(ivium) L(atinorum)*. *RIB* 2092
Castlesteads: altar of 209-11, rededicated 212-17, based on the text AUGGG, altered to
   AUG, i.e. for Severus and his sons, and then Caracalla alone. *RIB* 1978
Chesters: altar by *ala Augusta* for the Disciplina of Hadrian, 117-38. *Brit.* x (1979), 346, no. 7
Corbridge: base to Discipulinae Augustorum by *II Augusta. RIB* 1127
Corbridge?: slab to [Disci]p(ulinae) August[orum?] by *cohors I [fida Vardullor?]um* under [P.
   Calpu]rnius Victor. *RIB* asserts that this cannot predate 161-9, the first period of co-
   emperorship, but the relevant part of the text is not extant so this is only an inference.
   The same applies to the dedicant's name. *RIB* 1128
Greatchesters: altar. *RIB* 1723

Dolichenus, see **Jupiter Optimus Maximus Dolichenus**, and **Jupiter Dolichenus**

Domesticae, see **Matres Domesticae**

Domina Nemesis (Lady Nemesis)
Caerleon: lead curse (anonymous). *RIB* 323

Domus Divina (Divine Imperial House)
Brough-on-Humber: slab to Numina Augustorum M. Ulpius Januarius, *aedilis* of the
   vicus of *Petuaria*, to commemorate the new stage (*proscaenium*) for the theatre between
   140-61. *RIB* 707 (with Numinibus Augustorum)
Castlesteads(?): altar to Brigantia in honour of Caracalla and his divine house by M.
   Cocceius Nigrinus, *[pr]oc(urator) Aug(usti)*, between 212-17. *RIB* 2066 (with Nympha
   Brigantia)
Chichester: column base. *RIB* 89 (with Jupiter Optimus Maximus)
Chichester: slab recording the building of a temple to Neptune and Minerva in honour of
   the Domus Divina by the guild of smiths on a site given by [...]ens, son of Pudentinus,
   and by the authority of T. Claudius Togidubnus. *RIB* 91 (with Neptune and Minerva)
Old Penrith: slab to D(omus) D(ivinae) recording the rebuilding of a temple by Aurelius
   At[tianus?], prefect of *cohors II Gallorum. RIB* 916 (with Jupiter Optimus Maximus
   Dolichenus)
Vindolanda: altar by vicus inhabitants at Vindolanda. *RIB* 1700 (with Numina
   Augustorum and Volcanus)

Epona
Auchendavy: altar by M. Cocceius Firmus, centurion of *II Augusta. RIB* 2177 (with
   Campestres, Mars, Minerva, Hercules, and Victoria)
Carvoran: altar by P[...] So[...]. *RIB* 1777

Fatum Bonum (Good Fate)
Maryport: altar by G. Cornelius Peregrinus, tribune of the cohort and *decurio* of Saldae
   in Mauretania Caesariensis. *RIB* 812 (with Fortuna Redux, Genius loci, and Roma
   Aeterna)

Faunus (all on silver spoons unless otherwise mentioned)
Thetford: as Faunus Andicrose. *RIB* 2420.11
Thetford: as Faunus Ausecus (Faunus prick-ear/long-ear?). *RIB* 2420.12-13
Thetford: as Faunus Blotugus (Faunus Bringer of Spring Blossom or Fosterer of Corn?).
   RIB 2420.14

Thetford: as Faunus Cranus. *RIB* 2420.15-16
Thetford: as Faunus Medigenus (Faunus the Mead-Begotten?). *RIB* 2420.17-19
Thetford: as Faunus Narius (Faunus the Lord), see also **Narius** below. *RIB* 2420.20-1
Thetford: as Faunus Saternius (Faunus, Giver of Plenty?). *RIB* 2420.22

Fersomeri, see **Unseni Fersomeri**

Fimmilena et Beda (Alaisiagae)
Housesteads: shrine door jam by 'Germans, citizens of Twenthe'. *RIB* 1593 (with Mars
   Thincsus, and Numen Augusti)

Fontes (the Fountains)
Chester: altar by *XX Valeria Victrix*. *RIB* 460 (with Nymphs)

Fortuna
Balmuildy: altar by Caecilius Nepos, tribune. *RIB* 2189
Binchester: altar by M.Valerius Fulvianus, prefect of cavalry. *RIB* 1029
Birdoswald: altar. *RIB* 1873
Birrens: altar by *cohors I Nervana Germanorum*. *RIB* 2093
Birrens: statue pedestal by Celer, *libertus*, for P. Campanius Italicus, prefect of *cohors I[I]
   Tungrorum*. *RIB* 2094
Birrens: altar. *RIB* 2095
Bowes: altar by Virius Lupus, governor, restored a bathhouse for *cohors I Thracum*; work in
   charge of Valerius Fronto, prefect of *ala Vettonum*, between *c*.197-202. *RIB* 730
Caerleon: block by Julius [Ba]ssus, *praefectus castrorum* of (*II Augusta*?). *RIB* 317
Carlisle: miniature clay altar inscribed (on the top). *Brit.* xxiv (1993), 316, no. 6
Carrawburgh: altar by M. Flaccinius Marcellus, prefect of *cohors I Batavorum*. *RIB* 1536
Carrawburgh: altar by Vitalis. *RIB* 1537
Carvoran (probably): altar by Audac(ilius) Romanus, centurion of *VI*, *XX*, and *II Augusta*.
   RIB 1779
Castlecary: altar by vexillations of *II Augusta* and *VI Victrix*. *RIB* 2146
Greatchesters: altar to [F]or[t]u(nae) by a *vexillatio G(aesatorum) R(a)eto(rum)* commanded
   by the centurion Tabellius Victor. *RIB* 1724
Haltonchesters: altar. *RIB* 1423
Risingham: altar by G. Valerius Longinus, tribune. *RIB* 1210 (for this man again see
   Hercules, *RIB* 1214)
Slack: altar by G. Antonius Modestus, centurion of *VI Victrix*. *RIB* 624
York: altar by Sosia Juncina, wife of Q. Antonius Isauricus, imperial (legionary) legate,
   between. *RIB* 644
York: statue base by Metrob[ianus?], *li[b(ertus)*, for the benefit of Publius [Maesius]
   Auspicatus (Maesius is restored from the name of the beneficiary's son on the stone).
   RIB 645
Unprovenanced (British origin): altar. *RIB* 2217 (with Numina Augustorum)

Fortuna Augusta (the Emperor's Fortune)
Carvoran: altar dedicated for Lucius Aelius Caesar by T. Flavius Secundus, prefect of *cohors
   I Hamiorum sagittaria*, between 136-8. *RIB* 1778
Lanchester: altar by P. Aelius Atticus, prefect. *RIB* 1073
Risingham: altar by Aelia Proculina. *RIB* 1211

Fortuna Balnearis (Fortune of the Baths)
Kirkby Thore: altar to Fort[un]a Bal[n(eari)] by G. Caledius Frontinus of *n(umerus)
   m(ilitum) S(yrorum) s(agittariorum)*. *RIB* 764

Fortuna et Bonus Eventus, see **Bonus Eventus et Fortuna** above

Fortuna Conservatrix (Fortune the Preserver)
Chesters: altar by Venenus, a German. *RIB* 1449
Manchester: altar by L. Senecianius Martius, centurion of *VI Victrix*. *RIB* 575
Netherby: altar by M. Aurelius Salvius, tribune of *cohors I Aelia Hispanorum* (also named on *RIB* 978 at Netherby, in 222), about 222. *RIB* 968

Fortuna Populi Romani (Fortune of the Roman People)
Vindolanda: altar to Fortuna P(opuli) R(omani) by G. Julius Raeticus, centurion of *VI Victrix*. *RIB* 1684

Fortuna Redux (Fortune the Home–Bringer)
Chester: altar by the legate (presumably of *XX Valeria Victrix*) T. Pomponius Mamilianus. *RIB* 445 (with Aesculapius, and Salus)
Maryport: altar by G. Cornelius Peregrinus, tribune of the cohort and *decurio* of Saldae in Mauretania Caesariensis. *RIB* 812 (with Fatum Bonum, Genius loci, and Roma Aeterna)
Maryport: votive pillar. *RIB* 840 (with Roma Aeterna)
Risingham: altar by Julius Severinus, tribune, on completion of a bathhouse. *RIB* 1212

Fortuna Servatrix (Fortune the Deliverer)
Kirkby Thore: altar by Antonia Stratonis following a vision. *RIB* 760

Friagabis et Baudihillia, Alaisiagae
Housesteads: altar by *numerus Hnaudifridi*. *RIB* 1576 (with Numen Augusti)

Garmangabis
Lanchester: altar by *vex(illatio) Sueborum Lon(govicianorum) Gor(dianae)* between 238-44. *RIB* 1074 (with Numen Augusti of Gordian III)

God (in Hebrew form of Jahweh)
Caernarvon: amulet by Alphianos in Greek, apparently to the Hebrew God. *RIB* 436. See *Brit.* xxvii (1996), 456 for a revised translation of the text

Genius
Caerwent: altar. *Brit.* ii (1971), 353, no. 9
Chichester: altar by Lucullus. *RIB* 90
Cirencester: base by Attius [...?]. *RIB* 101
Ebchester: altar. *RIB* 1099
Old Carlisle: altar by Aurelius Martialis and Aurelius E[b]uracio(?). *RIB* 891
Vindolanda: altar by *cohors II[II] Gallorum*. *RIB* 1687 (with Jupiter Optimus Maximus and Custodes)

Genius alae primae Hispanorum Asturum (Genius of the ala)
Benwell: altar by Terentius Agrippa, prefect of *ala I Hispanorum Asturum*. *RIB* 1334 (with Matres Campestres)

Genius centuriae (Genius of the century)
Carlisle: altar by the century of Bassilius Crescens. *RIB* 944
Chester: altar. *RIB* 446
Chester: altar by Julius Quintilianus for the century of Aurelianus. *RIB* 447

Genius cohortis (Genius of the cohort)
Gloucester: altar by Orivendus (reading revised in *RIB95*). *RIB* 119
High Rochester: altar by T. Licinius Valerianus, tribune, for *cohors I fida Vardullorum*. *RIB* 1263 (with Signa cohortis)
Lanchester: altar by *cohors I Vardullorum* during the governorship of Antistius Adventus in c.175-6. *RIB* 1083, at the expense of the tribune Flavius Titianus (with Numen Augusti)

Genius collegii (Genius of the guild)
High Rochester: altar by Caecilius Optatus, tribune. *RIB* 1268 (with Minerva)

Genius collegii Apollinis (Genius of the college of Apollo)
Burrow-in-Lonsdale (Overborough): altar by [B]ellinus. *RIB* 611 (with Numina Augustorum)

Genius Domini Nostri/Dominorum Nostrorum (Genius of our lord/lords)
High Rochester: altar by Egnatius Lucilianus, governor, for the *Signa* of *cohors I Vardul[l(orum)* and *n(umerus) Explorator(um) Brem(eniensium) Gor(diani)* under the charge of Cassius Sabinianus, tribune, between 238-44. *RIB* 1262 (with Signa)
Old Penrith: altar by *cohors [II?] Gallo[r(um)], for Philip I and II, between 244-9. RIB* 915 (with Jupiter Optimus Maximus)

Genius Eboraci (Genius of York)
York: altar to Gen(io) Eb[or(aci?)]. *RIB* 657 (with Numen Augusti)

Genius huius Loci (Genius of this place)
Carrawburgh: altar by the Texandri and Suevae from a vexillation of *cohors II Nerviorum*. *RIB* 1538
Housesteads: altar by members of *II Augusta* on garrison duty. *RIB* 1583 (with Cocidius and Jupiter Optimus Maximus)

Genius Imperatorum? (Genius of the Emperors)
Caerleon: slab recording the possible restoration of a temple between 177 and 180. *Brit.* i (1970), 305, no. 1 (and Jupiter Optimus Maximus)

Genius legionis *II Augustae* (Genius of legio *II Augusta*)
Caerleon: pilaster given by [...], *primus pilus*, in 244 under the charge of Ursus, *actarius*, of *II Augusta. RIB* 327 (with Numina Augustorum)

Genius legionis *XX Valeria Victrix* D[eciana?] 'Genius of the XX legion'
Chesters: altar by Titus Vet[...] between 249-51. *RIB* 449

Genius loci (Genius of the Place), see also **Genius huius Loci**
Bath: altar by Torianus(?) of *VI Victrix?. RIB* 139
Binchester: altar by *ala Vettonum. RIB* 1032 (with Matres Ollotatae)
Carlisle: altar. *RIB* 945
Carrawburgh: altar by M. Hispanius Modestinus, prefect of *cohors I Batavorum. JRS* li (1961), 193, no. 9 (with Nymphae)
Castlesteads: altar by G. Verecundius Severus. *RIB* 1984 (with Jupiter Optimus Maximus)
Chester: altar by Flavius Longus, *tribunus militum* of *XX [Valeria Victrix]*, and his son Longinus, from Samosata. *RIB* 450
Clifton (found at Brougham?): altar by Subrius Apollinaris, *princeps* of *cohors IV[angionum?]. RIB* 792 (with Jupiter Optimus Maximus)

Daglingworth: slab. *RIB* 130 (with Matres)

Lincoln: altar. *RIB* 246

Malton: panel of exhortation to the slave of the *taberna aureficinam*. *RIB* 712

Maryport: altar by G. Cornelius Peregrinus, tribune of the cohort and *decurio* of Saldae in Mauretania Caesariensis. *RIB* 812 (with Fatum Bonum, Fortuna Redux, and Roma Aeterna)

Tilston: altar. *Brit.* xv (1984), 341, no. 14

Vindolanda: altar by Lupulus. *Brit.* iv (1973), 329, no. 10 (with Mogons)

York: altar. *RIB* 646

York: stone. *RIB* 647

York: altar by Q. Crepereius Marcus. *Brit.* iv (1973), 325-9, no. 5

Genius numeri Maurorum Aurelianorum Valeriani Gallienique (Genius of the *numerus* of Aurelian Moors of Valerian and Gallienus)

Burgh-by-Sands: altar by Caelius Vibianus, tribune of *numerus Maurorum Aurelianorum Valeriani Gallienique*, under the direction of Julius Rufinus, *princeps* between 253-8. *RIB* 2042 (with Numina Augustorum; the primary dedication to Jupiter Optimus Maximus is entirely restored in *RIB*)

Genius praesidii (Genius of the guard/garrison)

Housesteads: altar by Valerius, *miles* with *VI Victrix*. *RIB* 1577 (with Cocidius)

Genius praetorii (Genius of the commandant's house)

Lanchester: base by Cl. Epaphroditus Claudianus, tribune of *cohors I Lingonum*. *RIB* 1075

Vindolanda: altar by Pituanius Secundus, prefect of *cohors IIII Gallorum*. *RIB* 1685

Vindolanda: altar by Q. Petronius Urbicus, prefect of *cohors IIII Gallorum*. *RIB* 1686 (with Jupiter Optimus Maximus and 'other immortal gods')

Vindolanda: altar by *cohors IIII Gallorum*. *RIB* 1687 (with Custodes and Jupiter Optimus Maximus)

Genius sanctus centuriae (Holy Genius of the century)

Chester: altar by Aelius Claudianus, *optio*. *RIB* 448

Genius sanctus huius loci (Holy Genius of this place)

Cirencester: altar. *RIB* 102

Genius signiferorum legionis XX Valeria Victrix (Genius of the standard-bearers of *XX Valeria Victrix*)

Chester: base by T. Flavius Valerianus for his colleagues. *RIB* 451

Genius Terrae Britannicae (Genius of the Britannic land)

Auchendavy: altar by M. Cocceius Firmus, centurion of *II Augusta*. *RIB* 2175

Genius [...]vali (Genius of [...]valium; perhaps Luguvalium, i.e. Carlisle)

Hadrian's Wall (near mc 59): altar by [...] Martius, centurion of *cohors I Batavorum*. *RIB* 2015 (with Mars Cocidius)

Hammia

Carvoran: altar made by Sabinus. *RIB* 1780

Harimella

Birrens: altar by Gamidiahus, *arcit(ectus)*. *RIB* 2096

Herakles Tyrioi (Heracles, i.e. Hercules, of Tyre)
Corbridge: altar to Heracles of Tyre by Diodora the priestess (in Greek). *RIB* 1129

Hercules
Auchendavy: altar by M. Cocceius Firmus, centurion of *II Augusta. RIB* 2177 (with Campestres, Epona, Mars, Minerva, and Victoria)
Benwell: bronze ansate plaque by Marus, tribune of *XX. B* xxxii (2001), 392, no. 18
Brancaster: bronze tablet. *RIB* 2432.5
Burgh-by-Sands: altar by *cohors [...]. RIB* 2040 (with Numen Augusti)
Carvoran: inscription to (H)erc(u)l[i]. *RIB* 1781
Haile: altar by Primus, *custos armorum. RIB* 796 (with Silvanus)
High Rochester: altar to Herculens (sic). *RIB* 1264
Housesteads: altar by P. Aelius Modestus, prefect of *cohors I Tungrorum. RIB* 1580
Old Carlisle: altar by Sigilius Emeritus, or Sigilius, the *emeritus*, recording a division of spoils with the god. *RIB* 892
Risingham: altar by Julius Paullus, tribune. *RIB* 1213 (named as tribune of *cohors I Vangionum* at Risingham on *RIB* 1241)
Risingham: altar to (H)e[r]cul[i] by G. Valerius Longinus. *RIB* 1214 (see also *RIB* 1210 under Fortuna above for his full name)
Whitley Castle: altar by G. Vitellius Atticianus, centurion of *VI Victrix. RIB* 1199
York: slab by T. Perpet[...] Aeternus of York. *RIB* 648

Hercules Augustus (Imperial Hercules)
Brough-on-Noe: altar by the prefect Proculus, possibly referring to the restoration of a temple. *Brit.* xi (1980), 404, no. 3

Hercules Invictus (Invincible Hercules)
Carlisle: arched slab by Publius Sextanius, prefect of *ala Augusta*, celebrating the slaughter of a band of barbarians. *RIB* 946 (and see *B* 1999, 384–6 for a revised reading)
Risingham: altar by L. Aemilius Salvianus, tribune of *cohors I Vangionum. RIB* 1215

Hercules Magusanus (Hercules the magician?)
Mumrills: altar by Valerius Nigrinus, *dupli(carius)* of *ala (I) Tungrorum. RIB* 2140

Hercules Saegon[...]
Silchester: slab by T. Tammonius Vitalis. *RIB* 67

Hercules Victor (Victorious Hercules)
Whitley Castle: altar. *RIB* 1200 (with Menerva (sic))

Hospitales (Gods of Hospitality)
Newcastle-upon-Tyne: altar. *RIB* 1317 (with Jupiter Optimus Maximus and Numen Augusti)
York: altar by P. Aelius Marcianus, prefect of *cohors [...]* (*I Augustae Bracarum* has been suggested on the evidence of this man as its prefect on *ILS* 2738). *RIB* 649 (with Jupiter Optimus Maximus and Penates)

Hveterus/Hviteres, and variants; see also **Veteris** etc.
Carrawburgh: altar to the Hviteres. *RIB* 1549
Hadrian's Wall (exact location unknown): altar to the Hvitires. *RIB* 2069
Housesteads: altar to Hveteris by Superstes and Regulus. *RIB* 1602
Housesteads: altar to Hvitris by Aspuanis. *RIB* 1603
Netherby: altar to Hveterus. *RIB* 973

Hygiaea

Burrow-in-Lonsdale (Overborough): altar by Julius Saturninus. *RIB* 609 (with Aesculapius)

Chester: altar by Antiochos, *hiatros*. *JRS* lix (1969), 235, no. 3 (with Aesculapius and Panakeia)

Hypermenes (Saviour Gods)

Chester: altar by Hermogenes, a doctor (in Greek). *RIB* 461

Iao

Silchester: amulet. *RIB* 2423.16

Thetford: jasper gemstone. *RIB* 2423.15

West Deeping: lead tablet. *B* 1996, 443, no.10 (with Sabao and Adonai)

Ialonus Contrebis, see also Contrebis

Lancaster: altar by Julius Januarius, *emeritus*, former *decurio*. *RIB* 600

Invictus, see Hercules Invictus, Mithras Invictus, Silvanus Invictus, and Sol Invictus

Ioug[...]

York: slab to *Dea Ioug[...]* by *[...]sius, recording restoration of the shrine.* *RIB* 656 (with Numina Augustorum)

Isis

London: flagon of late first-century type recording the address *Londini ad fanum Isidis,* 'at London, by the temple of Isis'. The inscription could be much later than the vessel, which has survived intact, and thus could have been inscribed at any date during the Roman period. *RIB* 2503.127

London: altar recording the rebuilding of a temple of Isis by M. Martian[n]ius Pulcher, *leg(atus) Aug(ustorum)*, at some point in the third century. *Brit.* vii (1976), 378-9, no. 2

Iu[..]teris Fortunat[us]

Netherby: altar. *RIB* 969

Juno

Lullingstone: mosaic with a Latin couplet referring to Juno. *RIB* 2448.6

Juno Regina

Carlisle: 213-22 – altar by M. [Aurelius?] Syrio, military tribune with *XX Valeria Victrix.* *Brit.* xx (1989), 331-3, no. 5 (with Jupiter Optimus Maximus, Minerva, Mars, and Victoria)

Jupiter/Juppiter

Colchester: statuette by P. Oranius Felix. *RIB* 2432.8

South Shields: bronze belt plates. *B* 1996, 452, nos. 30-1

Stony Stratford: silver plate by Vassinus. *RIB* 215 (with Volcanus)

Jupiter Aeternus Dolichenus (Eternal Jupiter of Doliche)

Corbridge: altar by G. Julius Apolinaris (sic), centurion of *VI Victrix*, his name replacing someone else's. *RIB* 1131 (with Caelestis Brigantia and Salus)

Jupiter Augustus
Maryport: altar by M. Censorius Cornelianus, centurion of *[X Fr]etensis*, commander of
cohors I Hispanorum. *RIB* 814

Jupiter Optimus Maximus (Jupiter, Best and Greatest)
Auchendavy: altar by M. Cocceius Firmus, centurion of *II Augusta*. *RIB* 2176 (with
Victoria Victrix)
Aldborough: altar. *RIB* 708 (with Matres)
Binchester: altar by Pomponius Donatus, *b(ene)f(iciarius) co(n)s(ularis)*. *RIB* 1030 (with Matres
Ollototae sive Transmarinae) (N.B. another possibility at *Brit.* xxiii (1992), 314, no. 10)
Birdoswald: altar by *cohors I Aelia Dacorum* under the tribune Ammonius Victorinus. *RIB* 1874
Birdoswald: altar by *cohors I Aelia Dacorum* under the tribune Aurelius Faustus in 237. *RIB*
1875
Birdoswald: altar by *cohors I Aelia Dacorum* under Aurelius Saturninus. *RIB* 1876
Birdoswald: altar by *cohors I Aelia Dacorum* under Aurelius [...]. *RIB* 1877
Birdoswald: altar by *[cohors I A]el(ia) Da[corum]* under F[l(avius) ...]. *RIB* 1878
Birdoswald: altar by *cohors I Aelia Dacorum* under the tribune Funisulanus Vettonianus.
RIB 1879
Birdoswald: altar by *cohors I Aelia Dacorum* under Julius Marcellinus, centurion of *II
Augusta*. *RIB* 1880
Birdoswald: altar by *cohors I Aelia Dacorum* under the tribune Julius Saturninus. *RIB*
1881
Birdoswald: altar by *cohors I Aelia Dacorum*, commanded by the tribune Marcius Gallicus,
around the period 255-75 (see next entry for this man in post under Postumus). *RIB*
1882 (with Numen Augusti)
Birdoswald: altar by *cohors I Aelia Dacorum Postumiana*, commanded by the tribune Marcius
Gallicus between 259-68. *RIB* 1883
Birdoswald: altar with by Pomp[oni]us D[eside]rat[us], tribune commanding *cohors I
Aelia Dacorum Tetricianorum* between 270-3 (with primary anonymous dedication to
Cocidius). *RIB* 1885
Birdoswald: altar by *cohors I Aelia Dacorum Postumiana* under the tribune Probius Augendus
between 259-68. *RIB* 1886
Birdoswald: altar by *cohors I Aelia Dacorum* under the tribune Statius Longinus. *RIB*
1887
Birdoswald: altar by *cohors I Aelia Dacorum* under the tribune [...]us Con[...]. *RIB* 1888
Birdoswald: altars by *cohors I Aelia Dacorum* under [...]. *RIB* 1889-91
Birdoswald: altar by *cohors I Aelia Dacorum Antoniniana* between 213-22. *RIB* 1892
Birdoswald: altar by *cohors I Aelia Dacorum Gordiana* between 238-44. *RIB* 1893
Birdoswald: altar by *cohors I Aelia Dacorum* in the charge of [...]rinus, *beneficiarius*. *RIB* 1894
Birdoswald: altar by *cohors I Aelia Dacorum* under the tribune [...]. *RIB* 1895
Bowness-on-Solway: altar by Sulpicius Secundianus, tribune, between 251-3. *RIB* 2057
(and *RIB* 2058 recorded with an identical text)
Caerleon: slab recording the possible restoration of a temple between 177 and 180. *Brit.*
i (1970), 305, no. 1 (and Genius Imperatorum?)
Cappuck: altar by *ve[x]il(l)atio R(a)etorum Gaesat(orum)* commanded by the tribune Julius
Severinus. *RIB* 2117
Cardewlees: altar by (?), for the *numina* of Valerian I, Gallienus, and Valerian II as Caesar
under the charge of G. [C]arinius Aurelianus, centurion of *II Augusta*, between 253-5.
RIB 913 (with Numina Dominorum Nostrorum)
Carlisle: altar by M. [Aurelius?] Syrio, military tribune with *XX Valeria Victrix*, between
213-22. *Brit.* xx (1989), 331-3, no. 5 (with Juno, Minerva, Mars, and Victoria)
Carriden: altar by the vicus peoples of the fort of Velunia under the charge of Aelius
Mansuetus. *JRS* xlvii (1957), 229-30, no. 18

Castlesteads: altar by *cohors IIII Gallorum* commanded by the prefect of cavalry Volcacius Hospes. *RIB* 1980

Castlesteads: altar by *cohors II Tungrorum* commanded by the prefect Albius Severus, directed by Vic(...) Severus, *princeps*. *RIB* 1981

Castlesteads: altar by *cohors II Tungrorum* commanded by the prefect Aurelius Optatus, directed by Messius Opsequens, *princeps*. *RIB* 1982

Castlesteads: altar by *cohors II Tungrorum Gordiana*, commanded by the prefect T. Claudius Claudianus, work directed by [P.?] Aelius Martinus, *princeps*, in 241. *RIB* 1983 (with Numen Augusti Nostri)

Castlesteads: altar by G. Verecundius Severus. *RIB* 1984 (with Genius loci)

Castlesteads: altar. *RIB* 1985

Chichester: column base, and honouring the *Domus Divina*. *RIB* 89

Cirencester: column base by L. Septimius, *v(ir) p(erfectissimus) pr(aeses)*, and *rector*, of *Britannia Prima*. *RIB* 103 (**26**)

Clifton: altar by Subrius Apollinaris, *princeps* of *cohors I V[angionum?]*. *RIB* 792 (with Genius loci)

Cumbria: altar by Vitalis (reading of Jupiter Optimus Maximus in *RIB95*. *RIB* 1017 (with Mars Cocidius)

Dorchester-on-Thames: altar *cum cancellis* ('with screens') by M. Varius Severus, *beneficiarius consularis* of the governor. *RIB* 235 (with Numina Augustorum)

Godmanstone (nr Dorchester, Dorset): altar by Titinius Pines, of *[XX V(aleria)] V(ictrix)*(?). *JRS* lv (1965), 220-1, no. 2

Hadrian's Wall (between t 7b and mc 8): altar. *RIB* 1366

Housesteads: altar. *RIB* 1581

Housesteads: altar by *milites* of *II Augusta*. *RIB* 1582

Housesteads: altar by *milites* of *II Augusta* on garrison duty. *RIB* 1583 (with Cocidius and Genius loci)

Housesteads: altar by *cohors I Tungrorum*, under the prefect Q. Julius Maximus. *RIB* 1584 (with Numina Augustorum)

Housesteads: altar by *cohors I Tungrorum*, under the prefect Q. Julius [Cur?]sus. *RIB* 1585 (with Numina Augustorum)

Housesteads: altar by *cohors I Tungrorum*, under the prefect Q. Verius Superstis. *RIB* 1586 (with Numina Augustorum)

Housesteads: altar by (?), under the prefect [...]rius [.]upe[...]. *RIB* 1587 (with Numina Augustorum)

Housesteads: altar by [.....], prefect. *RIB* 1588 (with Numina Augustorum)

Housesteads: altar, anonymous dedication on behalf of Desidienius Ae[mi]lianus, prefect, in 258. *RIB* 1589

Lanchester: altar by *cohors I Lingonum* under the prefect [F]ulvius [Fel]ix. *Brit.* xix (1988), 492, no. 10

London: altar posssibly recording the rebuilding of a temple by Aquilinus, imperial *libertus*, Mercator, Audax, and Graecus. The dedication is not certain and may instead have been to Mithras or the Matres. *Brit.* vii (1976), 378, no. 1

Maryport: altar by [...]iana Hermione. *RIB* 813 (formerly read as Iuno)

Maryport: altar by *cohors I Hispanorum*, Hadrianic. *RIB* 815 (with Numen Augusti)

Maryport: altar by *cohors I Hispanorum*, commanded by the prefect L. Antistius Lupus Veranius. *RIB* 816

Maryport: altar by *cohors I Hispanorum*, commanded by the tribune G. Caballius Priscus. *RIB* 817

Maryport: altars by G. Caballius Priscus, tribune. *RIB* 818-20

Maryport: altar by P. Cornelius Ur[...], prefect of *cohors I Hispanorum*. *RIB* 821

Maryport: altar by Helstrius Novellus, prefect of *cohors I Hispanorum*. *RIB* 822

Maryport: altar by M. Maenius Agrippa, tribune of *cohors I Hispanorum*. *RIB* 823

Maryport: altar by M. Maenius Agrippa, tribune. *RIB* 824 (with Numen Augusti)

Maryport: altar by Maenius Agrippa, tribune. *RIB* 825 (with Numen Augusti)

Maryport: altar by Maenius [Agrippa], tribune. *RIB* 826

Maryport: altar by [L.?] Cammius Maximus, prefect of *cohors I Hispanorum* and tribune of *cohors XVIIII Voluntariorum*. *RIB* 827

Maryport: altars by L. Cammius Maximus, prefect of *cohors I Hispanorum*. *RIB* 828-9

Maryport: altar by T. Attius Tutor, prefect of *cohors I Baetasiorum*. *RIB* 830

Maryport: altar by L. Caecilius Vegetus, prefect of *cohors I Dalmatarum*. *RIB* 831

Maryport: altar by [Postumius] Acilianus, prefect of *[cohors I Dalmatarum]* between 138-61. *RIB* 833 (see *RIB* 832 under Jupiter Optimus Maximus Capitolinus)

Maryport: altar by [...], prefect of *cohors [...]*. *RIB* 834

Maryport: altar. *RIB* 835 (with Volcanus?)

Moresby: altar by *cohors II T(h)racum*, commanded by the prefect Mamius Nepos. *RIB* 797

Netherby: altar. *RIB* 969 (with Iu[...]teris Fortunatus?)

Newcastle-upon-Tyne: altar. *RIB* 1316 (with Victoria Augusti)

Newcastle-upon-Tyne: altar. *RIB* 1317 (with Hospitales and Numen Augusti)

Newstead: altar by G. Arrius Domitianus, centurion of *XX Valeria Victrix*. *RIB* 2123 (see this man again at Newstead under Diana Regina and Silvanus)

Old Penrith: altar by *cohors [II] Gallorum* between 244-9. *RIB* 915 (with Genius Dominorum Nostrorum)

Shakenoak: altar. *Brit.* ii (1971), 353, no. 8

Vindolanda: altar by Q. Petronius Urbicus, prefect of *cohors IIII Gallorum [Antoniniana]* or *[Severiana]*, between 213-35. *RIB* 1686 (with Genius Praetori)

Vindolanda: altar by *cohors IIII Gallorum*. *RIB* 1687 (with Custodes and Genius)

Vindolanda: altar by *[c]oh(ors) IIII G[al]l(orum)* under the prefect L. [...]gius Pudens. *RIB* 1688

Vindolanda: altars. *RIB* 1689-90

Hadrian's Wall (exact place unknown but probably Vindolanda): altar by *cohors IIII Gallorum* under the prefect Naevius Hilarus. *RIB* 2062

York: altar by P. Aelius Marcianus, prefect of *cohors [.....]* (*I Augustae Bracarum* has been suggested on the evidence of this man as its prefect on *ILS* 2738). *RIB* 649 (with Hospitalesand Penates)

Jupiter Optimus Maximus Capitolinus

Maryport: altar by Postumius Acilianus, prefect of *cohors I Dalmatarum* between 138-61. *RIB* 832

Jupiter Optimus Maximus Conservator (Jupiter, Best and Greatest, the Preserver)

Old Carlisle: altar. *RIB* 898

Jupiter Optimus Maximus Dolichenus (Jupiter, Best and Greatest, of Doliche)

Benwell: altar by M. Liburnius Fronto, centurion of *II Augusta*, between 139-61. *RIB* 1330 (with Numina Augustorum for the welfare of Antoninus Pius and *II Augusta*)

Bewcastle: slab recording the building of a temple. *RIB* 992

Birdoswald: altar to Jupiter Optimus Maximus [D(olichenus)?] by *cohors I Aelia Dacorum*, under the tribune Flavius Maximianus. *RIB* 1896

Birdoswald: altar by *cohors I Aelia Dacorum Maximini*, under the tribune Flavius Maximianus, between 235-8. *JRS* xlvii (1957), 229, no. 17

Birrens: altar to [Jupiter Optimus Maximus] Dol[iche]nus by Magunna. *RIB* 2099

Caerleon: altar by Fronto Aemilianus [...] Rufilianus, *legatus Augustorum* (possibly 161-9), of *II Augusta*(?). *RIB* 320

Carvoran: altar. *RIB* 1782

Chesters: altar by Galerius Ver[ecundus?] for the welfare of *Augustorum Nostrorum*, 'our emperors'. *RIB* 1452

Croy Hill: relief to [Jupiter Optimus Maximus Dolic]henus. *RIB* 2158

Duntocher: altar. *RIB* 2201

Greatchesters: altar by L. Maximus Gaetulicus, centurion of *XX Valeria Victrix*. *RIB* 1725

Greatchesters: altar by Regulus for(?) [...]ina, daughter of Sabinus. *RIB* 1726

Old Carlisle: altar to Jupiter Optimus Maximus [D(olicheno)?] by *ala Augusta* under the prefect Egnatius Verecundus about 197. *RIB* 895

Old Penrith: slab recording the rebuilding of a temple by Aurelius Attianus, prefect of *cohors II Gallorum*, and in honour of *D(omus) D(ivina)*. *RIB* 916

Piercebridge: altar by Julius Valentinus, centurion from Upper Germany, in 217. *RIB* 1022

Piercebridge: uncertain fragment, dedication conjectural. *RIB* 1023

Piercebridge: statue base by a vexillation of *VI Victrix*, the army of Germany, under the supervision of M. Lollius Venator, centurion of *II Augusta*. *JRS* lvii (1967), 205, no. 16

Risingham: slab. *RIB* 1219

Risingham: altar to [Jupiter Optimus Maximus] Dolochenus by G. Julius Publilius Prius, tribune. *RIB* 1220

Jupiter Optimus Maximus Heliopolitanus (Jupiter, Best and Greatest, of Heliopolis)
Carvoran: altar by Julius Pollio. *RIB* 1783

Jupiter Optimus Maximus Tanarus
Chester: altar by L. Elupius (or Elutrius) Praesens, of the Galerian voting tribe at Clunia (*Hispania Tarraconensis*), *princeps* of *XX Valeria Victrix*, in 154. *RIB* 452

Jupiter Serapis, see also **Serapis**
Kirkby Thore: altar by Lucius Alfenus Pal[...]. *RIB* 762

Lamiae Triades (Three witches)
Benwell: altar. *RIB* 1331

Latis
Birdoswald: altar. *RIB* 1897
Burgh-by-Sands: altar by Lucius. *RIB* 2043

Lenus Mars, see **Mars Lenus**

Loucetius Mars, see **Mars Loucetius**

Magusanus Hercules, see **Hercules Magusanus**

Maponus, see also **Apollo Maponus**
Hadrian's Wall (exact location unknown): altar by Durio, Ramio, Trupo, and Lurio, all Germans. *RIB* 2063 (with Numen Augusti)
Vindolanda: silver pendant. *RIB* 2431.2

Mars
Auchendavy: altar by M. Cocceius Firmus, centurion of *II Augusta*. *RIB* 2177 (with Campestres, Minerva, Hercules, Epona and Victoria)
Balmuildy: altar to [Ma]rti. *RIB* 2190
Bath: lead 'curse' tablet recording a gift to the temple of Mars by Basilia. Cunliffe (1988), no. 97
Benwell: altar by Lenuanus. *RIB* 1332

Birdoswald: altar by [...], tribune of *cohors I Aelia Dacorum. RIB* 1898

Birdoswald: altar by Aurelius Maximus. *RIB* 1899 (with Victoria)

Birrens: altar by *cohors II Tungrorum* under the prefect Silvius Auspex. *RIB* 2100 (with Victoria Augusti)

Bosence: pewter cup dedicated by Aelius Modestus. *RIB* 2417.1

Brough-on-Noe: altar. *RIB* 282

Brougham: altar to [Ma]rti. *RIB* 779 (with Victoria)

Brougham: altar by Januarius of the numerus equitum [St]ratonicianorum. *RIB* 780

Carlisle: 213-22 – altar by M. [Aurelius?] Syrio, military tribune with *XX Valeria Victrix. Brit.* xx (1989), 331-3, no. 5 (with Jupiter Optimus Maximus, Juno, Minerva, and Victoria)

Castlesteads: altar by Venustinus Lupus. *RIB* 1986

Castlesteads: altar by Paconius Saturninus, prefect of cavalry. *RIB* 1987 (with Numen Augusti)

Croy Hill: altar by Gaius D[...] B[...]. *RIB* 2159

Ebchester: altar. *RIB* 1100 (with Numen Augusti)

Fossdike: statuette by Bruccius and Caratius Colasunus. *RIB* 274 (with Numina Augustorum)

Gloucester: altar. *RIB* 120

Greta Bridge: altar by Enemn[o]genus. *RIB* 742

Greta Bridge: altar. *RIB* 743

Hastings: silver patera dedicated by Romulus, son of Camulogenus. *RIB* 2414.37 (with Numinibus Augustorum)

Housesteads: statue base. *RIB* 1590

Housesteads: altar by Q. Florius Maternus, prefect of *cohors I Tungrorum. RIB* 1591

Housesteads: altar by Vi[....]anus. *RIB* 1592

Housesteads altar by 'the Germans' of *cuneus Frisiorum Ver(covicianorum)* between 222-35. *RIB* 1594 (with Numen Augusti and Alaisiagae)

Housesteads: altar. *RIB* 1595 (with Victoria)

Housesteads: altar by [...], *custos armorum. RIB* 1596 (with Victoria and Numina Augustorum)

Housesteads: altar by Calve[...], a German. *RIB* 1597

Housesteads: pottery graffito. *RIB* 2503.128

Lancaster: altar by Sabinus, *praepositus,* and *numerus Barcariorum. RIB* 601

Lanchester: altar by Ascernus. *RIB* 1078

Lanchester: altar by Caurus. *RIB* 1079

Lanchester: altar by Sancidus. *RIB* 1080

Lanchester: altar. *RIB* 1081

Lincoln: altar to Ma[r]t[i]. *RIB* 248

Marlborough Downs: lead tablet bearing a curse text address to Mars. *B* 1999, 378 no. 3

Newtown (Powys): circular stone with incised image of the god and inscribed Matri, for Marti. *RIB* 2453.3

Old Carlisle: altar. *RIB* 900

Ribchester: base. *RIB* 585 (with Victoria)

Silchester: slab to Marti[...] (either the god or naming an individual) by guild of peregrini. *RIB* 71

Staincross Common: altar for the welfare of D(ominorum) N(ostrorum) Imp(eratorum) Aug(ustorum). *RIB* 622

Stony Stratford: silver plate. *RIB* 216

Stony Stratford: bronze plate. *RIB* 217

York: altar by G. Agrius Auspex. *RIB* 650

York: altar. *RIB* 651

Mars Alator
Barkway: silver-gilt plaque by Dum(...?) Censorinus. *RIB* 218
South Shields: altar by G.Vinicius Celsus. *RIB* 1055

Mars Augustus (Imperial Mars)
Birdoswald: altar. *RIB* 1900
Lanchester: gold plate by Auffidius Aufidianus. *RIB* 1077

Mars Barrex
Carlisle: altar by Januarius Ri[o?]reg[.]iau[...]. *RIB* 947

Mars Belatucadrus (with variant spellings) see also Belatucadrus
Bewcastle: altar. *JRS* xlvii (1957), 228, no. 11
Burgh-by-Sands: altar. *RIB* 2044
Carlisle: altar. *RIB* 948
Carvoran: altar to Mars Belatucairus. *RIB* 1784
Netherby: altar by [A]ur(elius?) [Ni]ca[n]or(?). *RIB* 970
Old Penrith: altar by Julius Augustalis, *actor* of Julius Lupus. *RIB* 918 (with Numina Augustorum)

Mars Braciaca
Bakewell: altar by Q. Sittius Caecilianus, prefect of *cohors I Aquitanorum*. *RIB* 278

Mars Camulus
Bar Hill: altar by *II [Au]g(usta)*. *RIB* 2166

Mars Cocidius see also Cocidius
Bewcastle: altar by Aelius Vitalianus. *RIB* 993
Cumbria (exact find-spot unknown): altar by Vitalis. *RIB* 1017 (with Jupiter Optimus Maximus; reading revised in *RIB95*)
Hadrian's Wall (near milecastle 59): altar by [...] Martius, centurion of *cohors I Batavorum*. *RIB* 2015 (with Genius [...]valium)
Hadrian's Wall (near milecastle 65): altar by members of two centuries of *II Augusta* commanded by the centurion Aelianus, work in the charge of Oppius Felix, *optio,*. *RIB* 2024
Lancaster: altar by Vibenius Lucius, *beneficiarius consularis*. *RIB* 602

Mars Condates
Bowes: altar by Arponatus. *RIB* 731
Chester-le-Street: altar by V[e]robnus. *RIB* 1045
Cramond: altar to M(ars) Con[dates]. *Brit.* ix (1978), 475, no. 15
Piercebridge: altar by Attionus Quintianus, *mensor* and *evocatus*. *RIB* 1024

Mars Conservator (Mars the Preserver)
Chesters: altar. *RIB* 454

Mars Corotiacus
Martlesham: bronze statue base, made by Glaucus, dedicated by Simplicia. *RIB* 213

Mars Lenus
Caerwent: statue base to Mars Lenus *sive* ('or') Ocelus Vellaunus by Nonius Romanus in 152. *RIB* 309 (with the Numen Augusti of Marcus Aurelius)
Chedworth: altar to [L]en(o) M[arti] with relief of the god. *RIB* 126

Mars Loucetius
Bath: altar by Peregrinus from Trier. *RIB* 140 (with Nemetona)

Mars Medocius Campesium (Mars Medocius of the Parade Ground?)
Colchester: bronze plaque by Lossio Veda, a Caledonian, between 222-35. *RIB* 191 (with
  Victoria of Severus Alexander)

Mars Militarus (Military Mars)
Maryport: altar by *cohors I Baetasiorum* under the prefect T. Attius Tutor (his full name
  appears on *RIB* 842, see Maryport under Victoria Augusti below). *RIB* 837
Maryport: altar by *cohors I Baetasiorum* under the prefect Ulpius Titianus. *RIB* 838

Mars Nodens/Nodons/Nudens, see also **Nodens**
Cockersand Moss: statuette by Aurelius [...]cinus. *RIB* 616
Cockersand Moss: statuette to M(ars) N(odens) by Lucianus for his colleague Aprilius
  Viator. *RIB* 617
Lydney Park: bronze plate by Flavius Blandinus, *armatura*. *RIB* 305
Lydney Park: bronze plate by Pectillus to *Nudente M(arti)*. *RIB* 307
Lydney Park: mosaic by T. Flavius Senilis, *pr(aepositus) rel(igionis)*, helped by Victorinus,
  interp(r)[e]tor. *RIB* 2448.3

Mars Ocelus, see also **Ocelus Vellaunus**
Caerwent: altar by Aelius Augustinus, *optio*. *RIB* 310
Carlisle: slab dedicated between 222-35. *RIB* 949 (with the Numen of Severus Alexander
  and Julia Mamaea)

Mars Olludius
Custom Scrubs, Bisley: gabled relief. *RIB* 131

Mars Pacifer (Mars the Peacemaker)
Ribchester: altar. *RIB* 584

Mars Pater (Father Mars)
Birdoswald: inscribed fragment to [Mar]ti Pat[ri...]. *RIB* 1901

Mars Rigas
Malton: base by Scirus. *RIB* 711

Mars Rigisamus
West Coker: bronze plaque by Iventius Sabinus. *RIB* 187

Mars Rigonemetos (Mars, King of the Grove)
Nettleham: slab by Q. Neratius Proxsimus, recording his arch. *JRS* lii (1962), 192, no. 8
  (with Numina Augustorum)

Mars Sediarum (Mars of the Sediae – presumably a place or tribe)
Markyate: on a small bronze or brass tablet with an inscription reading 'tessera of Mars
  of Sediae'. *RIB* 2408.1

Mars Thincsus
Housesteads: shrine door jam by 'Germans, citizens of Twenthe'. *RIB* 1593 (with the
  Alaisiagae: Beda and Fimmilena)

Mars Toutatis, see also **Toutatis**
Barkway: plaque by T. Claudius Primus, *liber(tus)*. *RIB* 219
Hadrian's Wall: bronze ansate plaque by Vinoma. *B* xxxii (2001), 392, no. 20

Mars Ultor (Mars the Avenger)
Corbridge: altar to [Deo Marti] Ul[tori]? by L(ucius) [...], *trib(unum)* [*militum*], during the
    governorship of Gn. Julius Verus (*c.*155-9). *RIB* 1132

Mars Victor (Mars the Victorious)
Benwell: altar by Vindex. *RIB* 1333
Carlisle: inscription recorded before 1125 on a Roman building. *RIB* 950
Risingham: altar by [J]ul(ius) Publilius [P]ius, tribune. *RIB* 1221
Risingham: altar by [...], under the charge of Au[r(elius)]. *RIB* 1222
Risingham: altar to [Mars Vi]ctor by [...], *libertus*. *RIB* 1223
Vindolanda: panel by [...] Caninius, commanding [....] (unit name lost but *RIB* restores
    cohors III Nerviorum from earlier readings). *RIB* 1691

Mater Div(or)um (Mother of the Gods)
Carvoran: altar by M. Caecilius Donatianus, prefect serving as tribune. *RIB* 1791 (with
    Virgo Caelestis, Pax, Virtus, and Ceres Dea Suria)

Matres (Mother Goddesses)
Aldborough: altar. *RIB* 708 (with Jupiter Optimus Maximus)
Backworth: silver patera dedicated by Fabius Dubitatus. *RIB* 2414.36
Binchester: altar by Gemellus. *RIB* 1033
Binchester: altar. *RIB* 1034
Carrawburgh: altar by Albinius Quartus, *miles*. *RIB* 1540
Castlecary: altar. *RIB* 2147
Cirencester: altar. *Brit.* iv (1973), 324, no. 1 (with Mercury)
Daglingworth: altar. *RIB* 130 (with Genius loci)
Hadrian's Wall (near milecastle 79): altar. *RIB* 2055
London: plinth recording restoration of, possibly, a shrine. *RIB* 2
Newcastle-upon-Tyne: altar. *Brit.* ix (1978), 475, no. 13
Ribchester: altar dedicated by M. Ingenuius Asiaticus, *dec(urio)*, to the Matres (dependent
    on Camden's reading in 1580). *RIB* 586
Ribchester: altar by Marulla (wife?) of Insequens. *Brit.* xxv (1994), 298. no. 3
Vindolanda: altar. *RIB* 1692 (with Numen Domini Nostri)
Walsingham: silver ring inscribed MATRIBUS I.R. *B* 1999, 32, no. 20
York: altar by M. Rustius Massa. *RIB* 654

Matres (variously) **Afrae, Britanniae, Italicae/Italae, Gallae, Germanae**
Dover: altar recording the building of a temple to the Matres Italicae by Olus Cordius,
    strator consularis. *Brit.* viii (1977), 426-7, no. 4
Winchester: altar to Matres Italae Germanae Gal(lae) Brit(annae) by Antonius Lucretianus,
    beneficiarius consularis. *RIB* 88
York: altar to Mat(res) Af(rae) Ita(lae) Ga(llae) by M. Minucius Audens, *miles* and *guber-*
    nator of *VI Victrix*. *RIB* 653

Matres Alatervae(?)
Cramond: altar by *cohors I Tungrorum*, directed by [...], centurion of *XX Valeria Victrix*. *RIB*
    2135 (with Matres Campestres)

Matres Brittiae (British Mother Goddesses)
Xanten (Germany): altar dedicated by L.Valerius Simplex of *XXX Ulpia Victrix*. *ILS* 4789

Matres Campestres (Mother Goddesses of the Parade Ground), see also **Campestres**
Benwell: altar by T(erentius?) Agrippa, prefect of *ala I Hispanorum Asturum*, in 238. *RIB*
    1334 (with Genius alae I Hispanorum Asturum)
Cramond: altar by *cohors I Tungrorum*, directed by [...], centurion of *XX Valeria Victrix*. *RIB*
    2135 (with Matres Alatervae)

Matres Communes (Mother Goddesses living everywhere)
Carrawburgh: altar. *RIB* 1541
Chesters: altar dedicated for the *decuria* commanded by Aurelius Severus. *RIB* 1453

Matres Domesticae (Household Mother Goddesses)
Catterick: altar by Julius Victor. *JRS* l (1960), 237, no. 6
Chichester: altar by ..., *arkarius*. *Brit.* x (1979), 339, no. 1
Hadrian's Wall (near milecastle 73): altar by a vexillation of *VI [Victrix]*. *RIB* 2050
Stanwix: altar by Asinius Senilis. *RIB* 2025
York: altar by G. Julius Crescens. *RIB* 652

Matres Germaniae (German Mother Goddesses)
Hadrian's Wall (exact provenance lost): altar by M(arcus) Senec[ia]nius. *RIB* 2064

Matres Ollototae (Mother Goddesses from other peoples)
Binchester: altar by Matres Ollototae *sive* ('or') Transmarinae by Pomponius Donatus,
    beneficiarius consularis. *RIB* 1030 (with Jupiter Optimus Maximus)
Binchester: altar to Matres O[l]lot(otae) by T. Claudius Quintianus, *beneficiarius consularis*.
    RIB 1031
Binchester: altar to [M]atres O[llotatae] by *ala Vettonum*. *RIB* 1032 (with Genius loci)
Heronbridge: altar by Julius Secundus and Aelia Augustina. *RIB* 574

Matres Omnium Gentium (Mother Goddesses of all races)
Castlesteads: altar to [Mat]ribu[s] Omnium Gentium by G. Julius Cupitianus, centurion
    commanding, on the restoration of a temple. *RIB* 1988

Matres Parcae (Mother Goddesses, the Fates), see also **Parcae**
Carlisle: base dedicated for Sanctia Gemina. *RIB* 951
Skinburness: altar. *RIB* 881
Vindolanda: silver ring inscribed *Matribu(s) Parc(is)*. *B* 1998, 440 no. 31

Matres Suleviae, see also **Suleviae**
Colchester: slab by Similis of the *Cant(iaci)*. *RIB* 192

Matres Tramarinae (Mother Goddesses from Overseas)
Binchester: altar to Matres Ollototae *sive* ('or') Transmarinae by Pomponius Donatus,
    beneficiarius consularis. *RIB* 1030 (with Jupiter Optimus Maximus)
Castlesteads: altar. *RIB* 1989
Old Penrith: slab by *[vexil]latio M[a]r[sacorum?]* between 222-35. *RIB* 919 (with Numen
    of Severus Alexander and Julia Mammaea)
Old Penrith: slab by *vexillatio Germa[no]r(um) V[o]r[e]d(ensium)*. *RIB* 920
Risingham: altar by Julius Victor (tribune of *cohors I Vangionum*; see for example *RIB* 1217
    under Jupiter Optimus Maximus above). *RIB* 1224

Matres Tramarinae Patriae (Mother Goddesses of the Overseas Homeland)
Newcastle-upon-Tyne: altar by Aurelius Juvenalis. *RIB* 1318

Matunus
High Rochester: altar by [G. Julius Marcus (deleted)?], governor, through Caecilius
   Optatus, tribune (of *cohors I Vardullorum*; see *RIB* 1272 under Mithras Invictus below),
   in 213. *RIB* 1265

Mercury
Birrens: statue base by Julius Crescens for the benefit of the *collegium*. *RIB* 2102
Birrens: statue base by a *collegium* of Mercury under the charge of Ing(enuius) Rufus. *RIB*
   2103 (with Numen Augusti)
Caerleon: statuette from Cur[...] and erected by Severus. *RIB* 321
Caister-on-Sea: bronze tablet by Aurelius Atticia[n]us. *RIB* 2432.2
Carlisle: relief to M(ercurius) by C(...) I(....) S(....). The incorporated *caduceus* confirms
   the expansion. *RIB* 952
Castlecary: altar by *milites* of *VI Victrix*, citizens of Italy and Noricum. *RIB* 2148
Cirencester: altar. *Brit.* iv (1973), 324, no. 1 (with Matres)
Corbridge: relief to Arecurio (sic), attributed to a mason misreading instructions, by
   Apollinaris. *RIB* 1123
Corbridge: relief. *RIB* 1133
Lincoln: inscription recording a guild of Mercury. *RIB* 270
Lincoln: face-pot with the inscription D(e)o Mercurio. *RIB* 2499.1
London: pottery graffito. *RIB* 2503.130
Old Harlow: lead sheet to Mercurius (on reverse) by the lover of Eterna. *Brit.* iv (1973),
   325, no. 3
Rocester: pottery graffito. *RIB* 2503.129
Stowmarket: silver ring. *B* 1996, 451, no. 29
Uley: bronze plaque from Severa [...] Felix. *RIB* 2432.6
Uley: bronze fragment. *RIB* 2432.7
Uley: lead curse addressed to Mercury. *B* 1996, 439, no. 1
Vindolanda: relief. *RIB* 1693
Wallsend: relief recording the dedication of a statuette of M(ercurius) by *cohors II
   Nerviorum*. The inclusion of a goat on the relief confirms the expansion of the deity's
   name. *RIB* 1303
Wallsend: slab to M(ercurius). *RIB* 1304
Wallsingham: silver ring inscribed MER. *B* 1999, 32, no. 18
York: relief. *RIB* 655

Mercury Andescociuoucus
Colchester: slab by Imilico, *libertus* of Aesurilinus. *RIB* 193 (with Numina Augustorum)

Mercury Propitius (Mercury the Favourer)
Leicester: inscription on column. *RIB* 244 (the authenticity of the inscription has been
   questioned)

Minerva, see also **Sulis Minerva**
Auchendavy: altar by M. Cocceius Firmus, centurion of *II Augusta*. *RIB* 2177 (with
   Campestres, Epona, Hercules, Mars, and Victoria)
Benwell: altar by Primus. *JRS* xlviii (1958), 151, no. 8
Birrens: altar by *cohors II Tungrorum*, under the prefect G. Silvius Auspex. *RIB* 2104
Caernarvon: altar by Aurelius Sabinianus, *actarius*. *RIB* 429
Carlisle: altar by M. [Aurelius?] Syrio, military tribune with *XX Valeria Victrix*, between

213-22. *Brit.* xx (1989), 331-3, no. 5 (with Jupiter Optimus Maximus, Juno, Mars, and Victoria)

Carrawburgh: altar by Quintus, *architectus*. *RIB* 1542

Carrawburgh: altar by Venico. *RIB* 1543

Carvoran: slab to [Mi]ner[vae] or Nep[tuno]. *RIB* 1788

Chester: altar by Furius Fortunatus, *magister primus*. *RIB* 457

Chichester: slab recording the building of a temple to Neptune and Minerva in honour of the Domus Divina by the guild of smiths on a site given by [...]ens, son of Pudentinus, and by the authority of T. Claudius Togidubnus. *RIB* 91

Corbridge: statuette base to M[inerva] by Titus Tertinius, *librarius*. *RIB* 1134

Ebchester: altar to [Miner]va by Julius Gr[...]nus, *actarius* of *cohors IV Breucorum Antoninianae*, between 213-22. *RIB* 1101

High Rochester: altar by Julius Carantus, *singularis consularis*. *RIB* 1266

High Rochester: altar by Flavius Severinus, tribune. *RIB* 1267

High Rochester: altar by Caecilius Optatus, tribune (of *cohors I Vardullorum*; see *RIB* 1272 under Mithras Invictus below), about 213. *RIB* 1268 (with Genius collegii)

Stonea: gold plaque to Mi(ne)rva. *RIB* 2430.1

Whitley Castle: altar to Menerva (sic). *RIB* 1200 (with Hercules Victor)

Minerva Sulis, see **Sulis Minerva**

Mithras, see also **Deus, Mithras Invictus, Sol Invictus**

Lanchester: altar to M(ithras). *RIB* 1082 (with Cautopates and Sol Invictus)

London: relief of Mithras (unnamed) to Ulpius Silvanus, *emeritus* of *II Augusta*. *RIB* 3

London: panel. *RIB* 4 (with Sol Invictus)

Verulamium: token adapted from a *denarius* of Augustus, struck 18 BC. *RIB* 2408.2

Mithras Invictus, see also **Deus, Mithras Invictus, Sol Invictus, Sol Invictus Mithras Saecularis**

Caerleon: base to [In]victus [Mit]hras by [...]s Iustus of *II Augusta*. *RIB* 322

Carrawburgh: altar to Inv(ictus) M(ithras) by L. Antonius Proculus, prefect of *cohors I Batavorum Antoninianae* between 213-22. *RIB* 1544

Carrawburgh: altar to In(victus) M(ithras) by A. Cluentius Habitus, prefect of *cohors I Batavorum*, after 198-211 on the evidence of the Severan titles in his home town's name. *RIB* 1545

Carrawburgh: altar to Invictus Mitras by M. Simplicius Simplex, prefect. *RIB* 1546

High Rochester: slab to Invictus by L. Caecilius Optatus, tribune of *cohors I Vardullorum*. *RIB* 1272 (with Sol)

Rudchester: altar to Invictus Mytras by P. Aelius Titullus, prefect. *RIB* 1395

Rudchester: altar to Anicetus (= Invictus) [Mithras] by Aponius Rogatianus. *RIB* 1397 (with Sol Apollo)

Mogons (N.B. there are several variants on this name, listed below, usually derived from the dative form *Mogonti*)

Old Penrith: altar to Mog(on)s. *RIB* 921

Vindolanda: altar by Lupulus. *Brit.* iv (1973), 329, no. 10 (with Genius loci)

Mogons/Mogonis Cad[...], see also **Mounus Cad(...)**

Risingham: altar to Mogonito Cad[...] by M. G(avius?) Secundinus, *[b](ene)f(iciarius) co(n)s(ularis)*, on his first posting at *Habitancum* (Risingham). *RIB* 1225 (with Numen Domini Nostri Augusti)

Risingham: altar by Inventus to Mounus Cad(...). *RIB* 1226

Mogons Vitiris
Netherby: altar by Aelius [....]. *RIB* 971

Mountis/Mountes
High Rochester: altar by Julius Firminus, *dec(urio)*. *RIB* 1269
Old Penrith: altar. *RIB* 922

Mounus, see **Mogons Cad[...]**

Narius, see also **Faunus Narius** above
Thetford: silver spoon. *RIB* 2420.23

Nemesis, see also **Domina Nemesis**
Chester: altar by Sext(ius) Marcianus, centurion, following a vision. *JRS* lvii (1967), 203, no. 5
Hadrian's Wall (exact location unknown): altar by Apollonius, *sacerdos*. *RIB* 2065

Nemetona
Bath: altar by Peregrinus from Trier. *RIB* 140 (with Mars Loucetius)

Neptune
Birrens: altar by Claudius [...]. *RIB* 2105
Castlecary: altar by *cohors I Vardullorum* under the prefect Trebius Verus. *RIB* 2149
Castlesteads: altar to [N]ep[tuno]. *RIB* 1990
Chichester: slab recording the building of a temple to Neptune and Minerva in honour of the Domus Divina by the guild of smiths on a site given by [...]ens, son of Pudentinus, and by the authority of T. Claudius Togidubnus. *RIB* 91 (with Neptune)
Frampton: mosaic with Latin couplet including a reference to Neptune. *RIB* 2448.8
Hamble estuary: lead curse addressed to Neptune. *B* 1997, 455, no. 1
Lympne: altar by L. Aufidius Pant[h]era, prefect of classis Britannica, *c.*115–40. *RIB* 66
Maryport: altar appropriated by L(ucius) Cass(ius) (secondary text). *RIB* 839
Newcastle-upon-Tyne: altar by *VI Victrix* (with *RIB* 1320, see Oceanus). *RIB* 1319
Vindolanda: altar. *RIB* 1694
York: arch and gateway to L. Viducius Placidus, *negotiator* from Rouen, in 221. *Brit.* viii (1977), 430, no. 18 (with Genius loci and Numina Augustorum; N.B. Neptune is restored on the stone and an alternative reading is IOM for Jupiter Optimus Maximus)

Nodens, see also **Mars Nodens**
Lydney Park: lead curse made by Silvianus against the ring-thief Senicianus. *RIB* 306

Numen
Netherby: altar to the Numen of Caracalla by *cohors I Aelia Hispanorum*, during the governorship of [G. Julius Marcus?] in *c.*213. *RIB* 976
Vindolanda: slab to the Numen of Severus Alexander(?) by *cohors IIII Gallor(um) [Severianae Alexandrianae]*, commemorating the restoration of a gate during the governorship of Claudius Xenephon between 222–35. *RIB* 1706

Numen Augusti/Numina Augustorum/Numen Domini Nostri (The Spirit of Augustus/Spirits of the Augusti/Spirit of our Lord)
Bath: altar to Numina Augustorum by G. Curiatius Saturninus, centurion of *II Augusta*. *RIB* 146 (with Sulis Minerva)
Bath: altar to Numen Augusti by G. Severius Emeritus, *c(enturio) reg(ionarius)*, recording the restoration of the holy place. *RIB* 152 (with Virtus)

Benwell: altar to Numina Augustorum by Aelius Vibius, centurion of *XX*. *RIB* 1327 (with Antenociticus)

Benwell: altar to Numina Augustorum, and naming Antoninus Pius, by M. Liburnius Fronto, centurion of *II Augusta*, between 139-61. *RIB* 1330 (with Jupiter Optimus Maximus Dolichenus)

Birdoswald: altar to Numen Augusti by *cohors I Aelia Dacorum*, commanded by the tribune Marc(ius?) Gallicus, around the period 255-75 (see *RIB* 1883 under Jupiter Optimus Maximus for this man in post under Postumus). *RIB* 1882 (with Jupiter Optimus Maximus)

Birdoswald: statue base to Numen Augusti by *cohors I Aelia [Dacorum?]*. *RIB* 1904 (with Signa)

Birrens: statue base of Mars(?) to Numen Augusti by a *collegium* of Mercury under the charge of Ingenuius Rufus. *RIB* 2103 (with Mercury)

Bollihope Common: altar to [Numina August]orum (primary text; for secondary, see Silvanus Invictus below). *RIB* 1041

Brough-on-Humber: slab to Numina Augustorum M. Ulpius Januarius, *aedilis* of the vicus of *Petuaria*, to commemorate the new stage (*proscaenium*) for the theatre between 140-61. *RIB* 707 (with Domus Divina of Antoninus Pius)

Burgh-by-Sands: altar to Numen Augusti by *cohors [....]*. *RIB* 2040 (with Hercules)

Burgh-by-Sands: altar to Numina Augustorum by Caelius Vibianus, tribune of *numerus Maurorum Aurelianorum Valeriani Gallienique*, under the direction of Julius Rufinus, *princeps*, between 253-8. *RIB* 2042 (with Genius *numeri Maurorum Aurelianorum Valeriani Gallienique*; the dedication to Jupiter Optimus Maximus is entirely restored in *RIB*)

Burrow-in-Lonsdale (Overborough): altar to Numen Augusti by Bellinus. *RIB* 611 (with Genius collegii Apollinis)

Caerleon: pilaster to Numina Augustorum by [...], *primus pilus* in 244. *RIB* 327 (with Genius legionis II Augustae)

Caerleon: altar to Numina Augustorum. *Brit.* viii (1977), 429-30, no. 16

Caerwent: statue base of Mars Lenus(?) and to Numen Augusti by Nonius Romanus in 152. *RIB* 309 (with Mars Lenus and Ocelus Vellaunus)

Cardewlees: altar to [N(umina)] D(ominorum) N(ostrorum) Va[leri]ani et G[allie]ni et Vale[ria]ni nob(ilissimi) C(a)es(ari) P(iorum) F(elicium) Augustor(um) by *numerus [...]* under the charge of G. [C]arinius Aurelianus, centurion of *II Augusta*, between 255-9. *RIB* 913 (with Jupiter Optimus Maximus)

Carlisle: altar to Numen Imp(eratoris) Alexandri Aug(usti) in 222-35. *RIB* 949 (with Mars Ocelus)

Carvoran: altar to Numina [Aug(ustorum)] by Julius Pacatus and Pacutius C[...], commemorating a new building. *RIB* 1786 (with Mars?)

Castlesteads: altar to Numen [Aug(usti)] by *cohors II Tungrorum Gordiana*, under the prefect T. Claudius Claudianus, in 241. *RIB* 1983 (with Jupiter Optimus Maximus)

Castlesteads: altar to Numen Augusti by Paco[ni]us Satur[ni]nus, prefect of cavalry. *RIB* 1987 (with Mars)

Castlesteads: altar to Numen Augusti by Aurelius Armiger, *decurio princeps*. *RIB* 1991 (with Vanauns)

Colchester: slab to Numina Augustorum by Imilco, *libertus* of Aesurilinus. *RIB* 193 (Mercury Andescociuoucus)

Chester: slate tablet to Numen Augusti. *RIB* 458

Chester: altar(?) to Numina Augustorum. *RIB* 459

Dorchester-on-Thames: altar *cum cancellis* ('with screens') to Numina Augustorum by M. Varius Severus, *beneficiarius consularis*. *RIB* 235 (with Jupiter Optimus Maximus)

Ebchester: altar to Numen Augusti. *RIB* 1100 (with Mars)

Fossdike: statuette of Mars and dedicated to Numina Augustorum by Bruccius and Caratius Colasunus. *RIB* 274 (with Mars)

Greetland: altar to Numina Augustorum by T. Aurelius Aurelianus, *magister sacrorum*, in
208. *RIB* 627 (with Victoria Brigantia)

Hadrian's Wall (exact location unknown): altar to Numen Augusti by Durio, Ramio,
Trupo, and Lurio, all Germans. *RIB* 2063 (with Maponus)

Haltonchesters: altar to Numina Augustorum. *RIB* 1425

Hastings: silver patera dedicated by Romulus, son of Camulogenus. *RIB* 2414.37 (with Mars)

Housesteads: altar to Numen Augusti by *numerus Hnaudifridi*. *RIB* 1576 (with Baudihillia
and Friagabis)

Housesteads: altar to Numina Augustorum by *cohors I Tungrorum*, under the prefect Q.
Julius Maximus. *RIB* 1584 (with Jupiter Optimus Maximus)

Housesteads: altar to Numina Augustorum by *cohors I Tungrorum*, under the prefect Q.
Julius [...]sus. *RIB* 1585 (with Jupiter Optimus Maximus)

Housesteads: altar to Numina Augustorum by *cohors I Tungrorum*, under the prefect Q.
Verius Superstis. *RIB* 1586 (with Jupiter Optimus Maximus)

Housesteads: altar to Numina [Augustorum], under the prefect [...]rius [.]upe[...]. *RIB*
1587 (with Jupiter Optimus Maximus)

Housesteads: altar to [Numina A]ug(ustorum). *RIB* 1588 (with Jupiter Optimus
Maximus)

Housesteads: shrine door jam to Numen Augusti by 'the Germans'. *RIB* 1593 (with Beda,
Fimmilena, and Mars Thincsus)

Housesteads altar to Numen Augusti by 'the Germans' of the cuneus Frisiorum
Vercovicianorum between 222-35. *RIB* 1594 (with Mars and the Alaisiagae)

Housesteads: altar to Numina Augustorum by [...], *custos armorum*. *RIB* 1596 (with Mars
and Victoria)

Lanchester: altar to N(umen) Gor[di]ani Aug(usti) N(ostri) by *vexillatio Sueborum
Lon(govicianorum) Gor(diana)* between 238-44. *RIB* 1074 (with Garmangabis)

Lanchester: altar to Numen Augusti by *cohors I Vardullorum* during the governorship
of Antistius Adventus, at the expense of the tribune Flavius Titianus (with Genius
cohortis), about 175-8. *RIB* 1083

Lincoln: altar to Numina Augustorum by G. Antistius Frontinus, *curator*. *RIB* 247 (with
Parcae)

London: slab to Numen C[aes(aris) Aug(usti)?]. *RIB* 5

London (Greenwich Park): slab dedicated to Nu[mini Aug?]. See next entry for the
evidence that this is plausible. *RIB* 38

London (Greenwich Park): small slab dedicated to [...Nu]min[i Aug...?] by [...
Cae]ciliu[s...]cus. If the identification is correct another slab from this site may now be
expanded (see previous entry). Minerva remains an alternative, but less likely, possibility.
Unpublished but forthcoming (found 15 July 1999)

Maryport: altar to Numen Augusti by *cohors I Hispanorum*. *RIB* 815 (with Jupiter Optimus
Maximus)

Maryport: altar to Numen Augusti by M. Maenius Agrippa, tribune. *RIB* 824 (with
Jupiter Optimus Maximus)

Maryport: altar to Numen Augusti by (M.) Maenius Agrippa, tribune. *RIB* 825 (with
Jupiter Optimus Maximus)

Nettleham: slab to Numina Augustorum by Q. Neratius Proxsimus, recording his arch.
JRS lii (1962), 192, no. 8 (with Mars Rigonemetos)

Nettleton: altar to Numen [A]ug(usti) N(ostri) by Aurelius Pu[...]. Wedlake (1982), 136,
no. 2 (with Silvanus)

Newcastle-upon-Tyne: altar to [Nu]men [Augusti?]. *RIB* 1317 (with Hospitales and
Jupiter Optimus Maximus)

Old Penrith: altar to Numina Augustorum by Julius Augustalis, *actor* of Julius Lupus. *RIB*
918 (with Mars Belatucadrus)

Old Penrith: slab to N(umen) Imp(eratoris) Alexandri Aug(usti) by the *vexillatio*

Marsacorum between 222-35. *RIB* 919 (with Matres Tramarinae)

Old Penrith: altar to [Num(ina) A]ug(ustorum) by a vexillation of *[X]X [Val](eria) Vic(trix)*. *RIB* 940

Risingham: altar to N(umen) D(omini) N(ostri) Aug(usti) by M. G(avius?) Secundinus, *beneficiarius consularis*. *RIB* 1225 (with Mogons Cad[...])

Risingham: altar to Numina Augustorum by *cohors IIII Gallorum*. *RIB* 1227

Scarcroft: altar to Num(en) [Aug(usti)?]. *JRS* lv (1965), 221, no. 6 (with Apollo)

Slack: altar to N(umen) Aug(usti) by T. Aurelius Quintus. *RIB* 623 (with Bregans)

Somerdale Keynsham: altar to Num(ina) Divor(um) Aug(ustorum) by G. Indutius Felix in the year 155. *RIB* 181 (with Silvanus)

South Shields: frieze to Numin[a Aug(ustorum)?] by Domitius Epictetus, recording a *templu[m]*. *RIB* 1056 (with another deity, name lost)

Ty Coch, near Bangor: milestone/honorific column dedicated to Num(ina) Aug(ustorum?) during the reign of Caracalla between 212-17. *RIB* 2264

Vindolanda: altar to Numina Augustorum by vicus inhabitants at Vindolanda. *RIB* 1700 (with Domus Divina and Volcanus)

Vindolanda: altar to Numen d(omini) n(ostri). *RIB* 1692 (with Matres)

York: altar to N(umen) Aug(usti) by Mat(...) Vitalis, centurion. *RIB* 640 (with Arciaco)

York: slab to Numen Augusti by [...]sius, recording restoration of the shrine. *RIB* 656 (with Ioug[...])

York: altar to Numen Augusti. *RIB* 657 (with Genius Eboraci?)

York: slab recording an arch and gateway dedicated to Numina Augustorum by L. Viducius Placidus, *negotiator* from the Rouen region, in 221. *Brit.* viii (1977), 430, no. 18 (with Genius loci and Neptune)

Unprovenanced (British origin): altar to Numina Augustorum. *RIB* 2217 (with Fortuna)

Nympha/Nymphae

Carrawburgh: altar to the [Nymp]hae by a vexillation of *[VI] Victrix*. *RIB* 1547

Carrawburgh: altar to the Nymphae by M. Hispanius Modestinus, prefect of *cohors I Batavorum*. *JRS* li (1961), 193, no. 9 (with Genius loci)

Carvoran: altar to the Nymphae by Vettia Mansueta and daughter Claudia Turianilla. *RIB* 1789

Castleford: slab to the Nymp(h)ae. *Brit.* xiv (1983), 337, no. 11

Chester: altar to the Nymphae by *XX Valeria Victrix*. *RIB* 460 (with Fontes)

Croy Hill: altar to the Nymphae by a vexillation of *VI Victrix* under Fabius Liberalis. *RIB* 2160

Greta Bridge: altar by Brica and daughter Januaria (name of the specific local Nymph unresolvable from the record of this stone). *RIB* 744

Risingham: altar to the Nymphae by the unnamed wife of Fabius. *RIB* 1228

Nympha Brigantia

Castlesteads(?): altar to Nympha Brigantia in honour of Caracalla and his divine house by M. Cocceius Nigrinus, *[pr]oc(urator) Aug(usti) n(ostri)*, 'procurator of our Emperor', between 212-17. *RIB* 2066 (with Domus Divina)

Nympha Coventina

Carrawburgh: altar to Nimfa (sic) Coventina by Maduhus, a German. *RIB* 1526

Carrawburgh: altar by [...]tianus, *decurio*. *RIB* 1527

Ocelus Vellaunus, see also Mars Ocelus

Caerwent: statue base by Nonius Romanus in 152. *RIB* 309 (with Mars Lenus and the Numen Augusti of Marcus Aurelius)

Oceanus/Ocianus
Newcastle-upon-Tyne: altar to Ocianus by *VI Victrix* (with *RIB* 1319, see Neptune). *RIB* 1320
York: bronze plate, texts in Greek, by Demetrius. *RIB* 663 (with Tethys) (attached to *RIB* 662, dedicated to Theoi Hegemonikos, 'gods of the governor's headquarters')

Panakeia
Chester: altar by Antiochos, *hiatros*. *JRS* lix (1969), 235, no. 3 (with Aesculapius and Hygeia)

Panthea, see also Silvanus Pantheus
Corbridge: altar. *RIB* 1135 (with Bona Fortuna)

Parcae (Fates), see also Matres Parcae
Carlisle: altar by Donatalis for his son Probus. *RIB* 953
Lincoln: altar by G. Antistius Frontinus, *curator*. *RIB* 247 (with Numina Augustorum)

Pax (Peace)
Carvoran: altar by M. Caecilius Donatianus, tribune serving as prefect. *RIB* 1791 (with Virgo Caelestis, Mater, Virtus, and Ceres Dea Suria)
High Rochester: base by the tribune Julius (Silvanus) Melanio. *RIB* 1273, see *RIB95*, p.781

Penates
York: altar by P. Aelius Marcianus, prefect of *cohors [.....]* (*I Augustae Bracarum* has been suggested on the evidence of this man as its prefect on *ILS* 2738). *RIB* 649 (with Hospitales and Jupiter Optimus Maximus)

Priapus
Birrens: slab inscribed *[P]riapi m(entula)*, 'phallus of Priapus', and a face of a god. The phrase seems to be exceedingly rare to the point of being unparalleled but Lewis and Short note *Priapo mentulatior* in a series of anonymous erotic poems collected for an 1878 edition of Catullus. The text is so unusual that some scepticism about its authenticity must be noted. *RIB* 2106 (but note also *RIB* 983 which is a specific and authentic reference to a phallus – *mentula*)

Ratis
Birdoswald: altar. *RIB* 1903
Chesters: altar. *RIB* 1454

Regina (Queen Goddess), see also Diana Regina, and Salus Regina
Lanchester: altar by Misio. *RIB* 1084
Lemington: relief to Dea Regina. *RIB* 125

Regina Caelestis (The Queen Caelestis), see also Bona Dea Regina Caelestis, Caelestis Brigantia and Virgo Caelestis
Carvoran: relief of altar by Aurelius Martialis. *RIB* 1827 (re-read, see *RIB95*)

Ricagambeda
Birrens: altar by men from *pagus Vellaus* ('Vellavian district'), currently with *cohors II Tungrorum*. *RIB* 2107

Roma
High Rochester: altar to D(eae) R(omae) by *dupl(icarii)* of the numerus exploratorum
Bremeniensium, under the charge of the tribune Caepio Charitinus. *RIB* 1270

Roma Aeterna (Eternal Rome)
Maryport: altar by G. Cornelius Peregrinus, tribune of the cohort and *decurio* of Saldae in
Mauretania Caesariensis. *RIB* 812 (with Fatum Bonum, Fortuna Redux, and Genius loci)
Maryport: votive pillar. *RIB* 840 (with Fortuna Redux)

Romulus
Custom Scrubs, Bisley: relief made by Juventinus and by Gulioepius. *RIB* 132

Salus (Health)
Binchester: altar by M. Aure[lius ...]ocomas, *me[dicus]*, for welfare of *ala Vet[tonum]*. *RIB*
1028 (with Aesculapius)
Chester: altar by the *liberti* and *familia* of the legate T. Pomponius Mamilianus. *RIB* 445
(with Aesculapius and Fortuna Redux)
Corbridge: altar by G. Julius Apolinaris, centurion of *VI Victrix*, his name replacing
someone else's. *RIB* 1131 (with Caelestis Brigantia and Jupiter Aeternus Dolichenus)
Ribchester: altar during the governorship of Gordianus(?) in *c.*216. *RIB* 590 (with
Victoria of Caracalla)

Salus Regina (Queen of Health)
Caerleon: altar by P. Sallienius Tha[la]mus, prefect of *II Augusta*, about 198-209 (see *RIB*
326). *RIB* 324

Sattada or **Satiada**
Vindolanda?: altar by the *curia* of the Textoverdi. *RIB* 1695

Senuna
Baldock: named on gold and silver votive plaques, probably from an open-air spring shrine.
Brit. xxxvi (2005), 489 no. 30 (see also *RIB* II 2422.3, now identified as Senuna)

Serapis, see also **Jupiter Serapis**
York: relief by Claudius Hieronymianus, legate of *VI Victrix*, recording the dedication of
a temple, late second/early third century. *RIB* 658

Setlocenia
Maryport: altar by Labareus, a German. *RIB* 841

Signa (Standards)
Birdoswald: statue base by *cohors I Aelia [Dacorum?]*. *RIB* 1904 (with Numen Augusti)
High Rochester: altar to *Signa cohors I Vardullorum* by Egnatius Lucilianus, propraetorian legate
for the *cohors I Vardullorum* and *numerus Exploratorum Brem(enensium)* under the charge of
Cassius Sabinianus, tribune, between 238-44. *RIB* 1262 (with Genius Domini Nostri)

Signa cohortis (Standards of the cohort)
High Rochester: altar by T. Licinius Valerianus, tribune, for cohors I Vardullorum. *RIB*
1263 (with Genius cohortis)

Silvanae [et] Quadrvae Caelestis (The Heavenly Silvanae nymphs and Quadruae)
Westerwood, Cumbernauld: altar by Vibia Pacata, wife of Flavius Verecundus, centurion
of *VI Victrix*. *JRS* liv (1964), 178, no. 7

273

Silvanus, see also **Vinotonus Silvanus**

Auchendavy: altar. *RIB* 2178

Bar Hill: altar by [C]aristanius [J]ustianus, prefect of *cohors I Hamiorum. RIB* 2167

Birdoswald: altar by venatores Bannie(n)sses. *RIB* 1905 (formerly believed to refer to Bewcastle)

Cadder: altar by L. Tanicius Verus, prefect. *RIB* 2187 (see *ILS* 8759b for a possible ancestor of this man in 80-1 in Egypt)

Carvoran: altar by Vellaeus. *RIB* 1790

Cirencester: altar by Sabidius Maximus. *RIB* 104

Colchester: bronze plate by Hermes. *RIB* 195

Corbridge: altar by a vexillation of *II Augusta* and *cuneus [...]. RIB* 1136

Eastgate: altar by Aurelius Quirinus, prefect of *cohors I Lingonum* at Lanchester, between *c.*238-44. *RIB* 1042 (datable from *RIB* 1091-2, naming this man under Gordian III)

Hadrian's Wall (milecastle 49): altar to [Si]l[v]an[us] by Flavius Marcellinus, *decurio. RIB* 1870

Haile (find-spot unknown): altar made by Primus, *custos armorum. RIB* 796 (with Hercules)

Kirkby Thore: altar by Ael[...]. *RIB* 763

Lanchester: pedestal by M. Didius Provincialis *beneficiarius consularis. RIB* 1085

Moresby: altar by *cohors II Lingonum*, commanded by G. Pompeius Saturninus. *RIB* 798

Netherby: altar. *RIB* 972

Nettleton: altar by [A]ur(elius) Pu[...]. *JRS* lix (1969), 235, no. 1, and Wedlake (1982), 136, no. 2 (with Numen Augusti)

Newcastle-upon-Tyne: altar by G(aius) Val(erius). *RIB* 1321

Newstead: altar by G. Arrius Domitianus, centurion of *XX Valeria Victrix. RIB* 2124 (see this man again at Newstead under Diana Regina and Jupiter Optimus Maximus)

Old Penrith: altars. *RIB* 923-4

Risingham: altar to Sil[vanus]. *RIB* 1207 (with Cocidius)

Somerdale Keynsham: altar by G. Indutius Felix in 155. *RIB* 181 (with Numina divina Augustorum)

Vindolanda: altar by Aurelius Modestus of *II Augusta*, and *beneficiarius consularis superioris Britannia Superior. RIB* 1696

York: altar by L. Celerinius Vitalis, *cornicularius* with *VIIII Hispana* before 120. *RIB* 659

Unprovenanced (now at Hereford): altar. *RIB* 303

Silvanus Callirius

Colchester: bronze plate by Cintusmus, *aerarius. RIB* 194

Silvanus Cocidius

Housesteads: altar by Q. Florius Maternus, prefect of *cohors I Tungrorum. RIB* 1578

Silvanus Invictus (Unconquerable Silvanus)

Bollihope Common: altar by G. Tetius Veturius Micianus, prefect of *ala Sebosiana*, recording a boar kill (secondary text). *RIB* 1041 (primary text for Numina Augustorum)

Silvanus Pantheus

High Rochester: altar to Silvanus [Pa]ntheus by Eutychus, *libertus*, for [Ru]fin[us], tribune commanding *[cohors I Vardullorum]* (from *RIB* 1288) and his wife (Julia) [L]ucilla. *RIB* 1271 (Rufinus' tombstone, *RIB* 1288, appears to record his wife's full name and by implication his career though in fact the deceased's name is lost)

Silvanus Vinotonus, see **Vinotonus**, and **Vinotonus Silvanus**

Sol (The Sun)
Housesteads: altar by Herion. *RIB* 1601

Sol Apollo Anicetus [Mithras] where *Anicetus* is the Greek for *Invictus*
Rudchester: altar by Aponius Rogatianus. *RIB* 1397

Sol Invictus (The Unconquerable Sun) (sometimes as Mithras)
Castlesteads: altar by S. Severius Salvator, prefect. *RIB* 1992
Castlesteads: altar by M. Licinius Ripanus. *RIB* 1993
Corbridge: slab by a vexillation of *VI Victrix* during the governorship of S. Calpurnius
  Agricola, *c.*163–6. *RIB* 1137
High Rochester: slab recording a building by L. Caecilius Optatus, tribune of *cohors I*
  Vardullorum, about 213. *RIB* 1272 (conflated with Mithras Invictus)
Lanchester: altar dedicated to S(ol) I(nvictus). *RIB* 1082 (with Mithras and Cautopates)
London: panel dedicated to [Sol] Invictus. *RIB* 4 (with Mithras?)
Rudchester: altar by T. Claudius Decimus Cornelius Antonius, prefect, to Mithras as Sol
  Invictus on the restoration of the mithraeum. *RIB* 1396

[Sol Invictus Elagabalus] (this name of the emperor, deified in his lifetime, is entirely
  restored on the inscription by *RIB*)
Chesters: slab recording the restoration of a building and by Septimius Nilus, prefect of
  ala II Asturum during the governorship of Marius Valerianus in 221. *RIB* 1465

Sol Invictus Mitras/Mytras Saecularis (The Unconquerable Sun, Mithras, Lord of
  the Ages)
Castlesteads: altar to Sol [Invi]ctus M[ith]r[a]s by M. Licinius Ripanus, prefect. *RIB*
  1993
Housesteads: altar by Litorius Pacactianus, *beneficiarius consularis*. *RIB* 1599
Housesteads: altar by Publicius Proculinus, centurion, in 252. *RIB* 1600

Sol Mitras (sic)
Castlesteads: altar. *RIB* 1994

Soteres (Greek Saviour Gods)
Chester: altar by Hermogenes, *hiatros* (= *medicus*). *RIB* 461

Sucabus
Hadrian's Wall?: slab by Cunovindus. *Brit.* ii (1971), 292, no. 14

Suleviae, see also **Matres Suleviae**
Bath: statue base by Sulinus, *scultor*, son of Brucetus. *RIB* 151 (see Cirencester below)
Binchester: altar dedicated by the *[ala] Vett[onum]*. *RIB* 1035
Cirencester: altar by Sulinus, son of Brucetus. *RIB* 105 (see Bath above). *RIB* 151, and
  under Sulis Minerva below. *RIB* 150)
Cirencester: altar by [P]rimus. *RIB* 106

Sulis
Bath: altar by Aufidius Eutuches, *libertus* of and for the good of M. Aufidius Maximus,
  centurion of *VI Victrix*. *RIB* 143 (see next entry)
Bath: altar by M. Aufidius Lemnus, *libertus* of and for the good of (M.) Aufidius Maximus,
  centurion of *VI Victrix*. *RIB* 144 (see previous entry)
Bath: altar by L. Manius Dionisias, *libertus*, for the good of G. Jav[olenus Sa]tur[nal]is,
  imaginifer of *II Augusta*. *RIB* 147

Bath: altar by Q. Pompeius Anicetus. *RIB* 148

Bath: altar by Priscus, *lapidarius*, from the Carnutes tribe (in Gaul, around Chartres), and son of Toutius. *RIB* 149

Sulis Minerva

Bath: fragment of inscribed frieze recording repairs at the expense of Claudius Ligur[...]. *RIB* 141(d)

Bath: altar by G. Curiatius Saturninus, centurion of *II Augusta*. *RIB* 146 (with Numina Augustorum)

Bath: altar by Sulinus, son of Maturus. *RIB* 150

Bath: base by L. Marcius Memor, *haruspex* of Sulis. *JRS* lvi (1966) 217, no. 1 (and Cunliffe & Davenport, 1985, 130, 9A.1)

Bath: pewter paterae. *RIB* 2417.5-8

Suria, see also Ceres Dea Suria

Carvoran: altar by Lic[in]ius [Cl]em[ens], prefect of *co]h(ors) I Ha[miorum]*, during the governorship of Calpurnius Agricola, between *c.*163-6. *RIB* 1792

Catterick: altar by Gaius N[...] O[...], *beneficiarius*. *RIB* 726

Tanarus, see Jupiter Tanarus

Terra Batavorum (Land of the Batavians) − now rejected

The sole instance of this supposed deity, on *RIB* 902, is now re-read as Brigantia Augusta. See above and *RIB95*

Tethys

York: bronze plate, texts in Greek, by Demetrius (see *RIB* for this man who may be a figure mentioned by Plutarch). *RIB* 663 (with Oceanus) (attached to *RIB* 662, see next entry)

Theoi Hegemonikoi (Greek: Gods of the governor's headquarters)

York: bronze plate, texts in Greek, by Scribonius Demetrius. *RIB* 662 (attached to *RIB* 663 dedicated to Oceanus and Tethys)

Toutatis, see also Mars Toutatis

Kelvedon: pottery graffito. *RIB* 2503.131

Walsingham: silver ring inscribed TOT. *B* 1999, 32, no. 19

Tridam[...]

Unprovenanced (now at Michaelchurch, Herefords): altar by Bellicus. *RIB* 304

Tutela Brigantia Augusta (Guardian Brigantia Augusta)

Old Carlisle: altar to T(utela) B(rigantia) A(ugusta) by T. Aurelius. *RIB* 902 (re-reading in *RIB95* of a stone formerly thought to refer to Terra Batavorum)

Unseni Fersomeri

Old Penrith: altar by Burcanius, Arcavius, Vagdavarcustus, and Pov[.]c[.]arus. *RIB* 926

Vanauns

Castlesteads: altar by Aurelius Armiger, *decurio princeps*. *RIB* 1991 (with Numen Augusti)

Verbeia

Ilkley: altar by Clodius Fronto, prefect of *cohors II Lingonum*. *RIB* 635

Vernostonus Cocidius
Ebchester: altar by Virilis, a German. *RIB* 1102

Veter/Veteres/Vheteris/Viter/Vitiris/Votris, variously male or female, singular or
  plural, and numerous other variants; see also **Hveteris**, and **Mogons Vitiris**
Benwell: altar to Vetris. *RIB* 1335
Benwell: altar to the Vitires. *RIB* 1336
Carrawburgh: altar to Veteris by Uccus. *RIB* 1548
Carvoran: altar to Veteris by Necalames. *RIB* 1793
Carvoran: altar to Veteris by Necalames. *RIB* 1794
Carvoran: altar to Vetiris by Julius Pastor, *imaginifer* of cohors II Delmatarum. *RIB* 1795
Carvoran: altar to Vetiris by Andiatis. *RIB* 1796
Carvoran: altar to Veteris. *RIB* 1797
Carvoran: altar to Viteris. *RIB* 1798
Carvoran: altar to Vitiris by Menius Dada. *RIB* 1799
Carvoran: altar to Vitiris by Milus and Aurides. *RIB* 1800
Carvoran: altar to Vitiris by Ne[ca]limes (sic, but see 1793-4 above). *RIB* 1801
Carvoran: altars to the Veteres. *RIB* 1802-4
Carvoran: altar to the Vitires by Deccius. *RIB* 1805
Catterick: altar to Vheteris by Aurelius Mucianus. *RIB* 727
Chester-le-Street: altar to Vitiris by Duihno. *RIB* 1046
Chester-le-Street: altar to the goddesses the Vitires by Vitalis. *RIB* 1047
Chester-le-Street: altar to the goddesses the Vit(ires). *RIB* 1048
Chesters: altar to Vitiris by Tertulus. *RIB* 1455
Chesters: altar to the Veteres. *RIB* 1456
Chesters: altar to Vitiris. *RIB* 1457
Chesters: altar to Votris. *RIB* 1458
Corbridge: altar to Vetiris. *RIB* 1139
Corbridge: altar to Vitiris. *RIB* 1140
Corbridge: altar to Vit(iris) by Mitius. *RIB* 1141
Ebchester: altar to Vitiris by Maximus. *RIB* 1103
Ebchester: altar to Vitiris. *RIB* 1104
Greatchesters: altar to Vetiris. *RIB* 1728
Greatchesters: altar to the Veteres by Romana. *RIB* 1729
Greatchesters: altar to the Veteres. *RIB* 1730
Hadrian's Wall (exact location unknown): altar to Veteris. *RIB* 2068
Housesteads: altar to the Veteres. *RIB* 1604
Housesteads: altar to the Veteres. *RIB* 1605
Housesteads: altar to the Veteres by Aurelius Victor. *RIB* 1606
Lanchester: altar to Vit(iris). *RIB* 1087
Lanchester: altar to Vitiris by [....], *princeps*. *RIB* 1088
Piercebridge: altar to Veteris. *Brit.* v (1974), 461, no. 3
South Shields: altar to Vitiris by Cr[...]. *Brit.* xviii (1987), 368, no. 7
Thistleton: silver plaque to Vete[ris] by Mocux[s]oma. *RIB* 2431.3
Vindolanda: altar to [V]ete[r]is. *RIB* 1697
Vindolanda: altar to Veteris. *RIB* 1698
Vindolanda: altar to the Veteres by Senaculus. *RIB* 1699
Vindolanda: altar to the Veteres by Longinus. *Brit.* iv (1973), 329, no. 11
Vindolanda: altar to the Veteres by Senilis. *Brit.* iv (1973), 329, no. 12
Vindolanda: altar to Vetir. *Brit.* vi (1975), 285, no. 6
Vindolanda: altar to Ve[ter]. *Brit.* vi (1975), 285, no. 7
Vindolanda: altar to the Vitirum. *Brit.* x (1979), 346, no. 8
York: altar to Veter by Primulus. *RIB* 660

Vicres
Old Penrith: altar by T(...) S(....). *RIB* 925

Victor, see **Hercules Victor** and **Mars Victor**

Victoria (Victory)
Auchendavy: altar by M. Cocceius Firmus, centurion of *II Augusta*. *RIB* 2177 (with
  Campestres, Epona, Hercules, Mars, and Minerva)
Birdoswald: altar by Aurelius Maximus. *RIB* 1899 (with Mars)
Brougham: altar. *RIB* 779 (with Mars)
Carlisle: altar by M. [Aurelius?] Syrio, military tribune with *XX Valeria Victrix*, between
  213-22. *Brit.* xx (1989), 331-3, no. 5 (with Jupiter Optimus Maximus, Juno, Mars, and
  Minerva)
Colchester: statue in existence by 60. Tacitus, *Annals* xiv.32
Colchester: bronze plaque to Victoria of Severus Alexander by Lossio Veda, a Caledonian,
  between 222-35. *RIB* 191 (with Mars Medocius Campesium)
Hadrian's Wall (1.25 miles south of mc 51): crag inscription recording *aurea per caelum
  volitat Victoria pennis*, 'golden Victory flies through the sky on her wings'. *RIB* 1954
High Rochester: base by Julius Silvanus Melanio. *RIB* 1273, see *RIB95*, p.781 (with
  Pax)
Housesteads: altar by [...], *custos armorum*. *RIB* 1596 (with Mars and Numina
  Augustorum)
Lanchester: altar by Ulpius. *RIB* 1086
Ribchester: base. *RIB* 585 (with Mars)
Ribchester: altar to the Victoria of Caracalla during the governorship of Gordianus(?) in
  c.216. *RIB* 590 (with Salus)
Rough Castle: altar by *cohors VI Nerviorum*, commanded by Flavius Betto, centurion of
  XX Valeria Victrix. *RIB* 2144

Victoria Augusti/Augustorum (Victoria of the Emperor/Emperors)
Benwell: altar by *ala I Asturum*, during the governorship of Alfenus Senecio, between
  c.205-8. *RIB* 1337
Birrens: altar by *cohors II Tungrorum* under the prefect Silvius Auspex. *RIB* 2100 (with
  Mars)
Castlesteads: relief. *RIB* 1995
Corbridge: altar by L. Julius Juli[anus]. *RIB* 1138
Greatchesters: altar by *cohors VI Nerviorum*, under the prefect G. Julius Barbarus. *RIB* 1731
Maryport: altar by *cohors I Baetasiorum*, under the prefect T. Attius Tutor. *RIB* 842
Maryport: altar by *cohors I Baetasiorum*, under the prefect Ulpius Titianus. *RIB* 843
Newcastle-upon-Tyne: altar. *RIB* 1316 (with Jupiter Optimus Maximus)

Victoria Augustorum Dominorum Nostrorum (Victoria of the Emperors, our
  Lords)
Maryport: altar. *RIB* 844

Victoria Brigantia (Victorious Brigantia)
Castleford: altar by Aurelius Senopianus. *RIB* 628
Greetland: altar by T. Aurelius Aurelianus, *magister sacrorum*, in 208. *RIB* 627 (with Numina
  Augustorum)

Victoria legionis VI Victricis (Victory of *VI Victrix*)
Tunshill Farm: silver plate dedicated by Valerius Rufus. The find-spot in a quarry makes
  it likely it had been removed from elsewhere in antiquity, perhaps York. *RIB* 582

Victoria Victrix (Victorious Victory)
Auchendavy: altar by M. Cocceius Firmus, centurion of *II Augusta*. *RIB* 2176 (with Jupiter Optimus Maximus)

Vinotonus
Scargill Moor, Bowes: altar by L. Caesius Frontinus, prefect of *cohors I Thracum*. *RIB* 733
Scargill Moor, Bowes: altar by V[inotono]. *RIB* 737

Vinotonus Silvanus
Scargill Moor, Bowes: altar by Julius Secundus, centurion of *cohors I Thracum*. *RIB* 732

Vinotonus Silvanus Augustus
Scargill Moor, Bowes: altar by T. [O]rbius Pri[mia]nus, prefect of *[cohors I Thracum?]*. *Brit.* xix (1988), 491, no. 7

Viradecthis
Birrens: altar by the Condrusi (a German tribe) serving in *cohors II Tungrorum*, under the prefect G. Silvius Auspex. *RIB* 2108

Virgo Caelestis (for Julia Domna), see also **Bona Dea Regina Caelestis, Caelestis Brigantia**, and **Regina Caelestis**
Carvoran: altar by M. Caecilius Donatianus, prefect, between 197-217. *RIB* 1791 (with Virtus, Mater, Pax, and Ceres)

Viridios
Ancaster: slab by Trenico, recording his making an arch. *JRS* lii (1962), 192, no. 7
Ancaster: slab dedicated to *Deo V(i)ridio Sancto* …, found forming part of a grave. *B* 2002

Virtus (Virtue)
Bath: altar by G. Severius Emeritus, *c(enturio) reg(ionarius)*. *RIB* 152 (with Numen Augusti)
Carvoran: altar by M. Caecilius Donatianus, prefect. *RIB* 1791 (with Virgo Caelestis, Mater, Pax, and Ceres)
Chesters: altar by *ala II Asturum* in 221-2. *RIB* 1466
Duntocher: relief of 139-61 by a vexillation of *VI Victrix*. *RIB* 2200
Maryport: altar by [...]iana Hermoniae, daughter of Quintus. *RIB* 845

Volcanus Vulcan
Barkway: silver votif leaf to Nu(mini) [Vo]lc(an)o. *RIB* 220
Maryport: altar to V[olcano?] (or Victoria). *RIB* 835 (with Jupiter Optimus Maximus)
Maryport: altar by Helstrius Novellus, prefect (of *cohors I Hispanorum*, see *RIB* 822 under Jupiter Optimus Maximus above). *RIB* 846
Old Carlisle: altar to V(o)lk(ano) by the *magistri* of the vicus inhabitants between 238-44. *RIB* 899 (with Jupiter Optimus Maximus)
Stony Stratford: silver plate to [Vo]lca(no) by Vassinus. *RIB* 215 (with Jupiter)
Vindolanda: altar by vicus inhabitants at Vindolanda. *RIB* 1700 (with Domus Divina and Numina Augustorum)

References and further reading

References

A	*Annales*, Tacitus
Agr	*Agricola*, Tacitus
ASC	*Anglo-Saxon Chronicle*, using G.N. Garmonsway's translation for the Everyman Library
B	*Britannia*, journal of the The Society for the Promotion of Roman Studies
BG	*Bellum Gallicum*, Caesar
CG	*City of God*, St Augustine of Hippo
DD	*de Divinatione*, Cicero
DA	*de Agriculturae*, Cato
DEB	*de Excidio Britanniae*, Gildas
DI	*Epitome Divinarum Institutionum*, Lactantius
DND	*de Natura Deorum*, Cicero
DRN	*de Rerum Natura*, Lucretius
DRR	*de Re Rustica*, Columella
E	*Epigrams*, Martial
HEGA	*Historia Ecclesiastica Gentis Anglorum*, Bede
H	*Historiae*, Tacitus
NH	*Naturalis Historiae*
SC	*Saturnalia Conversations*, Macrobius
SHA	*Scriptores Historiae Augustae*

Further reading

The following list is far from an exhaustive account of the available literature on the subject of religion in Roman Britain but provides a balanced reflection of the range of views held.

Adair, J., 1978, *The Pilgrim's Way. Shrines and Saints in Britain and Ireland*, London

Barley, M.W. & Hanson, R.P.C. (eds), 1968, *Christianity in Roman Britain 300-700*, Leicester

Birley, A., 1979, *The People of Roman Britain*, London

Blagg, T.F.C., 1979, 'The Date of the Temple at Bath' in *Britannia*, 10, 101 ff

Boon, G.C., 1960, 'A Temple of Mithras at Caernarvon-Segontium', *Arch.Camb.*, 109, 136-72

Brown, P.D.C., 1971, 'The Church at Richborough', *Britannia* ii, 225-31

Clarke, S., 1997, 'Abandonment, rubbish disposal and "special" deposits', in Meadows, K., Lemke, C. & Heron, J. (eds), *TRAC 96. Proceedings of the Sixth Annual Theoretical Roman Archaeology Conference Sheffield 1996*, Oxford, 73-81

Collingwood, R.G. & Wright, R.P., 1965, *The Roman Inscriptions of Britain. Volume 1: Inscriptions on Stone*, Oxford (see next entry for revised edition)

Collingwood, R.G. & Wright, R.P., 1995, *The Roman Inscriptions of Britain. Volume I Inscriptions on Stone* (second edition, with *Addenda and Corrigenda* by R.S.O. Tomlin), Stroud [this is the definitive publication of all inscribed slabs, altars and so on]. For Indexes to this work, see Goodburn and Waugh (1983) below

Cool, H.E.M., 2000, 'The Significance of Snake Jewellery Hoards', *Britannia* xxxi, 29-40

Cunliffe, B.W., 1984, *Roman Bath Discovered*, London, 1971, revised edition, London

Cunliffe, B. & Davenport, P., 1985, *The Temple of Sulis Minerva at Bath, Volume 1: The Site,* Oxford University Committee for Archaeology Monograph No. 7, Oxford

Cunliffe, B. & Davenport, P., 1988, *The Temple of Sulis Minerva at Bath, Volume 2: The Finds from the Sacred Spring,* Oxford University Committee for Archaeology Monograph No. 16, Oxford

Davies, J.A. & Gregory, A., 1991, 'Coinage from a Civitas', *Britannia* xxii, 65-102

de la Bédoyère, G., 1999, *The Golden Age of Roman Britain*, Stroud

de la Bédoyère, G., 2001, *Eagles over Britannia. The Roman Army in Britain*, Stroud

Detsicas, A.P., 1983, *The Cantiaci*, Gloucester, 60 ff (Springhead)

Downey, R., King, A. & Soffe, G., 1980, 'The Hayling Island Temple and Religious Connections across the Channel' in Rodwell, W. (ed), 1980, *Temples, Churches and Religion in Roman Britain*, B.A.R. (British Series) 77 (vol. i), Oxford

Fishwick, D., 1995, 'The Temple of Divus Claudius at *Camulodunum*', *Britannia* xxvi, 11-28

Ford, S.D., 1994, 'The Silchester Church: a Dimensional Analysis and a New Reconstruction', *Britannia* xxv, 119-26

France, N.E. & Gobel, B.M., *The Romano-British Temple at Harlow, Essex*, Gloucester, 1985

Frere, S.S., 1995, *The Roman Inscriptions of Britain. Volume II. Epigraphic Indexes*, Stroud

Frere, S.S. & Tomlin, R.S.O. (eds), 1991, *The Roman Inscriptions of Britain. Volume II, Fascicule 2. Weights, metal vessels etc (RIB 2412-2420)*, Stroud

Frere, S.S. & Tomlin, R.S.O. (eds), 1991, *The Roman Inscriptions of Britain. Volume II, Fascicule 3. Jewellery, armour etc (RIB 2421-2441)*, Stroud

Frere, S.S. & Tomlin, R.S.O. (eds), 1992, *The Roman Inscriptions of Britain. Volume II, Fascicule 4. Wooden barrels, tile stamps etc (RIB 2442-2480)*, Stroud

Frere, S.S. & Tomlin, R.S.O. (eds), 1993, *The Roman Inscriptions of Britain. Volume II, Fascicule 5. Tile Stamps of the Classis Britannica; Imperial, Procuratorial and Civic Tile-stamps; Stamps of Private Tilers; Inscriptions on Relief-patterned Tiles and graffiti on Tiles (RIB 2481-2491)*, Stroud

Frere, S.S. & Tomlin, R.S.O. (Eds), 1995, *The Roman Inscriptions of Britain. Volume II, Fascicule 7. Graffiti on samian ware (Terra Sigillata) (RIB 2501)*, Stroud

Frere, S.S. & Tomlin, R.S.O. (eds), 1995, *The Roman Inscriptions of Britain. Volume II, Fascicule 8. Graffiti on Coarse Pottery; stampe on Coarse Pottery; Addenda and Corrigenda to Fascicules 1-8 (RIB 2502-2505)*, Stroud

Goodburn, R. & Waugh, H., 1983, *The Roman Inscriptions of Britain. Volume I Inscriptions on Stone. Epigraphic Indexes*, Gloucester

Fulford, M.G., 2001, 'Links with the Past: Pervasive "Ritual" Behaviour in Roman Britain', *Britannia* xxxii, 199ff

Fulford, M.G., 2001, 'Timing Devices, Fermentation Vessels, Ritual Piercings?', *Britannia* xxxii, 293-6

Gillam, J.P., 1954, 'The Temple of Mithras at Rudchester', *Archaeologia Aeliana (4th series)*, 32, 176-219

Green, M.J., 1983, *The Gods of Roman Britain*, Aylesbury

Green, M.J., 1997, *The Gods of the Celts,* Stroud

Green, M.J., 1998, 'God in man's image: thoughts on the genesis and affiliations of some Romano-British cult imagery', *Britannia* xxix, 17-30

Handley, M., 2000, reviewing Thomas, C., 1998 (below), in *Britannia* xxxi, 463-4

Henig, M., 1984, *Religion in Roman Britain*, London

Henig, M., 2002, *The Heirs of King Verica. Culture and Politics in Roman Britain*, Stroud

Henig, M. & King, A. (eds), 1986, *Pagan Gods and Shrines of the Roman Empire*, Oxford University Committee for Archaeology Monograph No.8, Oxford

Hingley, R., 1982, 'Recent Discoveries of the Roman Period at the Noah's Ark Inn, Frilford, South Oxfordshire', *Britannia* xiii, 305-9

Horne, P.D., 1981, 'Romano-Celtic Temples in the Third Century' in Henig, M. & King, A., 1981, *The Roman West in the Third Century*, B.A.R. (International Series) 109, Oxford, 21-6

Horne, P.D., 1986, 'Roman or Celtic Temples?' in Henig & King, 1986, *op. cit*

Hull, M.R., 1958, *Roman Colchester*, London, 160 ff (Temple of Claudius)

Johns, C., 1996, *The Jewellery of Roman Britain*, London

Johns, C., 1997, *The Snettisham Roman Jeweller's Hoard*, London

Johns, C. & Potter, T., 1983, *The Thetford Treasure*, London

Jones, M.E., 1996, *The End of Roman Britain*, Ithaca

Irby-Massie, G.L., 1999, *Military Religion in Roman Britain*, Leiden/Boston

Leech, R., 1986, 'The excavation of a Romano-Celtic Temple and a Later Cemetery on Lamyatt Beacon, Somerset' in *Britannia* xvii, 259-328

Lewis, M.J.T., 1965, *Temples in Roman Britain*, Cambridge

Mayor, A., 2000, *The First Fossil Hunters*, Princeton

Meates Lt-Col. G.W., 1987, *The Lullingstone Roman Villa, Kent, Volume II – The Wall Paintings and Finds*, Maidstone

Milburn, R., 1988, *Early Christian Art and Architecture*, Aldershot

Mills, N., 2000, *Celtic and Roman Artefacts*, Witham

Morris, R., 1983, *Churches in British Archaeology*, CBA Res. Rep. 47, London

Muckelroy, K.W., 1976, 'Enclosed Ambulatories in Romano-Celtic Temples in Britain' in *Britannia*, 7, 173-91

Painter, K.S., 1977, *The Water Newton Early Christian Silver*, London

Rahtz, P., 1951, 'The Roman Temple at Pagans Hill, Chew Stoke, North Somerset', *P. Som. Arch. Soc.*, 96, 112 ff

Richmond, I.A. & Gillam, J.P., 1951, 'The Temple of Mithras at Carrawburgh', *Archaeologia Aeliana (4th series)*, 29, 1-92

Richmond, I.A. & Toynbee, J.M.C., 1955, 'The Temple of Sulis-Minerva at Bath' in *JRS*, 45, 97 ff

Rodwell, W. (ed.), 1980, *Temples, Churches and Religion in Roman Britain*, B.A.R. (British Series) 77, Oxford [contains a number of useful papers discussing various related topics]

Shepherd, J., 1997, *The Temple of Mithras: Excavations by W.F. Grimes and A. Williams at the Walbrook, London*, London

Smith, D.J., 1962, 'The Shrine of the Nymphs and the Genius Loci at Carrawburgh', *Archaeologia Aeliana (4th series)*, 40, 59-81

Thomas, C., 1981, *Christianity in Roman Britain to AD 500*, London

Thomas, C., 1998, *Christian Celts. Messages and Images*, Stroud

Webster, G., 1986, *The British Celts and their Gods under Rome*, London

Wedlake, W.J, 1982, *The Excavation of the Shrine of Apollo at Nettleton, Wiltshire, 1956-1971*, RRCSAL No. 40, London

Wheeler, R.E.M. & Wheeler, T.V., 1932, *Report on the Excavation of the Prehistoric, Roman and Post-Roman site in Lydney Park, Gloucestershire*, RRCSAL No. 9, London

Wheeler, R.E.M., 1943, *Maiden Castle, Dorset*, RRCSAL No. 12 Oxford

Wilson, D.R., 1975, 'Romano-Celtic Temple Architecture', *J. Brit. Arch. Assoc.* 38, 2-27

Woodward, A. & Leach, P., 1990, *The Uley shrines: excavation of a ritual complex on West Hill, Uley, Gloucestershire, 1977-9*, London

Index